MIDNIGHT IN WASHINGTON

MIDNIGHT IN WASHINGTON

HOW WE ALMOST LOST
OUR DEMOCRACY AND
STILL COULD

ADAM SCHIFF

RANDOM HOUSE | NEW YORK

Published in the United States by Random House, an imprint and division of
Penguin Random House LLC, New York.

RANDOM HOUSE and the HOUSE colophon are registered trademarks of
Penguin Random House LLC.

Hardback ISBN 978-0-593-23152-4
Ebook ISBN 978-0-593-23154-8

Printed in the United States of America on acid-free paper

randomhousebooks.com

2 4 6 8 9 7 5 3

First Edition

Book design by Susan Turner

To my beautiful wife, Eve, my fellow traveler, my loving, daring, and caring companion—no other Adam was ever so lucky,

To my mother and father, Sherrill and Ed, who gave me love and a sense of worth, and encouraged me to give back,

To my brother Daniel, who shared with me his passion for language, showed me what it meant to be devoted to a craft, and who led me to follow my dreams by fearlessly pursuing his own,

To my brother David, who enriched my life beyond measure when he became part of our family and I became part of his,

And to my daughter and son, Lexi and Eli, who make me as proud as a father could be and bring me nothing but joy (okay, mostly joy, almost complete joyousness, a whole lotta joy . . . omg not a dad joke in the dedication)

For truth is truth
To the end of reckoning.

—WILLIAM SHAKESPEARE, *Measure for Measure*

CONTENTS

WHY SHOULD I?

THE SENATE CHAMBER WAS SO MUCH SMALLER THAN I REMEMBERED. I
had tried an impeachment case against a federal judge ten years earlier and hadn't been on the Senate floor since. In the House, I could
see members on the other side of the chamber, but only dimly, their
faces indistinct in the distance. Some of the Republican members of
the House have been there for years, but sit in the far corner and are
not on any of my committees, and if I passed them at the airport,
I wouldn't know them from a stranger. Indeed, I *have* passed them
at the airport and not known who they were until they stopped and
introduced themselves. But as I walked onto the Senate floor again
after so long, I couldn't get over how intimate it was—how closely
I could observe each of the senators and their expressions, faces so
familiar to me even if I had never worked with them, or spoken with
them, before.

During the trial, with one glance I could tell how closely they were paying attention, or not paying attention—frowning, thoughtful, drifting off, engaged, moved, angered, or, worse, indifferent. You could see when their eyelids got heavy after lunch or long argumentation, or when their eyes glistened with emotion. We had twenty-four hours, spread out over three days, to make our case for the impeachment of a president, which didn't seem like much, which wasn't much, to sum up all of the reasons why Donald J. Trump posed a continuing danger to the Republic. We had spent two of those days making what I thought was a powerful case, my talented colleagues and incredible staff having put together a series of compelling presentations, integrating the testimony of the witnesses, documentary records, constitutional sources, and all of the powerful argumentation we could muster—but before the last argument of the day, one of my staff put his hand on my arm and stopped me.

"They think we've proven him guilty. They need to know why he should be removed."

I didn't have time to ask my staff who "they" were. We had been getting feedback during the course of the trial, sometimes directly from senators who would walk past us in the small lobby behind the Senate floor, going to and from lunch, or on a break, or who would wander up to our small table on the Senate floor when the day's presentations were done. But the best sources of information came from Senator Schumer's staff, passed on to my staff in whispers and handwritten notes. Were these questions coming from Democratic senators, like Joe Manchin from West Virginia, Kyrsten Sinema of Arizona, or Doug Jones of Alabama? If so, we were in trouble.

Or was this feedback coming from Republican senators, several of whom had kept their cards close to the vest? If the Republican senators were asking, that meant their minds were still open to conviction, and that was good, even though at this point in the trial they had yet to hear the defense case.

And still, what were "they" really asking? If senators believed that we had proven Trump guilty of withholding hundreds of millions of dollars of military aid from an ally at war in order to coerce that nation into helping him cheat in the upcoming election, wasn't that enough? Had the bar become so high with this president that *that* wasn't enough? It was like a juror in an extortion case involving the president asking the judge, "Okay, he's guilty, but do we really need to convict? Can't he just go on running the country?"

But as I walked to the lectern, I suddenly understood, in a way I hadn't fully appreciated until that moment, that this was the central question: Why should he be removed? He was the president of their party. He was putting conservative judges on the court. He was lowering their taxes. Why remove him? I had watched during breaks in the trial as the president's Senate defenders took to the airwaves to proclaim his innocence, and I had believed them—not their claims about the president's conduct, but that *they* believed what they were saying, that *they* believed there had been, to quote the president's mantra of defense, no quid pro quo. But I could see now that that wasn't it at all.

I should have known better. For the past three years, Republicans had confided, to me and to many of my Democratic colleagues, their serious misgivings about the president. Some would go on Fox News and bash me, only to urge me privately to keep on with the investigation. And it became clear that many Republicans felt someone needed to do it, someone needed to put a stop to it all, even if they couldn't, or wouldn't. And the question wasn't so much "Why should he be removed?" as "Why should I be the one to remove him? Why should I risk my seat, my position of power and influence, my career and future? Why should I? Why should *I*?"

There was only half an hour left of our case that day when I pulled my thoughts free of my staff to make those seven short paces from the House managers' table to the lectern, and I had no idea how I was going to answer that question. I had prepared to go through the record of the president's call again, the one in which he says "I want you to do us a favor, though"—because I had discovered there was so much more to that transcript, so much more now that we understood the whole scheme, and I had planned to go through it, line by line. It had become a practice of mine, during the hearings in the House, to do a kind of impromptu summary at the end of each proceeding, to try to distill the importance of what we had heard or learned, to try to express simply the significance of something that had struck me as particularly powerful or telling. It didn't even have to be all that important in its own right, as long as it spoke to something larger, something that shed light on the bigger issue, on what was at stake. But the call record now seemed insignificant, compared to the question: *Why should I?*

I needed time to think, and so I did go through the call record with the senators, pulling out a line here or there to explain its new significance. Most of the senators were listening politely after a long day, but not all, and their concentration was wandering, and so was mine. I was doing a kind of extreme multitasking, reading and speaking about the call but thinking about the question I needed to answer, and all the other questions that it presumed: What made this man so dangerous? What had he done to the country? How, in three short years, had he been able to so completely remake his own party, get it to abandon its own ideology, get my friends and colleagues to surrender themselves to his obvious immorality? How had he caused us to question ourselves, our values, our commitment to democracy, what the country even stood for? How had he been able to convince so many of our fellow citizens that his views were the truth, and that they should believe him no matter how obvious the lies?

When I was finished going through the call record, when I could delay no longer, I told the senators, "This brings me to the last point I want to make tonight." At the end of the trial, I said, I believed that we would have proven the president guilty—that is, he had done what he was charged with doing. But it was a slightly different question, I acknowledged, whether he really needed to be removed. Still, I was wondering, even as I was saying the words, how do I answer the question? In the few minutes I have left, what do I say? And all of a sudden, every senator seemed to be watching, alert and keenly interested in the answer. The moment stretched on in silence. "This is why he needs to be removed," I said at last, and did my best to tell them. . . .

. . .

IN THE YEAR AND A half since that day, I have thought a lot about what I might have said differently, or done differently, to persuade the senators of what a danger the now former president posed then, and poses still. Whether there was any course we might have taken, not just in the trial but in the years that preceded it, to prevent what was coming: a violent insurrection against the Capitol, a wave of antidemocratic efforts aimed at the heart of our democracy, and a full-out assault on the truth.

There is now a dangerous vein of autocratic thought running through one of America's two great parties, and it poses an existential danger to the country. In this we are not alone. All around the world, there is a new competition between autocracy and democracy, and for more than a decade, the autocrats have been on the rise. This trend toward authoritarianism began before Donald Trump and will not have spent its force when he steps off the political stage for good. The experience of the last four years will require constant vigilance on our part so that it does not gain another foothold in the highest office in our land.

The actions of our government, like the broader sweep of history, are not taken on their own, they are not the product of impersonal forces operating without human actors and agency. We made Donald Trump possible. We the voters, yes, but we in Congress even more so. He would not have been able to batter and break so many of our democratic norms had we not let him, had we not been capable of endless rationalization, had we not forgotten why we came to office in the first place, had we not been afraid. How does that happen? How do good people allow themselves to be so badly used?

As the pandemic hit and I was forced into seclusion, along with the rest of America, I set out to write a book about what I witnessed at that very human level, about the friendships I lost with colleagues on the other side of the aisle that I had long worked with and admired, about their failings and my own, about the heroism of people I had never met but who would enter my life and change it, sometimes with only a few words, like "Here, right matters." I tried to draw on my experience, not only in Congress, but growing up in a close-knit family that valued its immigrant history, as a prosecutor handling cases like espionage, and living overseas in a country broken up by the same kind of xenophobic populism we would see unleashed here.

Midnight is the darkest moment of the day, everywhere in the world. But it is also the most hopeful, because everything that comes after holds the promise of light. America has a genius for reinvention, and we must use it. As Lincoln said, we must "disenthrall ourselves" to save our country. From the same forces of bigotry that divided and nearly defeated the country in the Civil War, yes, without a doubt, but from something new to the American landscape as well, from a dangerous experimentation with a uniquely American brand of authoritarianism. We must all play our part. We must all confront the question—Why should I?

Here is my answer.

PART ONE

AGAINST OUR WILL COMES WISDOM

1

INSURRECTION

"PLEASE GRAB A MASK!" A CAPITOL POLICE OFFICER SHOUTED FROM the well of the House floor. Up until this point, I still wasn't sure what was happening outside the chamber and whether we were at serious risk. There were rioters in the building, that much I knew. How many of them, or how great a threat they posed, it was impossible to tell. I looked around at my colleagues to see if they were as perplexed as I was, and besides, what were we supposed to do in an emergency? I suddenly wished I had been paying more attention at freshman orientation twenty years earlier.

Sensing our confusion, the officer continued: "Be prepared to don your mask in the event the room is breached." He told us that we did not need to put the masks on yet, but tear gas was being deployed, so we should get them ready. "Be prepared to get down under your chairs if necessary. So, we have folks entering the Rotunda and coming down this way. . . . Just be prepared. Stay calm." I pulled a rectangular canvas pouch from under my seat and unzipped it. Inside was a strongly sealed plastic container with no obvious opening. I flipped it from side to side and upside down, trying to open the damned thing. Finally figuring it out, I helped the members around me open theirs, and we removed the plastic hoods. These hoods didn't resemble the gas masks you see police wearing during a riot; instead, they were a large polyethylene bag that you pulled over your head, with a small motor attached to circulate and filter the air. As you removed the hood from its packaging, the motor began running, and suddenly there was a din of dozens of these hoods buzzing, which only added to the growing sense of alarm.

"When you put on the hood," one of my colleagues and a former Marine, Ruben Gallego of Arizona, shouted, "breathe slowly." Ruben was standing behind me, and he could see the panic spreading from member to member. "Take slow, steady breaths. Your impulse will be to hyperventilate, but you need to breathe slowly." This was very helpful advice. I have a bit of claustrophobia, and the idea of pulling a bag over my head already had my pulse quickening. I resolved to wait until the last moment before I had to don the thing, since I wasn't smelling tear gas, not yet. "Breathe slowly when you put it on," Ruben intoned again, "or you will pass out. That is how people can die from wearing these." Okay, that wasn't so helpful.

"This is because of *you!*" yelled Representative Dean Phillips of Minnesota from the gallery at Representative Paul Gosar, who had been at the microphone. "Shut up!" came the Republican reply. "Call Trump, tell him to call off his revolutionary guards," screamed Representative Steve Cohen of Tennessee. He was also in the gallery, above me and to the right, his face red with anger. Other members tried to settle things down and not allow the recriminations to spread, but Phillips wasn't wrong. We were here for what should have been the ceremonial certification of the 2020 presidential election results, but instead we were now in danger. For months, GOP members of Congress had propagated the president's big lie about the elections, and you could draw a direct line between those lies and the threat we all now faced. Because of the pandemic, Phillips, Cohen, and other members had been required to wait in the gallery before their chance to speak, and they were the most exposed. Down on the House floor, we could barricade ourselves in, but upstairs there are multiple doors to the gallery and little to prevent the rioters from entering.

"Lock the gallery doors!" someone shouted from down below, but it wasn't clear to police upstairs which doors in the gallery remained open. "Not those doors—*those* doors!" came another excited shout. "Those doors over there!"

A police officer returned to the well again: He told us that they had secured an escape route and he wanted us to exit the chambers and proceed immediately down the stairs. Now. There are two sets of double doors behind the Speaker's chair and raised dais, and the doors to our right were pulled open. Members and staff quickly moved toward the exit and I was suddenly aware of just how many people had been on the floor, in the cloakroom or elsewhere, as they crowded by the exit and created a real logjam. I waited by my seat, still feeling relatively calm and wanting to give other members and staff a chance to go first. Besides, so many of the Republican members were not wearing masks, I wasn't eager to be jammed in with them shoulder to shoulder on my way out the doors. Eventually, I wandered over to the GOP side of the chamber and waited there alone, several rows above the well, until a young staff member approached me, perplexed why I wasn't leaving.

"Are you okay, Mr. Schiff?" she asked. I was astonished. She was all of about twentysomething and she was asking me if I was okay. What a remarkable calm amid the chaos. "I'm fine," I said, "just don't want to add to the melee. Thought I would let others go ahead." And then, as an afterthought, I asked her—"Are you okay?" She nodded.

Suddenly I could hear the crowd of insurrectionists outside the chamber. They had migrated from the Senate side of the building and were approaching the House floor from Statuary Hall, on the opposite side of the chamber from where members were exiting. And from the noise, it sounded like a lot of them.

Just then came a tremendous *thud*—something had been thrust against the doors not twenty yards away from me, battering them. *Thud.* A moment later, again: *thud.*

"You need to get out!" a police officer shouted. *"Move!"*

I made my way down to the well and joined the remaining members and staff filing out, looking back at the doors being hammered to the rear of the chamber, glass now shattering. Police officers pushed large cabinets in front of the doors and would soon draw their weapons.

"You can't let them see you," a Republican member said to me. "He's right," another Republican member said. "I know these people, I can talk to them, I can talk my way through them. You're in a whole different category." In that moment, we were not merely members of different political parties, but on opposite sides of a much more dangerous divide. At first I was oddly touched by these GOP members and their evident concern. But by then, I had been receiving death threats for years, and that feeling soon gave way to another: If these Republican members hadn't joined the president in falsely attacking me for four years, I wouldn't need to be worried about my security, none of us would. I kept that thought to myself.

As I made my way out of the back of the chamber, I took another look at the Republicans walking out with me. One had grabbed a wooden post with a hand sanitizer dispenser attached to it and was carrying it like a club, in case he needed it to defend himself against the rioters. "Are you that worried?" I asked him, as we began filing down the stairs from the Speaker's lobby and through the corridors below the Capitol. "Yes," he said agitatedly. "I think I just heard gunshots." He was right—only fifty feet away from the stairs, on the other side of the lobby, Ashli Babbitt, a fourteen-year veteran of the Air Force, had just been shot to death by a Capitol Police officer. In all the commotion, I had just assumed it was a tear gas canister.

"How long have you been here?" I asked the Republican.

"Seventy-two hours," he replied.

"What?"

"I was just elected. I replaced John Ratcliffe. I'm Pat Fallon."

I looked him in the eye and said: "It's not always like this."

Now down in the tunnels below the complex, Capitol Police were directing us to a secure location. I was taking my sweet time about it, because I still couldn't fully accept what was happening. There had been plenty of surreal moments over the last four years, but nothing like this. Could the U.S. Capitol really be under attack, and by our own people? I suddenly noticed there weren't many members ahead of me or behind. Where had they all gone? Representative Fallon was a few yards in front, and I was now walking with Sean Patrick Maloney of New York. He noticed the hand sanitizer post that Fallon was carrying and said, "Either that guy is really worried about his safety, or he's just really devoted to hand hygiene." I couldn't help but laugh.

"Hurry up, please," a police officer commanded. "You need to move." That brought us back to reality. I picked up my pace. The sudden air of crisis had me thinking back to September 11, during my first few months in Congress, and all the chaos that surrounded that day. September 11 had been a terrible tragedy, and it had brought Congress and the country together; this was going to be very different.

Months before the joint session of Congress, I had suggested to the Speaker that we assemble a small group of members to try to anticipate any postelection challenges to the vote, to the electors, or whatever else Donald Trump and the Republican Party might have in mind to overturn the results if we were successful on election day. She had agreed, and periodically we would conference with Representatives Zoe Lofgren, Jamie Raskin, and Joe Neguse on the multitude of contingencies that could result if the Electoral College was tied, or states designated more than one slate of electors, or the vice president refused to recognize a slate, or, God forbid, the election went to the Supreme Court to decide. We were determined to avoid the Court at all costs, and deal with any challenge to electors in the House, and not on a one state, one vote basis, but through the majority vote we controlled. Still, there were a dizzying array of possibilities, and we knew we could easily end up in uncharted territory.

But by early January 2021, the Electoral College results were settled, and the Trump campaign's endless legal challenges were over, so our rump group turned its focus to a far simpler task—organizing the opposition to GOP efforts to fight the electors of six states during the joint session of Congress at which the Electoral College results were to be counted and certified. Normally a sedate and purely ministerial event, the joint session would provide a last opportunity, however improbable, for Trump and his supporters to challenge the election results. Upon a written challenge to a state's electors that was signed by at least one House and Senate member, we would separate from the joint session into the House and Senate chambers to debate the challenge to that state's results.

During these individual sessions, the four of us planned to begin each debate period with broad, thematic opening statements, to be followed by House members from the state in question who could drill down on the bogus nature of the particular challenges to that state's election. Originally, I proposed an opening address that placed these challenges to the electors in the broader context of Trump's attacks on our democratic process, but the Speaker rejected the idea, and she was right. "Let's not make this about him," she said. "This is about our democracy, about the peaceful transition of power. Let's keep this very high-level, very dignified, befitting the seriousness of what we are engaged in."

The Speaker arranged multiple Zoom meetings each day with different state congressional delegations, where we discussed the arguments that Republicans would make to disqualify the electors from those states—false claims of fraud, or dead people voting, or Dominion voting systems, or decisions of elections officials that they would argue were in contravention of state law—and the members from each state would rebut them. I recommended to the state delegations that they avoid amplifying the president's false claims by repeating them if it wasn't necessary, and to wait for the Republicans to make certain arguments before shooting them down.

By the time that the morning of January 6 arrived, we thought we were well prepared for anything that could happen. I would be doing six opening arguments—assuming all six states we anticipated would be challenged by the Republicans—and six rebuttals, as would my three colleagues. I had written half of these opening statements and one rebuttal, and the rest I was prepared to do on the fly. I had no idea how ill-prepared we would turn out to be for what was coming.

Shortly after the joint session began with the reading of the first states, dozens of Republican House members, joined by several GOP senators, objected to counting the electors from Arizona, and we divided into our respective houses to debate the matter. When I spoke on the House floor in opposition to this challenge to the votes of millions of Arizonans, I wanted to emphasize that these Republican objectors were violating their oath to defend the Constitution, regardless of the outcome of their objection to the count, and doing grave damage to our democracy:

"Nor can we console ourselves with the intoxicating fiction that we can break that oath without consequence because doing so will not succeed in overturning the election. An oath is no less broken when the breaking fails to achieve its end," I said. Any who sought to overturn the election would do injury to our constitution, whatever the result. "For just as the propagation of that dangerous *myth* about this election made this moment inevitable, our actions today will put another train in motion. This election will not be overturned, but what about the next? Or the one after that?"

My original draft used the word *lie*, not *myth*, but I was mindful of the Speaker's injunction to make our arguments about the Constitution and not Trump, and I didn't want to risk the Republicans seeking to "take down my words"—an arcane legislative procedure used to take issue with a member's language on the floor. The president could lie for weeks about the election, but to say so was objectionable. And so I continued to focus on the danger of these bad-faith Republican challenges in more neutral terms, on how they were undermining our democracy and the work of the House in particular: "What shall we say when our democratic legacy is no more substantial than the air, except that we brought trouble to our own house, and inherited the wind?"

Although I did not know it, there *was* another train in motion. Nearby at the Ellipse on the National Mall, the president of the United States had incited a crowd of his supporters, repeating his big lie about the election, applauding the campaign to "stop the steal," telling them to "fight like hell" and that if they didn't fight, they wouldn't have a country anymore. He asserted that the vice president could overturn the results of a free and fair election in which over 155 million Americans had cast their ballots, if only he would be strong. And then he implored this mob to go to the Capitol and do something about it.

And they did.

I wasn't paying attention to what was going on down the Mall, as I was fixated on the speeches I was giving, the arguments the Republicans were making, and the need to rebut them. I was only dimly aware that people were gathering outside the building, and then I noticed other members increasingly on their phones watching television footage. "Do you know what's going on?" I asked another member, momentarily turning my focus away from the Republican who was speaking. "There are a bunch of people marching here from the rally," he said. I nodded, and thought little of it.

The first time I noticed that something was seriously amiss was when I looked up and noticed that the Speaker was not in her chair on the dais. I knew from our preparations that she planned to preside from start to finish, no matter how many hours the joint session went on, and so I assumed she was coming right back. A moment later, however, two Capitol Police officers rushed onto the floor, grabbed the Democratic majority leader, Representative Steny Hoyer of Maryland, and moved him so briskly out of the chamber that I recall thinking I had never seen Hoyer move that fast. Even then, I had been in Congress long enough to have witnessed lots of false alarms, when a plane mistakenly wandered into the airspace above, or suspicious packages had been left unattended.

I went up to the Speaker's chair, in which Representative Jim McGovern of Massachusetts was now presiding.

"Thank God," I told him, "we finally have someone disposable in the Speaker's chair." He looked at me and smirked—I clearly thought it was more amusing than he did. In fact, McGovern would be among the last to leave the chamber that afternoon, and in cellphone video taken by one of the rioters outside the Speaker's lobby, he can be seen through the glass doors only minutes before Ashli Babbitt was shot.

By the time I arrived at the secure location, the large room was already packed with members and staff, and several Capitol Police officers were guarding the entrance. "Please do not tell people where we are sheltering," we were instructed. "We don't know if rioters are in this complex, and we don't want them to know where you are." Members were soon buzzing about how one of our colleagues was nevertheless live-tweeting from the room. I was appalled that some-one would so quickly disregard what they were asked to do for our collective security, but then again, I wasn't surprised. Frankly, given the changes in Congress I had seen over the previous few years, the real surprise would have been to discover that no one had been tweeting about our location.

I am embarrassed to say that only then did I call my wife, Eve, to tell her that I was all right. She sounded fine and had been out running errands, getting home only when the breach of the Capitol was beginning. She ran to the television to watch and started getting texts from friends and family asking if I was okay, which worried her all the more. My daughter, Lexi, twenty-two, called, more on edge, and we merged the calls. I assured Lexi that I was fine and in a safe place. They wanted to know where I was, and I told them we were not supposed to say. *Never mind,* my son, Eli, eighteen, told the family. "I know where he is." Apparently, he used the "find my phone" feature to pinpoint my location.

I took a seat and exchanged glances with several of my colleagues. We were all stunned about what was happening, and a kind of sorting out was taking shape—Republican members and staff sought out their Republican colleagues, and Democrats did the same. Fear was receding and anger at the president was quickly taking its place. One of my Democratic colleagues came up to me and was the first to say what I would hear versions of for weeks to come:

"You said this would happen," she said.

"Well, I didn't say *this* would happen."

"You warned that he would try to cheat again."

"It didn't require any great clairvoyance," I replied, and then I added: "Someone really should have impeached that son-of-a-bitch."

In fact, several of my colleagues were already discussing the need to impeach Trump again for inciting this attack. For my part, I was more fixated on returning to the floor and finishing the joint session. "We really need to go back in and get this done. We can't let them stop us even for the day." My colleagues nodded. This was the universal sentiment in the room—we were not about to let the insurrectionists succeed or allow them to draw this out any more than they already had. Both our caucus chair, Hakeem Jeffries, and the Republican chair at the time, Liz Cheney, confirmed that we would return to session just as soon as police had cleared us to do so.

Meanwhile, the room had every hallmark of becoming a Covid-19 superspreader event, packed into tight quarters as we were, with no windows and lots of Republican members and staff not wearing masks. I recognized one GOP member who had been diagnosed with the virus only a couple of days before. She looked pale and unwell, and I couldn't imagine what she was doing at work that day, but having ignored the need to quarantine, she was now sheltering in place with a couple hundred of us.

Three hours later, we were still sheltering in place and hunger was starting to get the better of me. I realized I hadn't eaten anything since early that morning, and my stomach was complaining. We had not been given an all-clear, but I noticed the room was thinning, and I thought I might make a jail break. I had some food back in my office in the Rayburn Building, and I approached three of the police officers at the door. "Am I allowed to go back to my office?" I asked.

"We can't stop you," was his careful answer. It wasn't a green light, but it wasn't red either, so I decided to walk back to my office. During the pandemic, most of my staff had worked from home, but I had asked one of my staff to be present that day in case I needed anything on the floor. He did not feel comfortable remaining in my office alone, given the target I'd had on my back over the last four years, so he had been waiting in the neighboring office of Representative Carolyn Maloney. By this point, however, around six in the evening, I was glad to learn that he had been able to leave the building and go home. I locked the door to the office, turned on the television, then went to the window and gazed at Independence Avenue and the myriad national guardsmen, police officers, and police vehicles outside. My phone buzzed almost immediately with a text from Capitol Police. It read: "Capitol: Internal Security Threat: move inside office/lock doors, seek cover, and remain silent. USCP."

I turned off the television and forwarded the message to my staff. "I just left the secure location and went back to the office. Is this a new alert, or an old one?" I asked, although I already knew the answer: "It's new." Shit. I had picked a bad time to leave safety, but at least I had some food. I scrounged a few things out of my office refrigerator and wolfed them down, turned the television back on but kept the volume off, and waited.

A COUPLE OF HOURS LATER, I received a message that it was safe to return to the Capitol, and I walked back to the House floor. As the session recommenced, we voted down the objections to the Arizona electors, but an alarming number of Republicans still sought to overturn the results. It was incredible to me that after all this, after seeing the clear and violent implication of their conduct, with blood literally on the floor outside the chamber, these members were not finished with their oath breaking.

Late in the evening, I spoke again on the House floor. Remarking on the fact that Franklin Roosevelt had given his Four Freedoms speech in our chamber exactly eighty years earlier—highlighting the dangers of "poisonous propaganda" to our democracy—I called on Republicans to stop. I emphasized the need to come together in the face of the attempted insurrection and a pandemic that was killing thousands of us every day:

> This is the urgency that our new president must address, a virus that will claim more American lives than all our casualties during World War Two. To meet that moment will require unity, not discord, will require an abiding faith in our country, in our democracy, in our government's ability to function and provide for the needs of its citizens. The Members of this body cannot continue to challenge the merits of an election that was fairly conducted, and overwhelmingly won by Joe Biden. It must stop!

But it didn't stop. As the night gave way to morning, the objections continued and tempers began to flare. The most important speech, and the most surprising, came from Representative Conor Lamb, a conservative Democrat from western Pennsylvania. Gone was the caution he usually displayed. And, in light of the day's events, gone too was any sensitivity over the language we would use to push back against the continuing assault on the peaceful transition of power. He began by alluding to what he had planned to say, how he had planned to talk about how well the election was conducted in Pennsylvania, and how it was a Republican bill that had established the voting procedures that Republicans now complained about. He said that he had intended to address these issues as a sign of respect for his Republican colleagues, because that was how he was raised, to show respect—but that was now impossible.

"These objections don't deserve an ounce of respect," Lamb continued. "Not an ounce. A woman died out there tonight, and you're making these objections. Let's be clear about what happened in this chamber tonight. Invaders came in for the first time since the War of 1812. They desecrated these halls and this chamber and practically every inch of ground where we work. And for the most part they walked in here free. A lot of them walked out free. There wasn't a person watching at home who didn't know why that was—because of the way they look."

Republican members began muttering their disapproval, and Speaker Pelosi gaveled them down. "The House will be in order," she declared.

"We know that that attack today," Lamb went on, "didn't materialize out of nowhere, it was inspired by lies, the same lies you're hearing in this room tonight. And the members who are repeating those lies should be ashamed of themselves, their constituents should be ashamed of them."

It was a searing indictment, and Republican resentment started to boil over. GOP representative Morgan Griffith of Virginia soon interrupted Lamb, demanding recognition from the Speaker. "The gentleman said that there were lies on this floor here today, looking over this direction, I ask that those words be taken down."

"Get out of here," a Democratic member yelled in response, and shouts echoed around the chamber. The Speaker broke in and ruled the objection out of order as not timely. One of the Republicans shouted in frustration that the words should have been taken down, and the Speaker cast him aside, all too accurately: "Yeah look, you say that about me every single day, so just hold your tongue."

"The truth hurts," Lamb continued. "It hurts. It hurts them. It hurts this country. It hurts all of us." Republican lawmakers moved toward our side of the aisle and Democrats moved toward theirs, and there was a real risk of a brawl on the House floor. "Sit down," a Democrat yelled. "No, you sit down!" Representative Andy Harris of Maryland called back. "There will be order in the House," the Speaker insisted, banging the gavel. "There will be order in the House!" Democratic congressman Colin Allred of Texas, a former linebacker for the Tennessee Titans, moved toward the scrum. He was not someone you wanted to mess with. "Are you serious, man?" he asked. "Haven't you had enough violence for today?"

"The gentleman will clear the chamber," the Speaker ordered. "The gentleman will clear the chamber!"

"The truth hurts, but the fact is this," Lamb said, talking over the Republicans. "We want this government to work more than they want it to fail. And after everything that has happened today, we want that more than ever. We will make it work. They will not make it fail." When Lamb was finished, I leaped to my feet, as did most of the Democrats present, and we gave him a standing ovation. Conor Lamb, a former Marine, had shaken off his detached demeanor and said what we all wanted to say: that our colleagues' lies had brought us to this terrible end.

At around three in the morning, we voted on the baseless objections to the Pennsylvania electors. One hundred thirty-eight Republican members of the House, including a large majority of the Republican conference and their leadership, as well as seven Republican senators, voted to reject the votes of millions of Pennsylvanians. Impervious to logic, Republican members still maintained that the ballots were fraudulent even though they themselves had been elected on the very same ballots. As I pointed out during the debate, consistency mattered very little when it was weighed against ambition and the desire to keep power.

The following day, I felt a mixture of sadness over what our country had gone through, embarrassment at how we appeared in the eyes of the world, anger at the irresponsible actions of my colleagues who had spread lies about the election for months and brought this on themselves and the nation, and fury toward a president who had instigated the rebellion. But more than anything else, I was shaken by fear over what this meant for our future and a recognition of how long and difficult lay the road ahead.

Donald Trump bore responsibility for the mayhem that took place at the Capitol that afternoon. And every day that he would remain in office, he represented a clear and present danger to our democracy. But what took place inside our chamber, with the challenge to the electors, was every bit as much an attack on our democracy. The assault on our constitutional order was inspired by people wearing suits and ties and cloaked in the genteel language of congressional debate, but their purpose was no less ominous. We can fortify the defenses of the Capitol. We can reinforce the doors and put up fences. But we cannot guard our democracy against those who walk the halls of Congress, have taken an oath to uphold our Constitution, but refuse to do so.

That weekend, I remained in Washington, but many members of Congress traveled back home aboard the same planes and trains as the insurrectionists who had stormed the Capitol. As I watched footage of Democratic representative Lou Correa of Orange County, California, being shouted at and harangued at the airport, with angry maskless Trump supporters getting right in his face, I could not help but be struck by the conviction of these insurrectionists; they really believed the election had been stolen, they were completely taken in by the president's big lie. That is how powerful the words of a president are—relentlessly repeated and amplified by a complicit right-wing media. It infuriated me all the more that many of the Republicans in Congress continued to push that lie, because, unlike the insurrectionists, my colleagues had to know it was a lie. In that way, they were as culpable as anyone for the tragic events of January 6, and I wondered how I was ever going to work with them again. Prior to the Trump years, I cherished the relationships I had with many of the GOP members and worked closely with them on a range of issues and bills. Now it would be hard to even look them in the face.

2

THE ONE THING THEY CAN NEVER TAKE AWAY

IF THE PRESIDENCY OF DONALD TRUMP HAD TURNED ME INTO A LIBERAL lightning rod in a disastrously fractious country, I certainly didn't start out that way.

In a sense, I was born bipartisan. My family straddled the political divide. On my father's side was a long line of Democrats in the "yellow dog" tradition—so devoted to the Democratic Party that they would rather vote for a yellow dog than a Republican. I once asked my father, Edward, to explain this, and he said it was the product of our family's immigrant experience, and the hardships of growing up in Boston during the Great Depression. His grandparents Jacob and Bessie were Jewish immigrants from Lithuania who had come to the United States at the turn of the century after living in England for a few years. They were fortunate to leave Lithuania when they did; few countries suffered a greater loss of its Jewish population during the Holocaust, when more than ninety percent of its Jews were murdered.

Jacob and Bessie somehow managed to open a kosher butcher shop in South Boston while raising ten kids. They were Orthodox Jews, deeply grounded in their faith. When the oldest of their sons, Henry, was out delivering meat to a customer on his bicycle and held on to the back of a truck to be pulled along, he lost his balance and fell, hitting his head on the ground. He went to bed that night without eating, complaining of a headache, and the next morning he was dead. Henry had been only thirteen. My great-grandparents were grief-stricken, but rather than be embittered, Jacob thanked God for giving him thirteen years with their son. I admire that kind of faith, and envy the ability to look at the world that way, for the joy and love that it brings and not for what it takes away, even as I must acknowledge that my reaction to such loss would have been very different.

Their third-oldest son, Frank, was my grandfather. Without the resources to attend pharmacy school, he taught himself the trade, and by the time my father was born, in 1928, Frank had opened a small pharmacy of his own, just a few miles from the family's butcher shop. When the Depression hit, my father, his siblings, and their cousins worked around the clock to keep the pharmacy afloat. They kept the doors open twenty-four hours a day, seven days a week, knowing how lucky they were to have work. Even in the darkest years of the economic calamity, they provided medicine and supplies to families who couldn't pay. They were also profoundly grateful for the New Deal programs of the Democratic Party under Franklin Roosevelt. To them, the Republican Party didn't concern itself with working people. As my father told me simply, if pointedly, "The Democrats offered opportunity. The Republicans offered shit."

My mother's family was equally devoted to the Republican Party, notwithstanding a very similar immigrant experience. The Glovskys immigrated from Russia and Poland around the turn of the century, likewise to escape the pogroms that predated the Holocaust by a few decades. My mother's father, Harry, was a short and genial man, and he adored his wife, Marcie. I don't think I ever saw them walk together when they weren't arm in arm, her hand draped around his forearm as if they were reprising their walk down the aisle. My grandfather called her *mein gantze leben,* Yiddish for "my whole life."

My grandmother, Marcie, was a sweet and soft-spoken woman. She would watch us quietly at family gatherings, patting us on the hand or kissing us gently on the head, enjoying her grandchildren through our interaction with others. I did not get to know her charm, wit, and sense of humor until after my grandfather passed away, when she seemed to emerge, as if from behind a door. They too were products of the Depression, who lived in the same Newton, Massachusetts, apartment their entire adult lives, never really traveled, and saved what little they had in fear of being a burden to their children. When Harry passed, my mother was heartbroken to find that her parents had saved $300,000 and could have spent more than they did on themselves.

My mother's family was drawn to the Republican Party because in New England at the time, the party was home to many social progressives and moderates like the Rockefellers and the Lodges. Harry was actively engaged in politics, and when he joined the Massachusetts Republican Party, it was far more welcoming of Jews than the Democratic Party. As it was, I don't recall him ever having anything very positive to say about the Democrats, who welcomed some ethnicities but were strongly biased against others. When he did refer to the opposite party, it was always in the form of an alliterative epithet: "Those damn Dems."

By the early 1950s, my grandfather had become chairman of the GOP in Berkshire County and an elector for Dwight D. Eisenhower. I have an old black-and-white photograph from that period hanging on the wall of my office in Washington. In it, my grandfather is standing beside President Eisenhower and Republican senator Henry Cabot Lodge Jr. They are bathed in sunlight on a crisp day, a crowd around them, and my grandfather is wearing an enormous WIN WITH IKE button on the lapel of his suit. He appears to be introducing Eisenhower to someone, probably a local dignitary.

As a kid, I used to carry that photo in my wallet, and I would look at its folded and tarnished image, trying to imagine how he felt that day: the son of Jewish immigrants from Europe standing beside the president of the United States.

My parents would maintain their parents' party loyalties, but politics would be no impediment to their falling in love. They met at a party in Boston, when my mother was dating one of my father's friends. She was what they called at the time a real "head turner," and looked so much like the actress Suzanne Pleshette that she would get stopped on the street and asked for her autograph. She had beautiful dark silken hair, round cheeks, a playful smile, and a sense of fashion that she made up her own name for—*deg-re-zais*—a French-sounding invention connoting the height of couture. When my father saw her, politics was the last thing on his mind, and he was smitten. For her part, my mother was not so impressed by the self-assured clothing salesman making fifty dollars a week in the *schmata* business. At the time, my dad wasn't even really a salesman, only the "lumper"—the guy who carried the bag of swatches for the salesman. My mother also said that he was "geographically undesirable," since he was living in Boston and she still lived in the small Western Massachusetts town of North Adams. But as she would always tell us, "He wore me down."

After marrying, they settled in the Boston suburb of Framingham, where my brother, Dan, was born in 1958, and I followed two years later. My parents' political affiliations remained strong, but I don't remember them ever fighting over politics, and when the subject came up, it was characterized more by good-natured ribbing than anything else, with my father playing on the Boston Brahmin pretensions of my mother's family.

It was a childhood with lots of kids my age on our street, a protected woods adjacent to our house large enough to get lost in, ample trees to climb, backyards to sled in, and porches to jump off. My father was still on the road a lot, by then a traveling salesman for a large clothing manufacturer out of El Paso called Farah. Dan and I would play baseball in the street and go on long bike rides to a penny candy store called the Wayside Inn in neighboring Sudbury, baseball cards pinned to our spokes to make that nice *flap, flap, flap* sound as we pedaled. My mother stayed at home to raise us, hosting Cub Scout meetings, ordering pizza and KFC on special occasions, and dressing to the nines to go out with my dad on the weekends. My brother and I would disappear for hours at a time, admonished by our mother to "go out and play," and though we lived in a suburban neighborhood, she would summon us back for dinner with a cowbell. Because my father would be gone for long stretches on his sales routes, when he was home, my brother and I followed him from room to room or out in the garden just to be around him. When we were much older and had plans of our own, my dad would lament the loss of his "two shadows."

IF MY PARENTS SPENT LITTLE time debating politics, neither did they lecture us on issues of morality. They were not pedagogic in that manner, and I can recall no bromides about right and wrong. They preferred instead to teach us by their example, and on the few occasions when they did discuss matters of morality, it was generally framed in terms of our faith and our family. "We stand on the shoulders of those who went before," my father would tell us, and "we have an obligation to the next generation to leave things better off." They were particularly solicitous of strangers, since, as we learned during Passover, we were once strangers in the land of Egypt.

I did not always follow their good example, about strangers or about Egypt. A few doors down from our house, a family moved in and erected a tall metal fence around their property. Their yard became overgrown with large weeds and shrubs and took on a deeply forbidding air. The family, immigrants from Egypt, had two daughters who attended the same public elementary school that I did, and we all rode the same bus. On more than one occasion, the kids on the bus would sing a hateful nursery rhyme about those two little girls, huddled next to each other on a seat as if trying to ward off the hostile world, which they were. I regret to say that I joined in that ugliness, knowing it was wrong and only glad the song was not about me. When I think back on those bus rides, more than fifty years later, I still feel the shame.

My father had a certain stoicism that was true to his generation, but also part of his upbringing. My grandparents complained little, touted their accomplishments even less, and tolerated no idleness or self-pity. When Frank lay dying in the hospital with pancreatic cancer, they cut him open, found the cancer widespread, and closed him back up—my grandmother, Martha, never told him what they found. As a pharmacist, Frank was worried that he might become addicted to the morphine they were giving him, but my grandmother knew that he would not live long enough for that to be a problem. As she and my father left the hospital room, Frank's life ebbing away, my father started to cry. His mother slapped him across the face.

"There will be plenty of time for that later," she said.

My folks were insistent that their children get a good education, and they reminded us that "this is the one thing they can never take away from you." Left unsaid was who *they* were, or why *they* would want to take things from us, but we surmised my parents were referring to the pogroms and the Holocaust that followed. When the topic did turn to politics, my parents took pains to emphasize the value of hearing each other's opinions. Neither political party, they told us, has a monopoly on good judgment, and it was essential to exchange ideas with curiosity and respect.

When I was nine, my father was promoted to a management position in Scottsdale, Arizona, so we packed our bags and relocated to the edge of the Sonoran Desert. To cushion the blow, my parents bought motorcycles for Dan and me, which we learned to ride on the arid landscape nearby, getting airborne over small dirt hills and finding arrowheads on the ground when we paused to catch our breath. Two years later, another promotion took us to California, where we settled in the East Bay, about an hour from San Francisco.

We joined a Reform synagogue, having been members of conservative shuls in both Framingham and Scottsdale, completing the transition like so many Jewish families from Orthodox to Reform in a single generation. Unlike our neighborhood on the East Coast, we lived in a predominantly Christian community in Northern California. I recall telling my friends on a county all-star soccer team that I could not play in the championship game because of Yom Kippur, and seeing their blank and uncomprehending faces. This was not a principled decision on my part, but an edict set out by my parents that I was powerless to disobey. We had only eleven players, and if I didn't show up, the team would be one short. I didn't play, and the team lost.

I had decidedly mixed views of my religion, any religion, growing up. I was proud of being Jewish, and of the accomplishments of so many Jewish people in the arts, sciences, medicine, law, practically every field of endeavor. But I was also conscious of how pride in one's faith can be paired with prejudice against those of other faiths, and acutely aware of how much violence and warfare was born of religious differences. It would not be until I was much older that I could reconcile these conflicting impulses and would come to view faith as a uniformly positive force, and the turmoil, tragedy, and torment of religious conflict as a bastardization of faith.

My parents were conscious of anti-Semitism but never consumed by a fear of it. They seldom brought up the subject, and I did not grow up feeling that it would hold me back, let alone pose a physical threat to me, even as I would encounter its ugly face from time to time. This was not the universal view in my family. One cousin and my father's dear friend, Ken Rapley, had been on one of the last Kindertransports out of Germany in 1939, never to see his mother again. Born Kurt Rosenfeld, he and his sister, Lotte, would leave Judaism behind, convinced that it could "happen again" and that no one should be fooled into complacency by America's melting pot. Germany too, Lotte would remind the grandchildren, had been the most civilized of nations.

I remember my father getting emotional on the subject of anti-Semitism only once, when I was in high school and chastised him for telling a Polish joke. At the time, we were watching the *CBS*

Evening News together. Walter Cronkite was a staple in our home, his sonorous voice as much of a fixture in my childhood as any other sights and sounds of that era, and something on the broadcast about Poland must have triggered the jest. My father was stung by my criticism but ultimately relented, offering by way of explanation if not justification:

"Adam," he said, his voice quavering with sadness and anger, "the Poles turned in their Jewish neighbors, took their homes, their property, and their lives. And the Jews were butchered. I'm sorry, I know it's not right, but I have no use for the Poles." I couldn't understand why he felt more animus toward the Poles than the Germans, as if collaboration were a greater sin than engineering the final solution, but he did.

In high school, I developed a strong love of language, rhetoric, and history. My brother was a huge influence, as older siblings tend to be, and he was fascinated by the theater arts and Shakespeare, and the ability of words to move an audience. From the phonograph in his adjacent bedroom, I heard the wonderful voices of Laurence Olivier, Ralph Richardson, and John Gielgud performing *Hamlet, Richard III,* or *Henry IV.* He introduced me to Arthur Miller and Eugene O'Neill, and we would travel to Ashland, Oregon, for the Shakespeare festival. I loved seeing plays with him, stealing backstage to meet Jason Robards after *A Long Day's Journey into Night,* tears in Dan's eyes as he described the performance. His excitement, and the way he was so powerfully moved, was infectious.

Still, I was more interested in the words that moved nations, and when the voice of Richard Burton would pierce the thin wall between our rooms, I would answer back with recordings of John and Robert Kennedy, Winston Churchill, or Dr. Martin Luther King, Jr. Growing up in Boston, I was particularly enamored of the Kennedys, their call to service, and the beauty of their lofty rhetoric and ideals. I admired how unabashed they were about using literary references, never speaking down to their audiences but lifting them up, as when Robert Kennedy quoted Aeschylus after the death of

Martin Luther King: "Even in our sleep, pain which cannot forget falls drop by drop upon the heart, until, in our own despair, against our will, comes wisdom through the awful grace of God."

I MADE MY WAY TO Capitol Hill for the first time after my freshman year at Stanford, when I applied for congressional internships, eventually working in the Capitol or district offices of three members of the House of Representatives. Two were Democrats—Nick Mavroules of Massachusetts and George Miller of California. The third was Pete McCloskey, a Republican who represented Palo Alto and whose local office was a short drive from my dormitory.

But the most significant political experience I had in those years wasn't in a congressional office or a college lecture hall. It was the portion of my sophomore year that I spent abroad. In 1980, the university leased a beautiful estate on the river Thames, outside London, and I spent three months studying British constitutional law there. In small and ornate classrooms, once the preserve of dukes and earls, my professor expounded on Britain's unwritten constitution, comprised of Acts of Parliament, court judgments, and convention. It was astounding to me that a nation that could give rise to such strong principles of constitutional jurisprudence should rely so heavily on unwritten rules—not even the existence of the office of prime minister is codified, but rests only on a strong historical tradition. I thought that our Bill of Rights, and the checks and balances of our system, had a much more solid foundation, because they were laid out explicitly in a written document. Little did I understand how reliant our democracy was on its own conventions, and how easily those norms might be overthrown.

When the term was over, I bought a rail pass and traveled with three friends through a divided Germany and on to East Berlin. At Checkpoint Charlie, we stared at the barbed wire and imposing concrete walls that East Germany had erected, not to keep the West Germans out, but to keep their own citizens in. West Germany had prospered under a system of freedom and capitalism, while East

Germans were living in a police state, unable to express themselves freely, unable to choose their own leaders, and suffering from a poor economy and worse health. If there was ever a living proof of the dehumanization of Communism, this was it. In the United States, it was easy to engage in a partisan battle between Democrats and Republicans, secure in the knowledge that our differences were substantial but not foundational to our democracy and governance. But here, in the face of a Soviet-style dictatorship, I understood how lucky I was to live in a country where both political parties shared a commitment to the rights and dignity of the individual.

As my classmates and I returned to West Germany and continued our travels, the memory of Berlin haunted me. All of my reading about the Soviet Bloc, in newspapers and political science classes, had not prepared me for the visceral reality of a country in which everyone was imprisoned. I wanted to see more of the Communist system, and when my classmates were ready to return home, I decided to go back to the Soviet Bloc alone.

I made my way to Athens, and then Istanbul, meeting other travelers along the way. On a bus across the Turkish border, I met a group of Iraqi Kurds who shared their food and their aspirations for a homeland as one of the largest ethnic groups in the world without a country of their own. On a thirty-two-hour train ride, I sat beside an Iranian man, and we discussed the violent revolution that was under way in his country. Religious radicals in thrall to the Ayatollah Khomeini had recently seized power from the American-backed shah, and they were holding dozens of American citizens hostage in the U.S. embassy in Tehran. The man spoke limited English, and he was reluctant to talk about the standoff, but ultimately he made his views clear: "The shah was a killer-man," he said gravely, before adding, "Khomeini, also killer-man. No change."

At last I crossed behind the Iron Curtain into Bulgaria, arriving at its capital, Sofia. I had no plans, no one to contact, and nowhere to stay, but I was determined not to spend money in the downtown hotel operated by the Soviet government. I found a seat on the steps of a small factory, began eating some of the bread and cheese that had become my constant diet, and took out a map to explore what few options I had. After a few minutes, a man came out of the factory, sat beside me, opened his lunch, and without a word handed me a beer. We drank in silence for a minute or two, then he tried speaking to me in Bulgarian. I didn't understand, so I responded in English, which he didn't understand. Somehow we settled on French, which neither of us spoke well but we both spoke well enough. The beer helped.

His name was Michel Dusak, and he lived with his mother, Anastasia, and a young cousin. He invited me to join them for dinner, and having no other plans, I accepted. He returned to work, and I met him there again when he emerged at the end of the day. As we walked to his house, he pointed out the unmarked cars of the secret police, and I began to get a sense of the surveillance state he was living in.

Michel's family was warm and intimate, and our conversation was a mixture of politics and history. I spoke French with him and his mother and English with his cousin, and as the dinner drew to a close, I invited them to come visit me in the United States. The conversation then grew quiet, as they explained that wouldn't be possible; they were not members of the Communist Party, and travel outside the Eastern Bloc was a privilege reserved for party members.

Suddenly the front door swung open. The conversation immediately stopped, and the sense of alarm was palpable. Had someone been listening? We waited, but no one came in. Michel closed the door, and we gradually settled back down. Still, I began to wonder whether my visit might be endangering Michel's family. Getting up, I thanked them and returned to the train station for the night, lying down on the floor with my head on my backpack. I thought about how alien the Communist system was, how suffocating and demoralizing. "There is nothing like travel to make a patriot out of you," my father had told me before I left for Europe, and I could now see the wisdom of his words.

Back in the United States, I was certain I wanted a career in which I could be of service, but I wasn't sure how or even what field. I had developed an interest in medicine as well as government, and I enjoyed classes in physics and biology. In medicine, the public good was tangible, and it was brought about in a collaborative way, with doctors, nurses, and hospital staff all working toward the unmitigated good of saving lives. Politics could bring about systemic change, improving the lives of scores of people and on a scale that seemed far greater, but it was also contentious, messy, and sometimes corrupt. I procrastinated as long as I could, and when I decided on law school, my parents could not hide their disappointment.

My mother's family was already well populated with lawyers, and she was hoping, like all Jewish mothers, that her son would become a doctor. She knew I was interested in public policy, but she harbored a deep-seated distrust of politics and thought it was a dirty business. Part of this was born of her father's bitter experience after being promised a judgeship and passed over, a heartbreak she ascribed to anti-Semitism. The idea that her son might immerse himself in a world that had left her father so devastated was deeply troubling to her.

"As long as you are good at what you do," my father had once told me as a child, "there will always be a demand for you." This was a very liberating idea—that all I needed to do was focus on being good at my chosen profession and the rest would take care of itself. My brother would go on to become a playwright, no doubt encouraged by the same sound advice. But that was when we were young and the future seemed far off. Now my father likewise could not conceal his disappointment with my decision: "You say you are interested in law, and I would think that certain aspects of corporate law would be fascinating. But you say that you are interested in politics; that just makes me nauseous."

But my course was set. Months later, I arrived at Harvard Law School, excited to be back in the state of my birth. I sought out one of the most powerful legal minds on campus, Laurence Tribe, taking his class in constitutional law and serving as one of his research assistants. Tribe was a god among the Harvard faculty, enormously bright, fantastically articulate, and a frequent presence before the Supreme Court. I admired the way his mind worked, his ability to analyze and dissect an issue, to keep an organizational structure in his head, and to express complex thoughts in an erudite but digestible manner. I had no doubt that his training as a mathematician had something to do with his keen analytical ability, and he is one of the most gifted thinkers and orators I have ever met. I sat in awe of Tribe as a student, never imagining that we would remain in touch. To this day, he is one of the first people I call for advice on complex questions, as do so many of my colleagues. No law professor would play more of a role in shaping policy on a broad range of topics, from campaign finance reform to civil rights and freedom of speech. And there was certainly no one I would turn to more often when navigating the difficult waters around the shoals of impeachment.

3

TAKE OUT YOUR ROLODEX

LAW SCHOOL DOESN'T TEACH YOU HOW TO TRY A CASE, OR EVEN HOW to investigate one. And it certainly doesn't teach you how to tell a story, how to take a complex set of facts and weave them into a coherent and engaging narrative. And while you may learn how to present an argument to an appellate judge, there is nothing in the curriculum about speaking to a jury of your peers, and the heavy burden that accompanies asking someone to deprive another human being of their liberty. I learned those skills in Los Angeles, fresh out of a federal district court clerkship and a short stint in private practice, when I joined the United States Attorney's Office for the Central District of California in 1987.

I moved to Venice, California, after law school and found a rental on a quiet street near the beach. If you are going to live in Southern California, why would anyone choose to live anywhere but the beach? At least that was my thinking, and I loved breathing in the cool ocean air, people-watching along the boardwalk, and hanging out at the Rose Café. For a prosecutor, Los Angeles in the mid-1980s was a challenging place to be, with no shortage of serious crime, from carjackings and drug trafficking to defense contractor fraud and police corruption. The Central District included more than twelve million people, and the U.S. Attorney's Office consisted of over a hundred prosecutors who would handle any of the serious federal crimes that were committed in the region.

After an obligatory stint on "rookie row" trying cases involving bank robberies, stolen Treasury checks, large seizures of cocaine, and counterfeit cash, I joined the Public Corruption and Government Fraud section, where I handled cases involving bad cops, corrupt immigration officials taking bribes, environmental crimes, and more. One case would involve a pastor who was selling for profit surplus government food that he was supposed to be using to feed his flock, and another a ruthless Mexican drug lord complicit in the torture murder of an American DEA agent named Enrique Camarena that had my family worried over my safety.

But the most important case I would come to handle during my time in the U.S. Attorney's Office involved a different kind of danger. And it would introduce me to the shadowy world of espionage—how foreign powers targeted American citizens and preyed upon the vulnerabilities of greed, lust, and resentment—a vital education that would come in handy decades later in ways that I could not have imagined.

In the long history of the Federal Bureau of Investigation, none of its agents had ever been accused of betraying the country by spying for a hostile power. To be sure, the FBI had been implicated in the most egregious violations of civil rights under the autocratic rule of J. Edgar Hoover, but the idea that an FBI agent would be so corruptible as to sell out their country for money or sex was unthinkable. That is, until 1984, and an agent named Richard Miller.

Short, stout, and sloppily dressed, Miller appeared to survive on a diet of candy bars and soda. He was routinely admonished by superiors to comply with the bureau's standards for professional appearance, and he was considered by his colleagues to be equally slovenly in his work—taking three-hour lunch breaks at the local 7-Eleven, selling Amway products from the back of his car, and carrying on multiple affairs during work hours.

His apparent unfitness notwithstanding, Miller had one of the most sensitive positions in the office, as part of its counterintelligence squad. Counterintelligence is a confusing topic for the public, but it is how the U.S. government keeps an eye on foreign spies operating in our country, and acts to "counter" the intelligence-gathering efforts of our adversaries.

Given the particular importance of the FBI's counterintelligence work, as well as its essential access to classified information, many agents in the Los Angeles field office were mystified that Miller had been assigned to the unit. Yet there was an innate shrewdness and self-deprecation to Miller, and a manipulative ability that allowed him to ingratiate himself with others.

Miller's poor work ethic, financial problems, and promiscuity made him a prime target for the Kremlin. The Russian government doesn't waste time trying to corrupt those who are financially secure and of irreproachable character. Russian tradecraft deliberately focuses on those who already show signs of weakness, greed, or other vulnerabilities. Miller had been selected as a target by a young asset of the KGB named Svetlana Ogorodnikova (why do they always seem to be named Svetlana?), who, along with her husband, Nikolai, had immigrated to the United States from the Soviet Union. The Ogorodnikovs were unhappy in their new country and wanted to go back, but defectors were considered traitors by Soviet officials; in order to return, they needed to earn their passage home. Miller was Svetlana's ticket back.

Miller came into contact with Svetlana because she was a potential source of information for the bureau, since she was in contact with the Soviet émigré community in which Russian spies were likely to operate or conceal themselves. Svetlana was gregarious, flirtatious, and attractive, and Miller made an easy mark. What began as officially sanctioned contacts, documented and reported, soon became illicit meetings in which Svetlana had sex with him, first in his car and later at motels, and gave him money and gifts. In return, Miller smuggled classified and national security information out of the bureau and provided it to Svetlana for her KGB handler, a senior officer out of the San Francisco Russian consulate named Aleksandr Grishin.

At some point, Miller's colleagues at the FBI discovered that he had been meeting with Svetlana and not reporting it. Suspicious, they started following him shortly before Miller was to fly to Vienna to meet with a general in Russia's military intelligence unit, the GRU. As a counterintelligence agent, Miller was trained to detect surveillance and recognized that he was being followed by his fellow agents. Before he could be arrested, he went to his supervisor's office at the bureau and laid out what would prove to be a difficult defense to overcome—he had been secretly meeting with Svetlana as part of his efforts to infiltrate the KGB, in what he described as a "double-agent scenario."

Miller was charged with providing classified and national defense secrets to the Soviets, including the FBI's own manual on its counter-intelligence needs, methods, and requirements. The matter was of such significance to the Department of Justice that the U.S. attorney himself, Robert Bonner, would try the case. After a monthslong trial, the jury deadlocked, with some jurors believing that investigators had "browbeaten" Miller during interrogations and forced a partial confession. His second trial was overturned by an appeals court that objected to the prosecution's use of a failed polygraph test as evidence. By the time the case was returned to our office for a third trial, Bonner had accepted a position on the federal bench, and he needed to assign the case to someone else.

When I had interviewed with Bonner for a position in the office three years earlier, I had much less experience than most of the other applicants. "How long have you been in private practice?" he asked me after I had survived earlier rounds of interviews and scrutiny.

"Three months," I responded.

"That long!" he replied. "Why don't you stay in private practice awhile and get some trial experience. That way you won't be so eager to go back to the private sector after joining our office." I told him that I would get more trial experience in the U.S. Attorney's Office in three months than I would in a big firm in three years, and I asked him to take a chance on me. He did. But hiring me was one thing; entrusting me with the Miller case was another. This would be the last trial for the government and for Miller. Either the national security interests of the country would be vindicated, or he would walk. Bonner took another chance on me, and I was assigned to try the case.

With testimony from two prior trials and the grand jury, and thousands of exhibits, there was a mountain of evidence with which I had no familiarity. To prepare, I would need to spend months immersing myself in the record and interviewing Miller's former colleagues in the FBI. His private defense lawyers, Joel Levine and Stan Greenberg, were extremely capable and had the advantage of representing him during all of the prior proceedings. They were deeply skilled at drawing out inconsistencies in prior testimony and would be formidable opposing counsel.

By then I had tried many cases with the bureau, but nothing like this, and it brought me into close contact with dozens of agents working long hours to prepare for trial. I was impressed that these agents never tried to minimize Miller's conduct or hide the deficiencies in the bureau that his betrayal had exposed, and I developed a profound respect for the organizational culture that encouraged agents to pursue corruption in their own ranks. Dozens of them spent countless hours walking me through the details of their investigative process, explaining how the effort to ensnare Miller fitted into a larger pattern of Russian tradecraft. I came to understand how the Kremlin exploits the most basic human vulnerabilities: preying on those who feel unappreciated and resentful, who are fixated on money and success, who have a history of dishonesty and are prone to infidelity.

The case was assigned to Judge Robert Takasugi, a progressive judge who had been interned during the Second World War and who was known for his skepticism of the government and prosecutors. Levine and Greenberg wasted no time in waiving their right to trial by jury and allowing Takasugi to be the trier of both the facts and the law.

When the trial began, I pointed out that Miller's brand of espionage, like that of most spies, was not ideological, but was rather a crime of dollars and cents, of lust, of dissatisfaction, even of boredom. I emphasized why Miller was vulnerable to recruitment and why the Soviets would target him. The defendant was isolated from his church when he was excommunicated for adultery, and he was isolated from his wife and family. He was also isolated at work, with his field assignments taken away, relegated to endless hours of listening to wiretaps, and suspended without pay for failing to meet the bureau's weight standards. When an agent was suspended, it was a bureau tradition that other agents would take up a collection for his family, but none did. Miller not only was broke but felt betrayed.

One aspect of Russian tradecraft involves luring in a potential target by seeking incremental compromises that will eventually ensnare the victim. In Miller's case, it began with clandestine meetings with Svetlana against the explicit warning of his supervisor, enough to get Miller disciplined again if he was caught. Then sex with her, a firing offense, then small amounts of cash, a criminal matter, and finally the dangle of $50,000 worth of gold for classified information, a potential capital crime. She began by seeking the names of other Soviet defectors who were residing in Los Angeles that she could report to her KGB handlers. And later, she sought something even more significant, the Positive Intelligence Reporting Guide outlining the FBI's counterintelligence strategy.

In October 1990, after a seven-week trial, Judge Takasugi found Miller guilty on all six counts, sentencing him to twenty years in prison. I was proud to have helped the Department of Justice and the FBI finally deliver justice in the case, but I was also deeply concerned by what it revealed. While Miller was the first FBI agent convicted of spying, I knew that he wouldn't be the last. Indeed, during the same year in which Miller's spying came to an end, another FBI agent, Robert Hanssen, began a decades-long clandestine relationship with the KGB, something the Justice Department would come to call "possibly the worst intelligence disaster in U.S. history."

Our government is filled with patriotic and honorable public servants, but there will always be a small number who are vulnerable to foreign entreaties—and I now understood how determined the Russian government was to find them. Perhaps it was naïve of me at the time, but I little imagined that people of moral turpitude could occupy the highest positions of our government and make themselves targets of Russian tradecraft. But when an unscrupulous businessman later ran for president and surrounded himself with fellow grifters, I recognized both the target-rich environment it provided for Russian intelligence and the unmistakable hallmarks of their compromise. And the most terrible realization was not far behind: that a president of the United States could be so easily manipulated to serve the interests of our adversaries.

MY DECISION TO RUN FOR office came after the Miller trial. I loved my work in the office, the late nights and camaraderie, the war stories and strategizing over difficult cases. I won every case I brought, not because I was a good lawyer—there were many good lawyers—but because I was a careful one, only seeking indictment where I could prove guilt beyond a reasonable doubt, never overcharging a case, reasonable in plea negotiations, and honest with my judges and juries.

Still, my job as a prosecutor had its limitations. In a courtroom, I could deliver justice, but only after the fact. I started to take a strong interest in the juvenile justice system, in all the factors that led someone into a life of criminal conduct, and in the revolving door of our prison system. And I wondered whether it would be possible to exert a deeper influence on criminal justice through the political process. After three years as a prosecutor, I decided to leave the U.S. Attorney's Office in the hope of obtaining a new position that would allow me to be more proactive.

If the arc of my career was about to change, it was nothing as profound as what was taking place in my personal life. Two people would enter my life and change it indelibly. One would be a seven-year-old child living in nearby Inglewood and the other was a beautiful young woman I met on a tennis court.

When I moved to Los Angeles, I planned to stay for just the year of my clerkship, and wasn't sure that I liked the City of Angels. It was large and sprawling, with a downtown that most people avoided at night, and as dry as the desert that it was. What's more, it was confusing to hear Bruce Springsteen's version of "Santa Claus Is Coming to Town" when it was 85 degrees out. And it was even more disorienting to go to a Dodgers game and see half the stadium empty out before the game was over so people could beat the traffic. Diehard Red Sox fans would never dream of such a thing. But Los Angeles has a way of grabbing hold of you, and soon enough I found that I loved living in a community as diverse and vibrant as this one, with lots of unique neighborhoods, a fascinating history, exotic cuisine, and beaches and mountains only a short drive away.

Once I decided to settle in Los Angeles, I fulfilled a promise I had made to myself years earlier and walked into the office of Big Brothers of Greater Los Angeles. One of my law school classmates had been a Big Brother, and I vowed that I would do the same when I was living in one place long enough to make the commitment. The staff at Big Brothers told me that there was a long waiting list of little brothers in Los Angeles hoping to be paired, and that it was particularly long, several years long, for Black kids. They asked me how I would feel about being paired with an African American little brother, and I told them I thought that I would benefit from the experience. I was then given three little brother applications to look over, and I was immediately struck by one of them.

On the application, little brothers were asked what three things they wished for. Normally, a child would list the material objects they wanted—a bike, a skateboard, or a room of their own. But on one of the applications, the child made the following three asks: a big brother, a puppy, and a beautiful world. *A beautiful world.* What five- or six-year-old kid uses one of their precious three wishes for something as selfless and abstract as a beautiful world? David McMillan was his name.

David and I went on Big Brothers for a day, an outing designed to see how well you click together, a trial run. I took David to Venice Beach, where we walked along the boardwalk, stepped into the surf, and declared ourselves "the survivors." Indeed, we were. More than thirty years later, we remain family, seeing each other often, sharing many of life's experiences along the way: his graduation from Yale and USC film school, serving as a groomsman in my wedding, watching professional actors perform a play he wrote about the O. J. Simpson trial, dinners, movies, political events, campaigns. He has added more to my life than I could ever have imagined, and I could not be more proud of everything he has accomplished, the kind of man he has become, himself now a big brother, part of the same program that brought us together.

I met Eve a few years after becoming brothers with David, toward the end of the Miller case. I was still living in Venice, sharing a small house near the beach with a fellow prosecutor named Mark Byrne, when I was invited to join a friend for some doubles tennis. As with many stories of a first meeting, it almost didn't happen. I had said I would try to join my friend for some mixed-doubles tennis on Saturday morning, but after staying out late Friday night, I was tempted to pass. My roommate encouraged me, saying that these women I would be playing tennis with could be "hot" and I should go. That was incentive enough.

As it turned out, Mark was right, and I was immediately struck by Eve. She was smart, tall, brunette, beautiful, and with a killer double backhand. When the match was over and we all said our goodbyes, I promptly called her and asked her out. On our first date, we went to a kitschy Italian restaurant in Playa del Rey called Giovanni's Salerno Beach, the kind of place where Christmas lights are up all year long and where the owner sings opera and not very well, but with excellent food. Then we went to a jazz club in Santa Monica, listened to some good music, and got better acquainted. Eve had gone to college at UC Santa Barbara and done consulting with Arthur Andersen and was now in brand management at Carnation. Somehow, we got into a discussion about marriage, and I will never forget what she said. She was in no hurry to settle down, since it was hard enough to imagine "spending the rest of my life with the same person." Obviously, she hadn't met the right guy yet.

She was definitely not the committing type, but then neither was I. So we moved on to other weighty matters, like which sections of the newspaper we read first in the morning. I was a purist: front page, California, Sports, Opinion, Business, and last, if at all, View. *Who bothers to read the View section?* I scoffed. Without missing a beat, she said, "My father has had a syndicated column in the View section for years." I may have been clumsy—I was clumsy—but I was also entranced. She was beguiling, interesting, and delightfully playful. She made fun of me, and I enjoyed being made fun of. And did I say she was gorgeous? She was totally gorgeous (still is, by the way). I was lucky to get a second date.

My initial efforts at politics were not so fortuitous. I would lose my first two races for the state assembly, and if I had taken some early advice I received, I might never have run for office in the first place. Before my first race, I sought out one of the most experienced political hands in Los Angeles, Richard Katz, a hard-bitten Democratic leader in the state assembly.

"Take out your Rolodex," he told me, "and put a number next to every name. Then I want you to cross out that number, and write in half that amount. Then I want you to cross out that number, and write in half that amount. Then I want you to add up all those numbers. If they add up to three hundred fifty thousand dollars or more, you should run. If not, don't waste anybody's time."

When I got home I took out my Rolodex, and it didn't take me long to realize that my numbers were never going to add up to that amount or anything like it. But I pressed on anyway, and for the next two months, Eve and I walked through the district from morning to night, with me on one side of the street and Eve on the other, knocking on doors and introducing ourselves. And when my campaign coffers dwindled a few weeks before the election, I cashed out my retirement savings to keep the campaign going.

After the polls closed on election day, I not only lost, but finished eleventh out of fifteen candidates. It was a humiliating end to my first political campaign. As cynical as his advice had been, Richard Katz had been right. I couldn't raise the money and I didn't run a credible campaign.

When you win an election, it is an exhilarating experience. The phone rings constantly, and there is all the excitement of being sworn in, hiring your staff, and planning your agenda. Your victory also comes to have a certain inexorable character: "Well, of course he won, he did everything right." But when you lose, and lose badly, it takes on an equally obvious and debilitating tenor: "What on earth was he thinking?"

As I lay in my apartment, sun streaming through dirty window blinds and dancing on particles of dust in the air, the stillness was disorienting. The last two months had been a whirlwind of activity. Now, nothing. The phone was silent, my friends had moved on, Eve was at work, and I was alone to contemplate my loss and the future. I was disappointed, of course, but what really bothered me as I surveyed the election results was the realization that each of the candidates had placed in about the same order as their level of fundraising.

I didn't have long to stew on it—I was now broke and out of work. I spent a few days making phone calls to thank my friends and supporters, then I dialed the number of the U.S. Attorney's Office to see about getting my job back. As it turned out, there was a new and exciting opportunity for a senior prosecutor that immediately caught my interest. It was through a program known as the Central and Eastern European Law Initiative (CEELI), which had been created by the American Bar Association to provide legal assistance to countries formerly in the Soviet Union.

Since the collapse of the Berlin Wall, two years earlier, many regions of the USSR had broken off and declared their independence. The U.S. government was eager to help these emerging democracies establish norms in sync with our own. As part of that effort, the State Department and the U.S. Agency for International Development (USAID) were planning to select three federal prosecutors from around the country to spend six months of the coming year in Hungary, Romania, and Czechoslovakia. To return to the region a decade after my travels there as a student, and just as those countries navigated the path from authoritarian rule to democratic self-governance, would offer an extraordinary window on a profound moment in history. I applied immediately, and soon enough, I received a letter from USAID—its message was as exhilarating as it was succinct—*Pack your bags.*

4

A MAN MAY CHANGE HIS CLOTHES, BUT HE IS STILL THE SAME MAN

THERE ARE FEW THINGS MORE POWERFUL DURING TIMES OF ECONOMIC turmoil than xenophobic populism. And it was in Czechoslovakia that I would first witness the nation-altering impacts of an unscrupulous leader who could skillfully tap the anxieties and resentments of his fellow citizens to drive change. Vladimir Meciar would take the jarring increase in income inequality following the collapse of Communism and use it to propel not only his own rise, but a literal division of the country that only months earlier seemed fanciful. Like other populist movements, Meciar needed a real or imagined villain, an "other" to blame the nation's problems on, and he used hatred as an organizing tool. As a young lawyer working in the newly liberated Eastern Bloc, I thought that successful country-destroying autocrats like Meciar could only be found across the oceans from America, never imagining that such a dangerous populism could take root at home.

Pressed against the banks of the Danube River, about an hour east of Vienna, Bratislava is the Slovak capital and has served for centuries as a gateway between Western Europe and Asia. For the first time in their lives, Slovaks were grappling with the freedoms and frustrations of a market economy, learning to manage a checking account, to purchase property, and to establish a business while navigating a panoply of new risks in the form of organized crime, fraud schemes, and predatory lending.

I had been provided housing in the apartment of a professor who was out of the country, and I found the space unexpectedly cozy, with simple furniture, worn rugs, and a stereo that reminded me of the one I had in college. A woman named Lydia Durosova, who worked for the Slovak attorney general, had been selected to serve as my host. As I got to know Lydia and her husband, Jan, I tried to imagine how it felt to live through a period of such radical transformation. The drastic economic change the country was going through was spectacularly disruptive, turning doctors into taxi drivers and political dissidents into entrepreneurs. Almost nothing that Lydia and Jan had known of their country looked or felt precisely the same as it had only years earlier.

I spent six weeks immersing myself in the Slovak language with a private teacher before I arrived, and it was now sink or swim. Although Lydia and Jan spoke English, few of my Slovak interlocutors did, and I spent the next couple of months struggling to understand and be understood. On my first day at work, I was escorted to the attorney general's private office for an undrinkable cup of coffee. While Lydia was pleased to have a colleague from the United States to collaborate with, the attorney general himself was more aloof, and I began to wonder whether this was a partnership that he had requested or felt obligated to accept.

Outside of the office, Lydia introduced me to some of her friends and neighbors, and I struck up a friendship with a Jewish poet named Milan Richter. Richter's ancestors had lived in the region for centuries, and most of his family had been exterminated during the Holocaust. His poetry was provocative and unconventional, and for years, he had been denied publication by Communist Party apparat-chiks. Now that Communism had fallen, many of its former leaders had insinuated themselves into new positions of leadership. One of them, a former Communist leader who had been responsible for Richter's blacklisting, became the minister of education. "Do not be fooled by the façade," he warned when I described the warm greet-ing the minister had given me. "A man may change his clothes, but he is still the same man."

I was invited to tour the prisons in Slovakia, and discuss offender rehabilitation with the Ministry of the Interior. I soon discovered that prison officials were not in the habit of sharing coffee; they drank hard liquor, and at any hour. I remember pulling up to a prison one morning at 9 A.M., when the warden cheerfully invited me into his office and poured two shots of Slivovitz a strong plum brandy with enough alcohol to get a campfire started. One shot was for my health and the next for his. Then he poured a third round—I'm not sure whose health that was for!

After a tour of the facility, I left in a daze, and I still had two more prisons to visit that morning. I found the same welcoming rit-ual at each. By the time I went to lunch with prison officials, at a table laden with beer and wine, I had already drunk nine shots and my head was reeling. I somehow made it back to my apartment to lie down, watching the walls and ceiling spin around me. In the weeks to come, I learned to deflect many of the drinks I was offered, as I had but one liver to give for my country.

But the most intense phase of my immersion into Slovak public and private life would be the time I spent with judges and parlia-mentarians. This required me to travel frequently from Bratislava to Prague, which meant crossing the invisible line that separated Slo-vakia from the Czech Lands. The two regions had been combined into a single nation after World War I, but they were separated by ethnic and religious differences that proved difficult to overcome—and easily exploited for political gain. In the years leading up to World War II, as Hitler rose to power in Germany, he deliberately stoked those divisions to weaken the country. In 1939, with Hitler's encouragement, Slovakia broke away to declare its independence. The end of World War II brought the two nations back together in 1945, and a fragile union persisted under pressure from the Soviet Union. Even so, tensions lingered below the surface, and in 1968, the USSR permitted them a partial separation into semiautonomous jurisdictions. Finally, with the Soviet Union beginning to crumble in the 1980s, political leaders in both Slovakia and the Czech Lands began agitating for complete independence.

The separatist impulse in the Czech Lands was driven in significant part by economics. With a gross domestic product about 20 percent higher than Slovakia's, Czechs saw a substantial share of their taxes diverted to their poorer neighbors. For Slovaks, the push to independence was also tied to ethnic and religious differences, and a strong desire to be out from under the yoke of national leadership dominated by Czechs.

As I began getting to know Czech judges and parliamentarians, I found that many of them did not take the risk of a formal separation seriously. I remember meeting with the chief justice of the Supreme Court, a tall and distinguished older man named Milan Holub, who told me with great certainty that the Slovak threat to secede was purely tactical and designed to extract greater economic concessions. The ethnonationalist sentiment in Slovakia might be powerful, he admitted, but the tangible benefits to Slovakia of staying in the union were much stronger. Slovakia's separatist leader, Vladimir Meciar, was a crude and autocratic figure who railed against ethnic minorities with racist insinuations and xenophobic resentment in his campaign for Slovak prime minister, but Slovaks had to know they would suffer if parted from the Czechs. I shared Holub's profound aversion to Meciar, but I wondered if the teeming crowds at his rallies might be more indicative of Slovak sentiment than Holub was prepared to believe. Only three months later, and shortly after Meciar's victory at the polls, the Slovak government announced its formal separation from Czechoslovakia in what would be referred to as "the velvet divorce."

By the time that Eve arrived to visit me in Bratislava, the country that I had come to assist would soon no longer exist. It had been torn apart with startling efficiency by the divisive and populist rhetoric of Meciar, but the conditions that allowed Meciar to thrive were much deeper. I had seen the profound anxieties of daily life in Bratislava, as residents struggled to adapt in a period of radical economic change, and I had watched him skillfully stoke a sense of grievance among Slovaks—pinning blame for their economic distress on various minority groups and promising to restore prosperity by vanquishing the targets of his hatred.

As Eve and I began two weeks of travel by train through the nearby lands of my ancestors, I thought about the long and dangerous tradition that Meciar represented. In Lithuania, we visited the city of Panevezys, where Jacob and Bessie Schiff had lived a century earlier. My memories of Bessie resemble a silent film, black-and-white images of a stocky woman bustling in the kitchen on Jewish holidays, the scent of brisket in the air, soup boiling on the stove, challah toasting under the broiler. Jacob passed away before I was born, and I recall him only from a photograph, towering over Bessie and looking every bit the stern, goateed picture of Eastern European Judaism.

Neither Eve nor I spoke a word of Lithuanian, but most of the residents were fluent in Russian—which is similar enough to Slovak that I was able to communicate with them. I began asking people where we could find the city's old synagogues, and we quickly learned that only one remained, not as a temple, but as a basketball court. We found the building and went inside, and as I looked up to the balcony in the rear of the small building, I could imagine Bessie there, young and beautiful, looking down on Jacob below. And I could see my great-grandfather, not far from the ark—now sadly a basket and hoop—davening his thanks to God even as he planned his emigration.

Nearby Vilnius had been home to one of the largest Jewish communities in Europe. With more than a hundred synagogues, it was nicknamed by Napoleon the Jerusalem of the North. All of that came to an end in the 1930s and '40s as the Nazis prosecuted their campaign of extermination against Jews across the continent. In Vilnius, Christian residents turned on their neighbors with a staggering brutality, and by 1945, almost all of the city's Jews had been murdered—among the greatest losses of Jewish life and culture in Central or Eastern Europe. I understood the sinister backdrop of that genocide: how the Nazis had exploited the nexus between fear and hatred, casting blame on Jews for the economic distress after World War I and promising to restore stability by persecuting the "outsider."

The immense and growing popularity of Meciar in Slovakia was not to be equated with the rise of fascist leaders in the 1930s, but his methods in a period of economic turmoil—casting blame on the ethnic Hungarian minority and stoking fear of the impoverished Romany community—were a disturbing echo. Not all populists are kin, but the ability to stop those who would dehumanize others as a path to power depends on the will to resist, the durability of institutions, and fidelity to the law. Milan Richter had said that Slovakia's own brand of anti-Semitism was never far from the surface. The murder of his family had been aided and abetted by people who had been their neighbors. Were Slovak institutions strong enough now to resist the recurrence of such dangerous hatreds?

Of course, the problem of racism and tribalism was not far from the surface back home either. From Eastern Europe, I had watched in horror only months earlier as Los Angeles erupted in riots over the brutal assault on Rodney King by police officers. We held out the United States as a model of democracy to other nations, but our history was replete with ethnic discrimination and violence that included the enslavement of Black Americans, the wholesale slaughter of Native Americans, and the internment of the Japanese Americans during World War II. How many of our own racial divisions were still simmering, just below the boiling point of violence? To see my city engulfed in flames was shocking to me, but it was much more comprehensible to my brother David. On the phone from Los Angeles, he understood, in a way I could not, the immense frustrations of the Black community after decades of police violence against people of color, and the terrible persistence of systemic racism. Our country too was in a period of economic transformation, and for many of our political leaders, the temptation to exploit the divisions it was causing was proving irresistible.

In 1992, many seemed to believe that the decline of the Soviet Union would lead inexorably to the spread of representative government around the world; one of our country's foremost scholars had just published a book describing liberal democracy's ascendance as "the end of history." The titanic struggles of the twentieth century were over, and, the political scientist Francis Fukuyama theorized, fascism and Communism had been defeated, liberal democracy and free markets had won, and there would be no going back. Standing among the ghosts of Panevczys and Vilnius, after six months in a crumbling Czechoslovakia, and having witnessed my own city of Los Angeles riot and burn, it was difficult to share his confidence that mankind had made such dramatic progress.

TWO YEARS AFTER MY RETURN from Czechoslovakia, I ran for the state legislature again and would encounter my own challenge in confronting the power of xenophobic populism. My opponent was James Rogan, a former prosecutor in the Los Angeles County District Attorney's Office and later a state court judge. With a thick shock of brown hair combed to the side, a broad forehead, and sharp features, Rogan had a harsh aspect and spoke with the stridency of an angry pastor. He was smart, hardworking, articulate—a formidable opponent. And I was not just running against Rogan; I also had to contend with a xenophobic measure that Republicans placed on the ballot in 1994 to boost turnout.

Proposition 187 was a populist response to the 1990 recession, which sought to blame immigrants for the rise in unemployment and other societal ills. It required schools to verify and report the legal status of students and their parents, and it denied access by undocumented immigrants to all public services except emergency care. It was wildly popular in conservative districts, even those that were narrowly conservative, like the one in which I was running. I was against it, and it ran me over like a train.

The 1994 midterms brought a powerful Republican wave up and down the state and country, and I ended up losing the race by over 10 percent. I thought that was likely to be the end of my abortive political career. Compared to several Democratic legislators who lost their seats by even larger margins, I had done well, but after expending my time, energy, and resources on two unsuccessful runs for political office, I felt it was time to move on with my life.

Eve and I had become serious about each other and gotten engaged the previous December. She wasn't like anyone I had ever met or dated before. Very strong and adventurous, she had traveled alone in Africa and Asia and was fascinated with other cultures and languages. In college, she had taken a year off to study at the Sorbonne while working as a nanny to a family in Paris. She lorded her French over mine, made fun of my intellectual pretensions, and was a far better athlete. But more than anything else, I adored being with her and could easily imagine spending our lives together. She had made me the committing type. I proposed to her while we were visiting her folks in Del Mar, about two hours south of Los Angeles. I waited until she was out of the room to ask her father, Jim, for his permission to marry his daughter. His answer was appropriate for a man who had spent years writing a newspaper column (in the View section) entitled "Liberated Male." "I rather expect that's up to Eve now, isn't it?" he said. "But if she's amenable, I certainly won't object!"

Later that evening, Eve and I took a stroll along the dunes and I got down on one knee. My proposal wasn't a total surprise—she said I had been acting "a little weird" that night—but surprise or no surprise she said yes, and we began planning our life together.

Sometime later, we returned home one evening and found a message on the answering machine from a potential constituent who learned about our engagement. "I read about you, and what you are planning to undertake." At first, we thought he was referring to my running for office, but then he clarified. "Because I've been married for almost thirty-five years, and let me tell you something, it's a double-edged sword. It's no picnic." There was a long pause on the recording, before he said again, "No picnic." Eve and I looked at each other aghast—what were we getting in for—then broke out laughing.

It took some time for us to find a rabbi who would marry us. Eve was Catholic, but not especially devout, and we decided to have a Jewish wedding and to raise our children in the Jewish faith. On February 19, 1995, under a makeshift chuppah at the Altadena Town & Country Club, we were wed. My great-uncle Nate, a small, thin man with a pointed white beard, joyful smile, and sparkling eyes, held his hands high over our heads and said a Hebrew prayer over us. After the reception, a limousine took us to our hotel in Santa Monica. We checked in, then promptly went for a walk to get some pizza. We were starving.

Eve and I rented a small two-bedroom peach-colored stucco house in Burbank. It was filled with hand-me-downs: my parents' leather couch and easy chair, my grandparents' dining room table and bedroom furniture, and a swamp cooler that hardly worked. But it felt spacious compared to where we had been living, and we basked in our newfound domesticity. Eve was working at Nestlé in brand management, and I had begun practicing law at a private firm. On the weekends, we were adventurers, rollerblading from city to city along the beach and returning by moonlight, biking all day to Laguna Niguel for an arts festival, or scuba diving off the coast of Catalina. Having given up thoughts of running for office again, I was not expecting a call from Bill Lockyer.

"Senator Lockyer will be in Los Angeles on Wednesday," his staff member Cathy Keig told me over the phone, "and he would like to meet with you."

There was a state senate seat open in my area the following year, and the reason for his call was not a mystery, even if it was unexpected.

"I know why he's calling," I said, "and I don't want to take up his time. I have just started practicing law again, and I'm not interested in running."

"Just meet with him," Cathy said.

"I really don't want to waste his time."

"Just hear him out."

As the president pro tempore of the Senate, Bill Lockyer was the most powerful Democrat in the state. Of medium height, a solid girth, and equally quick to mirth or temper, he was an imposing figure. I met him at the AIDS Service Center in Hollywood, where he was touring the facility, and we found an office where we could talk privately. "I've done my research," he told me, "and you're the best person to run for this seat. You did well in your assembly race in a terrible year. 1996 will be a better year and we think you're the one who can win."

"I appreciate that," I responded. "But I just ran for the assembly and got no help from legislative leadership. I had to do everything on my own. I understand the reason, but even so, it left me to fend for myself. How serious are you about this race?"

"There aren't many competitive senate seats in California," he replied. "This is one of only two or three. I'm going to put a million dollars into this race whether I have a good candidate, a bad candidate, or no candidate at all."

I could tell that he was serious, and I told him I would think it over and get back to him. "Don't take too long," was all he said.

Anyone who has met Eve knows that I married well. She is supportive of my work without being subsumed by it. She jealously guards her privacy and her own identity, independent of mine. She is impressed by my work, but not too impressed, and keeps me grounded. She is more conservative than I am, less politically correct than I am, and less gregarious than I am. She doesn't like it when we are at receptions together and I offer to go get us drinks at the bar because she knows it may take half an hour for me to return, if I am able to break away from others at all. And she has always wanted me to pursue my passion for service, even after losing two campaigns in a row, and even though politics was not the career she would choose for me or the life she would choose for us, if it were left to her alone.

"If this is what you want to do," she said, "then do it."

So I did. And this time, I won, defeating a well-funded incumbent legislator named Paula Boland by seven percent.

THE CALIFORNIA ASSEMBLY HAD A detailed orientation for new members, but the state senate did not—presumably because nearly all of the senators came from the ranks of the assembly. I had none of that preparation, so I would have to make do on my own. I was simply shown to my office and told "Get to work." I was still just thirty-six years old, and looked younger. Constituents would often come by the office and ask if the senator was in. I would tell them that he was, and explain that he wouldn't go anywhere without me, and then I would introduce myself.

Two years into my tenure in the legislature, I became chair of the Senate Judiciary Committee. I wanted the committee to be deliberative and nonpartisan, so I began by changing some of the old rules. I allowed members to sit where they liked, not segregated by party, in the hope that they would develop better relationships, regardless of party. I also arranged for votes to be cast in alphabetical order, not by seniority, and I decided to cast my vote last so it wouldn't have undue influence on other members of my party. Finally, I felt it was important to consider every bill that was referred to our committee, whether it came from a Democrat or a Republican. This would give every member a chance to be heard, a reflection of my parents' conviction that neither party had a monopoly on good judgment.

The nonpartisan ethos I brought to my work was rewarded. In the four years that I served in the legislature, under governors of both parties, I wrote dozens of bills that became law each year. Those bills included measures to reform the child support system, create a patient's bill of rights, lengthen the school year, and guarantee up-to-date textbooks in schools. I was also proud to create a juvenile justice grant program that would match the funding we provided to police with an equal amount of support for preventive efforts.

Outside work, Eve and I were no longer the weekend warriors we had been. I was commuting to Sacramento every week and she was working long hours doing market research at a new firm. We contented ourselves with dinners out and movies on weekends. The trips to Catalina became less frequent, as did the long bike rides along the beach, but less than a year into my service in the legislature, we had even better things to anticipate—we were expecting our first child, due on the Fourth of July.

When Independence Day arrived, Eve was more than ready, but our child was not. Feeling robust, if about to burst, Eve had the stamina to join me for a community brunch, a block party, and three parades, during the last of which, through the small town of South Pasadena, organizers had us ride on an old-fashioned fire truck, "just in case."

Alexandra Marion Schiff was born a week later, on July 12, 1998, and her personality was apparent from the very beginning. Joyful, fun-loving, eager for life. With auburn hair, blue eyes, and a ruddy complexion, she was our bundle of happiness, our "angel baby," as we called her. I began to keep a journal for the first time in my life, in the form of letters addressed to her, and when she was two weeks old, I wrote: "I find you in your carriage at times when you are supposed to be asleep, eyes wide open, calm, just taking it all in."

A close friend told me that before their first child was born, they could not imagine loving something so much. He was right. The love of a parent for a child is a different kind of love than that between spouses, a love born of creation, a love filled with responsibility and a love of the future. "This morning . . . you sat on my lap and looked me straight in the eyes," I wrote to her several months later. "Do you know who I am? Could you understand what I meant when I said I love you?" Four years later, we would be blessed again, this time with a son, Elijah Harris, and our family would be wonderfully complete.

It is written in the Midrash that with the birth of a child, the world begins anew. Ours certainly did.

The blissful routine of being new parents would soon be interrupted, yet again, by a phone call. Less than six months after our daughter was born, and almost three thousand miles away, in Washington, D.C., President Bill Clinton was facing impeachment for lying under oath about his relationship with Monica Lewinsky and for obstruction of justice—and Democratic leaders were looking for a candidate to take on one of that impeachment's most vigorous champions.

AFTER DEFEATING ME IN THE assembly race in 1994, Jim Rogan had been elected to Congress and become a national darling of the conservatives. As one of the most aggressive of the House impeachment managers, he was also deeply controversial at home, where the district was evenly split between those who loved and those who hated him. During the winter of 1999, I was aware that someone had been in the field with a poll comparing the two of us in a head-to-head matchup, so I shouldn't have been surprised when House Democratic Minority Leader Dick Gephardt called. He had a simple request: "We want you to come to Washington and talk with us."

I arrived in Washington along with the biggest blizzard in recent history. The cab from the airport dropped me off at the home of Representative Patrick Kennedy, the chair of the Democratic Congressional Campaign Committee (DCCC). As I tramped into his house, stamping the snow off my shoes and brushing it from my jacket, Kennedy handed me a towel and a beer. "You guys don't play fair," I said, and gratefully accepted both.

As we sat down for the first of several meetings I would have on the trip, he told me that I had finished a few points ahead of Rogan in the poll they had done. Moreover, given Republican control of both houses of Congress, if we didn't flip the House—the Senate was considered less likely to change hands—it would be "lights out" for all of the things we cared about if George W. Bush were elected president. If I ran, I could be part of a historic takeover of the House and help improve the quality of healthcare, economic opportunities, and the environment.

It was heady stuff for a young state legislator, yet I was skeptical. I was up for reelection to the state senate and would have to give up that seat to run for Congress, so there would be no safety net. I knew that getting me to run was in the DCCC's best interests whether they got fully behind me or not, since it would force the National Republican Campaign Committee (NRCC) to spend a fortune defending Rogan's seat, rather than devoting those resources to defeating Democratic incumbents. As I made the rounds on the Hill in the days that followed, I heard only one completely candid assessment of the difficulty of the race. It came from George Miller, the same tall, white-haired, larger-than-life Irish congressman I had interned for in college. "A scared incumbent," he warned, "is a powerful thing. And Jim Rogan is scared of you."

I flew home two days later, excited but conflicted. On the plane, I wrote to my daughter, "I have a good opportunity to run—perhaps as good as anyone has a right to expect in life—but I do not relish the time, energy, and distraction of the next two years, your first two years. And so I agonize, and look at your photo and agonize some more."

"You're going to do it, aren't you?" Eve said when I got home.

"I don't know," I replied.

"Yes, you do. You're going to do it."

She was right. It was another big roll of the dice, but the risk of not running and regretting it was more than I was willing to bear.

The race turned out to be a real donnybrook. Rogan bragged that he had beaten me before and would beat me again, that I had "a glass jaw" and he would break it. As expected, Rogan drew support from all over the nation and raised a fortune—over $6.8 million. I wasn't too far behind, raising $4.3 million. Third-party groups also spent millions to support or oppose both of us. The pharmaceutical industry spent so much money on radio ads throughout Los Angeles that I would push the button on my radio to change the station to avoid the ad attacking me, only to find it playing on the next station.

Most of my fundraising events were local, but I did travel a couple of times to solicit support in other parts of the state. One of my earliest and most successful events was in San Francisco, and hosted by someone who would later play an outsized role in my career—Nancy Pelosi. She was even then a powerhouse, commanding the support of a well-heeled army of donors and the respect of her colleagues in Congress from coast to coast. Smart, strategic-thinking, and articulate, she was the hard-driving mother of five and our state's former party chair. No one would do more to help me get elected in 2000, or be more responsible for winning a host of other congressional seats up and down the state that year.

I beat James Rogan by 9 points in what became the most expensive House race in history. While the impeachment issue had attracted enormous sums of money into the race, both of our campaigns advised against raising the matter. The impeachment trial of Bill Clinton was an ugly memory for most Americans, and with our constituents evenly divided on the matter, I believed that the subject would alienate as many voters as it attracted. President Clinton had been impeached for sexual misconduct unrelated to the performance of his duties as president, and I found it hard to imagine that this was what the Founders had intended. The impeachment had been a torturous experience for the country, and I felt strongly that such a powerful and permanent remedy should be reserved for only the most egregious abuses of power.

Before Clinton, no president in 130 years had been impeached. Now I would be serving in the United States House of Representatives, the body with the sole provenance over impeaching presidents. Surely, we were good for at least another 130 years. *Surely*, for however long I might be in Congress, the necessity of removing a president from office was not something I would ever have to face.

5

YOU KNOW HOW IT GOES

It is tempting to imagine that all of the challenges we have experienced lately are the product of one man's dangerous contempt for anything but his own self-interest, and that the proliferation of conspiracy theories, the shattering of democratic norms, the politicization of our Intelligence Community, and the tearing down of our institutions can all be laid at the feet of Donald Trump. But the reality is far more complex. If Trump was the first since Watergate to batter down the wall of independence between the White House and the Justice Department, he was not alone in manipulating intelligence for a political end, as the Bush administration had done to justify an invasion of Iraq. The willingness to bend and break our democratic norms and traditions also preceded Trump's arrival in the Oval Office, as Mitch McConnell so graphically demonstrated when he withheld the nomination of Merrick Garland to the Supreme Court in a shocking act of constitutional disrespect for two other branches of government.

Without question, the most profound and relentless assault on our democracy would come during the years of the Trump presidency. But even then, it was the willingness of members of the legislative branch to go along with his serial abuses of power that enabled such devastation to take place. Republican Party leadership in Congress would embrace the most destructive of fantasies and falsehoods to gain or maintain a hold on power. And while this would reach its apotheosis in the Republican Party's embrace of the big lie, the willingness of Republicans to promote baseless conspiracy theories began before his 2016 election, even as it made his success in that election possible. The canary in the coal mine involved the death of four Americans, and the manipulation of that terrible tragedy in an unprecedented abuse of legislative power that came to be known simply as "Benghazi."

I was now the duly elected representative of the Twenty-seventh Congressional District of California, including the Los Angeles suburbs of Burbank, Glendale, Pasadena, and surrounding communities. A very diverse district, the twenty-seventh included large Latino, Asian, and Armenian populations, some very conservative areas like La Cañada, and some very progressive ones like Altadena. It was also home to iconic institutions like Paramount Pictures, Disney, Warner Bros., Dreamworks, and other studios as well as the Griffith Observatory, the Jet Propulsion Laboratory, and the Los Angeles Zoo. My congressional district was smaller than the area I represented in the state legislature, so I was already deeply familiar with the issues important to my constituents. And I was fortunate to keep my wonderful local staff, including my district director, Ann Peifer. We had established one of the best constituent service operations in the state, and I hoped to do the same now that I was in Congress. Working on legislation may be the higher-profile part of the job, but it's constituent service that is the key to reelection, and the foundation upon which all else rests. If I hoped to have a long career in Congress, and I did, I would do well to remember that.

Eve and I discussed whether to bring the family back to

Washington and decided that, for the time being, they would remain in Burbank while I commuted to the U.S. Capitol each week. It wasn't ideal, and would leave me in a permanent state of jet lag, acclimating to being on either coast only when it was time to fly back to the other. (Rogan would confide that he would wake on the plane and discover that he wasn't sure which direction it was pointed.) More important, it would mean that Eve would often be alone to look after our children and I would miss so much of their early childhood. After Lexi's birth, Eve had decided to leave the firm where she had been doing market research, to raise our kids full-time. I would grow deeply envious of my East Coast colleagues in Congress, who got to see a lot more of their families than those of us with long commutes. Three years later, we would bring the family to Washington, D.C.

When I arrived in Congress, I was seen as a dragon slayer, the man who beat Jim Rogan. I carried that appellation for about six to eight weeks, after which it seemed that few could remember who my predecessor had been—fame was indeed fleeting. I was going to have to strive to make a difference in people's lives and be content with that, knowing that the rest is ephemeral and matters very little in the end. That, in any case, was my assumption of the nature and purpose of public service. I would find out soon enough that while a substantial number of my colleagues felt exactly the same way, there were a great many others who had very different aspirations in mind.

The first time I set foot on the House floor, the sensation was electric. I don't know how else to describe the invigorating feeling of stepping onto that blue carpet, the shock of adrenaline that made me feel alive to every input, a kind of wonderful sensory overload. I did my best to take it all in, the darkened oil portrait of George Washington to the left of the entrance to the Speaker's lobby, where press would assemble and send small white cards to the members via the House pages when they wanted an interview. The concentric rows of wooden seats in semicircles facing the well below, long and wide in the rear and narrowing toward the front, as in a theater, giving each member an unobstructed view of the two narrow wooden lecterns where members would stand while speaking. And most imposing, the Speaker's chair, elevated above two levels of desks for the clerks and parliamentarians, above even the president when he addresses Congress during the State of the Union message, towering over the well and commanding respect even when empty.

I wrote to Alexa of the thrill to be in that place, so steeped in history, "to see what Lincoln saw" and "to stand where giants have stood." I thought of Franklin Roosevelt, calling December 7, 1941, "a date that will live in infamy" and asking Congress to declare war, and of Winston Churchill addressing a joint session only weeks later and remarking on his American heritage: "I cannot help reflecting that if my father had been American and my mother British instead of the other way around, I might have got here on my own." And of trailblazers like Shirley Chisholm and Father Drinan, Bella Abzug and Barbara Jordan. And I thought of the civil rights icon John Lewis, with whom I would now serve. I couldn't believe that I would soon take my place, however small and insignificant by comparison, among these historic figures, past and present.

Those first few weeks are a delirious blur of memories: a welcome dinner for new members in Statuary Hall, where Eve and I were seated with Dick Gephardt and his wife, Jane, laughing about how Adam and Eve were dining with Dick and Jane and discovering that our table was not far from where Abraham Lincoln had his desk as a member of Congress in the late 1840s; a dinner in Williamsburg, Virginia, accompanied by actors portraying our Founders; and getting back to the Mayflower Hotel one evening to find three messages on the hotel voicemail asking me to return a call from President Clinton offering congratulations.

After lobbying my new colleagues, I won a position on the House Judiciary Committee, and it was a far cry from my experience in California. Members sat by party, with Republicans on the left and Democrats on the right as one faced the chair, and we sat by seniority as well, with the most junior members sitting in rows most distant from the chair. And when we voted, we voted by party and in order of seniority, and almost without fail, the parties voted in lockstep.

It is a scheme designed to foster not collaboration but discord, and it is very good at it. The first time I departed from the chorus of "nays" coming at me from the Democratic members above me on the dais—and voted aye—an audible gasp came from Representative John Conyers of Michigan, the ranking Democrat on the committee and second-longest-serving member of the House. He practically levitated, then hustled down to where I was seated and castigated me in front of the whole committee and public. I was clearly not in the California legislature anymore.

Days later, I had lunch in the members' dining room with a long-time Hill veteran and complained about the partisan nature of the committee proceedings. "When I become chairman," I said, pausing, "twenty-five years from now, I'm going to do things differently." His response was unsympathetic: "Twenty-five years might be optimistic." After that lunch, I took to telling my constituents that I had discovered that the quickest path to power and influence on the Hill was to "eat right, exercise, and outlive the bastards."

It didn't take long for me to discover that the House was a big place, with its hundreds of members and innumerable areas of interest. I used to brag about how, as a state senator, I could work on anything under the sun, but in Congress, and now representing the Jet Propulsion Lab with its rovers on Mars and probes sent out into deep space, I could literally work on issues well beyond the sun. This was an enticement and an exhilaration, but also a trap; if you tried to do too much, or spread yourself too thin, you would end up accomplishing nothing, no matter how long you were privileged to serve in Congress. And so I set about to discover where, among these experienced and talented members, I could contribute the most.

On September 11, 2001, nine months into my first term, al-Qaeda attacked the United States using passenger planes targeting the World Trade Center, the Pentagon, and, we would later learn, the U.S. Capitol. I was walking along Pennsylvania Avenue on the way to the Capitol when the plane struck the Pentagon and a secondary explosion rocked the city. Crowds of people streamed past me in the streets as I called Eve to let her know I was okay, then tried to check on my staff and find out where Congress would be meeting to address the attacks.

It would be more than two years before the 9/11 Commission would issue its report documenting the intelligence failures that led to the deadliest attack on U.S. soil since Pearl Harbor. Our agencies had been stovepiped, the Commission concluded, and were unable to share information with one another that might have discovered the plot and stopped it. One agency knew that al-Qaeda was planning attacks, another that some of its operatives were already in the United States, and still another knew that Saudi foreign nationals were enrolling in flight schools and studying how to fly aircraft but with no apparent interest in how to land them.

The intelligence failures that led us into the Iraq War less than two years later were of a different nature altogether than those that led to 9/11. If we lacked the imagination to contemplate al-Qaeda using planes to take down our tallest buildings, it was all too easy to imagine Saddam Hussein transferring weapons of mass destruction (WMDs) to terrorists. After the trauma of 9/11, the Bush administration was so consumed with warding off another surprise attack that it searched for intelligence to validate its belief that Saddam's WMD program was real, advanced, and posed a grave danger to the United States. The administration would hype that intelligence, even as it downplayed or suppressed contradictory information, because it suited a narrative about Iraq that it wanted to believe and sell to the public.

I relied on that flawed intelligence to make the greatest mistake of my public life when I voted to authorize the Iraq War. It was a decision that would have grave consequences for the country, and for my constituents, many of whom would go off to fight there, and some of whom came home in body bags. I met these brave service members on frequent visits I made to that country, and I met their families when I was asked to speak at their funerals. No decision I would make in Congress would be more far-reaching, or catastrophic, and no decision I would make would more powerfully underscore how reliant we are on our intelligence agencies to help us make sound judgments, and the life-and-death consequences when they get it wrong or politicians are allowed to manipulate their work product. When an administration skews its intelligence to serve a desired policy—instead of using sound intelligence to inform policy—we get disasters like the Iraq War.

Defending the United States against those who would do her harm is the foremost job of the federal government, and ever since the Vietnam War, many Democratic candidates for president have struggled to meet the "commander-in-chief" test, historically one of the most important factors for voters. The problem is even more pronounced in Congress, where Republicans continually and often successfully paint Democrats as weak on defense. Part of this is the confusion of hawkishness and military adventurism with strength and principle. The GOP's willingness to spend endless amounts on defense budgets further confuses the issue.

National security and foreign policy had become keen interests of mine, and I soon discovered that there was a need in our party for members with a focus on these issues. Reps. Steve Israel of New York, David Scott of Georgia, and I cofounded a Democratic Study Group on National Security. We would invite authoritative voices on national security—former secretaries of state and defense and National Security Advisors, Democrats and Republicans alike, experts from academia and the press—to meet with us once or twice a month. We would organize lengthy floor speeches on terrorism, nuclear nonproliferation, the dangers posed by Iran and North Korea, and other key threats. And we would travel overseas together, and collaborate on legislative and oversight projects, all designed to strengthen Democratic credibility on national security.

In the midst of that work, and with the failures leading up to the Iraq War as a backdrop, I would be pulled into the world of intelligence gathering, though for another reason altogether, and it would require a set of skills I hadn't used since my days as a prosecutor.

· · ·

I WAS WALKING THROUGH THE Rayburn Room in the Capitol on an early evening in January 2007 when Speaker Pelosi stopped me.

"Can I talk with you for a moment?"

"What have I done?"

"No. No. It's all good. I want to talk with you about the Intelligence Committee," she said, referring to the Select Intelligence Oversight Panel, which helped set funding levels for the seventeen intelligence agencies that comprise the Intelligence Community. "We need to do an investigation into the destruction of the CIA interrogation tapes, and I think it would be good to have someone with your investigative experience on the committee. Think about it, and let me know if you're interested."

"I've just thought about it," I said on the spot, "and I'm interested."

When the public became aware of the CIA's use of so-called "enhanced interrogation techniques" (EITs) such as waterboarding, Congress began an investigation into the matter. Many agency witnesses were reluctant to cooperate, and they conveyed a sense that the country, whose security depended on their getting their hands dirty, was now turning its back on them when the threat seemed to have receded. The scope of our investigation was narrow—we were not investigating the use of EITs writ large, the Senate Intelligence Committee and the Justice Department were doing that—but rather the narrow issue of who destroyed the tapes of the interrogation sessions and why. Over a period of months, we struggled to get answers, but without the agency's full cooperation, our results were only partial and inconclusive. My participation in the investigation taught me important lessons about the difficulty of such inquiries and the need to use public pressure, coercive process, and every other tool legislators possess to get answers.

Not long after the tapes investigation, Speaker Pelosi asked me to serve on House Permanent Select Committee on Intelligence (HPSCI) as well. Although HPSCI has become most closely associated with the investigations it has conducted, the bread and butter of the committee's work is quite different. It conducts oversight to ensure that the Intelligence Community has the resources it needs to protect the country, that the agencies are working together, and to make certain they are doing so consistent with the law, the Constitution, and the privacy and civil liberties of the American people. These are not partisan tasks, at least they shouldn't be, and in practice the divide on many intelligence issues was not between liberals and conservatives, but on how to balance security and privacy interests, with libertarian Republicans often teaming up with very progressive Democrats to rein in the use of electronic surveillance. It was also an area where I felt that I could bring my background and skills to bear, since the questions we were grappling with often involved complex legal and constitutional issues.

Oversight of the intelligence agencies is an enormous challenge, and not just because it is their business to keep secrets. Our hearings with the agencies are almost always in closed session, and we do not have outside validators listening in on the testimony who can challenge any of the claims that are made. On the Transportation Committee, when a high-speed rail authority testifies about the great progress they are making on a project, third-party stakeholders and the press are watching and can inform Congress if the witnesses are not telling the truth. This is not true of closed Intelligence Committee hearings in the Sensitive Compartmented Information Facility (SCIF) three floors below the Capitol, and when there are problems, we are reliant on vigorous scrutiny of the agencies' work, self-reporting, opinions from the Foreign Intelligence Surveillance Court, and, above all, whistleblowers.

Because whistleblowers are such a vital source of information about problems within the Intelligence Community, Congress scrupulously protects their identities and defends them against any form of retaliation. At least, that had been the practice since the original whistleblower and inspector general protections were established after Watergate.

One of the many reasons I was attracted to the Intelligence Committee was that its work was less partisan than other committees. Notwithstanding the difficult policy issues over intelligence programs and capabilities, the committee conducted its oversight respectfully and produced a bipartisan Intelligence Authorization Act each year, to set the funding priorities and civil liberties protections governing all of the agencies. This was true during my first year on the committee, during the Bush presidency, and I hoped it would remain the case if Barack Obama was elected president.

In 2008, when Obama was in a hotly contested primary with Hillary Clinton, Eve and I packed up our two small children and drove the minivan to central Virginia to campaign for the senator from Illinois. We were assigned to canvass in a county that had a terrible history of racial segregation. When the Supreme Court ruled in *Brown v. Board of Education* and schools were forced to integrate, local officials in that county decided that they would get rid of school altogether. The public schools shut down, and the more affluent white children attended private school for the next several years. The Black children simply had no school. Many of our fellow canvassers were people who had lived in that area their whole lives and had been deprived of years of their education—now they were trying to elect the first Black president.

The Obama campaign managed to unite both sides of the Schiff family. My brother, Dan, parted company with John McCain after he chose Sarah Palin as his running mate. He thought Obama inexperienced, and he admired McCain, but "how can I vote for McCain now," Dan groused, "when that woman is only a heartbeat away from the presidency? I'm so disappointed." Meanwhile, my dad was doing his part in South Florida, fighting back against racist attacks on Obama claiming that he was a Muslim and people shouldn't vote for him for that reason. Receiving one such email that had been circulated to hundreds of recipients, my dad hit Reply All and said that Goebbels would be proud of their use of the Big Lie. "Son," my father explained, "dropping the Nazi bomb in South Florida is a pretty big deal, and some people are not going to be very happy with me. But you know something? I don't give a rat's ass."

"Dad," I said at the time, "you're eighty years old, I think you've earned the right to speak your piece and not give a rat's ass."

"Actually," he replied, "I've felt that way for several years now."

When Obama was sworn in, I was gratified to see that the work on the House Intelligence Committee remained reasonably nonpartisan. One contributing factor was the presence of a fellow Californian on the committee, Republican Devin Nunes, from the San Joaquin Valley. Nunes and I had a very good relationship, and shared something in short supply in Washington: an affinity for the Oakland Raiders. (I couldn't even get my son, Eli, to root for the Raiders. "They stink, Dad," he said when he was six. He had a point.) Nunes and I would occasionally text each other during games, or when the Raiders drafted a new quarterback, or suffered a devastating loss. When we began working together, Nunes had not been an ideologue, but was more in the mold of a country club Republican like his patron, John Boehner. During the height of the Tea Party movement, Nunes described these zealots as "lemmings with suicide vests."

When militants overran the U.S. diplomatic mission in Benghazi, Libya, on September 11, 2012, killing four Americans— Ambassador Chris Stevens, Information Officer Sean Smith, and CIA operatives Glen Doherty and Tyrone Woods—our committee would face its gravest difficulty yet.

The attacks in Benghazi took place during Hillary Clinton's tenure as secretary of state, making the consequences of our investigation especially fraught. Nevertheless, after a two-year examination, dozens of interviews, and the review of thousands of documents, our committee released a bipartisan report debunking any number of conspiracy theories surrounding the attack. There had been no delay in sending a rescue team, and "no evidence that there was either a stand down order or a denial of available air support." There was likewise no evidence that the CIA was secretly sending arms from Libya to Syria, and, most significant, no evidence that Secretary Clinton had somehow interceded to reduce security around the consulate.

In the past, during normal, sane periods of governance, members of Congress would come together to find out what had happened in a tragedy like this and take action to prevent it from happening again. And in our committee, this is just what took place. But the Republican House leadership had other ideas and wanted to turn Benghazi into a political bludgeon against Hillary Clinton and her campaign for the presidency. Our Republican committee chairman, Mike Rogers, understood this, and chose to release our report on the Friday before Thanksgiving, on November 21, 2014, to minimize attention to its apolitical and nonsensational conclusions. Even so, Rogers did not escape venomous attacks for not toeing the party line.

Just after the report was released, I appeared on one of the Sunday shows along with Senator Lindsey Graham. Before we went on air, the host said hello through my earpiece, a typical courtesy when appearing remotely. They then checked in with Graham, apparently without closing my line. When Graham was privately asked what he thought of the House Intelligence Committee's report, he was dismissive, not realizing I could hear him:

"It's crap. I don't believe a word of it."

"So you've read it?" the host inquired.

"No, I don't need to read it to know it's a bunch of crap."

Graham, who had served as a judge advocate in the Air Force, and I had once sought to work together on due process issues affecting detainees at the Guantanamo Bay detention camp, and he had been known to occasionally buck his party's worst impulses. But here he chose to embrace the conspiracy theories about Benghazi spun on Fox News and in the fever swamps of right-wing social media. To do so required him to make the calculated decision to reject our bipartisan findings and those of several other committees. In preferring alternative facts to the truth on Benghazi, Graham's posture was a portent of things to come. But when it came to the political exploitation of the tragedy in Benghazi, he could not hold a candle to two of my house colleagues, Kevin McCarthy and Trey Gowdy.

I LEARNED ALL I WOULD ever need to know about Kevin McCarthy on a plane, or, to be more precise, shortly after landing. About six months before the 2010 midterm elections, we were both headed back to Washington from California and happened to be seated together on a United Airlines flight. Although we are both from California, our districts are separated by almost a hundred miles and we never really had the opportunity to get to know each other. While Democrats were still in the majority, the elections were shaping up to be tight, our margin was small, and there was growing doubt about whether we would retain that majority. During the flight, I expressed confidence that the economy would remain positive and we would continue to lead the House. Not surprisingly, he took the contrary view. It wasn't much of a conversation, just the type of small talk you would have while waiting for a movie, any movie, to start on the plane. I thought nothing of it.

The next morning, I picked up one of the Hill newspapers. *Everyone knows that Republicans are going to win the House,* McCarthy had told a group of reporters after arriving at the Capitol from our flight. He said that he spoke to me on the plane and even I had admitted Republicans would take back the majority. My phone started ringing off the hook. Representative Chris Van Hollen, a good friend and at the time the chair of the DCCC, wanted to know why I would say such a thing to McCarthy. Of course, I hadn't. When first votes were called that morning, I made a beeline to McCarthy on the House floor. "Kevin, if we were having a private conversation on the plane, I would have thought it was a private conversation. But if it wasn't, you know I said the exact opposite of what you told the press."

"I know, Adam," was his reply, "but you know how it goes."

I was incredulous. "No, Kevin. I don't. You just make shit up, and that's how you operate?"

He just shrugged. That was simply how he operated, and how he still operates today. He was comfortable trafficking in his own "alternative facts" even before the advent of Trumpism.

To most Americans, Benghazi was a terrible tragedy in which four brave Americans lost their lives, but to McCarthy, it was also an opportunity. As secretary of state, Hillary Clinton had been one of the most widely admired women in the world, but now she was a candidate for president and McCarthy was determined to see her vilified. In addition to the House Intelligence Committee probe, three other bipartisan investigations of Benghazi failed to show that Clinton bore any personal responsibility for the deadly events of that day. Speaker Boehner was against another probe and called it pointless, but McCarthy had the support of the right-wing elements of his caucus and championing their cause would help cement his own leadership position. As McCarthy would later concede in an extraordinary public admission, the whole point of the new investigation would be to drive down Clinton's poll numbers. In this aspiration, it would shamefully succeed.

I was on *Fox News Sunday* again shortly after Boehner reversed himself and announced the formation of the new select committee to investigate Benghazi, and I was caught off guard when Chris Wallace asked me what I thought about it.

"Chris," I said, "I think it's a colossal waste of time. We've had four bipartisan investigations of this already . . . I don't think it makes sense really for Democrats to participate."

Wallace followed up, asking if I was suggesting that Democrats "should not appoint anybody to the special committee and let it simply be Republicans."

"You know," I replied, "that's what I would recommend. I don't know what leadership will ultimately decide. But I don't think it makes sense for us to give this select committee any more credibility than it deserves, and frankly I don't think it deserves very much. We've tread down this path so many times."

In Foxworld, I had just set off a hand grenade. SCHIFF CALLS ON DEMOCRATS TO BOYCOTT BENGHAZI PANEL, ran a characteristic headline in the right-wing media. My comments created no less controversy within the Democratic caucus, where there was a divide between those, like myself, who thought that Democratic participation would only give the proceedings a patina of respectability they didn't deserve, and others of my colleagues who thought that we needed to be "in the room." One of those members, Elijah Cummings, believed firmly that we needed to be present or there would be no constraint on the Republicans, no one to push back against any false allegations they might make or any efforts to simply use the committee to attack Hillary. In leadership meetings with Nancy Pelosi, now the minority leader, we argued our case. Elijah's view prevailed, and Democrats would join the proceedings. And my reward for suggesting the boycott was to be asked by Pelosi to be one of five Democrats on the roster.

Boehner chose Trey Gowdy to chair the select committee, and Pelosi chose Elijah as our ranking member. Gowdy reminded me a lot of Jim Rogan in his missionary zeal. Like Rogan, he was also a former prosecutor and has a sharp mind, good cross-examination skills, and a clever way of speaking that produces lots of good sound bites. Gowdy sported an ever-changing hairstyle that made him great fodder for memes, including innumerable comparisons with Draco Malfoy, the young villain from *Harry Potter*. During a break for votes on the floor, Democratic representative Derek Kilmer of Washington State offered me twenty dollars if I would refer to Gowdy as the Gentleman from Slytherin when we resumed one of our hearings. I didn't, but I was sorely tempted.

Gowdy's leadership of the committee struggled from the beginning, when we pressed him to establish a scope for our investigation and he proved unable. How do you define the scope of an investigation that covers the same ground as endless others and has no legitimate purpose except to diminish the leading Democratic candidate for president? You don't, and Gowdy wouldn't. Instead, Gowdy designed his investigation to be as open-ended as possible, and he sought hundreds of thousands of documents from the Obama administration.

Although the White House could have prevented the testimony of many top-level officials, it made them available to discuss the most sensitive deliberations and without invoking executive privilege, let alone a nebulous claim of some future privilege. As a result, we heard from National Security Advisor Susan Rice and Deputy National Security Advisor Ben Rhodes, among others. Initial intelligence reports, relied on by Rice, had suggested that the Benghazi incident might have begun as a protest. While we would subsequently learn that this view was wrong—it was more likely a premeditated attack—Republicans were falsely accusing Rice of lying.

One of the most revealing depositions in the select committee's investigation was with Michael Flynn, who had been the head of the Defense Intelligence Agency (DIA) at the time of the Benghazi attack. Since being forced out by the Obama administration—he was reportedly a terrible manager and had a predilection for direct-ing intelligence resources to prove "facts" not grounded in reality, something the intelligence analysts took to calling "Flynn facts"—he had become one of Obama's biggest detractors. Republicans on the committee felt certain that he would be a star witness, as he had such a clear animus toward the administration that had fired him and was publicly claiming that the Obama White House had politicized the intelligence around the attack.

When the Republicans were through with their first round of questions, it was my opportunity to question Flynn.

"What did you think of the DIA workforce?"

"At that time?"

"Yeah."

"Professional, exceptional, experienced . . ."

"I take it you didn't see evidence that they were trying to politi-cize their work product—"

"No."

"Did you have any indication during your tenure that—"

"None."

"—your analysts—"

"None."

"—were politicizing intelligence in any way?"

"No."

I then walked him through some of the intelligence produced by his own former analysts during the hours after the Benghazi attacks, which suggested that the attack had begun as a protest, a finding that Flynn had so angrily rejected in his public attacks on the administra-tion. Flynn was flummoxed that this had been written by his own people at DIA, and he looked to his staff and the Republican members for help, but none came.

"There was a protest. I mean, I think there was—" he stammered.

Facing this simple evidence, his testimony became an incoherent mess, and the Republican narrative of Benghazi, the narrative that Gowdy, Jim Jordan, and other committee Republicans were peddling, the very narrative that Flynn had been peddling, came into sharp conflict with reality once again.

In what struck me as a last ditch effort to exploit the tragedy in Benghazi for political gain, Gowdy called Hillary Clinton to testify, and she would, for eleven hours. By this time, in October 2015, the investigation had long since run out of steam. Republicans had kept it going for seventeen months and spent millions of dollars on the investigation, but nothing new of consequence had been learned, no new evidence had been produced to substantiate the conspiracy theories debunked by other committees, and Gowdy must have hoped that a dramatic confrontation with Clinton could change the committee's fortunes along with his own. The committee had revealed that Clinton used a private server for State Department business in violation of federal regulations, and, more seriously, that some of those emails may have contained classified references, but nothing in the emails shed any light on the issues we were examining. In that respect, the investigation had been a bust, and the expectations Gowdy had raised had thus far gone unrealized. Conservatives were gravely disappointed and had begun turning on him. The Clinton interrogation was his chance at redemption.

The stately Ways and Means Committee room was packed, with a line out the doors for additional spectators hoping for a chance to witness the historic confrontation. Never before had a candidate for president submitted to such unlimited questioning, let alone done so before a more hostile group of legislators. When Clinton arrived, she walked quickly to the dais and shook our hands before taking her seat, alone, at the witness table.

It wasn't long before Jim Jordan demonstrated what the GOP leadership really had in mind. A former wrestling coach at Ohio

State, Jordan is short and muscular and has a practice of not wearing a jacket and rolling up his sleeves to make it appear like he is hard at work. He thrives on media coverage and on mixing it up with colleagues, witnesses, and the press. It has always been my impression that to him, politics is just a game, a wrestling match in which anything goes and nothing matters but winning.

"Madam Secretary," he raged, after accusing her of hiding the truth, "Americans can live with the fact that good people sometimes give their lives for this country. They don't like it. They mourn for those families. They pray for those families. But they can live with it. But what they can't take, what they can't live with, is when their government's not square with them."

I am often asked whether my Republican colleagues believe what they are saying, or whether it is all an act. Of course, some of my GOP colleagues have deeply held ideological beliefs, but Jordan has never struck me as one of them. And many who I did believe were strongly guided by tenets of conservatism would soon completely abandon any such principles out of fealty to a corrupt president of their party, or ambition for higher office.

As with most important hearings, I had prepared questions in advance, but I also liked to leave myself open to new lines of questioning that only become apparent when listening to the witness. It is a mistake to cling desperately to questions written in advance and miss something far more important that might be staring you in the face. As I listened to Jordan finish his hostile questions and statements, I thought about the fact that among those killed in Benghazi were people Secretary Clinton knew and admired, like Ambassador Chris Stevens, and she was now being accused of complicity in his murder.

Clinton's poise had been frustrating to her tormentors as she remained calm and professional, refusing to be baited by their scurrilous accusations. Still, there was an aloofness about her demeanor, part of the armor she now wore after years of savage and dehumanizing attacks, and I thought she had been most effective in the moments when she had let us know how she was affected personally by the tragedy that night, and by all of the false allegations that followed. She of course had not been called before the committee to be humanized, but rather in an attempt to strip her of her dignity and destroy her politically. As we were witnessing, Republicans would go to any lengths to damage opponents they feared to face in a fair election.

When Jordan was finished and it was my turn to address Clinton, I said that as prosecutors, we are taught that every case should have a core theory, but I was struggling to understand what Republicans were trying to convey about the events of that tragic day. "I think the core theory is this," I said to Clinton, "that you deliberately interfered with security in Benghazi and that resulted in people dying.

"I know the ambassador was a friend of yours," I continued, inviting her to open up. "And I wonder if you would like to comment on what it's like to be the subject of an allegation that you deliberately interfered with security that cost the life of a friend."

The question elicited the most unforgettable moment in her marathon testimony. "Well, Congressman," she said, letting down her guard, "it's a very personally painful accusation. It has been rejected and disproven by nonpartisan, dispassionate investigators. But nevertheless, having it continued to be bandied around is deeply distressing to me. You know, I've—" She paused to retain her composure. "I would imagine I've thought more about what happened than all of you put together. I've lost more sleep than all of you put together. I have been racking my brain about what more could have been done or should have been done."

When she concluded her answer, Gowdy felt it necessary to respond, not to Clinton, but to me. "This is not a prosecution Mr. Schiff. You and I are both familiar with them. I've reached no conclusions, and I would advise you to not reach any conclusions, either, until we reach the end. There are twenty more witnesses, so I'll agree not to reach any conclusions if you'll do the same."

At this point in the hearing, Gowdy did not look well. He was perspiring profusely, drinking copious amounts of water, and his face was pale and covered in a glossy sheen. Clinton, on the other hand, was remarkably composed. After answering hours of difficult questions, she appeared as fresh as the moment she walked into the room. During the final hours of her testimony, I joked that if we kept her much longer, she would need to "take that three A.M. phone call from the committee room."

The hour was now so late that I was about to conclude my remarks without using the full limit of my time, but Representative Cummings sought my attention. I yielded to him, and afterward was very glad that I did.

Cummings began slowly, speaking more in sorrow than in anger. He talked about the witnesses who had come before his Oversight Committee and how their lives were sometimes upended by the experience. He talked about Clinton's staff, and how emotional they became in describing the secretary's actions in the aftermath of that tragedy, how it nearly brought them to tears.

"And it bothers me when I hear people even imply that you didn't care about your people." At this point, Cummings began to sway from side to side, as he would when he was warming to his topic. "That's not right." His voice rising, his tempo increasing, Cummings recalled her testimony that she had thought more about the events of that night "than all of you combined." Now that powerful voice rose more in anger than in sorrow, every part of him present in that moment. "I don't know what we want from you," he continued, almost shouting. "Do we want to badger you *over* and *over* again until you get tired, until we do get the *gotcha* moment that he's talking about? We are better than *that*. We are so much better! We are a better country. We are better than using taxpayer dollars to try to destroy a campaign. That's not what America is all about." Then calming, and with a trace of humor, he added: "You can comment if you like, I just had to get that off my chest."

The audience, sedate for hours, erupted into applause. Cummings gazed out at them, his eyes heavy and sorrowful, and waited for her response, but nothing could have been more powerful than his own statement. Afterward, I thanked Cummings for the master class and told him what a privilege it had been to work with him, to learn by his side. He was gracious, and pleased. I have often said of the time that I was compelled to work on the Benghazi Select Committee that I want those two years of my life back, but that is not completely true. I got to work with Elijah Cummings, got to know and admire and learn from him, and that was worth every moment.

CLINTON'S TESTIMONY HAD BEEN A debacle for the Republicans; after facing down a hostile committee of petty critics she had emerged unscathed. The hearing was not only a disaster for Republicans, it was a crisis for Trey Gowdy. Forced to concede to reporters immediately after the hearing that he had learned practically nothing new—a comment that was viewed as commentary on not just the hearing but the entire work of the committee—he seemed a broken man. Certainly, the experience would color his view of the risks inherent in any high-profile testimony and engender a deep distrust of the very public hearings he had craved.

But in a broader sense, the investigation had achieved its bad-faith objective for McCarthy and others. The object had never been to learn anything new or important, but to tear down Clinton. The hearing had failed to do that, but the incidental discovery that she used a private email server would provide endless fodder for GOP attacks and ultimately contribute to her undoing. Pelosi and Cummings had been right about Democratic participation on the Benghazi Select Committee, and I shudder to think of how much worse the conduct of that investigation would have been if we had not been present. Benghazi demonstrated the willingness of Republican leaders and their media allies to exploit the deaths of Americans and propagate baseless conspiracy theories to advance their political interests. If Donald Trump had been watching, he must have been encouraged by the eagerness of members of his party to embrace a destructive narrative so at odds with the facts.

Over the next four years, Trump would become so fixated on finding Clinton's email server and any personal emails that had been deleted from it that he would seek the help of Russia and then Ukraine to do so, imperiling his presidency and the security of our country. Destructive in its own right, the politicization of the attack on the U.S. diplomatic facilities in Benghazi was the bridge to a Republican future in which facts no longer mattered and those who exposed the truth would become enemies of the people. Up would be down. Black would be white. And American constitutional democracy would be in grave danger.

PART TWO

TRUTH ISN'T TRUTH

6

TWO STORIES

Republican exploitation of the tragedy in Benghazi was a warning to all who were paying attention that American politics had taken a terrible turn. The initial investigations were serious and bipartisan, but Republicans on the Benghazi Select Committee had a different objective altogether, and it was to construct a counternarrative—an alternate reality—in which their political opponents were indifferent to American lives, had acted with sinister intent, and then sought to conceal their betrayal. It was a model that Republicans in Congress would use over and over again in the next four years, and under the tutelage of a master who understood the craft far better than they did.

The story of the Russia investigation that followed Benghazi is really two stories, the first involving a campaign for president that eagerly sought help from a foreign adversarial power, made use of that help in every way it could, then lied and obstructed the investigation into that misconduct once the campaign had been successful. That tale is one of unprecedented corruption, and the willingness to denigrate American interests and the integrity of our elections in the headlong pursuit of power.

But there is another story, to which I was an even more direct witness, and that is the story of how a man skilled in deception and intrigue took over an entire political party and bent it to his will. The four years of the Trump presidency destroyed many friendships, and not a few marriages. But it also destroyed the Republican Party—once devoted to robust alliances, a healthy mistrust of executive power, and the expansion of democracy around the world—and turned it into something else, something unrecognizable, an antidemocratic party, a party willing to tear down the institutions of its own government, a party willing to give aid and comfort to a malign foreign power that wishes to destroy us, a party hostile to the truth.

From my vantage point in the Intelligence Committee offices three floors below the Capitol, I watched this transformation take place. I saw colleagues in the administration and in Congress that I admired and respected succumb to the deceitfulness and immorality of Donald J. Trump, I lost friends and a reputation for bipartisanship, and I felt the full fury of a president, his allies in Congress, and a vengeful right-wing media when I stood in the way.

The Russia investigation in the House Intelligence Committee began in the same way that the original Benghazi investigations had begun: with a bipartisan commitment to get to the truth. Within weeks, however, the Republicans would become willing accomplices in an effort to conceal the president's misconduct, and not just conceal it, but to construct a counternarrative that would devastate every truth in its path. The men and women of the FBI, lauded for decades by Republicans as the protectors of law and order, would become part of a deep state conspiracy against the president. The Intelligence Community, with dedicated officers around the world risking their lives to provide policymakers with information to keep the country safe, were now untrustworthy and corrupt, compared to the good words and deeds of Vladimir Putin and the Kremlin. Our free press was an enemy of the people and not to be believed over the president's transparent falsehoods. And Congress itself, with its essential role as a check on the executive, would be neutered by its own members in the service of the president.

That story—the story of how good people were persuaded to abandon their beliefs and ideology, their dedication to something larger than themselves and their ambition, and came to embrace an ugly nativism that their party had long held at bay—is the one that I wish to tell. By the time the Russia investigation was over, the Republican Party and its leadership in Congress would be broken. The Ukraine misconduct that followed was the logical consequence not only of Trump's belief that he had escaped accountability for seeking foreign interference in the 2016 campaign and lying about it, but also of his recognition that the Republicans in Congress would never confront him, never constrain him, and had been fully and successfully cowed. The die had already been cast, and as we would see following his acquittal during the first impeachment trial, each further proof of GOP acquiescence in his immorality would lead to further abuses of his power.

But first things first—what exactly did the Trump campaign do in the 2016 election and what was its relationship with Russia and its agents? Because the facts of the president's entreaties for Russian help and the campaign's innumerable Russian contacts leached into the public consciousness over a two-year period and were the subject of a relentless effort at obfuscation and cover-up, most Americans have only a dim sense of what actually took place. But the basic outlines of Trump's Russia-related misconduct are fairly simple, and had they all been exposed at the same time, instead of the drip, drip, drip of daily revelations, the totality of the campaign's collusion with Russia might have forced Trump from office long before the tragic end of that presidency.

These are the facts that the Republicans in Congress would do their best to prevent us from learning but were revealed through our investigation, the work of Robert Mueller and his team, intelligence professionals, investigative journalists, and others: Early in the 2016 presidential election, and prior to Trump's even becoming the Republican nominee, Russia's intelligence services hacked the Democratic National Committee (DNC) and stole tens of thousands of private emails, which the Russians believed they could strategically leak to assist the campaign of their preferred candidate, Donald J. Trump. In the same way that Soviet intelligence had identified Richard Miller as someone they could easily compromise, the Kremlin understood that a transactional and unscrupulous businessman like Trump would be a far more willing partner than Secretary Clinton.

In April 2016, the Russians used an intermediary to secretly communicate with the Trump campaign through one of its foreign policy advisers, George Papadopoulos. They told Papadopoulos that they possessed thousands of stolen Clinton emails and could assist the campaign by releasing them anonymously. At the time that the Russians informed the Trump campaign that they had the stolen emails, the Clinton campaign was not even aware that they had been hacked or by whom. But before releasing the emails publicly, it would have been important for the Russians to know that the Trump campaign would welcome the help.

In June 2016, the Russians made another approach to the Trump campaign, this time through the president's son, Donald Jr. Now using a business contact as an intermediary, the Russians informed Don Jr. that they could help his father in the election. The intermediary said the Russians had "official documents and information" that would "incriminate Hillary" and "be very useful to your father." The interlocutor further represented: "This is obviously very high level and sensitive information but is part of Russia and its government's support for Mr. Trump." A few minutes later, Donald Jr. responded, "If it's what you say I love it." Then he added that late summer would be the best timing. In subsequent correspondence, Don Jr. and the intermediary arranged the time and place of a secret meeting with the Russians—at the campaign's New York headquarters in Trump Tower.

By approaching the president's son through an intermediary and offering to supply dirt on his opponent, the Russians were again testing the waters. They dispatched a delegation from Moscow, led by a Russian lawyer, Natalia Veselnitskaya, who had ties to senior Kremlin officials but no official role. This was standard Russian tradecraft, giving the Kremlin plausible deniability if the Trump campaign refused the offer or, worse, reported it to the FBI. But the president's campaign did neither. To the contrary, the meeting was of such importance to the campaign that not only did Don Jr. attend, but he brought his brother-in-law, Jared Kushner, and the Trump campaign chairman, Paul Manafort. At the meeting, Veselnitskaya made it clear what the Russians wanted in exchange for help—relief from sanctions imposed over their human rights abuses under the Magnitsky Act.

That the Trump campaign at the highest level was receptive to help from the Kremlin sent a clear message to Moscow: Trump wants to play ball. Only days after the secret Trump Tower meeting, the Russians' preferred cutout, Julian Assange of WikiLeaks, would announce that he had received thousands of stolen Clinton emails and would be making them public. Having been given the green light, the Russians were doing exactly what they previewed to Papadopoulos, providing the emails to WikiLeaks and releasing them anonymously.

The Russians had gotten the message from Don Jr., but now they would get it directly from his father. On July 27, 2016, only seven weeks after the meeting in Trump Tower, Donald Trump, the Republican nominee for president, made his now-infamous plea to Moscow while speaking to reporters in Doral, Florida: "Russia, if you're listening, I hope you're able to find the thirty thousand [Clinton] emails that are missing. I think you will probably be rewarded mightily by our press." The Russians were in fact listening, and they attempted to hack a private server belonging to Clinton's personal office only hours later. WikiLeaks would launch its massive dumping campaign the same month, along with a Russian publisher, DC Leaks, and Trump would gleefully read the contents of the stolen emails at campaign stop after campaign stop.

Trump campaign associates would engage in communication with these Russian cutouts to discuss the timing of planned releases, and to help publish and amplify the damaging disclosures. These associates included Roger Stone, who predicted that Clinton campaign chairman John Podesta would soon have his "time in the barrel" over a month before WikiLeaks published emails stolen from Podesta's account. Stone would lie to our committee about these contacts and be indicted for his false statements and for trying to intimidate another witness into lying to cover up his contacts. But Donald Trump had a keen interest in what WikiLeaks was doing and when they were going to do it, and Stone was a key conduit in finding out.

Likewise, Don Jr. had repeated and secret contacts with WikiLeaks through private direct messages on Twitter, in which he coordinated efforts to publicize WikiLeaks' archives of stolen emails and exchanged information. In one particularly notable direct message that was a tragic harbinger of things to come, WikiLeaks wrote to Don Jr. to recommend that "If your father 'loses' we think it's more interesting if he DOES NOT concede and spends his time CHALLENGING the media."

The hacking and dumping operation was only one of the methods the Kremlin used to help Trump's election prospects—they also ran a large social media campaign out of St. Petersburg, Russia, designed to denigrate Clinton, elevate Trump, and turn Americans against one another. The Russian social media operation was extensive, generating content seen by tens of millions of Americans and leaving literally billions of views and impressions on Facebook, Twitter, YouTube, and other platforms. Unwitting Americans organized local protests against Clinton after being enjoined to do so by people they thought were neighbors but turned out to be Russians living half a world away.

In the midst of this clandestine social media campaign, Paul Manafort met repeatedly and had other contacts with a Russian intelligence agent named Konstantin Kilimnik, and provided Kilimnik with sensitive internal campaign polling data and campaign strategies in key midwestern states, which Kilimnik in turn provided to Russian intelligence services. Whether Manafort was supplying the Russians with that information so they could use it to target their social media efforts could never be confirmed since Manafort used encryted apps and destroyed his data, but Russian intelligence clearly coveted the information. Years earlier, Manafort had been representing pro-Russian interests in Ukraine, making millions by advancing Putin's interests there, and now he had been again serving Russian interests, this time during a U.S. presidential campaign. Manafort would also be charged with lying to investigators and suborning others to do the same, along with numerous other federal crimes.

After the election, President Obama imposed sanctions on Russia for its interference. Immediately thereafter, Trump's National Security Advisor designate, Michael Flynn, had secret discussions about the sanctions with Russian ambassador Sergey Kislyak, urging Kislyak not to respond. The implication was clear: The Russians had just helped Donald Trump become president, and Trump would return the favor by doing away with Russian sanctions. Flynn had been colluding with the Russians to undermine the bipartisan policy of the United States.

There was one last important element to Trump's secret contacts with Russia. Throughout the 2016 campaign, Donald Trump had claimed to have no business dealings with Russia. "I have nothing to do with Russia," he declared repeatedly, when asked about it. In fact, up until weeks before he seized the Republican nomination, Trump was actively trying to cement a deal that would likely be the most lucrative of his life—a Trump Tower in Moscow. When completed, the combination of luxury condos and retail shops would be the tallest building not only in Russia but in all of Europe. Trump stood to gain hundreds of millions of dollars if the project went through.

The Trump Organization had been in repeated contact with the Kremlin during the campaign, to seek their help in consummating the deal. They had even considered giving Putin a penthouse apartment at the top of the building as marketing or an inducement.

Michael Cohen, the president's personal lawyer, got on the phone with an assistant to Dmitry Peskov, a spokesman for the Kremlin and close confidant of Putin, and discussed the project at length. Peskov's assistant was well prepared for the call, and deeply familiar with the project. These secret negotiations gave the Russians additional and powerful *kompromat* on Trump. Donald Trump had been lying to the American people about his pursuit of a huge business deal in Moscow, and the Russians knew it. If Trump's campaign was successful, Kremlin agents could use any recording of the call with Cohen to potentially blackmail the president of the United States. Cohen, too, would lie to our committee and be indicted for his role in the cover-up.

When Donald Trump did become president, there would be no need for the Kremlin to blackmail him into betraying America's interests—to a remarkable degree, he would prove more than willing to do that on his own. And when he did, as when, in Helsinki, Finland, Trump stood next to Putin and took his side over his own intelligence agencies, the once proud party of Ronald Reagan publicly capitulated to this heir of the evil empire.

I NEVER EXPECTED DONALD TRUMP to win the Republican primary, much less to become president. When he descended a golden escalator and announced his campaign with a venomous attack on some of the most vulnerable and marginalized—calling Mexican immigrants drug dealers and rapists—I couldn't help but be struck by the familiar pattern of xenophobic rhetoric that I had witnessed in Czechoslovakia. While Trump's background had little in common with the penniless origins of a man like Vladimir Meciar, his political message was strikingly similar: Both stoked anger to mobilize support, both steered hostility toward ethnic minorities, and both promised a return to a bygone era. Classic demagoguery, from a dangerous and violent lineage. Not entirely unfamiliar in the United States, but never attempted at this scale, and never before with a Twitter feed reaching tens of millions.

I initially gave this ugliest of American campaigns no chance of success. As I used to tell audiences while out on the stump, "There are two reasons Trump will never win the Republican nomination: First, the GOP is not that suicidal. And second, the Democratic Party is not that lucky." I will forever be humbled by that blithe miscalculation. Clearly, we were witnessing something that none of us had seen before and didn't fully understand. Who could expect that a real estate celebrity who didn't pay his bills and couldn't tell fact from fiction would be taken seriously, let alone draw sustained support? But populism is potent, cultural resentment a powerful additive, and as we would all soon find out, both of these together can pose an existential threat to a democracy.

During the summer of 2016, I plunged into the Clinton campaign as a surrogate, traveling the country, delivering speeches, appearing on talk shows, fundraising for the candidate, and pointing out the many dangers of a Trump presidency.

Trump's national security policies were ill-informed and deeply contrary to our values. He was already proposing to ban Muslims from coming into the country, a policy both immoral and unconstitutional, at a time when we were dependent on our Muslim allies around the world to help us defeat a burgeoning threat from ISIS and when we needed the trust and assistance of Islamic communities at home to combat extremism. He was advocating for carpet bombing and torture and offering to meet with despots like North Korea's Kim Jong Un while berating our South Korean ally and threatening to withdraw our troops from the Korean peninsula if they didn't pay us more.

Trump was also seeking to tear down the international institutions and rules-based order that had allowed America and our allies to thrive since the end of World War II. There is no question that our NATO allies can and should contribute more to their defense and our collective security, or that the United Nations can be unwieldy, bureaucratic, and wasteful. But these institutions and others have contributed to our peace and security in innumerable ways, and no country has had a greater influence on their work or derived more benefit from them than the United States. The destruction of the rules-based order they represent would undermine our security and provide a windfall for rogue nations.

But no Trump foreign policy pronouncements were more alarmingly discordant than on the subject of Putin and Russia. Trump had nothing but praise for Putin, and seemingly nothing but disdain for our European and democratic allies. He suggested the United States recognize Russia's illegal annexation of Crimea from Ukraine, proposed an end to U.S. sanctions on Russia over its invasion of that country, claimed that NATO was obsolete and we might withdraw from it, and alleged that the Russians were fighting terror in Syria when they were merely trying to perpetuate the Assad regime and their own military presence in that country. As the top Democrat on the House Intelligence Committee, I traveled the world and heard the concern among our allies that Trump's policy positions were already endangering them by encouraging further Russian aggression and territorial expansion.

It was all so inexplicable—where did this fawning view of Putin's Russia come from, so at odds with reality, not to mention the GOP's own party orthodoxy? Soon my level of concern that Trump might betray our country's interests and security if he was elected president went from yellow to flashing red, and my concerns grew that far from a dispassionate interest in a Trump presidency, Putin might be secretly intervening in our election to bring it about.

By early June 2016, Russian intelligence services were hacking party organizations, think tanks, and private individuals, ostensibly to gather intelligence. Russia, China, and other countries with sophisticated cyber and other capabilities had long sought such information as a way of anticipating what a candidate's policies might be and how they would affect their own interests and security. These hacks were directed against both parties and opinion leaders from all along the ideological spectrum, and they followed a now well-worn playbook.

But later that month, matters took a much darker turn. A website called DC Leaks suddenly appeared online and began to publish emails stolen from Democratic officials. Then, three days before the Democratic National Convention in July, WikiLeaks published nearly 20,000 stolen emails related to the Clinton campaign. In the weeks to come, DC Leaks and WikiLeaks would publish more than 150,000 stolen emails. In the intelligence world, this was a three-alarm fire—what appeared to have been a foreign intelligence gathering operation targeting both parties had morphed into something quite different and far more sinister: an effort to weaponize the stolen information and influence the outcome of the presidential election. In an unprecedented escalation, the Russians had set aside any traditional risk aversion to getting involved in U.S. politics. Putin had picked a side.

"Are you seeing what I'm seeing?" Senator Dianne Feinstein asked me over a secure call that I took from the bunker. She was one of my home state senators and the top Democrat on the Senate Intelligence Committee, so we had worked closely for years.

"Yes," I replied. I knew exactly what she meant, even if we did not know of the most recent Russian assault on Clinton's computers.

"And are you as alarmed by it as I am?"

"I certainly am, Senator."

"What do you think we should do?" she asked.

Less than two years earlier, in November 2014, North Korea had hacked Sony Pictures before the studio released a film, *The Interview,* mocking the Dear Leader. The film was a poor satire, but the hack was no joke, destroying thousands of company computers and resulting in the theft of terabytes of data. The North Koreans fed salacious stolen emails about celebrities and studio executives to a press that was hungry for such fodder and eagerly published it. In this way, the press amplified the injury to Sony and rewarded the North Korean regime for its attack.

I took a deep interest in the Sony hack, both from a national security perspective and as someone who literally represented Hollywood, California, and urged the Obama administration to immediately attribute the attack to its indisputable source and impose real costs on North Korea through additional sanctions. I also urged them to use informational warfare and broadcast messages about the corrupt nature of the regime to the North Korean people in the same manner that South Korea responds after artillery attacks on its territory. I told the administration that if they left it at naming and shaming, we could expect other nations to conclude that cyberattacks—which are always deniable—are a cost-free way of influencing America's conduct. Our adversaries, I warned the administration, would be watching. Now, on the phone with Feinstein, I realized that they had indeed been watching, and the result was catastrophic.

"I think the administration needs to attribute the attacks to Russia," I told Feinstein, "and impose sanctions on them, otherwise we can expect a lot more of this. There is only one thing Putin respects, and that's strength."

Feinstein agreed, and we called on the administration to respond, making our request public to maximize the pressure to act. While we waited for an answer, the leaks kept coming, forcing the Clinton campaign off message. I was again deeply troubled by the role the press was playing in rewarding the hackers by publishing the stolen emails, just as the Hollywood press had done with North Korea's hack of Sony. My colleague Steve Israel, chair of the Democratic Policy and Communications Committee, and I got on the phone with the editor of *The New York Times* to make the case for stronger journalistic discretion and ethics. We're not saying that you should never publish stolen emails, we told the editor, but many of the emails you are publishing have little public value. And what's more, when you do feel that you need to reveal stolen information, you should always begin by putting the documents in the proper context—"in emails stolen by the Russian government in an apparent effort to influence our election, this is what we learned." All too often, the press would report any salacious new emails and only at the end of a long column of print would they include their likely provenance and add a disclaimer, "the Clinton campaign was contacted but declined to comment." Our appeal fell on deaf ears.

. . .

IN AUGUST, CIA DIRECTOR JOHN Brennan briefed me on intelligence that orders to interfere in our election were coming from the very top, Putin himself. This information was publicly disclosed by the Intelligence Community in 2017, and it may not seem exceptional now, but at the time it was a stunning revelation. Speaker Pelosi and I believed it was essential to warn state election officials that the Russians might seek to tamper with their registration databases and electronic voting machines. Russia had infiltrated databases in at least a couple of states, and there was a real danger that the Russians would go beyond seeking to influence voters and try to alter the actual vote count. There were still any number of counties in key battleground states that used voting systems with no paper trail—negligent on its face in the era of cyberintrusion—and the Russians could succeed in undermining our elections even if they didn't change the vote tally, by causing chaos on election day with missing registrations, or generally casting doubt on whether Americans could rely on the vote totals.

At a September meeting with top legislative leadership in the House SCIF below the Capitol, Secretary of the Department of Homeland Security Jeh Johnson discussed designating elections systems as critical infrastructure. And he pleaded with us, on a bipartisan basis, to alert the states to the danger of Russian cyberattacks and to encourage them to take advantage of the diagnostics DHS had to access the security or vulnerability of their voting systems and databases. (It would take days before we could agree on a bipartisan statement, and by then it would be so watered down as to be meaningless.) Senate Intelligence Committee chairman Richard Burr of North Carolina opposed designating elections infrastructure as critical, viewing it as a federal intrusion on the states' conduct of their own elections. Mitch McConnell was also vehemently against the idea and believed that the administration needed to be very careful about interfering in the election. Speaker Paul Ryan left the meeting early to attend to other business. I was mystified: What other business could he have that would be more important?

On the sidelines of the meeting, I urged Obama chief of staff Dennis McDonough and homeland security adviser Lisa Monaco to name Russia as the culprit and impose sanctions against the actors responsible for hacking the DNC. But Donald Trump was already claiming that the election was "rigged" to prevent him from winning, and the administration believed it would only play into that false narrative if it were to openly confront Russia over its actions. "That may be true," I acknowledged, "but there is no question the Russians are interfering to help decide the election and I think we can trust the American people with what to do with that information. Just think," I went on, "how incensed the public will be if they learn we saw this happening in real time and didn't say anything about it until after the election."

I could not persuade them. Feinstein and I decided to make a second announcement ourselves—but we knew that if we wanted the public to understand the danger, we had to explain that our concerns were grounded in classified information and not just the opinion of two Democratic lawmakers. To do so, we needed the approval of the intelligence agencies themselves, and the circumstances were unprecedented.

After several days of wrestling with a draft without securing agency approval, I happened to be on a panel at a defense conference where Brennan was speaking. We ended up meeting in the narrow unfinished hallways behind the stage, not far from the clamor of the kitchen staff and waitpersons, and he committed that if I would agree to a few final tweaks, he would give approval to go public. Back in the SCIF, I reviewed the final proposed language, and it was solid. On September 22, Feinstein and I released our new statement to the public:

"Based on briefings we have received, we have concluded that the Russian intelligence agencies are making a serious and concerted effort to influence the U.S. Election," we wrote. "At the least, this effort is intended to sow doubt about the security of our election and may well be intended to influence the outcomes of the election—we can see no other rationale for the behavior of the Russians. We believe that orders for the Russian intelligence agencies to conduct such actions could come only from very senior levels of the Russian government." I was relieved that we were able to get word out to the American people, but knew this would still not be enough. For the country to register the seriousness of the matter and gird itself for the foreign interference that was coming—had already come—it would be necessary for the president to speak out.

The Obama administration wouldn't make its own attribution until three weeks later, on October 7, acknowledging in a written statement that "the Russian Government directed the recent compromises of e-mails" and that these thefts and disclosures were intended to interfere in our election. But the written statement was just that, a press release with no more formal roll out behind it. Still wary of being perceived as trying to "rig" the outcome, agency heads let the written document speak for itself. It didn't work. WikiLeaks promptly dumped two thousand emails that Russia had hacked from the personal email account of John Podesta. These emails were explosive; they included excerpts of private speeches Clinton had made to Wall Street banks in which she suggested the banks knew best how to regulate themselves. Once again, the politically potent content of the emails overshadowed the fact that they had been stolen at the direction of the Kremlin.

On the campaign trail, Trump kept lauding the WikiLeaks disclosures, bringing them up more than a hundred times and disputing the fact that the emails were stolen by Russia. It could have been China or even a four-hundred-pound man on his bed, Trump claimed. At times he even denied that they were the product of a hack, and he accused Democrats of always blaming Russia. In this way, Trump was undermining the nation's intelligence agencies and the sanctity of our elections, as well as handing Putin a propaganda coup. If Trump could do all this as a candidate, I could just imagine what he was capable of doing as president.

Election day brought a stunning upset for Donald Trump. Given the broad and systematic intervention by an enemy foreign power into our affairs, we would have to get to the bottom of just what had happened. The future of our democracy depended on it. There was no way to know whether the Russian operation had changed the outcome of the race that would ultimately be decided by just seventy thousand votes scattered among a few key states. Nor could we know whether the Russians had engaged in this unprecedented attack on our democracy on their own or had had the help of Americans, but I was determined to find out.

Back in my personal office in Washington the following week, I found my staff devastated by the election. They were young and idealistic and desperately concerned about what it meant to the country and to our future. I gathered them in my office for a pep talk. "I know how worried you are about the election, and what the result means for all that we care about, and I just want to tell you, by way of encouragement . . . we're fucked." I smiled dejectedly, and said that I knew this was not the pep talk they were expecting, but that I just wasn't up to it, not yet, and I promised them that I would have more to say after I gathered my own bearings.

In early January, the leaders of the FBI, CIA, and NSA briefed our committee in the SCIF on the Intelligence Community Assessment (ICA) of Russia's interference in the election that it would soon make public. The Russians had massively intervened in our elections, denigrating Hillary Clinton and benefiting Donald Trump, and had done so under the orders of Vladimir Putin himself. And the ICA warned that the Russians would do it again.

Almost immediately, Republican members of our committee sought to contest the ICA assessment that the Russians favored Donald Trump. This was absurd, not only because the ICA on its face provided no basis for them to do so, but also because the Intelligence Community conclusion was so clearly borne out by the public evidence. Russian state media, its private trolls, the hacking and dumping operation—all of it so clearly hurt Clinton and helped Trump that any other conclusion seemed farcical. Certainly, there were efforts to incite both liberals and conservatives and promote general discord, but the Russian government preference for Trump was abundantly clear.

The president falsely claimed that the ICA found the Russian interference had no effect on the election; in fact, the ICA was very clear that the Intelligence Community was drawing no conclusion about the impact of Russian interference on the outcome. More broadly, though, Trump attacked the ICA and the Intelligence Community that produced it, and in doing so, gave Putin the strongest form of plausible deniability, further undermining the credibility of our agencies. Putin could tell the Russian people that not even the president of the United States believed U.S. intelligence, and that the ICA findings were merely the product of an anti-Russian establishment in the United States.

In February 2017, less than a month after Donald Trump was inaugurated president of the United States, I was invited to join Senator John McCain on a congressional delegation trip (CODEL) to Munich for the world's premier national security conference. Founded in 1963 and held at the historic Hotel Bayerischer Hof, the Munich Security Conference hosts heads of state, ministers and parliamentarians, business leaders, high-ranking military officers, and other leaders for a discussion of the world's paramount security challenges. For members of Congress, it is an extraordinary opportunity for bilateral meetings, where you can sit down with presidents and prime ministers in room after room without having to leave the hotel, let alone travel from country to country.

Concern over the Trump presidency at the conference was palpable. In office for only a few weeks, Trump had already battered our NATO allies, demanding greater financial contributions and questioning the relevance of the transatlantic alliance. Our democratic partners were in a panic, and Vice President Mike Pence, a speaker at the convention, did little to reassure them. Gathered in a conference room that was too small for the growing attendance every year, the audience sat shoulder to shoulder on small chairs in the hall and leaned forward on two levels of balconies above, listening in stony silence as Pence praised the president of the United States and said that he was making America respected as never before.

In sharp contrast, McCain's reception was effusive and emotional. Joining McCain in meetings with Afghan president Ashraf Ghani and other world leaders, I could see the immense respect they had for him, and how much they pinned their hopes on his ability to guide or constrain Trump's worst impulses. Ghani probably understood better than most the troubled relationship McCain had with Trump, but he and others were desperate for McCain's help, any help, in dealing with the erratic new American president.

One of the wonderful things about traveling with John McCain was that he could invite anyone he wanted to dinner, and they would usually come. One evening, we had dinner with Bono and Bill Gates—not my usual dinner company. In a private room, seated at a long wooden table with plenty of beer, wine, and heavy German food, McCain introduced me to his guests as "a good guy, for a Communist." It wasn't the first time he had introduced me in this fashion; when I'd joined McCain on CBS's *Face the Nation*, he had introduced me to host Bob Scheiffer as "a good guy who gets things right about zero percent of the time." I was flattered that he teased me this way; his staff told me that it's when he doesn't pick on you that you need to worry. That night in Munich, he introduced his closest friend, Lindsey Graham, by saying: "Everyone knows Lindsey; few people like him."

During dinner, we discussed the work that Bono and Gates were doing to fight disease and death in Africa and elsewhere, and, of course, Donald Trump. McCain was careful in his comments about Trump, not wanting to criticize our president while on foreign soil, and the rest of our delegation followed his example. As the night went on, we began telling jokes, and Bono told one about being Irish. Afterward, he grew serious and said: "I'm very proud to be Irish. I'm very proud of Ireland, but Ireland, like most countries, is just a country. America is also an idea."

The moment he said it, I realized that this is what was at stake with the Trump presidency: the very idea of America as a beacon of democracy. As we flew to Europe, Donald Trump had said, for the first time as president, that he believed the press was the enemy of the American people. I shouldn't have been shocked, but I was, and on ABC News that evening, I said that this was the kind of thing you would hear from a tin-pot dictator, not the president of the United States. But there it was, and it was only the beginning. Around the world—from journalists in their prison cells in Turkey, to protesters in Tahrir Squire, Cairo, who gathered by the hundreds of thousands to demand better governance, to inmates in Evin prison in Iran, to the victims of a campaign of mass extrajudicial killing in the Philippines—people looked to us as a beacon of liberty. But increasingly they did not recognize what they saw, and that was as terrible a tragedy for us as it was for them.

It was also a tremendous boon for Vladimir Putin. During an interview with Bill O'Reilly that aired that month and just before the Super Bowl, the conservative commentator asked Trump why he respected Putin, since Putin was a killer. Trump's response was reflexive, and it seemed to take O'Reilly aback: "You think our country is so innocent?" Trump asked, before suggesting we were also guilty of the same. In asserting a moral equivalency between the policies of the United States and Vladimir Putin—who had long since destroyed Russia's nascent democracy and made a practice of murdering his political opponents and journalists—the president was using talking points that might as well have been written in the Kremlin.

BACK IN WASHINGTON, D.C., I was informed that FBI director James Comey wanted to schedule a briefing for top congressional leaders, which was held on March 9. After ushering most of the staff out of the secure conference room and closing the heavy doors, the director shared some stunning information: The FBI had opened an investigation into four people associated with the Trump campaign to examine potential links between these individuals and Russia's government, and whether the campaign had coordinated with the Russian effort to subvert our election. I turned to my colleagues to see whether this information had landed on them with the same force it had hit me, and their stony expressions left no doubt. It was one of those "holy shit" moments, and the room was silent as we tried to take it all in, and figure out what it meant for the country.

I knew that the FBI investigation would complicate matters for a congressional probe of Russia's involvement in our election and issues of potential collusion—we would need to try to coordinate so that our actions did not interfere with one another—but I was determined to press forward with our own investigation. The FBI could determine whether people broke the law, and expose the counterintelligence risks posed by Trump campaign ties to Russia, but it wasn't required to share its full findings with Congress or the public, and it certainly couldn't take legislative redress to protect the nation going forward. Still, a decision by our committee to investigate the president's connections to a nation that had just meddled in our election, and perhaps decisively so, was not mine alone to make.

As the ranking member of the House Intelligence Committee, I could not launch an investigation of the Russian operation and use the committee's power to compel answers. That power belonged to Devin Nunes, now our chairman. Nunes and I discussed the matter at length, and he agreed that our committee had a duty to investigate the details of the Russian operation and any role played by Americans. Nunes had met Trump during the campaign when they traveled together in the Central Valley and had become part of the president's transition team, and I knew it would not be easy for him to pursue the investigation with the same intensity that I thought it deserved, but we had a good enough relationship that I was hopeful we could navigate the crosscurrents and do a thorough job.

Our first test came with discussions over the scope of the investigation. To his credit, and unlike with Gowdy during the Benghazi hearings, Nunes and I were able to agree on four parameters: "What Russian cyber activity and other active measures were directed against the United States and its allies? Did the Russian active measures include links between Russia and individuals associated with the political campaigns or any other U.S. persons? What was the U.S. government's response to these Russian active measures, and what do we need to do to protect ourselves and our allies in the future? What possible leaks of classified information took place related to the Intelligence Community Assessment of these matters?"

The last was an obsession of the Republicans, who seemed more concerned that evidence of Trump campaign connections with the Russians had been leaked than whether the Russians had made common cause with Americans during a U.S. presidential campaign to help sway the election. Leak investigations are exceedingly difficult, and they are conducted by the FBI and Department of Justice, not Congress, but this was a concession I had to make if I was to have any hope of persuading Nunes to examine the serious allegations of collusion between Russia and the Trump campaign.

In releasing our scoping document, Nunes said, "On a bipartisan basis, we will fully investigate all the evidence we collect and follow that evidence wherever it leads." My own statement was almost exactly the same, and we even held a joint press conference to announce our determination to move forward. Still, in private, I could sense his reluctance. Almost immediately he made that reluctance public as well, telling a reporter that "without any real credible evidence, we're not going to be bringing Americans into there [the SCIF] to be interviewed."

To distract from a daily drumbeat of news reports of previously undisclosed contacts between Russia and his campaign, Donald Trump began a vigorous counteroffensive, falsely alleging that the Obama administration had wiretapped his campaign and been spying on it, even implicating the British in his spurious allegations. In a tweet on March 4, he wrote: "Just found out that Obama had my 'wires tapped' in Trump Tower just before the victory. Nothing found. This is McCarthyism!" A few minutes later, he posted again: "How low has President Obama gone to tap my phones during the very sacred election process. This is Nixon/Watergate. Bad (or sick) guy!"

It was an audacious lie, but part of the Trump strategy of never defending, always attacking, turning your opponent's claim right back on them and truth be damned. It meant taking a wrecking ball to our intelligence agencies and their partners overseas, but he didn't care.

Notwithstanding the president's efforts to change the narrative, our committee's work was off to a promising start. The CIA had set up a special room at the agency where our members could begin wading through thick binders of information gathered by the Intelligence Community. I had already drawn up a proposed witness list, and for our first public hearing, Nunes and I agreed to summon FBI director James Comey and Admiral Mike Rogers, director of the NSA. At the time, I had no idea what Comey would say during the hearing, or how explosive it would turn out to be.

7

THE MIDNIGHT RUN

THE WEEKEND BEFORE THE COMEY HEARING, I WENT TO VISIT MY father in Boca Raton. My mother, Sherrill, had passed away several years ealier after a long battle with Alzheimer's disease. Excusing myself from a movie in the living room with my dad and his girlfriend, Claire, I retired to the guest bedroom to write my opening statement.

This would be no ordinary hearing. I needed to convince the viewing public why it was important that we investigate a foreign power's effort to influence our election, and most significant, whether that foreign power had had the help of American citizens. It may now seem self-evident that an investigation into the matter was essential, but I had no sense of that at the time, as Republicans were quickly growing hostile to the investigation. Their reflexive reaction to the

Intelligence Community Assessment that the Russians intended to help Trump had been a warning sign.

When I returned to Washington, I met privately in our underground hearing room with the Democratic members of our committee, each of them handpicked by Leader Pelosi for their work ethic and commitment to the nation's security. We discussed the need to prepare our questions in advance, to use them to tell a cohesive narrative of what happened, what we needed to find out, and why. There could be no freelancing; we needed to choreograph our presentation as succinctly and persuasively as possible.

The following day, as the audience packed into the same Ways and Means Committee hearing room where Hillary Clinton had faced down her Benghazi accusers two years earlier, Nunes and I met with Director Comey and Admiral Rogers briefly in a small anteroom. I asked Rogers about the impact the president's accusations were having on our relationship with British intelligence, and he was confident that the relationship would not be irreparably damaged. As for Comey, I had no expectation that he would disclose the FBI's ongoing investigation into the Trump campaign, and assumed he would merely sidestep any questions on that subject; certainly nothing he had said at that point suggested otherwise. Nunes and I took our positions on the dais and our witnesses took their places at the witness table.

Nunes began by acknowledging that the Russians' active measures during the campaign had been "deeply troubling," and that they "focused wide attention on the pressing threats posed by the Russian autocrat." And although he did not support the president's claims of wiretapping, he did suggest that "it's still possible that other surveillance activities were used against President Trump and his associates." Nunes also wanted "anyone who has information about these topics to come forward." I did not find these comments striking at the time, but in hindsight, he may have been foreshadowing an effort he was already engaged in to help the White House explain its otherwise inexplicable claims of espionage by the Obama administration.

I told Nunes my opening statement would be long, and then I set out to make the case for our investigation: "Last summer, at the height of a bitterly contested and hugely consequential presidential campaign, a foreign adversarial power intervened in an effort to weaken our democracy and to influence the outcome for one candidate and against the other. That foreign adversary was of course Russia, and it acted through its intelligence agencies and upon the direct instructions of its autocratic ruler, Vladimir Putin, in order to help Donald J. Trump become the forty-fifth president of the United States."

The Russian operation had begun at least a year earlier, escalating from a simple "spear phishing" attempt to collect information about the candidates to a highly sophisticated hack and continual leak of documents damaging to the Clinton campaign and helpful to Donald Trump, paired with an extensive overt and covert media strategy to denigrate the Democratic candidate. "We will never know whether the Russian intervention was determinative in such a close election," I said. "For the purposes of our investigation, it simply does not matter. What does matter is this: The Russians successfully meddled in our democracy, and our intelligence agencies have concluded they will do so again."

For eighteen minutes, I laid out the details that had been publicly reported—the efforts by Trump advisers like Roger Stone, Paul Manafort, and Michael Flynn to conceal their ongoing communication with Russian operatives, intermediaries and officials; Jeff Sessions's misleading testimony during his confirmation hearing about his contacts with the Russian ambassador; changes in the Ukraine provisions of the platform at the Republican convention to make it more Russia-friendly; Michael Flynn's efforts to undermine sanctions and his lies about it; and more. "Is it possible that all of these events and reports are completely unrelated, and nothing more than an entirely unhappy coincidence?" I asked. "Yes, it is possible. But it is also possible, maybe more than possible, that they are not coincidental, not disconnected, and not unrelated, and that the Russians used the same techniques to corrupt U.S. persons that they employed in Europe and elsewhere. We simply don't know, not yet. And we owe it to the country to find out."

As I yielded the floor back to Nunes, I could see frustration on the faces of my Republican colleagues. I had used my opening statement to lay out the scope of what we needed to investigate and why, and that seemed like more than enough to propel us forward. But what came next gave our investigation a momentum I never expected.

After a brief opening statement by Admiral Rogers, Nunes recognized Comey for an opening statement, and almost immediately—before I could even catch my breath—Comey made the secret thing public: "I have been authorized by the Department of Justice to confirm that the FBI, as part of our counterintelligence mission, is investigating the Russian government's efforts to interfere in the 2016 presidential election, and that includes investigating the nature of any links between individuals associated with the Trump campaign and the Russian government and whether there was any coordination between the campaign and Russia's efforts. As with any counterintelligence investigation, this will also include an assessment of whether any crimes were committed."

The announcement stunned the room, and much of the country, and as the questioning period began, I knew that Comey's testimony would dominate headlines for days to come. Any doubt that Republicans might try to plant about the necessity of our inquiry into the Russian operation would run headlong into the reality that the FBI deemed the situation sufficiently serious that they were conducting the same investigation. Nevertheless, we were not going to miss the opportunity to drive the point home. But first things first, I needed to address the president's repeated false claims that he, not Clinton, was the victim of spycraft, and not from the Russians, but from the Obama administration.

"Director Comey, I want to begin by attempting to put to rest several claims made by the president about his predecessor, namely, that President Obama wiretapped his phones. So that we can be precise, I want to refer you to exactly what the president said and ask you whether there is any truth to it . . . the president claimed, quote, 'Terrible. Just found out that Obama had my wires tapped in Trump Tower just before the victory. Nothing found. This is McCarthyism,' unquote. Director Comey, was the president's statement that Obama had his wires tapped in Trump Tower a true statement?"

If there was any answer that Comey had scripted out with precision in advance, it was this one. He looked down at his notes so that he could respond without a syllable out of place. "With respect to the president's tweets about alleged wiretapping directed at him by the prior administration, I have no information that supports those tweets, and we have looked carefully inside the FBI. The Department of Justice has asked me to share with you that the answer is the same for the Department of Justice and all its components. The department has no information that supports those tweets."

My Democratic colleagues walked systematically through all of the Trump/Russia contacts that merited investigation, tracking my opening statement. Seemingly oblivious to the magnitude of what Comey had disclosed, Republican members fixated on leaks and asked about little else. They were disorganized and unprepared. If the asymmetry in the presentations of the two parties was lost on the Republican members, it was not lost on their party leader, who watched it all from 1600 Pennsylvania Avenue, stewing. Trump's extreme displeasure would lead to an extraordinary chain of events that came close to destroying our committee's investigation within a matter of days.

I WAS SITTING AT MY desk in the bunker two days later when my communications director, Patrick Boland, appeared at the door. Boland is preternaturally gifted at his job, having developed in his twenties a better understanding of the media as an enterprise, as a business, and in all of its various and new incarnations than most elected officials will acquire in a lifetime. At six feet four, Boland is also an imposing figure and is sometimes mistaken for my personal security, a misconception that I was increasingly grateful for given the hostile nature of the calls and emails I was now receiving. Whenever I agreed to appear on Fox News, which was seldom, or prime time hosts Sean Hannity and Tucker Carlson were attacking me, which was frequent, the phones in our office would ring off the hook with profanity. Along with Emilie Simons, my talented press secretary, Boland and I were struggling to keep up with hundreds of press requests a week, sometimes a day. Capitol Police, for their part, were starting to investigate a growing number of threats on my life.

"Nunes is doing a presser in the well," Boland said with a concerned tone in his voice. "They won't tell us what it's regarding." This was unnerving for several reasons. Nunes and I had been doing our press appearances jointly, and nothing had been on the schedule for that morning. And what could possibly be the reason for keeping the topic of his briefing a secret? *What the hell was Nunes doing?*

Boland ducked outside to go watch the press conference, and I flipped on the television in my office and saw Nunes addressing a small group of reporters outside the SCIF, where a circular staircase winds two stories down from ground level in the Capitol Visitor Center. We often used the landing at the base of the stairs as a makeshift briefing room, so it was not surprising that Nunes had found reporters and cameramen waiting there. When you stand in the well, you are bathed in light from the skylights far above, while reporters stand in dark shadows along the wall. Some members of the media were assigned to wait in the stairwell all day to shoot footage and ask questions as we came and went from the SCIF, leading a cameraman to nickname the area the Pit of Despair.

Nunes was holding a sheet of white paper, which he began to unfold. "I'm gonna just read a very brief statement," he said. "At our opening hearing on Monday, I encouraged anyone who has information about relative topics, including surveillance on President-elect Trump or his transition team, to come forward and speak to the House Intelligence Committee. . . . I recently confirmed that on numerous occasions, the Intelligence Community incidentally collected information about U.S. citizens involved in the Trump transition . . . details with little or no apparent foreign intelligence value."

Over the next fifteen minutes, Nunes made a series of startling claims based on a "set of documents" that he had reviewed. He accused the Obama administration of conducting "surveillance" on members of the Trump campaign, and claimed that officials had abused their power to "unmask" the names of Trump campaign officials. "I want to be clear, none of this surveillance was related to Russia, or the investigation of Russian activities or of the Trump team," he said. "Who was aware of it? Why was it not disclosed to Congress? Who requested and authorized the additional unmasking?" He promised that the Intelligence Committee would find out the answers, then said, "I informed Speaker Ryan this morning of this new information, and I will be going to the White House this afternoon to share what I know with the president and his team."

In response to questions, Nunes was cagey about how and where he had received the documents. "I'm not going to go into sources or when it arrived," he said. He also claimed, "The administration isn't aware of this, so I need to make sure I go over there."

When Nunes was finished speaking, I turned to my staff. "Does anyone know what he's talking about?" No one did. I certainly wasn't aware of any evidence that would justify anything that Nunes had said. He had disavowed Trump's claim that Trump Tower had been wiretapped, but at the same time, he was now suggesting that Obama had been spying on his campaign in other ways. It struck me as a smokescreen, a not-so-subtle effort to give the president cover for the wild accusations that Comey and Rogers had just debunked. Or worse, like many a defendant in a criminal case that tries to put the prosecution on trial, Donald Trump was now attempting to try the Intelligence Community, and Nunes was helping him do so. This was a way of both undermining the investigation and turning it back on critics of the president.

National security agencies in the government routinely conduct surveillance of foreign adversaries, and it is hardly surprising that some of the people they target either call or mention American citizens in the course of their conversations. When they do, it is called "incidental collection," because the information about a U.S. person is picked up unintentionally. If that information is written up in a report, the names of Americans typically are "masked," that is, they are redacted, or given generic descriptors so that their privacy is protected. If a national security official who receives the report cannot understand its full import without knowing the redacted names, they may request the names be "unmasked." Such requests are adjudicated by career Intelligence Community professionals.

Without seeing the documents that Nunes described, I had no idea whether Obama officials had done anything improper. If Trump campaign officials had been surreptitiously communicating with a foreign power, they could have been incidentally the subject of collection on someone else. Nunes himself didn't seem to know whether anything was out of the ordinary, but he was clearly suggesting that something improper had taken place. What was worse, he made these allegations after reviewing documents that he hadn't shared with me, or, I would soon find out, his own Republican members. And now Nunes was going to the White House to share these documents with the president, when the president's associates were themselves the subject of our investigation? None of this made any sense. And it constituted a sudden threat to our investigation and our ability to work together. It also marked the beginning of what would become a disturbing and destructive pattern during the Trump presidency: Trump would say something that was utter nonsense, and rather than acknowledge that it was nonsense, his acolytes would work feverishly to make reality appear to conform to his ludicrous claims.

Nunes disappeared into the White House, emerging two hours later to hold another press conference in front of the West Wing. Once again, he refused to say anything about where he had gotten his information, and he insisted that he had an obligation to share what he knew with the president, whom he had just briefed personally. His comments were greeted with an appropriate level of skepticism by reporters. "Why is it appropriate for you to brief President Trump, given it's his own administration or campaign associates that are a part of this investigation?"

"Because what I saw has nothing to do with Russia and nothing to do with the Russia investigation," Nunes claimed. "It has everything to do with possible surveillance activities, and the president needs to know that these intelligence reports are out there—and I have a duty to tell him."

"What did the president tell you?" another reporter asked.

"I think the president is concerned, and he should be," Nunes said.

"Can you rule out the possibility that senior Obama administration officials were involved in this?"

Nunes looked pensive. "No. We cannot."

"Can you tell us who brought you this information?"

"Well, I can tell you this," he said. "We've been asking for people to come forward. And they came through the proper channels. They had the proper clearances. And I'm just going to leave it at that."

Late that afternoon, I sought out Nunes in his office in the bunker. "Devin, what's going on? I haven't seen these documents that you're talking about, none of us have. And I don't see how you can go share them with the White House without even telling us what they are."

He stared back at me impassively, repeating the claim that he had a duty to inform the president. When I asked what kind of documents they were, and why he thought something improper had been done by the prior administration, he claimed that many of the names in the documents he had seen were masked, but that he could figure out who they were. This was even more perplexing to me, since that is often the case when a foreign party is speaking about a prominent American. If two Chinese nationals are discussing the potential election of "U.S. Businessman 1," it is not difficult to figure who they are discussing, but there is nothing even remotely improper about that. I left Nunes's office in despair. I needed him to be the chairman of an independent investigation, but in my view he was acting more like a surrogate of the White House. And he might have just destroyed the credibility of our investigation.

My Democratic colleagues on the committee were apoplectic

about what Nunes had done, and several gathered shoulder to shoulder in my small office to ask me whether I thought we should call on Nunes to step down. One of them was already on my TV screen demanding exactly that. "I don't know," I said. "He's put us in an awful position. We can ask him to step down but he won't, and then where will we be? At this point, I think the Republicans would be happy to see the whole investigation go away. I would still like to see if we can salvage this."

The following morning, March 23, Nunes asked to meet with committee members in our hearing room, outside the presence of staff. As we took our seats in two concentric rows of plush leather chairs, the room was perfectly still. We looked at one another and then at Nunes. He said that he wanted to explain his handling of the surveillance issues. He had made a judgment call to brief the president before talking to the committee, he said apologetically, and then assured us that he really wanted the investigation to be bipartisan. It is a rare thing for a member of Congress to express regret to his colleagues, but Nunes did, and as I listened attentively, I wondered if the situation might be salvaged after all.

Later that night, Nunes appeared on Fox News and made a striking admission to Sean Hannity. He said the reason he felt he had a duty to tell the president about the documents was that the president was "taking a lot of heat in the news media." As I feared, this whole thing was about giving the president cover. For his part, Trump was very pleased, and claimed that the Nunes documents had "somewhat" vindicated him. And I would soon learn that his mea culpa notwithstanding, Nunes's actions were far worse than I knew.

The following day, March 24, I heard some disturbing rumors. While Democratic and Republican members of the committee have separate staffs, many of those staff members come out of the agencies and had worked amicably together for years. One of the Republican senior staff informed a member of my staff that the evening after the Comey hearing, Nunes had been in a car with him when he received a message on his phone. Nunes abruptly ordered the staff to pull over, stepped out, and hailed an Uber. Neither the aide that he left in the car nor anyone else on his staff seemed to know where Nunes had gone.

With so many reporters covering Nunes's allegations against the Obama administration, it was no surprise when news of his mysterious Uber ride was published in *The Daily Beast* only days later, and in greater detail. Reporters were chasing down a report on Nunes's mysterious destination on the evening of the Midnight Run, as it was now called, the place where he had obtained the mysterious documents. Soon enough, Nunes was forced to make another remarkable admission. In a statement through his spokesman on March 27, Nunes admitted that he had gone to see the documents at the White House. The information that he felt compelled to brief the president about had come not from an intelligence agency, or from a whistleblower, but from people who worked for and close to the president. "Chairman Nunes met with his source at the White House grounds in order to have proximity to a secure location where he could view the information provided by the source," his spokesman said. With that revelation, it was now clear that Nunes's dramatic press conference as he left the Capitol to inform the president of the existence of the documents was a charade, and Nunes was allowing himself and the committee to be used to launder documents supplied by the White House.

In light of his bizarre and inexplicable behavior, it was clear to me that there was no way we could conduct our investigation if Nunes remained in charge. That evening, I released a statement to the press: "After much consideration, and in light of the Chairman's admission that he met with his source of information at the White House, I believe that the Chairman should recuse himself from any further involvement in the Russia investigation, as well as any involvement in oversight of matters pertaining to any incidental collection of the Trump transition, as he was also a key member of the transition team. This is not a recommendation I make lightly, as the Chairman and I have worked together well for several years."

To no one's surprise, Nunes responded that he had no intention of stepping down. Instead, he doubled down by canceling our next open hearing with former deputy attorney general Sally Yates, former Director of National Intelligence (DNI) James Clapper, and John Brennan, and ordering the indefinite suspension of all interviews in the investigation, effectively killing off the only investigation of Trump's campaign ties to Russia that had been authorized to proceed in the House.

Days later, on March 30, even more damaging information came to light when it was reported that not only had Nunes met his alleged "source" at the White House, but the source was actually two of the president's most shameless partisans. One was Ezra Cohen-Watnick, the senior director for intelligence programs on the National Security Council, who had been fired two weeks earlier by National Security Advisor H. R. McMaster (and reinstated only when Steve Bannon and Jared Kushner appealed to the president on his behalf). The other source was a national security assistant named Michael Ellis, who had previously worked for Nunes as a staff member on our committee. These were hardly the whistleblowers Nunes had led people to believe—they were among the president's most ardent and unscrupulous defenders.

The air of scandal around Nunes was now palpable. It seemed to me that his whole world was caving in, and not even his Republican colleagues wanted to defend him. Everywhere he went, he was trailed by a phalanx of reporters shouting questions about the "Midnight Run," and I would see him in the corridors below the Capitol, hurrying to escape the press, looking beleaguered and afraid. Physically, Nunes appeared weighed down by the daily revelations against him. It brought me no pleasure, far from it. If not friends, we had been friendly, and we had worked productively together for years. And even if we hadn't, there is nothing pleasant about the rapid disintegration of someone's life and reputation, even when they had brought it upon themselves.

But there was a more profound implication of Nunes's apparent humiliation over the Midnight Run—the trauma of the experience would seem to bind him even more closely to Trump. Trump's own message of aggrievement now had a far greater resonance, and

Nunes soon developed the same intense hostility to the mainstream press. Embracing the more extreme elements of the GOP that he had previously disdained, Nunes would make himself into one of the president's greatest champions, and no one would more aggressively or effectively carry Trump's conspiratorial counternarrative.

ON THE AFTERNOON OF MARCH 31, I was sitting in my underground office with a White House press briefing on the television screen. These conferences had become a font of misinformation with daily dissembling by Press Secretary Sean Spicer. The dishonesty had begun quaintly enough, with lies about the size of Trump's inauguration crowd, but since then his falsehoods had only grown more brazen. Trump adviser Kellyanne Conway would coin a new term on *Meet the Press* for the administration's propensity for untruth; they weren't lies, but "alternative facts." Our institutions depend on a shared experience, and every press conference from the Trump White House was an assault on that common understanding.

I scarcely watched them anymore, but I knew that reporters were likely to ask Spicer about the Midnight Run, and I wanted to hear his response. Sure enough, once the question period began, a reporter asked Spicer to identify which members of the Obama administration had requested the unmasking of names in what people were now calling "the Nunes documents." "I don't know," Spicer said. "I've tried to make it a comment not to get into the specifics." But everything that Nunes had done was "routine and proper," he said. "If there were people violating civil liberties to unmask, and spreading classified information to places they weren't supposed to, it should concern every American," Spicer claimed. People "misused, mishandled, and potentially did some very, very bad things with classified information. . . . Chairman Nunes and Ranking Member Schiff, who I understand is expected here later today, both possess the appropriate credentials and clearances. We've invited Democrats here, and I've been told that material they will see will shed light on the investigation."

"You said Congressman Schiff is coming today?" a reporter asked. That was news to me.

"He has made contact and is trying to arrange a time," Spicer said.

There had been no discussion between my office and the White House about scheduling a time to do anything, much less to view the Nunes documents.

"What is he talking about?" I asked my staff, who shook their heads. "We never received an invitation from the White House to see the documents, did we?" The clerk of the committee walked into my office at that very moment—"You mean this invitation?" Sure enough, the White House had just emailed me an invitation to come review the documents, which they must have sent while Spicer was still talking.

"It's a trap!" Tim Bergreen, my deputy staff director, said excitedly, and many of the other staff shared his skepticism. "If you go review the documents, they are going to say that they show things they don't, and you won't be able to contradict them, because it's classified. You will be damned if you say anything, and damned if you don't."

"It may be a trap," I said, "or it may not be a trap. But I can't refuse to go, or they will say that I was demanding to see the documents and now I'm refusing. Let's try to set it up for later this afternoon, after votes."

I drove to the White House with my staff director and we found a parking spot a few blocks away. We walked toward the entrance on Seventeenth Street and approached the security guard. "I'm Congressman Schiff and this is Michael Bahar," I said as we took out our government IDs. "We have an appointment." He looked them over and slid them back under the heavy glass.

"You can come in," the security officer said to me, buzzing the gate. "But he's not on the list." I explained to the guard that I had been invited to the White House for a meeting and asked him to check again.

I called the office and reached Tim. "They won't let Michael onto the grounds. Can you call the White House and get this fixed? We are waiting at the gate."

"It's a trap!" he said. "I told you it's a trap!"

"Tim," I said, "you're freaking me out here. We made the decision to go, and we're going."

But there was no way that I was going inside without a witness. We stepped away from the booth and waited another twenty minutes while Tim negotiated with the president's staff to put Michael on the list. At last they did, and we passed through security and stepped onto the White House grounds.

Our contact would be John Eisenberg, the top lawyer for the National Security Council, who also happened to be Michael Ellis's boss. Eisenberg's own role in the Midnight Run was unclear, but it was hard to imagine that Ellis would have engaged in such a subterfuge without Eisenberg's knowledge and approval. We found Eisenberg's suite in the Eisenhower Executive Office Building and waited a few minutes in the sitting room before Eisenberg emerged. A diminutive man with glasses, he looked like every kid I hadn't liked in law school. We barely said hello before he jabbed a finger in Bahar's direction and growled, "He can't see the documents."

"Why not?" I asked.

"He's not approved."

"Approved by *whom*?"

"He's not seeing them," Eisenberg said.

"You are the ones who invited me to come and see the documents—now you are going to turn me away?"

"I'm not turning you away, only him."

While Eisenberg and I were arguing the matter, the president's deputy chief of staff, Sean Cairncross, came into the room. "The president would like to see you in the Oval Office," Cairncross said. "But," he said, looking at Bahar, "he can't come." Bahar knew Cairncross from an earlier point in both their careers, but it didn't matter, the president wanted to see me and me alone. It really was starting to feel like a trap. I couldn't refuse to see him, but I also couldn't trust how he might mischaracterize anything that was said in the meeting. "Okay," I replied finally, and I walked with Cairncross across the small walkway to the entrance to the West Wing.

I had been in the Oval Office several times over the years, for meetings with both Barack Obama and George W. Bush, and there is no acclimating to the pulse-quickening sensation of stepping into that room. Small, sunlit, and bright, the rich carpet absorbing ambient sound, the room is both majestic and intimate at the same time. I had a moment to adjust to being in that remarkable place, before focusing in on Donald Trump. He was sitting behind the desk called Resolute, a gift from Queen Victoria to Rutherford B. Hayes in 1880, made from the oak timbers of a ship that had explored the Arctic. The image of Trump sitting behind that desk, a desk that John F. Kennedy once toiled at, his children frolicking around its massive and intricately detailed form, was jarring. Trump looked so out of place. Here was a man who had pretended to be a successful and decisive businessman on reality television, and I couldn't shake the impression that he was still pretending, only now he was pretending to be president.

He stood up and approached me in the middle of the room. "You know, you do a good job," he said, shaking my hand. There was an awkward silence, while he seemed to be waiting for me to return the compliment. During the campaign, Trump would gush that Vladimir Putin had called him a "genius" and "brilliant." "If he says great things about me, I'm going to say great things about him," he had said. Clearly, flattery worked on the president. Maybe he assumed it worked on everybody. I couldn't bring myself to do it.

"Thank you," I said, self-consciously, "I appreciate that."

He directed me to one of the chairs while he took a seat behind Resolute again. "There should be things that we can work together on, right? Things we can get done?"

"Absolutely," I replied. "I know you support a major infrastructure bill, and we do too. It would be a great thing for the country. I think you would find a lot of bipartisan support for rebuilding our roads, bridges, electrical grid—"

He cut me off. "You Democrats, you really like your infrastructure."

"Yes, we do, Mr. President. And we could work together on lowering the cost of prescription drugs. I know that's a priority of yours, and it is for us too."

"Yeah," he broke in again, clearly wanting to be the one talking. "I've talked to Elijah Cummings about that. I like him, and I think he likes me. He says a lot of nice things about me."

I had never heard Elijah say anything nice about Trump, but I knew that my colleague was making a major push to permit reimportation of prescription medication and supported allowing Medicare to bargain with drug companies over price. But mostly, I was just happy that we were talking about anything other than Russia, and tried to steer the conversation to safe topics. Finally, he asked me: "So, are you getting everything you need?"

"Well, no, actually, I'm not. I have my staff director with me, and the NSC lawyer won't allow him to accompany me while I review the documents. We have a policy on the Intelligence Committee not to review classified information outside the presence of staff," I explained. I wanted to tell him that was why Nunes was in such trouble, but refrained.

"Well, I don't have a problem with that. You can bring your staff. The whole committee can see these documents."

I heard groaning from behind me. Until that point, I had felt that we were the only ones in the Oval Office, but I now realized that several of the president's men, including his chief of staff, Reince Priebus, were standing behind me along the back wall. The president heard the groaning and picked up on it.

"If they're okay with it," he said, now qualifying his approval, "I'm okay with it."

The meeting broke up shortly thereafter, and I was relieved that the president never got into the substance of the Russia investigation. There would be little for him to misrepresent, and his comments might even help break the logjam over access to the documents. But when I returned to Eisenberg's office, he still refused to allow my staff director to join me in reviewing the materials.

"The president doesn't have a problem with it," I said.

"No, but I do," was his reply.

"And why is that?"

"I don't have the agency's approval to let him see the documents."

That was absurd, and we both knew it. The chair and ranking members of the House and Senate intelligence committees, along with the Speaker and majority leader in the House and the Senate majority and minority leaders, are all part of the "Gang of Eight" and receive the most highly classified reports and briefings not available to any other members of Congress. My staff director attended Gang of Eight meetings with me, and he had access to all the same top secret and compartmentalized information that I did. Eisenberg would have known that, but he was making excuses, and not particularly good ones.

"That's bullshit," I said to Eisenberg. "There's no way the agencies have a problem with my staff director reviewing these documents. If you have a question about that, call them."

Eisenberg frowned. "I don't know how long it would take me to get ahold of them," he said.

"You're the fucking White House," I said. "I think you can get them on the phone." I turned around and took a seat while Eisenberg returned to his office, ostensibly to call the agency whose documents we would be reviewing. After making me wait about twenty minutes, he returned. "He can come in."

On a table inside Eisenberg's office was a large binder filled with reports and other records. All of them were classified, and some were highly classified. Bahar and I spent the next two hours reading through the materials, and while I cannot divulge their contents, a few things were almost immediately apparent. First, some of the documents were relevant to our investigation, and Nunes either hadn't read them very well, didn't understand their relevance, or was just trying to mislead the public. Even more obvious, these reports were of great foreign intelligence value—and Nunes's denial of that fact was just plain wrong. Finally, on their face, none of the reports and materials contained any suggestion of wrongdoing by the Obama administration. There was no reason to imply, as Nunes had, that this binder contained evidence that Obama had been spying on the Trump campaign, or improperly unmasking the identities of Americans, or disseminating the information to people for an illegitimate or partisan reason. If there existed evidence of any such improper practices, it was not here. And Nunes should have known it.

By the time I returned to the Capitol, I was more certain than ever that Nunes could not continue to lead the Russia investigation. It would take another week in the media spotlight, and a pair of blistering ethics complaints, before he finally announced on April 6 that he was stepping down from the investigation. Going forward, the investigation would be led by the second most senior Republican on the committee, Mike Conaway. He was a soft-spoken former accountant from rural Texas, and I knew him to be a decent man with strong religious beliefs. I could only hope that unlike Nunes, he would work with me to conduct a thorough and credible investigation.

8

KEEP DOING WHAT YOU'RE DOING

The spring of 2017 brought with it a sense of foreboding that the cherry blossoms were powerless to dispel. The president's basic immorality and his disdain for democratic institutions seemed to be spreading like a virus throughout the administration and federal government. Congress was not immune to this virus. And it wasn't just Devin Nunes who succumbed; I began to see a change in many of my Republican colleagues as they walked away from their commitment to our institutional responsibility as a coequal branch of government, not to mention their own party's ideology, to gratify the president. Meanwhile, the threat to our country from Russia was metastasizing. Like the clever former KGB officer that he is, Putin had Trump's number and was playing him for a fool, trading compliments for concessions that benefited Russia magnificently, at America's expense.

We had lost precious time with Nunes's Midnight Run and all the noise in its wake, but now we really needed to get moving with the investigation. Nunes had betrayed the integrity of our investigation in the most unforgivable way, but I was considerate about his decision to step down, telling the press that I appreciated how difficult a decision that was and that I still looked forward to working with him on other issues before the committee.

I also publicly expressed my "great admiration and respect" for Mike Conaway, and we got off to an encouraging start, with immediate discussions about doing joint press availabilities as I had originally done with Nunes, and a pledge to resume hearings. Nevertheless, he had two requests at the outset that he claimed would help facilitate a reset of the committee's investigation, and one of them was deeply problematic.

The first request was that the Democratic members of the committee do less press about the investigation. This was not unreasonable, and I told him that I would discuss it with my colleagues. But I also made it clear that the reason we had been so public about the investigation thus far was because Nunes had been acting to subvert it, and that was not something we could remain silent about. The majority controlled every aspect of the investigation—which witnesses would be called, when or whether subpoenas would be issued, the timing and pace of interviews, everything. The only tool the minority had to make sure things were done properly was to call public attention to any effort to impede its results. As a measure of good faith, I told Mike I would ask my members to dial it back for a while to give us a fresh start. We were heading into the two-week recess for Easter, and the time away from it all would be good for us anyway.

Conaway's second request was not so well intentioned. He asked that I fire my staff director, Michael Bahar. Conaway did not have a good explanation for this extraordinary demand, merely saying that his members did not have confidence in Bahar. That wasn't going to cut it—I wasn't about to let the Republicans decide who my staff should be or let go of someone as talented and bright as Bahar for no reason. It seemed like the Republicans were only making this ask because they wanted a pound of flesh for Nunes's removal from the investigation. I would not give it to them.

Later that day, I texted Conaway that I had asked our members to take a break from all the media hits over the recess and to be gracious about the chair's decision, but I told him that I could not accommodate his request on Bahar. I suggested we huddle in a couple of weeks and chart the best course forward. Conaway said he appreciated that and looked forward to our restart.

During the recess, I called Conaway to follow up on getting our next open hearing scheduled. Conaway raised the possibility of doing bicameral hearings with the Senate Intelligence Committee, and I told him that I liked the idea. In fact, I had proposed it to Nunes weeks earlier. After 9/11, House and Senate intelligence committees did a joint investigation of that tragedy, and it prevented a lot of duplication of effort. Conaway agreed to raise it with Chairman Burr.

Burr would decline, and given the circus that had taken place with our committee, I could hardly blame him. Burr was serious about conducting a thorough and credible investigation, and I had been envious of Senator Mark Warner, the ranking Democrat on that committee, for having such a good partner. As it turned out, I would again not be so lucky. Weeks passed by, and Conaway wouldn't take even the most basic step of rescheduling our open hearing, let alone bringing in additional witnesses to testify in closed session. I kept bringing up the need to "pick a date" for our next hearing, and Conaway kept demurring. Something was going on, and I couldn't tell what.

"You need to talk to Gowdy," Conaway said, finally, after he grew exasperated by my repeated requests.

"Why?"

"He's opposed to doing open hearings."

"But he's not running the investigation, you are," I replied.

"You need to talk to him."

"Okay, I will talk to him."

Later that day, I sought out Gowdy on the House floor but couldn't find him anywhere. He was voting—I could see that from the board above the floor that shows how members have cast their votes in bright green and red lettering—but he must have been disappearing somewhere after each vote. "He's in the cloakroom," one of the Republicans told me, and I went to look for him there. The Republican cloakroom is just off the House floor on the GOP side. It has comfortable leather couches, a small snack bar, and a bank of telephone booths where members can make private calls. It is a mirror image of the Democratic cloakroom, and although there is no rule that members of each party stick to their own cloakroom, I had rarely been inside theirs, and as I walked inside, it felt as if I was in the other team's dugout. I spotted Gowdy at the far end, talking with Representative Tom Rooney of Florida, another Republican member of our committee, who, along with Gowdy, had been designated by Nunes to help Conaway with the investigation.

"Trey, have you got a second?" I asked. "Mike suggested I talk with you about the open hearing with Yates, Clapper, and Brennan. We have been trying to get it on calendar for weeks and I wanted to find out if there was a problem."

"I think open hearings are a bad idea," Gowdy responded. "You get much better work done in closed hearings, where the testimony is private, and witnesses can't line up their stories. It's much more productive."

I told Gowdy that I certainly agreed that many—probably most—of our interviews would be in closed session but that we couldn't conduct them all that way. The public would surely lack confidence in the results of our investigation if it was undertaken entirely in secret and the public could not measure its progress. The Senate Intelligence Committee recognized the importance of public hearings and our committee always had, too, which is one of the reasons that, before the Trump administration, we did an annual open hearing on World Wide Threats. "Besides," I said, "the Comey open hearing was very important for the public's understanding of what's going on."

Gowdy looked at me as if I didn't understand something basic, and he was right: "Our members thought the Comey hearing was an unmitigated disaster," he said.

Now things began to make a perverse sense. There was no reason for the Republicans to feel the Comey hearing was disastrous. Sure, they had been unprepared and too fixated on leaks, but that couldn't account for the vehemence of Gowdy's reaction. No, the hearing was a disaster in their eyes precisely because the public learned that Trump campaign officials were under investigation, and that was evidently a fact that some of the Republican members of our committee would have preferred to remain secret. It was also clear to me that after Gowdy's demoralizing experience with the open hearing before his Benghazi Select Committee, in which Hillary Clinton made his members look so small, the Comey hearing had been the last nail in the coffin.

With our committee at a standstill, the Senate Judiciary Committee conducted two major open hearings in early May, including a hearing with Yates and Clapper and a second blockbuster hearing with James Comey. When Comey was asked to justify his decision to reveal the existence of Anthony Weiner's laptop and additional Clinton emails eleven days before the 2016 election, he claimed that the choice he faced was to "speak or conceal." This was a flagrantly self-serving frame, and he had to know it. Department of Justice practice prohibited the discussion of an investigation in the run-up to an election and for good reason—it might influence the result and it would embroil the FBI in a political process in which it didn't belong. Comey's real choice was between following DOJ policy and ignoring it; he chose to ignore it, placing his own interests over those of the bureau and doing great damage to both in the process.

Comey's testimony about the continuing investigation into ties between the Trump campaign and Russia would have an explosive impact. Trump watched, furious, from the White House. Days later, he fired Comey.

Trump celebrated Comey's firing in the Oval Office the next day, with Russian Foreign Minister Sergey Lavrov and Ambassador

Kislyak. Trump told his White House guests that Comey was "crazy, a real nut job." He added that firing Comey had "taken off" the "great pressure" from the Russia inquiry. The Russians were only too happy to publish photos from the Oval Office of the president smiling and laughing with Lavrov and Kislyak. The meeting had been closed to the American press, but a photographer from a state-run Russian news agency had been allowed in. Putin couldn't resist involving himself in the growing scandal, offering to provide a transcript of the White House meeting—if the House and Senate would like a copy. No one took him up on the generous offer. I was once again astonished at Trump's brazen disregard for the nation's interests, and that he would carry on this way with our adversaries. And I was deeply concerned about what Comey's firing meant for the FBI's Russia investigation. My Republican colleagues felt differently.

Notwithstanding the obvious and growing damage that Trump was doing to our national security and the FBI, some Republicans in Congress, including those on our committee, rushed to Trump's defense. The president has a right to fire the FBI director if he chooses, they argued, even though directors are appointed for ten-year terms that are meant to span administrations, in part to allow directors to maintain their independence from the White House. This was the first of many times to come that my GOP colleagues would affirm the president's power to take a certain action while ignoring the unethical motivation behind it.

What's more, the claim wasn't true. A president may have the power to fire an FBI director, but that doesn't mean he has the power to do so for a corrupt purpose. If Trump fired Comey to subvert an investigation into his own potential wrongdoing or that of those around him, it was not only impermissible, it was a potentially criminal act of obstruction of justice. But I was deeply skeptical that the Trump Justice Department would hold the president accountable, given another troubling set of facts: Both the attorney general and his deputy had willingly supplied an alibi, and both had serious conflicts.

Trump claimed to have fired Comey on the basis of a memo

written by Deputy Attorney General Rod Rosenstein and with the advice of Attorney General Jeff Sessions. I went to see Rosenstein at the Justice Department shortly after the firing and sat down with him at a table in his office. Rosenstein and I had attended the same law school, although several years apart, and in his wire-rimmed glasses, he looked every bit the studious lawyer.

The room was dark, or maybe it was just the mood, and I could tell that he was uncomfortable. So was I. In his three-page memo to Sessions, entitled, without any sense of irony, "Restoring Public Confidence in the FBI," Rosenstein echoed many of the arguments I had made about Comey's poor handling of the email investigation, the violation of DOJ policy with his decision to discuss it in the waning days of the campaign, and the false dichotomy between "speaking" and "concealing" that Comey had tried to use as justification. The problem with Rosenstein's memo was not with its accuracy, but with the unmistakable fact that it was used as a pretext for a firing based on something completely different, and Rosenstein knew it.

"I am troubled by the memo you sent to Sessions about Comey's firing," I told Rosenstein. "First of all, why would you involve Sessions in a decision over whether to fire the FBI director? Comey's most important investigation was the Russia investigation, and Sessions was supposed to be recused. How can Sessions advise the president whether Comey should be removed when he isn't supposed to be making any decisions affecting the investigation?"

Rosenstein stared at me, expressionless, and gave a terse response. "I understand your position."

"Well," I continued, "I hope you will encourage the attorney general to play no role in choosing Comey's successor." Again Rosenstein gave a nonresponsive reply, and I had no confidence that he would ask Sessions to stay out of the next decision affecting the Russia probe. Finally I got to the meat of the matter. "I don't disagree with what you wrote in your memo. Comey made terrible and costly mistakes in his handling of the email investigation, and I have said so for months. But you had to know how your memo would be used."

Rosenstein said he stood by his memo, which was another dodge, and I knew I would get nothing further from our meeting other than the opportunity to convey how poorly his actions were being received by many on Capitol Hill. Nevertheless, I made a final plea to Rosenstein—to appoint a Special Counsel. "I know there are a lot of great career lawyers in the department who could handle an investigation of this importance," I said, "but the reality is that in the absence of a Special Counsel, the public will not have confidence in the result." I left Rosenstein's office discouraged, and without any expectation that Rosenstein would bring in a special prosecutor.

As I drove out of the underground parking lot at the Justice Department and into bright sunlight, I wondered what had happened to Rod Rosenstein. He had been appointed U.S. attorney for the District of Maryland by George W. Bush, and he was the only Bush-appointed U.S. attorney in the country who had been retained by Barack Obama. Over the years he had served at high levels in the Justice Department, and he had a solid reputation as a career prosecutor. But Rosenstein had never been tested before, not the way he had been under Trump, and he was failing the test. Robert Caro, one of my favorite biographers, once took issue with Lord Acton's dictum that power corrupts and absolute power corrupts absolutely. Instead, Caro said, "Power *reveals*—it doesn't always reveal you for the better, but it reveals." Power, and the desire to keep it, was revealing Rod Rosenstein not as a bad or corrupt person, but as someone not strong enough to stand up to someone who was bad and corrupt. He would soon have a lot of company.

Days later, my staff informed me that Rod Rosenstein and the acting FBI director, Andrew McCabe, were coming to the Hill to give top congressional leadership a briefing. The Justice Department didn't specify the topic, but they didn't need to—we were still demanding answers on the Russia investigation and how it would continue without further interference from the White House, and I was eager to hear what they had to say. But even before the briefing began, we had a problem—Nunes was waiting inside the SCIF to join the meeting.

"What's he doing here?" Chuck Schumer, the Senate minority leader, wanted to know. The Speaker, Warner, and I all were wondering the same thing. Nunes was recused from the Russia investigation and should have had no part in any briefing on the subject. Outside the room, I raised my concern with McCabe, and he and Rosenstein conferred on the matter. It was Speaker Ryan's decision, they said. Nunes would stay.

When the doors were closed, McCabe told us that the FBI had opened an investigation into the president of the United States for possible obstruction of justice. Around the room, everyone was silent. I looked at McConnell, who took the news with a mix of stoicism and alarm, much like the rest of us. Rosenstein had authorized the appointment of a Special Counsel, in an announcement to be made shortly. There have been more than a few times when I was really conscious of being present at a moment in history, when, as if on a tether, the world swung wildly in a new and uncertain direction. As we filed quietly out of the room, I could tell that this was one of those moments.

ON MAY 17, ROD ROSENSTEIN announced that former FBI director Robert Mueller would assume control of "the investigation confirmed by then–FBI Director James B. Comey in testimony before the House Permanent Select Committee on Intelligence." Mueller's appointment letter granted him broad authority to examine "any links and/or coordination between the Russian government and individuals associated with the campaign of President Donald Trump" along with "any matters that arose or may arise directly from the investigation." (In his report, Mueller would conclude that the scope of his appointment was broad enough to allow him to investigate the president for obstruction of justice.) I knew Mueller from our many interactions when he was leading the FBI, and I had great respect for him. He was smart, ethical, and knowledgeable and had an impeccable reputation.

Conaway and I soon met with Mueller and his top aides in the

SCIF to discuss how to—if not coordinate, then at least deconflict—our efforts. I emphasized to Mueller that our committee had an important responsibility to investigate the president's contacts with Russia with an eye to informing the public and taking any legislative steps necessary to protect the country. We could not hold our investigation in abeyance until Mueller concluded his own work, but we were interested in making sure that nothing we did would interfere with his efforts to bring people to justice or address the counterintelligence risks that he was also supposed to investigate.

As a former prosecutor, I knew that Mueller's team would have concerns about witnesses we were interviewing that they would be taking before the grand jury, and the chance for inconsistencies in testimony that might emerge during a trial. Mueller was appreciative of our willingness to deconflict, but also very tight-lipped about his investigative plans. This was not surprising; in his place, I would have been equally opaque. He did not ask us to hold off, nor did he wish to preview the first witnesses they would be interviewing, so we arrived at a compromise: We would let Mueller know who we were bringing in and when, and if his team had a concern, they would let us know. Although it did not come up at the time, I also resolved that we would confer with Mueller before offering a witness immunity, something that could effectively derail a criminal prosecution, as a grant of congressional immunity had done during the Iran-Contra investigation decades earlier.

As it would turn out, the conflicts over witnesses would be not between our committee and Mueller but within our own committee. Just prior to Mueller's appointment came explosive press reports about a private White House dinner shortly after the inauguration during which Trump had asked Comey to pledge his personal loyalty. More disturbing, Trump had brought up the investigation into Mike Flynn and told Comey, "I hope you can see your way clear to letting this go, to letting Flynn go." Flynn was under investigation not only for lying to the FBI about his communications with Ambassador Kislyak, but also for unreported income from Russian business entities, and for undisclosed lobbying on behalf of the government of

Turkey. The president had leaned on Comey to drop the Flynn case, then fired him when he wouldn't do as he was told. This appeared to be a textbook case of obstruction of justice and demanded investigation. In the Senate, Burr and Warner issued subpoenas to Flynn's companies demanding documents, and Burr made it clear he was serious about getting a response and would pursue all avenues to make that happen. "At the end of that option is a contempt charge, and I've said that everything is on the table," he told the press.

I urged Conaway to follow suit with our own subpoenas and encountered nothing but delay. This was a recurrent problem now, with Conaway agreeing to pursue a matter, then sitting on it. I couldn't tell whether he was just stringing me along, or whether Nunes was still running the show and Conaway was powerless to get things done. In a normal investigation, you request documents from a witness before you depose them, so that you have the benefit of that information to form your questions. And while we had sent out letters to several witnesses, I could not get Conaway to insist on getting the documents before bringing them in for questioning. We agreed to a forty-eight-hour rule, in which either of us would respond to the request of the other within forty-eight hours so that we could act more nimbly as a committee, but he was already violating the agreement, and it was maddening.

"We should probably try to act on this Thursday," I wrote to him on May 23, on the subject of the Flynn subpoenas. "Invoking our 48 hour rule!"

"In conversations with Devin on mechanics," he replied. "Let's talk tomorrow."

Nunes of course had recused himself from the matter and should not have been playing any role in issuing subpoenas, or in anything else related to the investigation. No wonder Conaway had been dragging his feet on everything. I urged Conaway to get Nunes to delegate his subpoena authority in the Russia investigation to Conaway. That night, I gave a press interview where I emphasized the need to get answers on the allegations involving Flynn and said that we should issue a subpoena and explore holding him in contempt if necessary. This was in line with what Burr was saying, but it was nonetheless too much for Conaway.

"You are trying my patience with this front running on what the committee 'might' do," Conaway texted me the next morning. "Why did you feel compelled to announce a decision in progress. Let's discuss."

"And you are trying mine," I replied. "Burr and Warner have no problem working expeditiously. We agreed to issue subpoenas when voluntary compliance was refused. . . . We do need to talk. Our members are losing patience and I am in agreement with them."

It took another week, and Conaway finally got approval from Nunes for the subpoenas, but it wasn't long before Conaway and I were butting heads again, and over the same problem. Comey had written extensive memoranda documenting his meetings with Trump, leading Trump to suggest in a tweet that "James Comey better hope that there are no 'tapes' of our conversations before he starts leaking to the press!" I recommended to Conaway that we write to the White House and request any such recordings or memoranda. He agreed, and on June 9, we sent a joint letter to White House Counsel Don McGahn asking whether any "recordings or memoranda of Comey's conversations with President Trump now exist or have in the past," and requesting that he produce them to the committee if they did.

Two weeks later, we received a cursory response from the assistant to the president for legislative affairs saying that the president's subsequent tweets spoke for themselves, when Trump acknowledged he had "no idea whether there are 'tapes' or recordings" and that he did not make "any such recordings." But this did not answer the question of whether recordings or memoranda existed, and I persuaded Conaway to join me in another letter to the White House, this time making clear that "should the White House not respond fully, the Committee will consider using compulsory process to ensure a satisfactory response."

When you threaten to use a subpoena if a party does not comply with a request for information, you darned well better be prepared to do it, or you reveal your investigation to be toothless. Weeks later, when the administration missed our second deadline for the return of documents or information, I warned Conaway that if we allowed the White House to ignore our subpoena threat, they would conclude that they could stonewall us on other things, maybe on everything. He didn't disagree, but he still wouldn't move forward. It was then that I realized that Conaway wasn't in control of the investigation at all. Nunes was—and he had other objects in mind.

In fact, without my knowledge, Nunes had issued three subpoenas on his own, demanding information from the CIA, FBI, and NSA on details of any requests by former Obama administration officials to "unmask" the names of Trump campaign personnel inadvertently picked up in foreign surveillance. There was no need for Nunes to subpoena the agencies, which were complying with our oversight requests voluntarily. Clearly, he intended to conduct a counterinvestigation to advance the president's counternarrative. Nunes wanted to step on news about the progress of the Russia probe, and instead put the intelligence agencies on trial. What's more, Nunes was now claiming that he never recused himself from the investigation, and that "this was essentially made up by the media."

While Conaway and I were fighting over White House denials of our requests for information and learning of Nunes's rogue investigation, news broke that Jared Kushner had met with the Russian ambassador during the transition and proposed "a secret back channel" using a Russian diplomatic facility. This was unprecedented. Immediately following an election in which the Russians had covertly and overtly helped elect Donald Trump, his son-in-law was proposing a mechanism to open a line of communications with Moscow, with the intent of keeping those conversations secret from our own government.

The president's second national security advisor, H. R. McMaster, gave an interview in which he attempted to defend Kushner, saying that he was not concerned about back-channel communications, that historically there have always been back channels. This was preposterous. Yes, there are times when the United States government has used back-channel communications with nations like Cuba or Iran, when we have no diplomatic relationship or there is a need for great secrecy. We might have a back channel to the Taliban to negotiate the release of a hostage. But those back channels are designed to facilitate communication for our government, not to conceal information from our government, and for McMaster to suggest otherwise was more than disingenuous, it was dangerous.

I had met McMaster in Afghanistan and been impressed with him and his commitment to our Afghan partners. I was visiting Kabul to oversee rule-of-law issues, and he dressed down a colonel in front of me for suggesting that Afghans were inherently corrupt. "They are no more inherently corrupt than we are, and they are fighting and dying beside us every day, so you should show some respect," he told the officer in a blistering critique. He had written a seminal work on the leadership mistakes we made in Vietnam, *Dereliction of Duty*, which was required reading in the military academies. What was happening to him now?

The back-channel news was followed only days later by the first reports of the June 2016 Trump Tower meeting between the senior campaign staff and the Russian delegation promising dirt on Clinton. Up until the revelation of the secret meeting in New York, the evidence of Trump campaign collusion had been mostly circumstantial, but this was more than circumstantial; this was direct evidence, in writing, of an attempt to conspire with the Russians. I was stunned by how flagrant the emails were, how unequivocal the Russians were about their intentions to help Trump win, and by Don Jr.'s warm embrace of their corrupt offer, even spelling out the best timing of disclosures to assist their campaign.

Evidence of illicit contacts between the Trump campaign and Russia was now coming to light every week and sometimes several times a day. In a healthy democracy, that would have resulted in a growing and bipartisan imperative to uncover the truth. But that required Republicans to put the interest of the country first, rather than their party affiliation. Some of the greatest heroes of the Watergate scandal were members of Richard Nixon's own party, who were people of conscience before they were Republicans. In our own time, we have not been so lucky. With every new discovery, the degree of Republican obstructionism only grew, and by the summer of 2017, it was clear that as long as Donald Trump was in the White House, it would be harder and harder to find people of conscience in his party.

BACK IN CALIFORNIA FOR A week, I was invited to give a keynote address at the state party convention in Sacramento. I told the crowd of activists that over the last 120 days I had come to see just how fragile our democracy really was, just how much the proper functioning of its checks and balances depends not on the operation of law alone, but upon the observation of certain norms of behavior, and a very basic level of decency. All of that was threatened by a president who lacked that essential quality and was fundamentally indecent. And I said that I found myself in a role to which I was not accustomed, and to which I did not aspire, but which was now required of all of us who were unwilling to stand idly by and watch the undoing of all we cherish, and that was the role of resistance.

I spoke about the other challenges facing the country, and the enormous economic disruption caused by automation and globalization. About the media revolution that was causing fear and lies to travel with virality and balkanizing the country. When you looked at the map of our country, with its red states and its blue, geography seemed like destiny. The middle of the country was a sea of almost uninterrupted red, the coasts a vivid blue. Had we now become two nations, living together in the same landlocked household, and with differences so irreconcilable that we can never again be made whole?

To win back those voters we had lost to Trump, we needed to answer the question of a parent in coal country, or a young man in the inner city, or the mother in the steel mill, and the father of four whose job was shipped overseas and whose pension was lost after he had spent his whole life working for the same company. "And that question is this: In a world that is changing so fast, that is small and yet global and where machines can do the work of our fathers and mothers, what can you offer that will give me the hope that my life will be better, that my children's lives will be better, that we will have a fighting chance?" We desperately needed to win back those voters and reclaim a Democratic majority if we had any hope of rescuing our democracy.

DURING THE SUMMER AND FALL of 2017, the pace of our investigation picked up dramatically, and we finally began deposing witnesses, sometimes several days a week. The Republicans were not eager to do so but felt compelled by growing public pressure. In a closed session on June 22, the committee interviewed Dan Coats, who had been confirmed as the DNI in mid-March after being recruited for the role by Mike Pence, and now oversaw the entire Intelligence Community. Before his appointment as director, he had spent twenty-four years as a Republican member of the House and Senate from Indiana, and we had interacted a few times. I found him genial and civil, and I wondered if he would have the independence required of the job. On that day, I would learn that he did.

Gowdy began by asking a question that he would repeat in almost every interview—"Have you seen any evidence of collusion or coordination or conspiracy between the Russians and any member of Trump's official campaign?" Coats answered in the negative, but then explained that he had not been part of Trump's campaign—he had been a Rubio supporter—and was not currently involved in the investigation and had no desire to be. Gowdy would have known this, as I did, but he was using a defense counsel tactic of asking summary, opinion, or legal questions to witnesses that were not in a position to answer them, so that their testimony could be used to mislead. This was another disturbing, but not surprising, indication that Gowdy was more interested in protecting the president than in learning the truth.

It wasn't until the end of Gowdy's questioning that he asked something useful, probably because he was expecting a very different answer: "Did the president ever ask you to publicly state that there was no evidence of collusion between him and his campaign and the Russians?" Coats was in the midst of telling us about a phone call from Trump on a Saturday night, while Coats was watching a Final Four basketball game at his son's house. When the call came in, he stepped outside to speak with the president on a secure phone in his security detail's vehicle. Trump was not calling to discuss sensitive intelligence or national security affairs. He was upset that media organizations were reporting on the contacts between his campaign and the Russian government. Trump listed several public officials who said they had not seen conclusive evidence of collusion between his campaign and Russia. "He mentioned Dianne Feinstein. He mentioned Mark Warner. He mentioned Richard Burr," Coats recalled. "He said: Is that something you can do?"

"And I said: 'Mr. President, in my job . . . I don't think it is appropriate for me to do that.'" Coats explained further: "To tell you the truth, I was sitting there thinking: Here is the president of the United States sitting in an empty White House. His wife is in New York. His family is in New York. On a Saturday night, that has got to be a lonely thing to do."

I followed up on this line of questioning and Coats revealed that Trump's phone call was not the only time he had been urged by the president to publicly deny evidence of collusion, even though Coats was not privy to the investigation. Trump had also taken him aside during a meeting in the Oval Office to make the same ask, and got the same answer.

Coats had been remarkably candid, and he would be throughout his tenure. By Robert Caro's maxim, power had revealed Dan Coats to be a person of great character, willing to speak the truth, even if it cost him his job, which, eventually it did. Others proved all too willing to hide the truth, or bend it to the president's purposes. When Mike Pompeo had been nominated as CIA director, I praised his intellect but warned of his acute partisanship. He would need to set that aside if he was going to run the nation's premier intelligence agency. But Pompeo had other ambitions, and he quickly learned to flatter and deceive. Speaking at the Aspen Security Conference in his first months in office, he downplayed Russian interference in the election, saying the Russians had also interfered in the election "before that, and the one before that," and many weeks later he would repeat the president's lie that the Intelligence Community concluded that Russia's interference had no effect on the outcome of the election. These may have been his first acts of deception in the Trump administration, but there would be all too many to come.

With his remarkable candor, Coats would prove the exception, not the rule, and in the weeks ahead, several of the president's men filed into the SCIF and lied to us. Others, like Keith Schiller, the president's longtime security staff and body man, and Rhona Graff, his secretary at Trump Tower, had a remarkable lack of recall. Still others, like Attorney General Jeff Sessions, White House chief strategist Steve Bannon, Communications Director Hope Hicks, and Campaign Manager Corey Lewandowski, refused to answer questions on the basis of new and invented privileges, which even then they never bothered to invoke, or merely because they chose not to. Don Jr. would claim that his conversations with his father were protected by attorney-client privilege—a bewildering suggestion, since neither was an attorney, nor the client of the other. To my great frustration, Conaway adopted a laissez-faire attitude toward these and other witnesses, and my threats to force answers with subpoenas became increasingly ineffective.

When Jared Kushner testified before the committee in late July, for example, we still hadn't received a fraction of the documents we had requested from him months earlier. His lawyer, Abbe Lowell, chose the timing for the interview—not the committee—and set the conditions: He would appear for two hours, but not to worry, he would come back if necessary. Kushner entered the freezing conference room where we conducted our interviews (I would soon take to wearing a topcoat over my suit or a flannel vest under it), saw me, and came over for a private conversation. "You know," he said, "you do a really good job on TV." I thanked him, but given that Trump was attacking me for doing too much press, I added, "I don't think your father-in-law would agree." He leaned in: "Oh, yes, he does, and that's why."

It was an interesting insight into why the president was so frequently attacking me, but more interesting to me was why Kushner was sharing it. Plainly, he was trying to ingratiate himself. He was a smooth operator, not at all the naïf he was often made out to be. When I asked him about his discussions with Ambassador Kislyak over establishing a secure back channel, he played on this perception of himself as inexperienced, a babe in the woods.

"Was the goal," I began, "to secure the information from the U.S. government; that is, provide a channel in which the U.S. government would be unaware of the communication?"

"It could have been to keep it from the Chinese," Kushner replied, which made no sense whatsoever. "It could have been to keep it from anyone else who listens to the calls. Again, at that point in time, I did not have a security clearance. I had not been briefed on secure communicating practices."

Conaway asked a few questions of Kushner and left the heavy lifting to Gowdy, who adopted the same summary line of questioning he had used with Coats, but here it was even more absurd. "To your knowledge," Gowdy asked, "did anyone officially connected with the Donald Trump for President campaign collude, coordinate, or conspire with Russian officials to impact, influence, or interfere with the 2016 election cycle?"

"No," was all Kushner had to say. If Kushner was being candid, he might have said: "Of course, didn't I just tell you that I attended a secret meeting with a Russian delegation set up by Don Jr. for the explicit purpose of receiving their help in the 2016 election cycle? If that's not evidence of collusion, I don't know what is." But Gowdy wasn't looking for candor or the facts, only to help out the president and his allies. And he didn't stop with asking his pointless questions, but encouraged Kushner to stop answering our questions altogether.

"I want to compliment you," Gowdy told Kushner, "and tell you how much I appreciate your willingness to stay until my friends run out of questions. But I have to let you know: That's never going to happen. The longer you stay in here, the narrative will be how important and significant a witness you were, hence the fact that they kept you in here all day long. . . . And I really appreciate your willingness to say you're going to stay. But unless you want to cancel your weekend plans, they're never going to run out of questions."

We had been interviewing Kushner, a key witness, for a little over two hours, and the man who forced Hillary Clinton to testify for eleven hours was suggesting that we were taking too long, and the witness could leave any time he desired. Most depositions last all day, sometimes more, as Kushner's attorney, Abbe Lowell, understood only too well. Nonetheless, Lowell picked up on what Gowdy was offering and tried to cut off the questioning. "I think we've probably reached the end of what a useful session is," Lowell said, soon thereafter.

"Well," I replied, "I appreciate your opinion on where the end of a useful session is. We haven't reached the end of the questions that we have for you today. And I appreciate Mr. Gowdy's advocacy on your behalf. That's really not the role of the committee, though." Gowdy turned red in the face. "It's not advocacy on his behalf, Adam. . . . No, you're not going to make an allegation and then not let me respond to it. It's not advocacy on his behalf. It's called fundamental fairness." But call it what you will, after only a couple of witness interviews, the pattern had already been established: Gowdy would ask questions he thought were helpful to the president, then remind witnesses that they were appearing voluntarily and could refuse to answer and were free to leave whenever they wanted.

That the Republicans simply did not want to know the truth was now beyond dispute, and they didn't want the public to know it either. Like Ahab after the white whale, Gowdy and other Republicans had circled the earth looking for evidence that didn't exist of Clinton complicity in the deaths of the four Americans in Benghazi. But when faced with indisputable evidence of Trump campaign efforts to collude with the Russians, the Republicans on our committee were telling witnesses that they could come and go as they pleased, that they could provide documents or not provide them, and that answering questions was purely optional. They just didn't seem to care that the Russians had interfered in our election, because it helped the candidate of their party.

But occasionally, in quiet chance encounters, other Republicans let me know that they did care, and that they wanted me to get to the bottom of the Trump campaign's collusion with Russia. Even a Republican chairman walking past me in halls of the Capitol paused for a moment to lean in and whisper: "Keep doing what you're doing."

9

IF I COULD ONLY SPEAK TO A COUPLE HUNDRED MILLION PEOPLE

WHILE MY DEMOCRATIC COLLEAGUES ON THE COMMITTEE AND I were doing our best to investigate the president's web of corrupt ties to Russia, Donald Trump was not remaining idle. He launched a major counteroffensive, and his strategy was simple—lie, deny, and attack. His most important target was Mueller, since his investigation could not be stonewalled with the same ease as our committee. And besides, Mueller's work could result in the president's indictment, if not while in office, then as soon as he was out.

The president relentlessly went after Mueller and his team, sometimes several times a day. He characterized Mueller as corrupt, biased, and without a legitimate mandate, and the investigation he was conducting as a "witch hunt" or a "hoax." Trump attacked the investigation hundreds of times in a two-year period, denying any evidence of collusion and claiming that Mueller's team consisted of "12 angry democrats."

Trump also tried to undermine Mueller's investigation by dangling pardons for people he believed were willing to lie to cover up for him, like Roger Stone and Paul Manafort. Speaking more like an organized crime figure than the president of the United States, he praised Manafort for not "flipping" and condemned those who were cooperating with authorities, like his former lawyer Michael Cohen, as "a rat." Trump was sending an unmistakable message to witnesses of his misconduct in the Russia investigation: Keep your mouth shut and the president will protect you.

But while Mueller operated in secret and was seldom seen, I was the very public face of the investigation of the president.

"Sleazy Adam Schiff, the totally biased Congressman looking into 'Russia,' spends all of his time on television pushing the Dem loss excuse!" the president tweeted in the middle of July, when our committee was beginning dozens of interviews. This was the first time that the president had gone after me on Twitter, and it was a doozy. Boland, Simons, and I debated how I should respond, while I got helpful suggestions from my colleagues. Democratic representative Mike Thompson of Napa stopped me on the House floor to suggest, "Adam, you should tweet back: Mr. President, when they go low, we go high, go fuck yourself!" How I would have loved to do that.

In a normal world, being called sleazy by the president of the United States would be a big deal. My daughter was nineteen and old enough to laugh it off, but my son was still only fourteen and away at tennis camp. I hoped that he wouldn't have heard about it from someone else—they take the kids' cellphones away when they arrive at camp—because I wasn't sure how he would react. When my wife and I went to pick him up at the end of session, I told him that there was something I needed to share that had taken place while he was away at camp. It wasn't anything to worry about, I assured him, but I wanted him to hear it from me. "The president called your father sleazy," I said. He paused for a moment, taking it in, then looked up at me and asked:

"Can I call you sleazy?"

"Not unless you want me to call you sleazy junior," I said. I guessed he was going to be okay with the news after all.

My father, now ninety, was getting into arguments at the club in Boca Raton, Florida, although that wasn't particularly new. Life in his small community was like a scene out of *Seinfeld*. While eating in the bar, he asked the only other person present if he could change the channel from golf coverage on ESPN to one of the news shows. The other man, who hadn't been watching television, demanded to know what channel he would put on. "Andrea Mitchell," my dad replied. "I hate Andrea Mitchell" was his answer. "Okay," my dad said, "how about CNN?" "That's even worse," the man replied.

"What do you want to watch, Fox?" my father asked, losing his patience. The man said nothing, but my dad believed he had sized up the real objection and it had more to do with me than the channel. "You're an asshole," my father said.

"No, *you're* an asshole," the man replied, "and so is your son."

The man reported my dad to the club management and he was hauled before the board to explain himself. "If we let you off with a warning," he was asked by a sympathetic board member, "do you promise not to call anyone an asshole again?"

My dad thought it over before replying: "I'll do my best, but I'm not sure I can give you an ironclad guarantee."

But this was just the beginning of the attacks against me by the president, not to mention nicknames. "Leakin' monster," "Shifty Schiff," "little Adam Schiff," "corrupt politician," "pencil neck," "Adam Schitt"—the childish taunts came fast and furious. The nicknames were so cartoonish that they didn't bother me, except to the degree that he was debasing the office of the presidency. At times I couldn't help but be astounded at the buffoonery. Once, he attacked me as "liddle' "Adam Schiff, and called out CNN for omitting the apostrophe in his tweet (inaccurately calling it a hyphen). "To show you how dishonest the LameStream Media is, I used the word Liddle', not Liddle, in discribing (sic) Corrupt Congressman Liddle' Adam Schiff. Low ratings @CNN purposely took the hyphen out and said I spelled the word little wrong. A small but never ending situation with CNN!" Was this really the president of the United States?

The president's constant attacks and all the attendant attention raised my visibility even further, and in an odd way only added to my stature. Visiting my daughter in New York, where she was interning at a talent booking agency, I couldn't believe how many people recognized me even though I was wearing blue jeans, a canvas jacket, and sunglasses. As I walked down the street on the Upper West Side, people were stopping me for selfies, shouting out comments, or trying to engage me in conversation. This was becoming irksome to Lexi; after all, there was to be only one center of attention in our family, and it sure wasn't me. The final straw came when someone asked her to hold their beer while I took a photo with them. "What am I now," Lexi asked plaintively, "the beer holder?"

"I'm just amazed," I responded, "that anyone can even recognize me. I don't look anything like I do on TV."

"Well, Dad," Lexi replied, not missing a beat, "it's the pencil neck."

While the nicknames were sophomoric, there were other Twitter attacks that were much more concerning, and went to the substance of the Russia investigation. In the beginning, I felt the need to respond immediately. His tweets were going out to tens of millions of Americans and I didn't want them to go unanswered. I had learned from my earliest campaigns that it was essential to answer or the negative narrative would take hold. But the attacks became so frequent that Boland, Simons, and I concluded that we couldn't respond to them all, and shouldn't give some of them any greater amplification. Part of this decision was borne of futility; he had a massive megaphone and there was simply no way that I could compete with his bully pulpit, or reach his audience.

As the president increased his attacks, so did Fox. Hannity, Carlson, Dobbs, and others, with some of the largest cable viewerships on television, began blasting me on a nightly basis, amplifying whatever false smears the president threw my way and coming up with several new ones on their own. At times, they would devote large portions of their shows to attacking me, and I suddenly had an even greater appreciation for how Nancy Pelosi had been demonized by the right wing for years. I stopped her on the House floor to tell her that I had been receiving a lot of threats lately. "Welcome to the club," she said.

Prior to Trump's presidency, I was certainly not a household name, but I was a relatively well-known member of the House and a frequent guest on the Sunday morning talk shows, the Beltway index for members of influence. My appearances were focused on national security, foreign policy, and intelligence issues, and I wasn't particularly controversial. Now the people stopping me on street corners, in airports, and at bus stations held radically different views of my performance in office.

I remember stepping off the train in New York's Penn Station and barely setting foot on the platform when the first New Yorker stopped me. "Are you Adam Schiff?" he asked excitedly. "I just want to shake your hand. You're my hero." That lasted about a millisecond before the next New Yorker came up to me: "Well, you're not *my* hero," he said angrily. "Why are you eavesdropping on our conversations and leaking them to the press?" Everywhere I went, I got both extremes. At home in Burbank, I heard shouting: "There's that asshole!" In the distance, almost a block away, a man was crossing the street with his wife. "What's the matter, honey?" his wife was imploring him. "What's wrong?"

"There's that son-of-a-bitch Adam Schiff!" was his reply.

On social media, critics were even more unrestrained. One commenter on my Facebook page wrote that he hoped my family and I would "go back to Auschwitz." The diatribe was not anonymous, and it included a smiling profile photo of its author. The first time the president accused me of being a traitor, it was only a matter of hours before one of his supporters would respond: "Shifty Shiff needs to be hung." Another Trump supporter said they wanted me hanged in a football stadium so that the public could watch. Still another longed for the "good old days when traitors like Schiff would be hanged by the neck until dead." One man left a voicemail at my Burbank office threatening to put three bullets in the back of my head, then proceeded to describe the gun he would use to do it.

Over time, I started to get advisories from the Department of Justice that they were investigating threats against my life, several of which would result in charges. The alerts were sometimes accompanied by mugshots, if the suspect was on bail, or there wasn't sufficient evidence to make an arrest. I shared them with my wife, in case we ever found anyone loitering around our house. We did our best to shield our kids from any discussion of what was going on, but there was no shielding Eve, and at times, the constant attacks left her unnerved. "I just can't stand how they hate you so much," Eve said, as I held her in the kitchen one night during the height of the Russia investigation, her eyes moist with tears. Her friends and family would text and email her to see how she was doing, and in a way, that made her feel worse. "They feel sorry for me," she said. "I don't want them to feel sorry for me."

IN ADDITION TO TEARING MUELLER and me down, Trump was aggressively trying to flip the script. He wasn't colluding with Russia, Hillary was; he hadn't done anything wrong, the FBI had; the Justice Department shouldn't be investigating him, they should be investigating the FBI. To a shocking degree, this strategy was successful. The Justice Department launched an investigation of Andrew McCabe, and they put it on a fast track so that he could be deprived of part of his pension, just as the president was urging. I told Rosenstein that the investigation into McCabe would be tainted, regardless of what it found, because its original purpose was improper and political. Trump had been using the Justice Department as a shield to protect him, but now he was using it as a sword to go after his enemies, and this was a far more sinister abuse. This is what they did in developing countries, not in the United States.

In addition to enlisting the Justice Department, the president also wanted Congress to investigate his growing enemies list, and to be more aggressive in pushing his counternarrative. Nunes was happy to oblige. A central villain in the counternarrative was the former British spy Christopher Steele, author of the now infamous "dossier," a trove of raw intelligence compiled during the campaign. Deep state enemies at the FBI knew the dossier was Russian disinformation, the story went, but used the dossier as a pretext to investigate the president. That wasn't true, but Trump believed that if he could discredit Steele and the dossier, he could argue that the whole investigation was illegitimate, no matter how many of the president's confederates Mueller was indicting, or how incriminating the evidence turned out to be.

In Nunes's efforts to advance the president's conspiracy theories, his partner was a Republican staff member named Kash Patel. Patel had been hired by the House Intelligence Committee in 2017 after a lackluster stint in the Justice Department. While working on a counterterrorism case in January 2016, Patel was castigated by a judge, who told him to "act like a lawyer," then demanded to know "what you have to contribute" before concluding, "You don't seem to know anything about trying a case." The judge ejected Patel from his chamber and later issued an "Order of Ineptitude" lambasting "pretentious lawyers" from the Justice Department who neither "knew what they were doing" nor "had the humility to ask for help."

Patel would receive a much warmer welcome among House Intelligence Committee Republicans, and Nunes in particular seemed to regard him as a kindred spirit. Nunes would go so far as dispatching Patel to London, without informing Conaway or me, in a failed effort to confront Steele at his lawyer's office. The 2017 trip, nicknamed "London Calling," was a fiasco, and when discovered, it did nothing but throw the committee's investigation into further disrepute.

While strongly resistant to the issuance of subpoenas in the investigation of the Trump campaign's contacts with Russia, Committee Republicans had no such hesitancy when it came to the use of compulsory process to advance the counternarrative, particularly involving Steele. In August, Conaway texted me: "Adam. Tomorrow or Wednesday we will issue subpoenas to the DOJ and FBI requesting records related to FISA court applications for Trump and associates or Russia investigations and records concerning Christopher Steele's work as an FBI informant. I'll be able to discuss tomorrow afternoon but I wanted you to know before the subpoenas are actually sent." This was a disturbing new escalation by Nunes that was already, apparently, a fait accompli. Nevertheless, I tried to get Conaway to stop it, texting back:

> Mike, we should definitely discuss before anything goes out. This is the first we are hearing of this and will likely prompt similar blowback as the Steele office visit and damage to the committee's reputation. . . . Unless you can help me understand what's going on, we won't be able to defend it and that will fall to you. . . . There is also the issue of how this will affect our cooperation with special counsel. So let's think this out and talk first. You and I are doing our best to hold things together, and I'm concerned with the path this may put us on.

This time Conaway didn't even bother to respond, and the subpoenas went out two days later as Nunes had planned. Whatever grip Conaway had had on the reins—and it was limited from the start—appeared completely gone.

As Nunes pursued all things Christopher Steele, Fox News drove the counternarrative to its millions of viewers nightly, to the point where Republicans not only believed it but started to have a negative view of the entire FBI—a remarkable turn for a party that had always claimed to be the "law and order" party. Positive news coverage among conservative outlets had also resurrected Nunes's fortunes; he went from pariah status after the Midnight Run to hero worship in the conservative tabloids, and became a top fundraiser in the GOP.

On the eve of Mueller's first indictment of a Trump associate, Trump went on another Twitter diatribe, bemoaning the lack of progress in the investigation of his rivals and ending with "DO SOMETHING!" Trump wanted an investigation into Hillary Clinton, and House Republicans again complied, opening yet another bogus probe into the former secretary even though she hadn't held office for years, this time dealing with a far-right conspiracy theory involving the sale of a company called Uranium One. The Justice Department would likewise open its own investigation of Uranium One to mollify the president, and spend more than two years on it before concluding that there was nothing worth pursuing.

By the end of 2017, Nunes was no longer content to wage his counterinvestigations on the president's behalf, he wanted the real investigation shut down. Conaway began scheduling witness interviews multiple times a day, including some in other cities and on dates when we had critical votes and it was impossible for members to attend. And the Republican practice of allowing witnesses to refuse to answer questions became more and more egregious. When Erik Prince, a major Trump donor and the former CEO of Blackwater, refused to answer a relevant question about his back-channel contacts with a Russian state banker in the Seychelles, Representative Quigley turned to Conaway for help. "Mr. Chairman," he said, "I would ask that you respectfully ask the witness to answer."

"The witness is here on a voluntary basis," Conaway said. "If he answers, he answers. If he doesn't, he doesn't." Then he told Quigley, "The gentleman's time has expired."

Spurred on by the Republicans' complete deference to the president, administration witnesses became even more emboldened in their defiance of the committee. Steve Bannon showed up for testimony one afternoon with a list of only twenty-five questions he would deign to answer in the entire investigation, notwithstanding the fact that he was a key witness. More stupefying, he admitted that the list had been written by the White House, complete with a one-word answer to each—"no." This was too much even for Gowdy, but Republicans still refused to do anything about it.

Nevertheless, they could not conceal a growing body of evidence, including dozens and dozens of illicit contacts between the Trump campaign and Russian entities and an extensive effort by the president to cover them up. Since most of the Republican members didn't bother coming to the Russia interviews, or would leave shortly after their attendance was recorded, I began to wonder whether they were simply unaware of the facts. "Mike," I said to Conaway one day in the SCIF, "I think it would be a good idea to get the whole committee together to go over the evidence we have accumulated so far. Most of your members haven't been coming to the interviews, and we would like an opportunity to explain why we think the evidence is so troubling. It would also be a good opportunity to clear the air." Conaway agreed, but as the weeks went by and I repeated the request, it became obvious that such a meeting was never going to take place. Nunes wouldn't have it.

For the public, the issue was not one of willful ignorance, as it had been with my GOP colleagues, but rather the degree to which information was now siloed, and the lack of access to conflicting views. As a college student, I had rushed back to my dormitory one evening to watch Walter Cronkite's last broadcast. He had been one of the most trusted voices in the country, along with the anchors of the other two networks that provided most Americans with their news. That was a time in which there was a large body of agreed-upon fact. We might differ with what to do with those facts, but at least we agreed that there were "facts" and "truth." In the 1990s, we moved to a model in which many Americans got their news from cable and tuned in only to the news they wanted to hear.

Now we were living in a world in which most people got their news on their phones and from social media. Algorithms knew exactly where we lived, how old we were, our race and ethnicity, our likes and dislikes, and what we shared and didn't share, and in an effort to keep us on their platforms, they showed us the news we wanted to see, curated just for us. During a hearing with technology executives that fall of 2017 to discuss the extensive nature of the Russian social media campaign, I asked representatives from Facebook, Twitter, and YouTube whether their algorithms were having the effect of balkanizing the public and deepening the divisions in our society. "We recognize the concerns," Colin Stretch, vice president and general counsel of Facebook replied. "The data on this is actually quite mixed."

Maybe that was so, but it didn't seem very mixed to me. The news in my Twitter feed was very different from that of my neighbor, or if not my neighbor, it was certainly different from that of someone living in another part of the country. Outside an airport one evening in Charlotte, as I waited by the curb for an Uber, a stranger approached me and said in a soft, conspiratorial tone:

"You're Adam Schiff, right?" The man was in his midthirties, short, and with a pronounced Southern accent.

"Yes."

"You can tell me—there's nothing to this 'collusion' stuff, is there?"

"Let me ask you a question," I responded. "What if I was to tell you that we had evidence in black and white that the Russians approached the Clinton campaign and offered dirt on Donald Trump, then met secretly with Chelsea Clinton, John Podesta, and Robby Mook in the Brooklyn headquarters of the campaign to deliver it. Then Hillary lied about it to cover it up. Would you call that collusion?"

"I think I see where you're going here," he said, hesitantly.

"Now, what if I also told you that after the election, former National Security Advisor Susan Rice secretly talked with the Russian ambassador in an effort to undermine U.S. sanctions on Russia after they interfered to help Hillary win. Would you call that collusion?"

He paused for a moment, thinking it over, then said: "You know, I probably would."

His car arrived and he took off, leaving me at the curb. It had been one of those "eureka" moments, and I remember thinking, "Now, if I can only speak to a couple hundred million people."

On March 12, 2018, Conaway left me a voicemail informing me that he was ending the committee's Russia investigation, after refusing to interview dozens of witnesses that remained on our witness list. "Got your message," I texted him. "But in a fitting coda to our investigation, first learned of the decision to shut down by reading it in the paper before your call. This is a sad chapter for the Congress and our committee. I really feel it is an abdication of our responsibility."

In announcing the end of the investigation, Republicans on the committee declared: "We have no evidence of collusion, coordination, or conspiracy," and then went further, even attacking the idea that the Russians were trying to help the Trump campaign. "The Russians did commit active measures," Conaway conceded, but the committee majority rejects "the narrative that they were trying to help Trump." Committee Republicans were not only denying collusion but rejecting the unanimous conclusion of the intelligence agencies—not to mention all of the evidence we had gathered—that the Kremlin had intervened to undermine Clinton and boost the candidacy of Donald Trump.

Naturally, the president claimed vindication in an all-caps tweet:

THE HOUSE INTELLIGENCE COMMITTEE HAS, AFTER A 14 MONTH LONG IN-DEPTH INVESTIGATION, FOUND NO EVI-DENCE OF COLLUSION OR COORDINATION BETWEEN THE TRUMP CAMPAIGN AND RUSSIA TO INFLUENCE THE 2016 PRESI-DENTIAL ELECTION.

Days later, the Republicans completed a report that claimed to reveal our "findings," which they adopted in another party line vote. It was a transparent whitewash, and not even a very good one. The majority report was riddled with misrepresentations and distortions in a further effort to vindicate Trump, while ignoring the unanimous dissent of Democratic members. Most disappointing was the fact that Representative Will Hurd—a former CIA clandestine officer whose independent cast had set him apart from most other Republicans—had vouched for the report, including its baseless attacks on the Intelligence Community's conclusion that Russia had interfered to help Trump. House Intelligence Republicans stood alone in that shameful assertion; not even their Republican counterparts on the Senate Intelligence Committee would back them up. But for Hurd to join in attacking the Intelligence Community as a way of protecting Trump was all the more inexplicable. I had expected more from Hurd, and had tried to work with him, and this would not be the last time he would revert to partisan form.

In a particularly galling passage, the majority's report even cited Gowdy's summary questions as evidence of the scrupulous attention to detail by Republican members. "The Committee cast a wide net, generally asking each witnesses (sic) whether they had evidence of any 'collusion, coordination, or conspiracy' between Russia and candidate Trump or any of his associates," the report said. "None produced any evidence. For example, Trump's son-in-law and senior adviser Jared Kushner stated categorically that the Trump campaign 'did not collude, cooperate, whatever other "C" words you used, with any foreign governments.'"

The implication was that if self-interested witnesses like Kushner—who personally attended a meeting to get help from the Russians—denied wrongdoing, then that negated all of the evidence of collusion. It was the oversight equivalent of asking: Who are you going to believe, Kushner or your lying eyes? On March 26, the Democratic members issued a rebuttal to correct the record. "The Majority's report reflects a lack of seriousness and interest in pursuing the truth," we wrote.

> By refusing to call in key witnesses, by refusing to request pertinent documents, and by refusing to compel and enforce witness cooperation and answers to key questions . . . the Majority hobbled the Committee's ability to conduct a credible investigation that could inspire public confidence. The Majority's conduct has also undermined Congress' independent investigative authority . . . and is unworthy of this Committee, the House of Representatives, and most importantly, the American people, who are now left to try to discern what is true and what is not.

We made a motion to release all of the unclassified transcripts of our interviews—something that Nunes had committed to doing whenever the investigation concluded—but the Republicans voted us down. No doubt they did not want the public to witness their duplicity or see the incriminating substance of what we had learned. Instead, they would send the transcripts to the Intelligence Community for a declassification review—even for the vast majority of witnesses who had no access to classified information and for which such a review was pointless—and insisted that no transcript could be released publicly until all were released. The White House demanded to have a role in approving the release of our transcripts—an outrageous intrusion on the congressional prerogative over our own work product—and the Republicans allowed them to do so. The result was that the Trump administration was able to keep all of the transcripts bottled up for the next year and a half.

As our rebuttal got picked up by the media, I hoped that it would serve as a useful tool for journalists and future historians. We had not only documented the disgraceful whitewash by Intelligence Committee Republicans but also set out the many incriminating links between Trump and Russia that they had worked so hard to conceal. But I had no illusion that public scrutiny of our report would chasten my Republican colleagues. They had never wanted to investigate the Russian operation, let alone collusion by the Trump campaign, and now that they had closed the inquiry, nothing would make them reopen it.

What we had learned in the investigation was far worse than I had imagined when we began. If someone had told me then that we would discover emails between the president's son and intermediaries with the Russian government documenting an effort to collude by secretly providing dirt on Hillary Clinton, I would not have believed it. "No one would be stupid enough to put that in writing," I would have said. And yet we found exactly that.

We had not been able to conduct the investigation in the bipartisan way I had hoped and that I believed the public deserved, and I wondered whether there was anything I could have done differently. But given the Republican determination to protect the president at all costs, it seemed the only way our investigation could have been bipartisan was if Democrats had agreed to abandon a pursuit of the truth and call it progress.

If there was to be a real House investigation of the Trump ties to Russia, and of the danger that Trump was compromised by his financial interests, personal history, or the hopes of doing business in Russia in the future, we would have to occupy the majority ourselves. With the midterm election seven months away, that seemed increasingly possible. The vulgar transformation of the GOP under Trump had alienated many conservatives, and dozens of House Republicans had already announced that they would not seek reelection. The exodus culminated on April 11, when Speaker Paul Ryan added his name to the list. Just three years earlier, Ryan had been widely regarded as the future of the Republican Party: a fiscal conservative from the Midwest who received the vice presidential nomination in 2012 and was drafted by his colleagues three years later to serve as Speaker. Now he too would be gone.

I liked Ryan personally, but he had proved all too pliable in the face of Trump's attacks on our democracy. When he was asked, for example, what he thought of Trump's threat to revoke NBC's broadcast license, the most he could say was that he was for the First Amendment. "I'm a constitutional conservative, and I'm just going to leave it at that." I took that to mean he was very conservative in his support for a free press when politically inconvenient. But the criticism that Ryan received from Democrats was trivial in comparison to the rage that he inspired in the emerging populist right. Three years after his colleagues had begged him to lead their caucus in the House, he had become the villainous face of a Beltway establishment that Donald Trump was anointed to destroy.

For all my differences with Ryan, I felt some measure of sympathy for his predicament. I had spent two decades in public life, working with Republicans to bridge the political divide. I still believed deeply in the bipartisan ethos of my parents, and the unshakable conviction that a healthy democracy depends on the exchange of competing ideas. None of my Republican colleagues would have imagined before 2016 that I would become a lightning rod for partisan attacks. Yet the metamorphosis of the GOP under Trump had forced me to take on a different and more controversial role, putting me in direct and often daily conflict with an American president who lavished praise on dictators, alienated our closest allies, disparaged minorities, denigrated women, attacked the rule of law and our democratic institutions, lined his pockets with the fruits of his office, and colluded with a foreign adversary to undermine our election. There was nothing partisan in my doing so. His actions did not reflect Republican values, at least not as a generation of Republicans had expressed them. Trump learned to inflame his base by casting his own critics as the enemy, no matter what party they occupied. It was a political tactic that I knew well, and the hallmark of autocrats everywhere.

As I reflected on this turning point in the Russia investigation, what I found most disturbing was not the attempt by Kremlin agents to influence our election, or even the evidence of collusion by the Trump campaign. It was the realization that the greater danger to our democracy now came not from Russia or any other external adversary, but from within. One by one, Trump had been tearing down our institutions. The Judicial branch was only legitimate when courts ruled in his favor, otherwise judges were corrupt, subject to attack over their ethnic backgrounds, or only "so-called" judges. The legislative branch was to be treated with contempt, its subpoenas ignored, and witnesses instructed to refuse to answer questions without asserting any applicable privilege. Trump was caught in secret discussions with the postmaster general in an effort to browbeat her into raising postal rates on Amazon as a way to punish *The Washington Post*. He was not only criticizing the press, but using the instruments of state power to silence the press. The Justice Department operated like the president's personal law firm, to protect him from criminal or civil liability and to go after his enemies. Intelligence community leaders needed to adhere to the president's preferred narrative of events or risk losing their jobs. In Trump's view, America's elections were not free and fair, but rigged and illegitimate, if they didn't go his way.

With remarkable speed, Donald Trump had undermined the foundation of our democracy and projected his warped vision of America onto the world. He had also completely remade one of America's two major political parties in his own flawed image, and my Republican colleagues weren't courageous enough to try to stop him. So many of the principles they claimed to hold dear had fallen away in the service of this man, and in their effort to preserve their places in office or at the seat of power. Our political system depends on Congress to hold the president accountable. When the Founders established three branches of government, they anticipated friction between them. Indeed, the friction was by design. By allowing each branch to constrain the others, to set ambition against ambition, they created a barrier to concentrated power. But in the age of Trump, the Founders' check on the executive branch was failing, and Congress was subordinating itself to the president. Republicans in Congress would not challenge a president of their party even as he denigrated and demeaned them, and the institution in which they served.

There were exceptions, of course, and one of the most courageous was Republican senator Jeff Flake of Arizona. Jeff and I are friends; we had come to Congress together, traveled together, and worked together on civil liberties and environmental issues. Because Jeff was a man of principle, there was no room for him in a party dominated by a characterless president. Announcing his decision to retire on the Senate floor, Jeff said: "We were not made great as a country by indulging in or even exalting our worst impulses, turning against ourselves, glorifying in the things that divide us, and calling fake things true and true things fake. And we did not become the beacon of freedom in the darkest corners of the world by flouting our institutions and failing to understand just how hard-won and vulnerable they are." Rejecting the gravitational pull of politics and party loyalty, Jeff declared, "I have children and grandchildren to answer to."

10

THE BARR DECEPTION

With the committee's official investigation over, we had to take on a much more defensive role. The president was pushing for an end to Mueller's probe as well, and concerns over Mueller's potential firing soon reached a peak. Bipartisan legislation had been introduced months earlier to prohibit his removal without cause, but it had gone nowhere, and Republicans were now even less willing to confront the president. The relentless pounding of Mueller had also taken a further toll on his support, with public approval among Republicans down to 41 percent.

The New York Times reported in April that Trump had ordered Mueller fired, and only backed down when he was assured by Mueller's team that they had not subpoenaed Trump's records at Deutsche Bank. This concerned me greatly, not only because of the president's willingness to entertain firing Mueller, but also because it suggested that Mueller was observing a red line the president had drawn around his finances. Mueller's scope included any connections between Trump and Russia, and if the Russians had been laundering money through the Trump organization, that was profoundly compromising and needed investigation. To do otherwise would leave our national security at the risk of Russian financial leverage. And besides, the president had no business telling Mueller what he could or could not investigate.

The president was also escalating his attacks against both Sessions and Rosenstein. He had been pressuring Sessions to retake control of the Russia investigation, to "unrecuse" himself, even though doing so would violate the advice of ethics lawyers at the department. Trump said that Sessions would be a "hero" if he did. And he was urging Rosenstein to open another investigation into his investigators, which Rosenstein was, sadly, willing to do. "If anyone did infiltrate or surveil participants in a presidential campaign for inappropriate purposes," Rosenstein said in announcing the probe, "we need to know about it and take appropriate action."

Republicans were also trying to subpoena investigative files from the Justice Department so that Trump's legal team could make use of them. One of the president's personal lawyers, Rudy Giuliani, made no bones about the fact that he expected to see whatever Republicans obtained from their investigation of the investigators. That summer I took to the House floor to fight back in the only way I knew how. "When this chapter of history is written," I warned, "it will condemn the actions of a president who little understands or respects the institutions of our democracy. But it will reserve some of the harshest criticism for this Congress that enabled him. This Congress that knew its responsibility but failed to live up to it. Wake up, Republican Party! Wake up, my colleagues, the country needs you . . . Wake up, my colleagues, and do your jobs!"

It would take a profound and humiliating act of presidential betrayal before any of them would be stirred to say a word. In June 2018, as he prepared for a summit with Putin in Finland, Trump again cast doubt on whether Russia had been responsible for hacking the 2016 election, calling it all a hoax and suggesting that it was time to invite Russia back into the G-7 group of nations, even though Russia had done nothing to merit its reintegration into that influential body. It turns out that in addition to all else, Donald Trump was also a lousy dealmaker—whatever leverage he might have had going into this summit he squandered days before the meeting even began.

Soon enough, Trump stood next to the Kremlin dictator in Helsinki to answer questions from the assembled journalists and was asked to denounce the Russian attacks against our democracy—it should not have been a difficult question, and yet it was. Trump said that he didn't "see any reason why" Russia would be responsible for the hacking of our election. "I have great confidence in my intelligence people, but I will tell you that President Putin was extremely strong and powerful in his denial today." Continuing the Kremlin narrative of false equivalence, Trump said that it was the Special Counsel's investigation, not the Russian meddling, that had "kept us apart," and he suggested he might even be willing to surrender U.S. diplomats to Russian interrogation as part of their own "investigation" into the matter.

I was watching the conference while on the set at CNN in Washington, shaking my head and running out of adjectives and expletives. It was too much even for several Republicans. Paul Ryan criticized the president's remarks and said, "There is no moral equivalence between the United States and Russia, which remains hostile to our most basic values and ideals." Senate Foreign Relations Committee chairman Bob Corker went further, saying that Trump "made us look as a nation more like a pushover." Even on Fox News, Trump's obsequious display was more than they could stomach. One characteristic headline ran PUTIN EATS TRUMP'S LUNCH IN HELSINKI. McCain said it better than anyone else, describing Trump's role as "one of the most disgraceful performances by an American president in memory."

But most Republican members remained silent and simply avoided talking to the press. And when push came to shove, they fell right back in line. Trump's public comments in Helsinki followed a lengthy private meeting in which Trump had asked all of his top personnel to step out of the room, leaving him alone with Putin and their interpreters. If Trump's public comments and commitments had been so detrimental to U.S. interests, there was no telling how much worse the private agreements had been. Not even Director Coats knew what was discussed in Trump's private meeting with Putin, which put him at a serious disadvantage compared to the Russian intelligence services, who unquestionably did. In committee, I made a motion to subpoena the interpreter's notes, an extraordinary proposition but one necessitated by the degree to which Trump had already betrayed our country's interests to Russia. Not surprisingly, Republicans uniformly voted it down. Occasional criticism was one thing, but voting against the president was another; and besides, did they really want to know what went on behind closed doors?

The clear message to Putin from the summit was this: Donald Trump was too weak a president to confront him. And the Russians could intervene in our politics as much as they liked, as long as they favored Trump. In fact, he would probably welcome their help again. Sure enough, the Russians were already interfering in the 2018 midterm elections. They were using spear phishing attacks against Democratic candidates in pivotal Senate races like that of Missouri Democratic senator Claire McCaskill. Trump had called for McCaskill's defeat in August 2017, and not long thereafter, the Russians tried to hack her campaign. Had they been listening to Trump again?

The best way to harden our defenses against election interference would involve developing a national consensus that both parties would reject foreign meddling—no matter who it helped or hurt. But such a consensus proved impossible as long as Trump was in office. As the midterm elections approached, I campaigned for our candidates all over the country, flying constantly, visiting about two dozen states. In a year of unrelenting and grim tidings, one ray of bright light shone through—we had the most extraordinary class of candidates running for Congress in modern history. Many of them were veterans of the armed forces, the State Department, and the

Intelligence Community. In the same way that thousands of patriotic Americans had joined the service after 9/11 to defend our country, these veterans were now running for office to help defend our
democracy.

Between campaign events, I would return to the departure gate
of an airport or retreat to my room in some nondescript motel,
watching the television with a knot in my stomach as the president's
latest bombast pierced the air. On October 2, before a crowd in conservative DeSoto County, Mississippi, Trump mocked Dr. Christine
Blasey Ford, the woman who had accused Supreme Court nominee Brett Kavanaugh of sexual assault when they were teenagers.
Despite having claimed he found her credible days earlier, Trump
engaged in a satiric dialogue with himself:

"I had one beer!" he shouted, impersonating Ford.

"How did you get home?" he asked, in another voice impersonating a questioner at the hearing.

"I don't remember!" he replied as Ford.

I watched the crowd behind Trump, standing on risers as the
president's backdrop. They loved it, laughing and applauding as the
president mocked this victim of sexual assault. Ford had testified
that one of the most haunting memories of her assault—in which
Kavanaugh forced her on a bed, climbed on top of her, and started
groping her—was that of Kavanaugh and his friend laughing about
it, and now so was this crowd. As I watched the glee on their faces, I
could not help but think that the virus of this amoral president had
now infected not just the whole of government but the rest of the
country as well.

As the election approached, our prospects of winning the House
continued to rise. There was an extraordinary rebirth of activism
and I could see it everywhere. As I was flying back to Washington
on United Airlines, the woman next to me said: "I am part of an
eleven-thousand-strong group of women online. We call ourselves
'law mommas.' We are lawyers, we are mothers, and we are pissed.
And we're going to do something about it." If eleven thousand law
mommas had found themselves online and were this engaged, I

thought to myself, there was something really powerful and organic going on. In my district, constituents organized an effort they called Civic Sundays, gathering in someone's living room every Sunday for two long years to work on the election, writing postcards, making calls, and texting.

When election day arrived, the result was an overwhelming repudiation of Trump and of the Republicans in the House who supported him. In the suburbs in particular, Republicans were wiped out and new members were elected who would soon become household names, like Katie Porter, Mikie Sherrill, Elissa Slotkin, Abigail Spanberger, and more. I was thrilled and relieved. From the day after Trump's inauguration, when millions gathered in the women's march, to the midterms two years later, people remained engaged and they had brought about a massive victory. The House would be in Democratic hands and able to serve as a vital backstop against Trump's autocratic drive and familial corruption. I was also about to become chairman of the Intelligence Committee, and our committee could finally undertake its investigative work in a credible and competent way. Should the president engage in further misconduct with a foreign power, we could do whatever would be necessary to stop him.

THE DAY AFTER THE ELECTION, the president fired Jeff Sessions, still furious over Sessions's early decision to recuse himself from the Russia investigation. In a pattern that would repeat itself endlessly, Republicans who previously warned the president not to take certain destructive actions—like firing Sessions—were now silent or, worse, welcoming of the changes. Just a year earlier, Senator Lindsey Graham had said that there would be "holy hell to pay" if Trump fired Sessions. Now that the dirty deed was done, he said merely: "I look forward to working with President @realDonaldTrump to find a confirmable, worthy successor so we can start a new chapter at the Department of Justice."

That "worthy" successor would be William Barr. Six months

earlier, on June 8, Barr had written a nineteen-page letter to Rosenstein taking issue with the Mueller investigation, and particularly its examination of the president's many acts of obstruction of justice. "Mueller should not be permitted to demand that the President submit to interrogation about alleged obstruction," Barr argued, in what came to be considered his job application. Without even knowing the facts or the legal theory Mueller might apply to those facts, Barr opined that "Mueller's obstruction theory is fatally misconceived" and "premised on a novel and legally insupportable reading of the law."

A strong believer in a unitary executive in which the attorney general serves the president's interests, whatever they may be, Barr argued, "the president may exercise his supervisory authority over cases dealing with his own interests; the president transgresses no legal limitation when he does so." Barr's overt hostility to the Mueller investigation, his belief in boundless presidential power, and his lengthy conservative pedigree proved irresistible to Trump, and on December 7, he nominated Barr to be his next attorney general.

During his confirmation hearings, Barr said he would seek the advice of ethics lawyers as to whether he should recuse himself from the Russia investigation, given his obvious bias. Tellingly, he would agree only to ask the ethics lawyers their opinion, but he would not commit to following it, arrogantly asserting that he would make his own judgment as to whether they were right. Of course, the whole point of consulting ethics lawyers is the realization that you are not the best judge of how your actions will be perceived, and public officials must avoid not just impropriety but the appearance of impropriety. But Barr had no intention of removing himself from the case. In Barr's view—and Trump's—that was Sessions's mistake.

Just as disturbing, Barr would not commit to making the Mueller report public, and said he might provide only his own summary of the matter. Under those circumstances, there was no way Barr should have been confirmed, and I said so. Nevertheless, Barr was approved on a vote of 54–45, with three Democratic senators voting "yea." If I had been aghast at how the Justice Department had compromised its independence and integrity under Sessions, I had no idea how much worse the problem was about to become—we hadn't seen anything yet.

Just five days before Christmas, Trump announced that he would not sign an appropriations bill to fund the federal government unless it provided $5.7 billion for construction of his border wall—the one that Mexico was supposed to pay for. The demand was outrageous, but hardly surprising. His campaign for the presidency had been defined by the xenophobic pledge to thwart immigration, and many of his supporters were incensed that two years later, the wall had not been built. I had never forgotten the repugnance that I felt as a young man facing the Berlin Wall, and I had no intention—then, or ever—of reproducing such a structure at home.

When Congress refused to approve the full funding he requested, Trump announced he was declaring a national emergency and would divert military appropriations to construct his wall. In seeking to do an end run around Congress's power of the purse, Trump was usurping our most effective means of serving as a check on the administration, any administration. For this reason, even McConnell privately urged the president not to declare an emergency or circumvent Congress, but when he did, once again McConnell fell in line. Not since McConnell blocked the nomination of Merrick Garland had he supported an action so deleterious to our constitutional scheme. Ever the sycophant, McCarthy was more than content to go along with the president. Both Republican leaders were sacrificing the most important of Congress's powers to please the president. If they were willing to do that, I recall thinking, when would they ever defend the institutions of our democracy?

Early in the new year, I sat down with the Democratic members and staff of the Intelligence Committee to discuss the Russia investigation. Robert Mueller was close to wrapping up the Special Counsel's investigation, and I had carefully followed the subpoenas Mueller was issuing and the indictments he was obtaining, searching for clues as to what he was investigating and what he was not. As the new chairman of the Intelligence Committee, I had no interest in re-creating the work that he was already doing, and with greater resources behind the effort. But as I scrutinized the public record, I grew increasingly concerned that the counterintelligence investigation was being ignored as Mueller pursued the criminal investigation. There is a lot of activity that, while not criminal, is nonetheless a real danger to the country, and if Mueller wasn't pursuing that, as Comey had been charged to do, then our committee needed to do so or the country would be left at risk.

ADAM SCHIFF'S PLANS TO OBLITERATE TRUMP'S RED LINE read a headline in *The New Yorker*, over a piece outlining my intentions to subpoena financial and other records to determine whether there was any entanglement that could compromise our interests. Trump's sons had bragged about getting money from Russia, including the claim by Eric Trump that "We don't rely on American banks. We have all the funding we need out of Russia." For his part, Don Jr. claimed that "in terms of high-end product influx into the U.S., Russians make up a pretty disproportionate cross-section of a lot of our assets." At a minimum, it was important to find out whether these statements were true and the Russians exerted undisclosed financial leverage over the president of the United States.

"An economic miracle is taking place in the United States," Trump declared in his State of the Union address that February, "and the only things that can stop it are foolish wars, politics, or ridiculous, partisan investigations." As I sat in the chamber listening, heads turning in my direction to see if I thought he was talking about me and to gauge my reaction, I resisted the impulse to shake my head. A few days later, he made explicit what he thought was a ridiculous, partisan investigation, tweeting: "So now Congressman Adam Schiff announces, after having found zero Russian Collusion, that he is going to be looking at every aspect of my life, both financial and personal, even though there is no reason to be doing so. Never happened before!"

. . .

By late February or early March, rumors were circulating that Mueller would not be seeking any further indictments and would soon be issuing his report. Immediately, Trump and his allies claimed exoneration and went on the attack. On March 23, Rudy Giuliani tweeted: "@AdamSchiff said 'there is significant evidence of collusion involving Trump campaign.' I trust he is relieved there is no collusion. And I hope he will apologize for his mistake. We all make them. The real virtue is to admit it. It would help us heal."

That Sunday morning on his program, George Stephanopoulos asked me if I was going to apologize. Declining, I pointed out the distinction I had always made between collusion and proof beyond a reasonable doubt of the crime of conspiracy. The president's campaign could, and did, try to collude with the Russians to get help in the election. Whether Mueller believed he could satisfy a jury that all of the elements of the crime of conspiracy had been met was another matter, and that would be up to him. But Giuliani was in the vanguard of another Republican assault on the truth that would explode in the coming days, and it was engineered by President Trump's new attorney general. And as Giuliani's statement presaged, one of the main targets of this assault would be me.

Later that day, I was pulling my car into a parking spot beside Amoeba Music in Hollywood when my cellphone pinged with the news that Attorney General Bill Barr had just delivered a summary of the Mueller report to Congress. The timing could hardly have been worse. My daughter, Lexi, and her boyfriend, Eric, were visiting me in Los Angeles, and we had been planning a hike in the hills above Griffith Park after a quick stop at the record store. Now I would be inundated with requests from the media to comment on whatever the Barr summary said. Boland and Simons were on the other side of the country and we would have to coordinate our response remotely; with news this big, that was far from ideal. Giuliani's attack the day before made more sense now—and suggested that Barr was coordinating with the White House, if not with the Trump defense team directly.

I told Eric and Lexi, "You guys head in, I'm going to need to deal with this. I will meet you inside." I never made it into the record store. Instead, I sat alone in the car reading the summary letter, my heart racing. "I am writing today to advise you of the principal conclusions reached by Special Counsel Robert S. Mueller III," it began. "On Friday, the Special Counsel submitted to me a 'confidential report explaining the prosecution or declination decisions' he has reached." Barr explained that Mueller's report contained two parts. The first examined the Russian attack on our election, including possible coordination by the Trump campaign. The second examined the president's conduct during the investigation, and whether he tried to obstruct Mueller's work.

According to Barr, both parts of the Mueller report vindicated Trump. The first part directly exonerated his campaign of conspiring with Russia in their election interference. "The Special Counsel's investigation did not find that the Trump campaign or anyone associated with it conspired or coordinated with Russia in its efforts to influence the 2016 U.S. presidential election," the letter said. The second part, Barr acknowledged, was indirect. Mueller "did not draw a conclusion" on the question of obstruction, but in the absence of a conclusion by Mueller, Barr claimed the right to make a determination himself. "After reviewing the Special Counsel's final report on these issues," he wrote, "Deputy Attorney General Rod Rosenstein and I have concluded that the evidence developed during the Special Counsel's investigation is not sufficient to establish that the President committed an obstruction-of-justice offense."

By the time the kids emerged from the store, I had yet to wrap my head around the full import of Barr's summary. But one thing was immediately clear: The letter from Barr had given Republicans all the ammunition they needed to condemn the Russia investigation as a hoax. Frantic messages were pouring in from Boland that I was getting pummeled on conservative media. As we made the short drive to the Griffith Observatory and began our hike, the barrage of messages continued. It was a beautiful day, with an immaculate blue sky and a gentle breeze—and I was an abysmal hiking companion, perpetually falling behind, agonizing over poor cellular reception, and hastily responding to the crush of emails on my phone.

"Mueller did not find sufficient evidence to establish conspiracy, notwithstanding Russian offers to help Trump's campaign, their acceptance, and a litany of concealed interactions with Russia," I tweeted, in response to the news. "I trust Mueller's prosecutorial judgment, but the country must see the evidence. Mueller spent two years investigating obstruction of justice and found evidence that 'does not exonerate' Trump. Barr took two days to set aside that evidence. The entire report must be published and evidence provided to Congress so the American people can judge for themselves."

Early that evening, I sat distracted at dinner with Lexi, Eric, and my nephew, Raffi, at one of my favorite restaurants, Jitlada in Thai Town. Later, while the kids went outside and waited by the car, I remained at the table agonizing over the Barr letter. I had no idea what the Mueller report actually said, but I was deeply skeptical that Barr had accurately described it. If the report was hundreds of pages, Mueller must have written his own summary, so why would Barr feel the need to draft one? Thirty years earlier, while leading the Office of Legal Counsel at the Justice Department, Barr had written a legal opinion that authorized a U.S. president to abduct people in foreign countries. The administration of George H. W. Bush relied on that memo to justify a mission in which commandos invaded Panama and captured its leader, Manuel Noriega—but when Congress demanded to see the legal basis for the abduction, Barr refused to show them. Instead, as *Just Security* documented, he prepared a shorter document for Congress that he said "summarizes the principal conclusions" of the memo. When the actual memo was finally made public—years later—it became clear that Barr's account had left out some of its most important elements. Now he was promising to "summarize the principal conclusions" of the Mueller report and history was about to repeat itself, but in an even more insidious fashion.

Barr's summary was the first draft of the history of the Special

Counsel's investigation of the president, and it was a deliberate and monstrous deception. With it, Trump and his allies seized control of the narrative, and they used it to bury the truth. They also used it to try to bury me. Sean Hannity and Tucker Carlson filled the airwaves with condemnations of the "Russia hoax," portraying me as a sinister conspiracist whose fertile imagination defamed and imperiled the president of the United States. I remember watching Kellyanne Conway hold forth on *Fox and Friends* in the morning, saying, "Adam Schiff should resign. He has no right, as somebody who has been peddling a lie day after day after day! Unchallenged! Unchallenged, and not under oath! Somebody should have put him under oath and said, 'You have evidence? Where is it!'"

For his part, the president, meeting in the Oval Office with Israeli prime minister Netanyahu, suggested that those who had been probing his Russia ties were guilty of treason and should be investigated. "There are a lot of people out there that have done some very, very evil things, some bad things, I would say some treasonous things against our country," he said. "And hopefully people that have done such harm to our country—we've gone through a period of really bad things happening—those people will certainly be looked at." A few days later, he made it clear who he believed at least one of the traitors was, tweeting: "Congressman Adam Schiff, who spent two years knowingly and unlawfully lying and leaking, should be forced to resign from Congress!"

Appearing on CNN for the first time since the summary was released, I faced a skeptical Chris Cuomo, who asked, "You think that you're really going to be surprised by the report itself? You think the AG would hide any material findings of Bob Mueller? I mean, it would be pretty foolish to do so." Foolish or otherwise, that is exactly what Barr was doing, but as long as he withheld the report from the public, his preferred narrative of the events would set in. And I could see how powerless I would be to defend myself.

11

YOU MIGHT THINK IT'S OKAY

Back in Washington, D.C., four days after the Barr summary was released, I was on my way to an open hearing of the Intelligence Committee. It was a beautiful, brisk spring morning, and I opted to walk outside from the Capitol to the Rayburn House Office Building rather than take the tunnels beneath. The day's proceedings would be broadcast on television from the majestic chamber of the Education and Labor Committee. Given the clear orchestration of the attacks against me by the president and his allies in the media and on Capitol Hill, I suppose I should have anticipated what happened next. But I didn't.

As I stepped into the hearing room a few minutes ahead of schedule, I was surprised to see that all of my Republican colleagues were already there. They stood on the dais at the front of the room, whispering in a huddle. While the GOP members were present in force, my Democratic colleagues were late, only amplifying a sudden unease. Were they planning to make a motion to end our investigation of the counterintelligence risks of Trump's innumerable Russian contacts? If I brought the gavel down when the hearing was set to begin at 9 A.M., Democrats could have been outvoted on any motion brought by the Republicans. For fifteen long minutes, I waited in the anteroom, jotting down notes if I needed to defend the investigation or myself, and waiting until we reached parity so that I could begin the hearing.

I crossed the chamber and took my seat at the center of the dais. None of the Republicans looked up to meet my gaze, so I turned my attention to the witness table before us. Three of the world's leading experts on Russia were among the witnesses, including Michael McFaul, a former U.S. ambassador to Russia; Steven Hall, a former chief of Russian operations at the CIA; and Heather Conley, a former diplomat and Russia scholar, whose book *The Kremlin Playbook* had inspired the title of our hearing: "Putin's Playbook—the Kremlin's Use of Oligarchs, Money and Intelligence in 2016 and Beyond."

I had chosen a broad scope for the hearing to avoid unnecessary rancor, but I had a sinking feeling that that was no longer possible as I called the room to order. "Today, the House Permanent Select Committee on Intelligence will hold an open hearing," I said, "to discuss how the Kremlin uses financial leverage and corruption as tools of intelligence operations and foreign policy." I gave a brief explanation of the link between Russian oligarchs and the Russian state, using money to corrupt and compromise foreign politicians and businesspeople. "This notion of compromise, or *kompromat* in Russian, can be subtle," I said. "It can be witting or unwitting, and it can take many forms."

After Nunes gave a brief statement about how it was the Republicans who had sounded the alarm about Putin, I heard the voice of Mike Conaway trying to interject.

"Mr. Chairman," he said, staring down to read a letter and not able to look me in the eyes, "since prior to the inauguration of

President Trump in January of 2017, you have been at the center of a well-orchestrated media campaign, claiming, among other things, the Trump campaign colluded with the Russian government." The letter claimed that I had abused my position on the committee, damaged its reputation, and undermined public trust in democratic institutions. Using the Barr summary as a proxy for the unreleased Mueller report, Conaway's letter—which had been signed by every Republican member of the committee—accused me of making false allegations against the president, and also, paradoxically, of leaking classified information that supported the allegations. "Your actions both past and present," he read, "are incompatible with your duty as Chairman of this Committee, which alone in the House of Representatives has the obligation and authority to provide effective oversight of the U.S. intelligence community.

"As such," Conaway concluded, "we have no faith in your ability to discharge your duties in a manner consistent with your Constitutional responsibility—and urge your immediate resignation as Chairman of the committee."

I pride myself on having a thick skin, and by then I had been the subject of innumerable presidential attacks—but these were my peers, people I had worked hard to get along with and was still trying to salvage a working relationship with. To have them blindside me with a call for my resignation was wounding, as deeply personal as it was unexpected. After three years of their deliberate falsehoods and endless capitulation, it was also more than I could take. As my Democratic colleagues looked to me for my answer, I could feel the heartbreak inside—years of effort developing bipartisan relationships had come to naught. But I could feel something else rising within me. I could feel the anger.

The letter Conaway read was filled with dishonest claims about me, our investigation, and our committee. The assertion that our investigation had "found no evidence" of collusion between the Russian government and the Trump campaign was, like the president's mantra of "no collusion, no obstruction," as false as it was a brazen attempt to turn fiction into fact through sheer repetition. But it was

more than that. Underlying their argument was the insidious suggestion that anything the Trump campaign had done to conspire with
Russia was perfectly acceptable if it stopped just short of criminality.
They were attempting to draw a new ethical line for themselves and
for the country, one that tolerated—even invited and exploited—
foreign intervention unless it was indictable. This was more than
wrong, it was dangerous. With the hearing broadcast on live television to viewers across the country, I knew it was essential to set the
record straight.

"My colleagues may think it's okay," I began, "that the Russians offered dirt on a Democratic candidate for president, as part
of what was described as the Russian government's effort to help
the Trump campaign. You might think that's okay. My colleagues
might think it's okay that, when that was offered to the son of
the president—who had a pivotal role in the campaign—the president's son did not call the FBI. He did not adamantly refuse that
foreign help. No, instead that son said that he would *love* the help
of the Russians."

I glanced at Conaway and the other Republicans sitting to my
right. They stared forward, expressionless.

"You might think it's okay that he took that meeting," I continued.

You might think it's okay that Paul Manafort, the campaign
chair—someone with great experience in running campaigns—
also took that meeting. You might think it's okay that the president's son-in-law *also* took that meeting. You might think it's
okay that they concealed it from the public. You might think
it's okay that their only disappointment after that meeting was
that the dirt they received on Hillary Clinton wasn't *better.* You
might think that's okay.

You might think it's okay that when it was discovered a year
later, they lied about that meeting and said it was about adop-
tions. You might think it's okay that the president is reported
to have helped dictate that lie. You might think that's okay. I
don't. You might think it is okay that the campaign chairman

of a presidential campaign would offer information about that campaign to a Russian oligarch in exchange for money or debt forgiveness. You might think that's okay. I don't.

You might think it is okay that that campaign chairman offered polling data—campaign polling data—to someone linked to Russian intelligence. I don't think that's okay. You might think it's okay that the president himself called on Russia to hack his opponent's emails if they were listening. You might think it's okay that, later that day, in fact, the Russians attempted to hack a server affiliated with that campaign. I don't think that's okay. You might think that it's okay that the president's son-in-law sought to establish a secret back channel of communications with the Russians through a *Russian diplomatic facility*. I don't think that's okay. You might think it's okay that an associate of the president made direct contact with the GRU, through Guccifer 2 and WikiLeaks—that is considered a hostile intelligence agency. You might think that it's okay that a senior campaign official was instructed to reach that associate and find out what that hostile intelligence agency had to say, in terms of dirt on his opponent. You might think it's okay that the National Security Advisor–designate secretly conferred with the Russian ambassador about undermining U.S. sanctions. And you might think it is okay he lied about it to the FBI.

You might say that's all okay. You might say that's just what you need to do to *win*. But I don't think it's okay. I think it's immoral. I think it's unethical. I think it's unpatriotic. And, yes, I think it's corrupt and evidence of collusion.

Now, I have always said that the question of whether this amounts to proof of "conspiracy" was another matter. Whether the Special Counsel could prove beyond a reasonable doubt the proof of that crime would be up to the Special Counsel, and I would accept his decision, and I do. He is a good and honorable man, and he is a good prosecutor. But I do not think that conduct—criminal or not—is okay. And the day we *do* think that's okay is the day we will look back and say, "That is the day

America lost its way." And I will tell you one more thing that is apropos of the hearing today: I don't think it's okay that during a presidential campaign, Mr. Trump sought the Kremlin's help to consummate a real estate deal in Moscow that would make him *a fortune;* according to the Special Counsel, hundreds of millions of dollars. I don't think it is okay that he concealed it from the public. I don't think it is okay that he advocated a new and more favorable policy toward the Russians even as he was seeking the Russians' help—the Kremlin's help—to make money. I don't think it's okay that his attorney lied to *our committee.* There is a different word for that than collusion. And it is called "compromise." And that is the subject of our hearing today.

I directed my attention to our first witness, former ambassador McFaul. We had already wasted too much of his time. "Mr. Ambassador," I said, "you are recognized for your opening statement." Before I could finish the sentence, I heard the voice of Republican Mike Turner trying to cut in.

"Will the gentleman yield?" he asked, repeating the question twice in a combative tone.

"I will not yield," I said, keeping my attention on McFaul. I tried again to recognize the ambassador for an opening statement, but Turner continued to interrupt.

"You just said some things about all of us that I think we all should get the opportunity to respond to," he said loudly.

I struck the gavel to demand order.

"Mr. Turner," I said, "you are not recognized. Ambassador McFaul, *you* are recognized."

Turner slumped into his seat as McFaul leaned forward and began speaking.

In my experience, it is very difficult to tell when something you've said will resonate with people. This did. There were Americans all over the country who had watched with horror the slow but steady degradation of civility, decency, and ethical conduct and wondered whether anyone else felt that way or were they just crazy. Hearing someone tell them that what they were seeing wasn't right, wasn't moral—wasn't okay—struck a nerve in a way that I certainly hadn't expected. My Democratic colleagues took to telling me that the Republicans should call on me to resign more often.

ALMOST THREE WEEKS AFTER RELEASE of his summary, Bill Barr was still withholding the Mueller report from Congress and the public, and I was still twisting in the wind. It was excruciating. The Speaker and my colleagues in the Democratic caucus were strongly supportive, but so many of the attacks were directed at me personally that I faced the futile task of countering the president, the attorney general, Republicans in Congress, and the right-wing ecosystem. Eric Swalwell, also a former prosecutor and deeply familiar with the facts and law surrounding Trump's misconduct, was enormously helpful in pushing back, but that only succeeded in putting the target on his back as well as mine.

In the SCIF, we were hearing disturbing reports that Mueller had strongly objected to Barr's characterization of his report. During an April 9 hearing before the House Appropriations Committee, Representative Charlie Crist of Florida told Barr, "Reports have emerged recently, General, that members of the Special Counsel's team are frustrated at some level with the limited information included in your March 24 letter, that it does not adequately or accurately necessarily portray the report's findings." Then Crist asked: "Do you know what they're referencing with that?" Barr's answer was "No, I don't." That was deliberately false. In fact, at the time of this testimony, Barr had already received a letter and a phone call from Mueller complaining that his summary "did not fully capture the context, nature, and substance" of his work and conclusions, and asking for the immediate release of his own summary. Barr had refused.

But at the time, I knew nothing concrete about the Mueller team's strenuous objections or that Barr had just perjured himself before Congress, and I had little way to counter the false narrative that he and the president were pounding into the public consciousness day after day.

Donald Trump, Jr., appearing on Fox News, participated in the pummeling, claiming the Mueller report demonstrated the Russia investigation was a hoax and disparaging me as the "leader of the tinfoil hat brigade."

When Barr finally released a redacted copy of the Mueller report, on April 18, the onslaught of partisan spin had been under way for weeks, and many Americans had already locked in to a fixed view of what the report said. Even then, Barr was not content to release the report without a further attempt to mislead the public about its contents. Holding a press conference at the Justice Department, with Rod Rosenstein and his deputy Ed O'Callaghan flanking him, Bill Barr painted a sympathetic portrait of a sincere president besieged by investigations and a hostile press and cooperating fully with the investigation. I had seen all of the witnesses before our committee refuse to answer questions at the president's direction, and I knew this was a lie, but it was the least of Barr's deceits.

Barr went on to claim, over and over, that Mueller had found no evidence of collusion. This too was clearly wrong, but Barr was counting on the public to take his word for it rather than read the lengthy report. Finally, Barr claimed that there was insufficient evidence of obstruction of justice—when in reality the report would provide a factual basis to charge the president with multiple crimes of obstruction.

Once he was finished, Barr fielded questions from reporters. "Why is he [Mueller] not here, this is his report obviously that you are talking about today," a reporter asked.

"No, it's not," Barr responded. "It's a report he did for me as attorney general."

"Is it an impropriety for you to come out and sort of, what appears to be, sort of, spinning the report before the public gets a chance to read it?" the reporter asked.

"No," was Barr's abrupt answer, Rosenstein smirking at this side. And with that, they left the stage.

Back in my Burbank office for meetings with constituents, I turned off the television in disgust. Donald Trump had always wanted a lawyer at the Justice Department like Roy Cohn—Joseph McCarthy's chief counsel—someone aggressive, unscrupulous, and willing to do his bidding, and now he had found him. There had been few signs of Barr's mendacity during his tenure as attorney general during George H. W. Bush's presidency. Surrounded by people in that administration, including the president himself, who were of good character and integrity, Barr's true nature remained concealed. By Donald Trump's side, he appeared a different man altogether, willing to sacrifice the interests of the Justice Department and the public and sully his own name for a continued opportunity to be at the seat of power. It was not, I supposed, that he was really a different man now, but only that power had revealed who he really was, and tethered to a man of low character, he showed himself to be the same.

As I opened the Mueller report, one of the first things I noticed was that Mueller had written his own summary, and one very different from Barr's. Within the first few pages, Mueller made it explicit that he would not be addressing whether the Trump campaign colluded with Russia. The introduction also made it clear that although Mueller did not believe he could prove every element of conspiracy, that was not the same thing as saying there was no evidence of conspiracy. In fact, the report disclosed considerable evidence of an attempt to conspire with the Russians to gain derogatory information on Hillary Clinton. No wonder Mueller's team had been so furious. Barr's summary—and his press conference—was replete with falsehoods.

Mueller's report also outlined numerous instances in which Trump and his close advisers almost certainly broke federal law in order to impede the investigation—by firing Comey, instructing others to fire Mueller, and telling still others to lie to cover it up, among other acts. But because Mueller did not believe he had the power to indict a sitting president, he was not willing to assert that Trump broke the law, a determination he no doubt intended to leave to Congress. But failing to do so left the report to the whims of Bill Barr, and the report's ambiguity on that score would prove catastrophic. The weeks Bill Barr spent misrepresenting the report before it was public, amplified endlessly by the president and right-wing media, had been spectacularly successful. The false narrative of "no collusion, no obstruction" had sunk in, as indelible as if it had been written by Mueller himself.

As disappointed as my Democratic colleagues were in the Mueller report, many of them—and at least one Republican, Justin Amash of Michigan—believed the report made a strong case to begin impeachment proceedings. Mueller himself seemed to suggest as much, invoking the power of impeachment repeatedly in each volume, and implying that his reluctance to reach a conclusion on whether Trump should be indicted was partly because he did not want to "preempt" the impeachment process. The base of the Democratic Party overwhelmingly favored impeachment, as I would find when I was again invited to address my state party convention in San Francisco. When I followed Representative Maxine Waters onto the stage (she had been one of the earliest proponents of impeachment in Congress), the audience greeted my arrival on the podium with chants of "Impeach Forty-five! Impeach Forty-five!" But that was not something I was prepared to endorse.

The president was clearly guilty of impeachable offenses, and I was convinced that he should be removed from office. But Barr's deception had been so effective that out in the country, the impetus for impeachment, never high, seemed to decline further. An impeachment based on the Mueller report alone would not have popular support and was doomed to failure in the Republican Senate. This put Congress in the midst of a dilemma in which the strongest argument for impeachment was also the strongest argument against it. If Congress failed to impeach a president who had solicited and made use of illicit foreign assistance in his campaign—in effect, cheated his way into office—and then obstructed the investigation into that misconduct, then we risked setting a precedent that such behavior was compatible with holding the office. And yet if we impeached the president and he was acquitted in the Senate, then we would have established that such misconduct was unimpeachable.

Almost exactly a year earlier, I had written an op-ed in *The New York Times* entitled "Democrats: Don't Take the Bait on Impeachment." In the piece I described the legal standard for impeachment—high crimes and misdemeanors—and a second, much more practical and political standard: "Was the president's conduct so incompatible with the office he holds that Democratic and Republican members of Congress can make the case to their constituents that they were obligated to remove him? If they cannot, if impeachment is seen by a substantial part of the country as merely an effort to nullify the election by other means, there will be no impeachment, no matter how high the crime or serious the misdemeanor."

This was a very high bar, but the bar should be set high for removing a president. Still, every day the president seemed to underscore the need to remove him, and to demonstrate his incapacity to defend the country and its interests. Appearing with George Stephanopoulos in mid-June, the president falsely claimed that his campaign rebuffed Russian offers of assistance in 2016 and that it was Hillary Clinton who had colluded with the Russians. Then Trump was asked about his plans for 2020.

"Your campaign this time around," Stephanopoulos inquired, "if foreigners, if Russia, if China, if someone else offers you information on opponents, should they accept it, or should they call the FBI?"

Trump responded: "I think maybe you do both. I think you might want to listen, there's nothing wrong with listening. If somebody called from a country, Norway, 'we have information on your opponent.' Oh, I think I'd want to hear it."

"You want that kind of interference in our elections?"

"It's not an interference. They have information. I think I'd take it."

After all that Trump had put the country through in the last two years, he was telling us that he would do it all over again. When Stephanopoulos asked Trump about FBI director Christopher Wray's recent testimony before Congress that anyone who received an offer of campaign assistance from a foreign government should report that contact immediately to the FBI, Trump bridled. "The FBI director is wrong."

In fact, Christopher Wray was one of the few remaining agency heads appointed by Trump who was still willing to speak truth to power. I admired the way he defended the men and women of the bureau, answered questions in a straightforward manner, and never dissembled. He didn't go out of his way to contradict the president, but he nonetheless maintained a high level of integrity. In one of our first meetings, I had warned him about how many good people the president had chewed up and spat out. "I don't need this job," he confided. "And I would leave it before I ever felt the need to do something that wasn't right." Wray was doing his best to walk an ethical line. Unlike so many, he was succeeding.

There was one more opportunity to persuade the public of the seriousness of the president's offenses, and that required us to have witnesses testify in open session. The Mueller report was not evidence, but a summary of the evidence, and the public needed to hear from those who directly observed Trump's misconduct. And most important, they needed to hear from Robert Mueller. For two years, Mueller had conducted the investigation in almost complete secrecy, only emerging when indictments were returned and even then the cases were handled by members of his team. If Mueller could bring his report to life, it might be compelling.

AT WHAT SEEMED LIKE THE peak of tensions with the president, I was more than a little surprised when I received an invitation to the White House. I had had little contact with the president since my meeting with Trump in the Oval Office following the Midnight Run. My only face-to-face contact with other administration officials had consisted of a few short meetings with the new White House counsel, Pat Cipollone, as when we were fighting over release of the HPSCI transcripts. But this invitation had nothing to do with Russia.

During the summer of 2019, Iran responded to the administration's "maximum pressure" campaign of increased sanctions by attacking shipping in the Strait of Hormuz. The Iranians denied any role in the attacks on tankers, but there was little doubt of their complicity; one of the limpet mines they had placed on a tanker failed to detonate and they were forced to go back and try to retrieve it. Notwithstanding their dangerous interference with the freedom of navigation and the impact on the shipping of other nations, Secretary of State Pompeo had been unsuccessful in marshaling the support of our allies to stand up to Iran. Our allies had warned us that we could expect exactly these kinds of actions if we reneged on the Iranian nuclear deal, and perhaps far worse if the Iranians resumed their enrichment program, which they did. Now that Tehran was escalating the situation, our allies did not want to lock arms with us in what they perceived as our race to war. They simply no longer trusted us.

The flashpoint came when Iran shot down an American drone flying in international airspace with a surface-to-air missile. Prodded to take military action by Pompeo and National Security Advisor John Bolton, Trump invited about a dozen members of the congressional leadership to the White House to consult with him on the U.S. response.

When I arrived at the White House, I was shown into the Cabinet Room, where I was joined by the leadership of the Armed Services, Intelligence, and Foreign Affairs committees in the House and Senate as well as Chuck Schumer, Kevin McCarthy, and Mitch McConnell. Vice President Pence, Pompeo, Bolton, and other cabinet officials filled the seats opposite us. The Speaker was late, still trying to detach herself from a meeting back in the U.S. Capitol with a foreign leader, and we eyed one another guardedly while we waited. The president soon took up a position almost directly across from me along the long table. When he looked over to see who was gathered there, I was the first person he saw—and he winced.

His staff must have told him which congressional leadership had been invited, using our titles rather than our names, because he clearly wasn't expecting me. "I'm glad you're here," he said, awkwardly. "I'm glad I'm here too," I responded. "I appreciate the invitation." As we waited for the Speaker and struggled to fill the silence, I noticed that both the outgoing secretary of defense, Patrick Shanahan, and his replacement, Mark Esper, were sitting at, or behind, the table on my left. I had known Esper for over a decade, and liked him. I wasn't sure that he had the background or gravitas to become secretary of defense—that was undoubtedly why Trump chose him (there would be no more Mattises)—but he never struck me as partisan or particularly ideological. In the scheme of things, that made him about the best choice we could hope for.

"Mr. President," I said, to fill the void, "I think you've made an excellent choice for defense secretary. I've known Mark for a long time, and think he will do a fine job. I hesitate to say so, because I wouldn't want you to hold it against him." The president nodded and looked at Esper but didn't otherwise respond. The conversation drifted to other matters, and then the president turned back to me, and without a hint of humor, asked: "Just how long have you known Esper?" *Oh my God,* I thought, *have I just killed his nomination?*

When the Speaker arrived, the discussion began in earnest and the president laid out his thoughts on what the Iranians had done and what he was considering as a response. After the House and Senate leadership expressed their views, I interjected to share mine.

"Mr. President," I said, "I appreciate that you are consulting with Congress on a matter of this importance. I know you don't want war, and I don't think the Iranians do either. The risk is that we end up at war because of a miscalculation. As a threshold matter, I do not believe that you are authorized to use force against Iran by any of the existing AUMF's (authorization to use military force) and think my Democratic colleagues feel the same way." I could see Schumer, Pelosi, and other Democrats nodding. "I strongly support taking action to protect the freedom of navigation in the Strait of Hormuz, but I think it's essential that whatever action we take is proportional, and that we take it in concert with our allies. These attacks have been on several nations and we should act together. The Iranians are hoping that these provocations can drive a wedge between us and our allies. We shouldn't let them succeed."

Trump listened respectfully to my points and those of others. Pompeo felt at liberty to chime in from time to time, with remarks that were, not surprisingly, bellicose. But interestingly, Pence remained silent until the end of the meeting, when he felt the need to ask the president's permission before he could comment, and whatever he said was so inconsequential as to escape my memory completely. It was also clear that the president had no interest in Bolton's opinion, never asking him for his thoughts or making eye contact with him, nor did Bolton feel comfortable speaking. Only at the end of the meeting did Bolton have anything to say, and even then it was only to underscore how important it was that our discussions not leave the room.

The president kept his cards pretty close to the vest, only once intimating that he might already have made up his mind. Representative Michael McCaul, the ranking Republican member on the Foreign Affairs Committee, expressed support for taking out the Iranian missile batteries that were responsible for downing the drone, and the president responded by saying, "I think you're going to like what you see."

I was genuinely surprised that the president was interested in our views—even mine—and seemed to be giving them serious consideration. I had the impression, watching the body language of those on his side of the table, that he felt pressured by what Pompeo and Bolton were advocating, and was seeking more diverse input than he was receiving from his own cabinet. For all of the tough guy talk and posturing, Trump appeared not to want to bring us into another war, even as he was trying to extricate us from the two we were already in.

Later that night, and at the last minute, Trump called off a retaliatory strike on Iran, acknowledging that it was not "proportionate to shooting down an unmanned drone." In doing so, Trump had reconsidered a decision that might have led us into a dangerous cycle of escalating violence and possible war. He had asked our opinion and he appeared to have listened to it. I'll be damned.

A conflict with Iran seemingly avoided, at least for the moment, I returned my focus to securing Mueller's testimony. Ever since the release of his report, my staff had been in contact with his team to arrange for his appearance. Mueller was deeply reticent. In a rare press conference over a month after the release of his report, he stood alone behind the lectern at the Department of Justice for just under ten minutes, saying that his report was his testimony and that an appearance before Congress would yield nothing beyond it, before attempting to disappear, J. D. Salinger–like, back into obscurity.

No doubt, Mueller hoped his short utterance would satisfy the public hunger for his testimony. Of course, it did not. I sat down at my desk and handwrote him a note. I thanked him for his years of public service, and for accepting a task that he must have known would be difficult and subject him to scorn. Nonetheless, I told him that "you have one more service to perform," and that that was his testimony, and that I awaited his reply.

For some time, he didn't respond, and I reluctantly told my staff to prepare a subpoena. This is not the way I wanted Mueller's career to end, compelled to testify against his will, but the matter was one of cardinal importance to the country, involving the misconduct of the president of the United States, and he would be heard, willingly or otherwise. It was not that I thought Mueller's testimony would be transformative, or would lead a stampede to impeachment, and I tried to set expectations appropriately. But I did feel he could bring a sense of urgency to his findings that his report had not.

Finally came word: Mueller would accept a subpoena, and he would testify. This began an endless set of negotiations with his staff over how long he would testify and under what conditions. Not since our committee's hearing with James Comey would we have such a consequential witness testify in open session. My colleagues and I disappeared into the bunker for long practice runs, so that we would get it right. One of the key staff in our efforts to prepare was a former assistant U.S. attorney from the Southern District of New York named Dan Goldman.

Just prior to the midterms, I had been in New York for a live appearance on Rachel Maddow when I ran into Dan in the green room. Dan had left the U.S. Attorney's Office in the Southern District of New York (SDNY) and was now doing legal commentary on MSNBC. I had seen him discuss complex legal issues during his many appearances and had been very impressed with his knowledge, analysis, and ability to communicate. I knew that this was not a full-time gig for him and asked about his plans, and he told me that they were still up in the air. "If we win the midterms," I said, "and I get to chair the Intel Committee, we will need more people trained in investigations. I'm one of the most experienced investigators we have, and that's not a good thing. We should talk." He seemed interested and we exchanged cards. Now he was in the SCIF, and playing the role of Robert Mueller in our version of "mock trial."

We had studied Mueller's prior testimony before our committee and others during his long service as FBI director, and we tried to adapt our questions to his distinctive manner. Mueller was famous for delivering terse answers in his testimony to Congress, rarely uttering a word more than he felt was required. Especially now, at the center of a political firestorm where the presidency itself might be at stake, I expected him to be more guarded than ever. If we asked yes-or-no questions, we would get "yes" or "no" for an answer, and he would volunteer little or nothing. We had to find a way to draw him out and let him tell the public the significance of what he had found in a manner that was compelling, even if it was not new.

Dan sat, ramrod straight, behind the witness table in our hearing room, face devoid of expression, and made a spectacular Mueller. His answers were short, tightly aligned with the report, and precisely accurate. He gave no more than he had to. It was exasperating, and it was excellent preparation. We had to laugh at just how well he nailed it, and we refined our questions to be more specific, more direct, and more likely to elicit useful and vivid information.

My plan for the Mueller hearing was much like that for the Comey hearing. I wanted to lay out the themes in my opening statement—even if I wasn't going to take eighteen minutes—and then help the members organize their five minutes to draw out these themes in each round of questioning. Tell them what you are going to tell them, tell them, and then tell them what you told them. To the degree that Mueller would not go beyond the narrow confines of his report, we would use him to bring out all of the key facts in a narrative of Trump's Russia-related misconduct.

While we were getting prepared for the next day's hearing, Trump underscored its importance once again. Giving a speech at the conservative Turning Point USA conference, he went on another tirade against Robert Mueller and how he, Trump, could have stopped the investigation any time he wanted. "I have an Article Two," he said, "where I have the right to do whatever I want as president."

THERE WOULD BE TWO MUELLER hearings—early in the day in the Judiciary Committee, and later that afternoon in the Intelligence Committee. And on the morning of his long-awaited testimony that July, I asked the members of my committee to join me in the SCIF so we could watch his appearance before Judiciary together, in case we needed to make any adjustments. As we did, the immense gravity of the moment was clear. All across the country, Americans were tuning in to hear from one of the most important figures of our time, and one who had spoken publicly for less than ten minutes in two years.

The hearing began, and within minutes, I knew that something was wrong. Seriously wrong. After opening statements by Chairman Jerry Nadler and Ranking Member Doug Collins, Nadler began the first round of questions. "Director Mueller," he said, "the president has repeatedly claimed that your report found there was no obstruction, and that it completely and totally exonerated him. But that is not what your report said, is it?"

"Correct," Mueller said. "That is not what the report said."

"Now, reading from page two of volume two of your report that's on the screen, you wrote, 'If we had confidence after a thorough investigation of the facts that the president clearly did not commit obstruction of justice, we would so state. Based on the facts and the applicable legal standards, however, we are unable to reach that judgment.'"

Mueller seemed to be furrowing his brow as he tried to follow the short preamble to the question, but when Nadler concluded by asking, "Does that say there was no obstruction?" Mueller straightened in his chair.

"No," he said firmly.

"In fact, you were actually unable to conclude the president did not commit obstruction of justice, is that correct?" Nadler asked.

"Well, we, at the outset, determined that we . . ." Mueller seemed to lose his train of thought and paused. "When it came to the president's culpability, we needed to—we needed—we needed to go forward, only after taking into account the OLC opinion that indicated that a president—a sitting president—cannot be indicted."

I felt myself stiffen. In more than a decade of speaking with Mueller, I had never heard him grope for words. Yet as Nadler continued to ask him questions, Mueller seemed increasingly halting, and uncertain. When Nadler asked, "Did any senior White House official refuse a request to be interviewed by you and your team?" Mueller's eyes darted left and right, visibly searching his memory. "I don't believe so," he said.

Now I was alarmed. Nadler's question was almost rhetorical; anyone following the investigation could have answered it. The most senior White House official of all—President Trump—had strung them along for over a year before refusing to speak with Mueller's team.

I could see that Nadler was equally puzzled. He raised his eyebrows in disbelief, and said slowly, "The president . . ."

Mueller raised a hand in recognition of his error. "Well, I take—let me take that back," he said.

Nadler tried again. "Did the president refuse a request to be interviewed by you and your team?"

"Yes," Mueller said quickly.

Nadler soon reached the end of his time and yielded to Collins for the first round of Republican questions. Collins was not interested in a discussion of the evidence contained in the report. He was focused on trying to undermine Mueller and discredit the investigation, peppering Mueller with a series of rapid-fire questions that focused little on the substance of his findings.

"Since closing the Special Counsel's office in May," he began, "have you conducted any additional interviews?"

"In the—in the—in the wake of the report?" Mueller asked.

"Since the closing of the office in May," Collins said.

Mueller frowned. "And the question was, have we conducted . . ."

"Have you conducted any new interviews, any new witnesses, anything?"

"No," Mueller said.

"And you can confirm you're no longer Special Counsel, correct?"

"I am no longer Special Counsel."

Over the next five minutes, Collins asked Mueller arcane details: how many FBI agents contributed to the investigation, how many lawyers worked for his office, how many search warrants he executed, how many subpoenas he issued. Mueller obviously did not know the numbers and was clearly struggling to respond. Collins didn't make it any easier for him, speaking in staccato bursts and often stammering his own questions. Mueller had to ask Collins to repeat himself, saying things like "That went a little too fast for me," to which Collins would reply, "Okay, in your report—I'll make this very simple" or "We'll walk this really slow if we need to."

I winced at the sight of this and turned to my Democratic colleagues. It was heartbreaking to see Mueller, this person whom I so admired, having difficulty answering some of the most basic questions. Even on a bad day, Mueller had been capable of performing better than ninety-nine percent of the witnesses I had heard testify in my decades of public service. But this was not the Bob Mueller I knew. Two years had brought a striking change, and I suddenly understood not only his own reluctance to testify, but the protective instincts of his dedicated staff. Had I known how much he had changed, I would not have pursued his testimony with such vigor—in fact, I would not have pursued it at all.

We would have to scrap everything we had planned to ask and prepare instead for a very different interview. "We need to cut our questions down," I told my colleagues. "We have to cut the number and the length." Instead of open-ended questions to prompt fully developed answers, we would pose the shortest and most direct questions possible. "No questions calling for a narrative answer," I told them. "No multipart questions. If you think your question may be too long, it is. Cut it down." The members pored through their materials with a sense of urgency, flipping the pages, crossing out lines, simplifying the language. I was rushing to do the same.

My colleagues and I walked silently over to the Rayburn Building and the Judiciary Committee room, where our hearing would also take place. I took my seat behind the rostrum and waited. As the minutes ticked by, my staff grew increasingly anxious. The Judiciary Committee session had run much longer than they promised Mueller, and his staff was furious. Maher Bitar, my committee general counsel, came and whispered in my ear: "It may be helpful if you go talk with him. Mueller and his staff are in the small anteroom." I made my way behind the hearing room and found Mueller and a couple of his staff sitting around a small table. He stood up as I approached, and we shook hands. "Thank you for coming," I told him, and he nodded. "I really appreciate your service to the country. I hope you got my note."

"Yes," he said, "thank you."

"I know the Judiciary Committee ran over, and I can assure you, we won't. We will follow our agreement to the letter. See you shortly."

When it was our committee's turn, we tried our best to accord Mueller the great respect he deserved, especially for what seemed certain to be his last such public appearance. In a perfect illustration of the chasm between the two parties, I framed my opening remarks in a way that I hoped would help convert a four-hundred-page report into something much simpler, more visceral, more easily understood and digested—a tale of disloyalty, greed, and lies. When it came his turn, Devin Nunes said, "Welcome everyone, to the last gasp of the Russian collusion conspiracy theory."

Mueller seemed to relax as we settled into a staccato rhythm of questions and answers—and as the hearing continued, he spoke more forcefully about the findings of his investigation.

These were the occasional gems that our members were able to harvest by keeping their questions simple and direct, not pushing Mueller too hard for answers that he was unlikely to give. Our members always had the exact page references ready—thanks to excellent staff work—so that if Mueller faltered they could direct him to an exact paragraph, backing up the answer they sought.

And that is how the afternoon went, back and forth between objective reality and the Trumpian alternate reality into which all the Republicans on the committee seemed to have descended. Mueller recovered from the morning's stumbles and did his duty, with the help of my remarkable Democratic colleagues. It would be Representative Peter Welch who drew the most notable response of the day, asking Mueller whether we could now expect that candidates who were offered foreign help would accept it, rather than feel a sense of duty or legal obligation to report it to the FBI. "I hope that this is not the new normal," Mueller responded, his brow again furrowed and his gaze focused on my colleague seated to his far left, "but I fear that it is."

His words hung heavy in the air, and I later picked up where Welch left off. "From your testimony today, I gather that you believe that knowingly accepting foreign assistance during a presidential campaign is an unethical thing to do?"

"And a crime."

"And a crime," I repeated, surprised by his willingness to go beyond the report.

"And to the degree it undermines our democracy and our institutions, we can agree that it's also unpatriotic?"

"True."

"And wrong."

"True."

"We should hold our elected officials to a higher standard than mere avoidance of criminality, shouldn't we?"

"Absolutely."

"You have served this country for decades, you've taken an oath to defend the constitution, you hold yourself to a standard of doing what's right."

"I would hope" was all that Mueller would say.

PART THREE

IMPEACHED FOR LIFE, IMPEACHED FOREVER

12

CROSSING THE RUBICON

JUST AFTER 9 A.M. ON JULY 25, THE DAY AFTER ROBERT MUELLER TESTI-fied, an exultant Donald J. Trump was on his phone. He believed that Mueller's testimony had bombed, not the climactic prelude to impeachment that many Democrats hoped, but a very anticlimactic denouement in which he had been, if not vindicated, at least confi-dent he had finally escaped the jailer.

The call was with President Volodymyr Zelensky of Ukraine, and it started off with perfunctory congratulations. Zelensky, like Trump, had been an entertainer before running for office, and formed a new political party, Servant of the People, named after a television series in which he starred. He then defeated the incumbent, Petro Poro-shenko, earning more than 73 percent of the vote. Trump congratu-lated him on his win, and Zelensky flattered the American president in return. "I would like to confess to you that I had an opportunity to learn from you," Zelensky said. "We used quite a few of your skills and knowledge and were able to use it as an example for our elections."

Had the call stopped there, the course of American history would have been very different.

AFTER MUELLER'S TESTIMONY, NO ONE should have been under any illusion; the only way Trump was going to be removed from office was at the ballot box. The Speaker felt much the same way. She said that the members of our caucus needed to make up their own minds on impeachment; that it was a decision of conscience and members should be guided by what they thought best for their constituents and the country.

One Florida constituent I knew felt very strongly about the matter. "Adam," my father said, leaving me a message on my voicemail, "the man is a liaah (his full Boston accent coming out with the word)—"he is a liaaah, and you all need to call him a liaaah. If he walks like a duck and he quacks like a duck, he's a liaaah." My father spoke for many, but we would need to do more than change our messaging if we were to hold the president accountable.

Congress was entering the long summer recess and I headed back to my district for a diverse series of events and constituent meetings. No sooner had I arrived than the country was rocked by a shooting in El Paso, Texas, on August 3, when a white nationalist terrorist opened fire on the largely Hispanic patrons at a Walmart, killing twenty-three and injuring twenty-three more. He had been inspired by another white nationalist who gunned down fifty-one people at a mosque and Islamic Center in Christchurch, New Zealand, earlier that year.

Appearing at a multidenominational gathering at All Saints Church in Pasadena, I talked about what was fast becoming the predominant terrorist threat in the country, not international terror, but homegrown terror—and motivated primarily by the scourge of white nationalism. Addressing the rising tide of hate-motivated violence in the country, I spoke of the president's role, his comments about Charlottesville, and his dehumanization of immigrants, calling them invaders or an infestation, language echoed by the killer in El Paso. "White supremacy is inside the White House!" screamed a very large man in the rear of the church. "But you can't hold the president accountable for his violations of the law!" Church security moved to escort the man out, and as he left the building, you could still hear his voice trailing, "Who are you afraid of?"

The following afternoon, August 6, I was on San Vincente Boulevard in West Los Angeles, traveling between events with Boland in his beat-up 2004 Green Camry, when I got a call from our committee's legal staff back in Washington.

"Yes," I answered.

"Sorry to bother you," they said. "We want to make you aware of something." Someone had reached out to the committee about a potential abuse of power by the president or senior White House officials. It involved foreign officials in Ukraine and also a presidential call. The person hadn't decided what they would do about it. My staff advised them to consider contacting the Intelligence Community Inspector General and retaining a lawyer.

Hanging up the phone, I was skeptical. We frequently received what might be considered "hot tips" from call-ins, walk-ins, you name it, and much of the time the information didn't pan out. As the chair of the Intelligence Committee, I had grown accustomed to people contacting my offices in Burbank and Washington with all kinds of conspiracy theories, and while this must have been different in kind to warrant a call from my staff, I really didn't think much of it.

Months earlier, Rudy Giuliani had been planning a trip to Ukraine, but he was forced to cancel it when his plans became public, and my staff proposed digging into the matter further to discover just what Giuliani had been up to. At the time, Giuliani had claimed he was going to Ukraine not because he was meddling in the election, but because "we're meddling in an investigation." When I became chairman, I had hired a very bright and talented woman out of the Center for American Progress named Diana Pili-penko. Diana was the associate director for anticorruption and illicit finance, and I brought her on to help our team "follow the money" in the Russia investigation. But Diana had another unique skill that was critical to our work: She had obtained her master's degree from Harvard in regional studies—Russia, Eastern Europe, and Central Asia—and was fluent in Ukrainian and Russian. Since May 2019, she had been scouring Russian and Ukrainian open media, and she didn't like what she was seeing. For one thing, there had been a con-certed smear campaign against the U.S. ambassador to Ukraine, Marie Yovanovitch, and Giuliani appeared to play some role in it. Why would Giuliani be involved in trying to oust our ambassador to Ukraine? The House Foreign Affairs Committee was also concerned with what it was seeing and hearing, and our two committee staffs began comparing notes.

The last ten days of August I reserve every year for family time. My son and I began a tradition when he was little of going on annual father/son road trips, first with an overnight train ride from Burbank, California, to Klamath Falls, Oregon, and a long drive back along the coast. In subsequent years, we drove an RV around the national parks and beach communities of Southern California, becoming, we liked to joke, the first two Jews to rent an RV. One very hot summer, we biked the Florida Keys, getting mauled along the way by horseflies before settling into a hotel and scuba diving for the remainder of the trip. This year, Eli decided that we should go on our first father/son cruise, and we boarded a ship in Miami headed for the Caribbean to do more scuba diving, and some body surfing.

The trip was bittersweet. Our father/son adventures always involved nonstop quality time, just the two of us, and with the hurly-burly of my job, I savored every moment I could get with him. Each year, as he got older, I wondered whether that trip would be the last and dreaded the day Eli would tell me, "Dad, sorry, but I just don't want to go this year, I want to hang out with my friends." I suppose I had been the same way, but as a kid Eli didn't often share his thoughts with me; he saved his most expansive moments for car rides with his mother, sitting in the back of the minivan, the window down, no pressure of a face-to-face conversation, his thoughts bubbling to his lips as Eve listened without interruption. But on my road trips with him, we would lie awake telling stories, or laugh easily with each other while on horseback, the horses skittish from the scent of bear, and I was in heaven. Here on the boat, though, there were lots of cute girls to occupy his attention, and I often found myself alone.

Each night, as Eli ambled off to meet up with his posse of fellow teens, I grabbed a book and headed to one of the isolated spots on a deck overlooking the water. I love being on the ocean and have always felt a certain kinship with the sea. My last name, after all, is German for "ship," and I found the sight of that endless ocean to be at once terrifying and exhilarating. In the face of its enormity, our problems seem so very small. John Kennedy put it best, in a speech I have always loved:

> I really don't know why it is that all of us are so committed to the sea, except I think it's because in addition to the fact that the sea changes, and the light changes, and the ships change, it's because we all came from the sea. . . . We are tied to the ocean. And when we go back to the sea—whether it is to sail or to watch it—we are going back from whence we came.

For the entire week, the skies were blue and inviting, and the seas were steady. I had no reason to know it, but this was the calm before an immense storm.

MONDAY, SEPTEMBER 9, BROUGHT AN abrupt end to the summer recess. It would be a fall like no other.

Based largely on Diana's research over the summer, my staff had been working for weeks with the Foreign Affairs and Oversight committees on plans to announce a joint investigation into "reported efforts by President Trump and his associates to improperly pressure the Ukrainian government to assist the president's bid for reelection."

They had prepared a three-committee letter announcing the investigation the previous week but decided to hold off on releasing it until I was back in town. The decision to initiate the investigation, the letter said, was based on "a growing public record . . . that, for nearly two years, the president and his personal attorney, Rudy Giuliani, appear to have acted outside legitimate law enforcement and diplomatic channels to coerce the Ukrainian government into pursuing two politically-motivated investigations under the guise of anti-corruption activity."

Giuliani's plotting had two objects: First, Giuliani was hoping to persuade the Ukrainians to prosecute individuals who had supplied evidence to the U.S. government of Paul Manafort's pro-Russian activities in Ukraine, in an effort designed to discredit the Mueller investigation. The second matter was meant to denigrate Joe Biden and his son Hunter. Our investigation was predicated on open sources, including the Ukraine government's readout of the July 25 call between Trump and Zelensky, which Diana discovered shortly after the call, suggesting that Trump was focused on these investigations, telling Zelensky, according to the Ukrainians, that he was "convinced that the new Ukrainian government will be able to quickly improve [the] image of Ukraine, [and] complete [the] investigation of corruption cases, which inhibited the interaction between Ukraine and the USA."

Our letter also made reference to a *Politico* story, dated August 28, reporting that Trump had threatened to withhold hundreds of millions of dollars of security assistance that Congress had already appropriated for Ukraine: "If the President is trying to pressure Ukraine into choosing between defending itself from Russian aggression without U.S. assistance or leveraging its judicial system to serve the ends of the Trump campaign," we wrote, "this would represent a staggering abuse of power, a boon to Moscow, and a betrayal of the public trust." We demanded a broad range of documents from the State Department and the White House, including a transcript of the president's call, and no later than September 16.

The investigation we announced in our letter drew a predictable reaction from the president's lawyer. "They are amateurs at what I'm a professional at: investigating crimes," Giuliani told the press after learning of the investigation. "This is even dumber than calling in Mueller." But the investigation gained a sudden urgency later that morning, September 9, when we received a letter in the SCIF from the Intelligence Community Inspector General (ICIG), Michael Atkinson. The letter was addressed to me and Nunes, and it informed the committee that a whistleblower complaint was being withheld from our committee in violation of the law. My staff told me that I needed to come down to the SCIF urgently, and I made my way there as soon as I could and read the letter.

Under the Intelligence Community whistleblowing statutes, once a complaint is filed, the inspector general has fourteen days to do a preliminary investigation. If he finds it to be urgent and credible, it is presented to the Director of National Intelligence, who has seven days to review it before the statute says that it "shall" be provided to our committee. The director may include his or her own thoughts on the matter, but the transmittal is not discretionary—it must be provided to Congress. The complaint had been filed on August 12, which meant that even if the inspector general and DNI had used the full period authorized by statute, it should already have been provided to our committee. It hadn't been.

Atkinson's letter said that he had received "a disclosure from an individual" alleging "a serious or flagrant problem, abuse, violation of the law or Executive order, or deficiency relating to the funding, administration, or operation of an intelligence activity" within the responsibility of the DNI and involving classified information. During his preliminary review, Atkinson had concluded that the complaint met the criteria of an urgent concern and was credible. On August 26, he had sent the complaint and the results of his review to the act-ing DNI, Joseph Maguire, but "it is my understanding that the Acting DNI has determined that he is not required to transmit my determi-nation . . . or any of the Complainant's information." Maguire's with-holding of the complaint was inconsistent with past practice, in which all complaints were transmitted to Congress even if the ICIG himself determined they fell short of the statutory criteria.

The following afternoon, September 10, I met with Atkinson in the SCIF to discuss the impasse with Maguire. I wanted to know why the DNI was violating the law. When we met in the small conference room, Atkinson was nervous, and I could see, without his needing to say it, that he was putting his career on the line. But he was doing his duty as he saw it; while he would not convey anything about the substance of the complaint, I could tell that the matter was urgent, and not merely in the statutory meaning of that term.

Later that afternoon I wrote a private letter to Maguire: "The House Permanent Select Committee on Intelligence . . . has learned that, contrary to your express obligations under the law, you are withholding from the Committee an authorized and protected whistleblower disclosure." In an unprecedented departure from past practice, the DNI had not only failed to transmit the complaint but also failed to even notify the committee "of the fact of the disclosure or your decision not to transmit it." Instead, he had effectively over-ruled the independent determination of the ICIG and taken the law into his own hands.

"We do not know whether this decision to withhold the disclosure was made only by you," I continued, "or whether it involved interference by other parties, including the White House. The Committee's recent experience has heightened concern of improper White House efforts to influence your office and the Intelligence Community." My letter demanded immediate production of the full complaint, or the committee "will resort to compulsory process" and will also "require your appearance before the Committee to testify publicly about this matter."

I HAD BEEN PLEASED WHEN Maguire was chosen as Acting DNI only weeks earlier, and I believed that his most important job would be to maintain the independence of the Intelligence Community in the face of any political pressure to align their analyses with the president's agenda. Trump had finally tired of Dan Coats's contradicting his dangerous delusions about Kim Jong-un, and his unwillingness to bend on Russia's malign intentions, and forced him to resign, along with Sue Gordon, Coats's very capable number two. Trump had initially nominated Representative John Ratcliffe, a junior member of our committee, to serve as the new DNI, having been pleased by Ratcliffe's audition during the Mueller hearings, where the congressman from Texas had insisted that volume two of Mueller's report, which outlined the findings of the investigation into obstruction of justice, "was not authorized under the law" and "was written in violation of every DOJ principle." This was credential enough to run the intelligence agencies, as far as Trump was concerned. But Ratcliffe was almost immediately forced to withdraw, when he was found to have padded his résumé, and even Republican leaders were lukewarm to his strident partisanship and lack of experience. Trump then settled on Maguire.

In contrast to Ratcliffe, Maguire had a sterling record and reputation, as a former Navy SEAL, leader of the Naval Special Warfare Command, and later the director of the National Counterterrorism Center. When he retired from the Navy in 2010 after thirty-six years of service, he had earned the rank of vice admiral. After a short career in the private sector, Maguire ran a nonprofit serving the needs of the families of wounded or killed special forces, until he was selected by Trump to serve as acting DNI. I found it hard to imagine why someone of Maguire's background and stature would withhold the complaint, but then I had seen other good military men, like General H. R. McMaster and General John Kelly, make their own troubling concessions to the unscrupulousness of the president and his agenda.

I had my staff arrange for me to speak with Maguire, and around noon on September 12, I talked by phone with Maguire and his general counsel. "The law is very clear," I told him, "and requires you to turn over the complaint. It is not discretionary." He made it plain that he could not, or would not, and was elusive about why. "Is this your decision, or are you being instructed not to turn it over?" I asked.

Initially, Maguire said that it was his decision, but he went on to say that his hands were tied and that there were issues about whether it was within his jurisdiction. I could tell that he was trying to be a good soldier and take responsibility for some kind of advice or edict that he had received. When I asked if the White House was involved in his refusal to provide the complaint, he demurred, and then made reference to a higher authority, "someone above."

I told him that if he did not release the complaint to us, I would require him to come before our committee in open session and tell the whole country why he was the first DNI in the history of that office to withhold a whistleblower complaint from Congress. He asked for more time and said that he was trying to resolve the matter, which involved the Justice Department but also, potentially, issues of privilege. I repeated what Atkinson had told me about the urgency of the matter and said that we didn't have the luxury of time. Finally, I asked: "I know you won't tell me what the complaint is about, but does it concern a matter the committee is currently investigating?"

"No" was his quick answer. Jason Klitenic, his general counsel, suddenly interjected, "You can't answer that." Klitenic would have been aware of the letter our committee had released days earlier announcing our investigation into Ukraine, while Maguire might not have seen it. As I hung up the phone, I had the strong impression that our Ukraine investigation and the whistleblower complaint were connected.

If the subject of a complaint filed with the Intelligence Community Inspector General somehow involved someone *outside* the Intelligence Community, as the DNI was suggesting, and outside the authority of the DNI because that person was *above* the DNI, *and* that someone could make a claim of executive privilege, the list of potential targets was very short indeed. And if the DNI sought advice from Bill Barr's Justice Department and his Office of Legal Counsel as to whether to turn it over to Congress, I was also confident that their opinion would likely not be worth the paper it was written on.

The Intelligence Committee is uniquely dependent on whistle-blowers, because of the classified nature of our work. Without them, we would be almost completely reliant on the intelligence agencies to self-report any problems. And since someone who witnesses official wrongdoing can't take a classified complaint to the press, Congress may be the only effective remedy. Take away a whistleblower's access to Congress and the whole system fails.

The following day, September 13, we received a letter from Klitenic declining to turn over the complaint. Klitenic's letter referenced a consultation with the Justice Department, which meant that there might be a secret Office of Legal Counsel (OLC) opinion justifying their refusal. If this was true, the consequences were potentially dire: Not only could the DNI keep the complaint from Congress, but neither Atkinson nor any other inspector general could look any further into the allegations. This meant that the malefactor, whoever it was, was being shielded from examination or oversight.

I wrestled with what to do and discussed various options with my staff. I was convinced that we needed to subpoena the director, and that we needed to go public. Up until this point, all of the back-and-forth with Maguire and Atkinson had been done in private, and the world spun on oblivious to the showdown being fought out below the Capitol. But if we were going to escalate, it would affect the whole caucus, and that was ultimately a decision above my pay grade. I went to see the Speaker and told her my suspicions about the complaint, and what it might involve. As I always did in our conversations, I tried to give her the full picture so that she could evaluate the risks. No one had seen the complaint, and there was always the chance that we would go to the mat fighting for something that turned out to be a lot less than advertised.

"So what do you think?" the Speaker asked off the House floor, after I teed up the issue. I told her that I didn't think Atkinson would say it was credible if it wasn't credible, and I didn't think he would say it's urgent if it wasn't urgent. As little trust as I had in the administration to be an honest broker on matters of privilege, the Speaker had even less. By this point in the administration, there was no one in Congress who prayed harder for the president, or felt he was in more need of prayer. "Then do it," she said, of the subpoena.

That afternoon, Friday the thirteenth, we put the finishing touches on the subpoena and a long letter to accompany it. The subpoena compelled Maguire to immediately provide the complaint and accompanying materials, or appear before our committee in six days to explain his failure to follow the law. In the letter, I set out the history of my private interactions with the DNI, and the correspondence between us as well as with the inspector general. "The Committee can only conclude," I said in the letter, "based on this remarkable confluence of factors, that the serious misconduct at issue involves the President of the United States and/or other senior White House or Administration officials." By Friday night, the letter and subpoena had still not been released, and I kept texting Boland every thirty minutes—Is it out yet? Is it out now? Boland had a rule about Friday press releases: Never send one out after two o'clock or forget about getting press attention. It was not until 7:37 P.M. that the subpoena, letter, and release were finished and Boland could finally hit Send. Not surprisingly, press reaction was a bit confused—why would we release information on a Friday night? That was normally the time you tried to bury information. Nevertheless, much of the press quickly understood the significance, and the pressure on the DNI to release the complaint increased.

Now that the matter was public, Maguire asked for another call with me and again pleaded for more time, saying, "You have my word I'm going to try to get this resolved." I believed that he would try, but ICIG Atkinson had described the whistleblower's complaint as urgent, and there was no time to waste. I told Maguire that I would agree to postpone the hearing for one week if he would commit to attending and testifying without a fight. He did. And I wanted his word on one more thing: "I need to know that you will protect the whistleblower from retaliation." "Mr. Chairman," he assured me, "you have my word."

Meanwhile, out in the world, the story was building in intensity. On September 18, *The Washington Post* reported that Trump's communications with a foreign leader were part of the whistleblower complaint. Citing two former U.S. officials, the story alleged that

"Trump's interaction with the foreign leader included a 'promise' that was regarded as so troubling that it prompted an official in the U.S. intelligence community to file a formal whistleblower complaint."

I FLEW BACK TO CALIFORNIA that weekend for a series of district events, and when I wasn't in meetings, I was on the phone with my House colleagues. During the course of the last year, I had grown close to a group of new women members who called themselves the Badasses. Representatives Elaine Luria, Chrissy Houlahan, Mikie Sherrill, Elissa Slotkin, and Abigail Spanberger were all veterans of the military or CIA, and all represented very challenging districts. Several came from communities that had strongly supported Trump in the 2016 election, and they had been buffeted by the demands of progressives that they impeach the president and by moderate voters from both parties who wanted them to put party politics aside. We would meet in my office, along with fellow veterans Jason Crow and Gil Cisneros, and I would hear out their concerns, share my own thoughts on the investigations, and try to give them insights into what the Speaker might be thinking. Above all, they hoped not to be surprised by any decisions of the leadership.

Several of the Badasses called me over that weekend to gauge my thoughts. Were the Ukraine allegations—and the unlawful withholding of the complaint—changing my calculus on impeachment. Yes, they were, I explained. If, after all that Trump had put the country through by seeking foreign help in the 2016 election and lying to cover it up, he was once again trying to get illicit foreign intervention, and violating the law requiring whistleblower complaints to be turned over that might expose it, I told them that I thought it was time to open an impeachment inquiry. To my surprise, so did they. They were working on an op-ed for *The Washington Post,* and doing some final due diligence before they finished drafting it.

There are two kinds of jobs in Congress—the measure isn't whether you are a representative from a Democratic district or a representative from a Republican district. Rather, it is whether you are a representative from a safe seat or from a swing seat. Since I had defeated a Republican incumbent in my first congressional election, as many of the Badasses had, I knew exactly how difficult their responsibilities were in balancing the needs and desires of their constituents. In one of our first meetings in my office, I told them a story about the legendary House Speaker Sam Rayburn. In the early days of the Kennedy administration, Lyndon Johnson was telling Rayburn how well educated and successful the Kennedy cabinet was shaping up to be. As David Halberstam records in *The Best and the Brightest,* Rayburn replied dismissively, "You may be right and they may be every bit as intelligent as you say, but I'd feel a whole lot better about them if just one of them had run for sheriff once." Listening to the debates among my colleagues in Congress from time to time, I wished that all of them had run in a competitive general election just once. These Badasses were about to risk their hard-won seats on a vote of conscience, and I respected their courage and dedication to country.

The most important of my conversations that weekend was with the Speaker, on Saturday morning, September 21, and not long after I landed at LAX. I was in the car with Patty Horton, my campaign manager, when I received a call from Pelosi, and signaled to Patty to pull into an empty parking lot so that I could concentrate. We spoke for about forty-five minutes about a wealth of new public reporting that the president might have withheld hundreds of millions of dollars in military aid to pressure Ukraine into investigating Joe Biden; about our conversations with other members; and about the road ahead. "So, what are you thinking?" she asked, finally, on the decision before us. "I think it's time to move forward on impeachment," I said. "And I'm doing a Sunday show tomorrow, but I don't want to get out ahead of you." She assured me that I would not be. "You just tell 'em what you think." The president was abusing his office in the most reprehensible ways, and she was determined that we do everything in our power to stop him. "Are you ready to do this?" she asked, so there would be no ambiguity. "I am," I responded.

"All right," she replied, determinedly, "good."

The following morning, Sunday, September 22, Trump admitted discussing Joe Biden in his call with Zelensky but said that it was perfectly appropriate that he do so. Appearing on *State of the Union* at the same time, I told Jake Tapper that we were going to get the whistleblower complaint, and if the new allegations against the president were true, it would be the most profound violation of his oath of office yet. "I've been very reluctant to go down the path of impeachment . . ." I reminded him, "but if the president is essentially withholding military aid at the same time that he is trying to browbeat a foreign leader into doing something illicit—that is, providing dirt on an opponent during a presidential campaign—then that may be the only remedy that is co-equal to the evil that conduct represents. . . . We may very well have crossed the Rubicon here."

The very next day, the administration admitted delaying the military support to Ukraine prior to the president's call with Zelensky, although the president was claiming—in what would become a new mantra—"no quid pro quo." Late that night, I had a conference call with the Badasses, who had a message for me: If we were going down the road to impeachment, they wanted to make sure I played a leadership role. The previous week, Corey Lewandowski had testified before the Judiciary Committee in what many members of our caucus described as a "shit show" where he arrogantly refused to answer questions, traded insults with members, and exhibited a shocking level of disdain for Congress. I knew how difficult a witness Lewandowski was from our own proceedings with him, and Chairman Nadler did an admirable job trying to control his belligerent personality. But the GOP members of that committee—Jim Jordan, Doug Collins, Louie Gohmert, and others—wanted to turn the hearing into a circus, and they succeeded. If the Badasses were going to stick their necks out on an impeachment investigation, they wanted to avoid any future "Lewandowskis."

The following morning, September 24, I had a lunch event off the Hill, and my staff met me there for a "walk and talk" on the way back. I was in a hurry to get back to the office and we walked quickly. The administration was hinting that it might make the call record public, and the prospect now, suddenly, unsettled us. Our whole strategy was to use the hearing with Maguire to get the whistleblower complaint if we could, and then leverage that to get the transcript of the call. If they were going to release the call record now, did that mean it was far less telling than we had imagined? Or inconsistent with what we had learned about the complaint from the press? My general counsel had worked on the National Security Council, and he informed me that the "transcript" might not be a verbatim record, since staff monitoring a call might leave out items that were immaterial to the purpose of the call or embarrassing to the president. Several different versions of a call record might be taken by different staff on the call—maybe they were going to provide the least incriminating. And of course, with this crowd, we could not exclude the possibility that they would redact or even doctor the transcript.

Back at the Capitol, I joined the Speaker in her office along with the other five chairs of the investigatory committees. In any impeachment inquiry, the Speaker said, it was vital that we keep our focus on the president's Ukraine misconduct, which could be easily understood by the public. She wasn't ruling out articles of impeachment based on other presidential misconduct, like his obstruction of justice during the Mueller probe, but for now she wanted our investigative work to zero in on Ukraine. That meant the locus of the impeachment investigation would be in my committee, and I was more than aware of the heavy responsibility she was now placing on my shoulders.

At a full Democratic caucus meeting that afternoon, the Speaker asked me to address the members, and, knowing my comments might be leaked, Boland accompanied me to take notes. The room was packed and there was an electric sense of expectation among the members; we all understood that this was a day on which we might make history. I told the members that it was bad enough when Trump was soliciting foreign interference as a candidate, but now he could use the full power of his office to browbeat the leader of another nation into helping him cheat in the election. The Speaker had taken to telling us, in the words of Thomas Paine, that "the times have found us." Well, the times had found us, I said. And we know what we have to do.

Immediately following our caucus meeting, Speaker Pelosi called a press conference and announced that the House of Representatives was moving forward with an official impeachment inquiry, and she was directing the six committees that had been probing the president's conduct to proceed with their investigations under that umbrella.

The following morning, I was in my office in the SCIF with two large-screen televisions on my right displaying the news feed from CNN and MSNBC. I was trying to prepare for the hearing with Maguire scheduled for the next day, when one of my senior staff, Rheanne Wirkkala, yelled, "It's out!" Wirkkala brought me a copy of the call record, which had been sent to us by the administration simultaneously with its public release. I muted the TVs, and before I knew it, five or six of my staff had gathered in my small office to read their copies along with me. They stood around me, in front of my desk and to the side, transfixed, others gathering in the two doorways, peering in while frantically reading.

"Holy shit," I said as I read through the first couple of pages. "Oh my God," exclaimed one staff member. "Jesus Christ," blurted another. We were all racing through the document, and it was a chorus of expletives and biblical references. "Have you gotten to page four yet?" "No, I'm still trying to wrap my head around page two." "Do you see where Zelensky's asking about the Javelins?" " 'I would like you to do us a favor, though'—can you believe he said that?" As for me, I kept muttering the same thing, over and over. "Holy shit. Holy shit. Holy shit." And finally, "I can't believe they would release this."

13

I WOULD LIKE YOU TO DO US A FAVOR, THOUGH

THE PRESIDENT'S RELEASE OF THE CALL RECORD WAS A STRATEGIC blunder of historic proportions. For all of the completely spurious claims of privilege the administration made—or threatened to make—during the Russia investigation, Trump could have made a plausible argument in court that his conversations with another head of state enjoyed a presumption of confidentiality. Before an unbiased Supreme Court, that claim would likely have failed when weighed against Congress's need to know in an impeachment proceeding, just as Nixon's claim of privilege over the Watergate tapes had failed. But Trump could have tied us up in the courts for years before we would have prevailed. And while you can say many things about the present Supreme Court, "unbiased" is not one of them.

But now we had the call record, and it was damning. Almost immediately, Trump begins by telling the Ukrainian president how much the United States does for Ukraine, compared to Europe. But while the United States "has been very very good to Ukraine," the president says, "I wouldn't say that it's reciprocal." Zelensky agrees with the president, at least insofar as his critique that other countries need to do more, but then pivots to his need to purchase more Javelin antitank weapons from the United States. Immediately, the president responds by saying: "I would like you to do us a favor, though. . . ."

The favor involves two asks by President Trump. First, he wants Zelensky "to find out what happened with this whole situation with Ukraine, they say Crowdstrike . . . The server, they say Ukraine has it." What Trump is referring to here is a conspiracy theory that posits that Russia didn't interfere in the 2016 elections, Ukraine did, and on Hillary Clinton's behalf, and that the DNC's cybersecurity firm Crowdstrike absconded with a Clinton server containing the evidence of this plot as well as her missing emails. That the president of the United States was spouting this propaganda was startling enough, but that he appeared to believe it was even more unnerving. Trump then asks Zelensky to have his people work with Attorney General Barr "to get to the bottom of it." Trump goes on to criticize the former United States ambassador to Ukraine, Marie Yovanovitch, telling Zelensky that she "was bad news and the people she was dealing with in the Ukraine were bad news."

Trump next turns to the second part of the favor, and the most disturbing. "The other thing, there's a lot of talk about Biden's son, that Biden stopped the prosecution and a lot of people want to find out about that so whatever you can do with the attorney general would be great. Biden went around bragging that he stopped the prosecution so if you can look into it . . . It sounds horrible to me." Here, Trump is referring to a spurious allegation that Biden sought to stop an honest prosecutor from investigating corruption in order to shield his son's role on the board of the energy company Burisma from scrutiny. In reality, the prosecutor was corrupt, and it was the official position of the United States that he should be removed as part of rule-of-law reforms. There was nothing at all nefarious about Biden's actions.

Zelensky promises Trump that he is bringing on a new prosecutor who "will be one hundred percent my person. . . . He or she will look into the situation, specifically to the company that you mentioned in this issue." Zelensky then goes on to bash Yovanovitch as well, saying that "she was a bad ambassador" and "her attitude towards me was far from the best."

"Well," Trump replies, "she's going to go through some things." Trump then promises to have Giuliani and Barr reach out to him so they can "get to the bottom of it." As they approach the end of the call, Zelensky brings up an invitation to visit the United States and his desire to meet with the president personally. "On the other hand," Zelensky says, evidently connecting the two, "I also want to ensure you that we will be very serious about the case and will work on the investigation."

The call record was more damaging than I imagined, far more. The ease of Trump's corruption was stunning. I couldn't get over how overt the president had been about seeking dirt on his rival, and how often he connected his "favor" with the requests that Zelensky was making. Zelensky wanted military support in the form of Javelins, and Trump brings up the investigations. Zelensky wants a meeting with Trump, and Zelensky feels the need to bring up the investigations. Over and over, Trump tells Zelensky to talk to Giuliani—his personal attorney. The references to Barr were equally numerous and troubling; once again the attorney general of the United States was being used as the president's personal lawyer and consigliere. But there was something else bothering me about the call record, a cloud that hung over my thoughts, its outline dark and amorphous, its meaning unclear. Finally, I settled on what was troubling me: *Zelensky wasn't surprised by Trump's requests.* Nothing Trump asked for took him aback, and he never once asked what these investigations were really all about. He knew. Someone had prepared Zelensky for exactly what the president would be asking.

While I was studying the call record, Trump was in New York at the United Nations, sitting down with Zelensky in an awkward and uncomfortable meeting—at least for Zelensky. Asked by reporters whether he felt any pressure to investigate Biden, Zelensky struggled for an answer: "I think you read everything. So I think you read text. I—I'm sorry, but I don't want to be involved in Democratic, open, elections—elections of USA. No, you heard. We had I think good phone call. It was normal. We spoke about many things. So, I think, and you read it, that nobody pushed, pushed me." Trump then added his own interpretation: "In other words, no pressure."

Later, I met in Pelosi's office with the five other chairs to discuss the week's events. It was only Wednesday, and yet it already seemed like a different world than the one we lived in a few days earlier. "I can't believe they released the call record," I said, still in some wonder about it. "He's so blatant."

"Can you imagine?" the Speaker asked, herself incredulous. "They're at war with the Russians and he's bringing up Joe Biden like that— He's a disgrace." We still didn't know exactly what was in the whistleblower complaint, I pointed out, although Trump was bragging that "everyone" had seen it and they were all laughing about it. But if they handed it over as they were now saying they would, it could give us a pretty good road map of next investigative steps. We would want to bring in the whistleblower and identify other potential witnesses, and we would need to work as fast as we could.

At the U.S. Mission to the United Nations, the president was asked whether he was ready for the impeachment proceedings that now lay ahead. His answer was telling, and it shed light on why he'd felt so free to press Ukraine for help in the election on the day after Mueller testified. "I thought we won," he said, plaintively. "I thought it was dead. It was dead." The following morning, Trump would suggest the whistleblower or their source was like a spy, and issued a thinly veiled threat: "You know what we used to do in the old days when we were smart? Right? The spies and treason, we used to handle them a little differently than we do now."

After the chairs meeting with Pelosi, I returned to the SCIF to meet with the Democratic members of our committee and finish drafting our questions for the hearing with the DNI. Just as we were strategizing over how to handle Maguire, a credible witness and highly decorated veteran who was nonetheless in defiance of the law, we received a call from the DNI's office that they would soon be hand-delivering a classified copy of the whistleblower complaint for the committee to review. They would not leave it with us, and we would only be allowed to read it in their presence. When the representatives of the DNI arrived in the SCIF, they did not have nearly enough copies for our committee members, Democrats and Republicans, who were quickly gathering in the hearing room to read the document. Under the watchful eyes of the DNI staff, we quickly ran off a bunch of copies and handed them out.

For the next hour, the SCIF was silent but for the flipping of pages. Members came and went as they read the materials, seldom saying anything above a whisper. I sat in the front of the room, as if I were a witness testifying before the committee, and read, and reread, the weighty complaint. From time to time I would look up and make eye contact with one of the Democratic members, and we would nod, or raise an eyebrow, as if to say, "It's all here in black and white."

THE WHISTLEBLOWER COMPLAINT WAS EXCEEDINGLY well written and equally well documented. The author was smart and professional, and they knew what they were doing. Moreover, it was a perfect roadmap for our investigation, naming names, identifying where we could find additional evidence, and, importantly, never speculating or exceeding the witness's knowledge. No wonder Atkinson had found the whistleblower and their allegations credible—even without fourteen days to do a preliminary investigation, I could tell that just by reading it. Besides, we already had the most powerful form of corroboration: Just about everything the whistleblower said about that July 25 call—and they'd said a lot—was already borne out by the record that the White House had released that morning.

The nine-page document began with a startling summary: "In the course of my official duties, I have received information from multiple U.S. Government officials that the President of the United

States is using the power of his office to solicit interference from a foreign country in the 2020 U.S. election. This interference includes, among other things, pressuring a foreign country to investigate one of the President's main domestic political rivals. The President's personal lawyer, Mr. Rudolph Giuliani, is a central figure in this effort. Attorney General Barr appears to be involved as well."

The facts in the complaint had been provided by more than half a dozen officials, and while the whistleblower was not a direct witness to most of the events, the account was compelling and credible because "multiple officials recounted fact patterns that were consistent with one another." The whistleblower then described the July 25 call between Trump and Zelensky, and not only was their description remarkably consistent with the call record now in our possession, but the whistleblower further revealed that White House lawyers instructed that the record of the call be loaded onto a "separate electronic system that is otherwise used to store and handle classified information of an especially sensitive nature," and that this was a potential abuse of that system because "the call did not contain anything remotely sensitive from a national security perspective."

The complaint then elaborated on the circumstances leading up to the call, Giuliani's interactions with numerous Ukrainian officials, his interest in securing their help on two investigations, efforts to sideline Ambassador Yovanovitch, concerns by State Department officials with Giuliani's "circumvention of national security decisionmaking processes to engage with Ukrainian officials and relay messages back and forth between Kyiv and the President," and, most significant, how "Ukrainian leadership was led to believe that a meeting or phone call between the President and President Zelenskyy would depend on whether Zelenskyy showed willingness to 'play ball' on the issues that had been publicly aired by Mr. Lutsenko [a corrupt former Ukrainian prosecutor] and Mr. Giuliani." Finally, the whistleblower revealed that they had been informed that the order to suspend the military assistance to Ukraine "had come directly from the President" and that Office of Management and Budget officials "were unaware of a policy rationale."

No wonder Zelensky had not been surprised by Trump's request for a "favor" on the July 25 call. The whistleblower confirmed my deep suspicion that Zelensky was fully prepared to receive the president's request, and went further: The call itself was predicated on the understanding that Zelensky would be receptive to the president's demands that he investigate the Bidens. We didn't need to prove a quid pro quo, but if the whistleblower's allegations could be corroborated, it now appeared that the presidential call, a White House meeting, and hundreds of millions in military assistance might all have been conditioned on Ukraine's agreement to help Trump's reelection.

As significant as these allegations were, there was one more pivotal aspect of the complaint: The whistleblower named names. Three that drew my immediate attention were Ambassador Kurt Volker, Ambassador Gordon Sondland, and Energy Secretary Rick Perry. It would be essential to find out what role each of them may have played in outreach to the new Ukrainian president and the degree to which they were either aware of, or participated in, Giuliani's efforts to get him to "play ball." The "Three Amigos," as we would later learn Sondland had dubbed the trio, were among the first witnesses we would need to depose.

Just before eight o'clock the next morning, while putting some finishing touches on my opening statement for the hearing with DNI Maguire, we finally received the unclassified version of the whistleblower complaint. The DNI's office informed us that they were not going to make it public but had no objection if we did. We certainly would, but now the question was timing. My staff and I debated whether to release it immediately or after the hearing, mindful that if we released it now, it would completely overshadow the hearing and people would be reading it instead of listening to what Maguire had to say. "Put it up on our website," I said, after listening to everyone's point of view. "The whole point of this hearing was to compel them to give us the complaint. They have. In that respect, our hearing has succeeded even before it begins."

With the release of the call record and the whistleblower's

complaint in quick succession, our committee—and the whole world—had a sudden and vivid understanding of what Trump had done. There was no effort to hide his coercion of Zelenksy; Trump spoke in the manner of mob bosses everywhere. And of course we also had a much clearer appreciation of why it was so problematic for Maguire to rely on the opinion of the president's lawyers in withholding the complaint. When the hearing began, I used my opening statement to highlight this profound conflict of interest and ask Maguire why he "chose to allow the subject of the complaint to play a role in deciding whether Congress would ever see the complaint." And I mocked the president's words in his phone call, like he was running a racketeering operation, rather than the most important office in the land.

The call record, I said, "reads like a classic organized crime shakedown," and then I proceeded to demonstrate what it must have sounded like to the Ukrainian leader. "In not so many words, this is the essence of what the president communicates: We've been very good to your country, very good. No other country has done as much as we have, but you know what, I don't see much reciprocity here. I hear what you want. I have a favor I want from you, though. And I'm going to say this only seven times, so you better listen good. I want you to make up dirt on my political opponent. Understand? Lots of it, on this and on that." I continued in this mocking way for another moment, summarizing the gist of the president's shakedown and his desire for Zelensky to talk to the attorney general and Rudy, before underscoring that "this is in sum and character what the president was trying to communicate with the president of Ukraine."

I didn't think much of it at the time, but Trump would seize on my caricature of his call to say that I had "illegally made up" things and should be "questioned at the highest level for Fraud & Treason." That was of course a willful misrepresentation of what I had said, and a richly ironic one, considering that Trump was constantly mocking all of his enemies, real or perceived.

The more important thing that I remember from the early part of the Maguire hearing is that we spent far too much time focused on Maguire's defiance of the law in refusing to turn over the whistle-blower complaint, failing to understand that the world was much more interested in the dramatic revelations of the president's abuse of his office. We now had the complaint in hand. The situation was moving fast. And I had been slow to adapt.

By midhearing, we were getting feedback that commentators couldn't understand why we were so focused on process, and they were right. Boland rushed up from his seat behind me to tell me that we were getting clobbered on social media, so much so that he spilled coffee on one of the other staff. We quickly pivoted to the substance of the complaint. We would adopt the same approach we used in the Comey open hearing two years earlier, and walk Maguire through the charges one by one, highlighting why it was so important they be investigated. Beginning with Representative Mike Quigley, that is exactly what we did through the remainder of the hearing. During the last twenty minutes, I took over the questioning and did nothing but walk this reluctant witness through key sections of the complaint, airing its damning allegations and making the case to investigate them.

"The whistleblower further says that the president 'sought to pressure the Ukrainian leader to take action to help the president's 2020 reelection bid.' You would agree that should be investigated?" I asked Maguire.

"Not necessarily, sir . . . it was investigated by the Federal Bureau of Investigation."

"No, it wasn't," I responded. The Department of Justice had taken one look at the complaint and concluded it didn't merit investigation. Given that Bill Barr was mentioned numerous times in the call itself, it wasn't hard to see why. Since DOJ had declined, I asked Maguire whether he would agree that "someone should investigate this." Maguire replied that if he didn't think someone should investigate the matter, he wouldn't have referred it to the FBI in the first place.

At the end of the hearing, I addressed myself to the people of Ukraine who might be watching, and told them how distressed I was that while they were trying to liberate themselves from Russian oppression, while they were trying to root out corruption in their country, they should be asked to engage in corrupt acts on behalf of our president. What they were witnessing in the actions of our president was not democracy. It was the very negation of democracy. Growing emotional, my voice starting to tremble, I said, "*This* is democracy. What you saw in this committee is democracy. As ugly as it can be, as personal as it can be, as infuriating as it can be, this is democracy. *This* is democracy."

As Maguire made his way out of the hearing room, I returned to the conference room, feeling deflated. Soon the Democratic members rejoined me there, and I did my best to put on a good face. We had a lot of hard work ahead of us. With the call record and complaint in hand, and a fine road map for our investigation, we would be wasting no time. "Rest up," I told them, "for the real work begins now."

As they filed out, I remained behind, still agonizing over the hearing. The parody had been unnecessary and gave the Republicans another opportunity to attack me. But more important, I had been too slow to move off the focus on process. Maguire had been a deeply sympathetic witness, and as much as we tried to take issue with his decisions and not his integrity, I was afraid we didn't get the balance quite right. I felt that I had let down my colleagues on the committee, who had come to place great trust in me and in my judgment. More than that, I felt that I had let the caucus and the Speaker down. They wanted me to lead the impeachment investigation because they felt I knew how to conduct a hearing, and this was a poor start.

IF I WAS UPSET ABOUT the hearing, there was someone else even more greatly displeased. "I just watched a little bit of this on television," Trump told reporters. "It's a disgrace to our country. It's another witch hunt. Here we go again. It's Adam Schiff and his crew making up stories and sitting there like Pious, whatever you want to call them. . . . The Democrats are going to lose this election. They know it. That's why they are doing it. And should never be allowed what happened to this President."

But what most particularly disturbed the president was my mocking him like an organized crime boss. Claiming that I was trying to deceive the public by parodying his remarks in the call, Trump tweeted "Rep. Adam Schiff totally made up my conversation with Ukraine President and read it to Congress and Millions. He must resign and be investigated. He has been doing this for two years. He is a sick man!"

In the weeks and months to come, he would go even further, inventing a whole new version of events, one in which I had somehow received a copy of the call record before it was public and thought I could mislead the country about what it really said, but Trump had foiled me by ordering the release of the transcript. He would tell this fanciful story gleefully at rallies, and his allies in Congress took up the cause, even introducing a resolution to censure me over the faux outrage.

If it hadn't been apparent to me before, it was readily clear to me now—Trump needed a villain and I was it. Mueller was a thing of the past. The legislative battles were secondary to Trump's fixation on his potential impeachment, so I supplanted our leadership as the White House's public enemy number one. Following me on PBS just after the Maguire hearing, Kellyanne Conway demonstrated how the gloves, never fully on, had come off: "I listened to Chairman Schiff and he's lying to you and to all of your viewers tonight. When he says a president was using the sanctity of the office to dig up dirt on a political opponent, where is that? I'm looking at the telephone conversation here. It simply isn't there. At no time was it mentioned of aid being withheld. . . ." If that was what the administration's propaganda ministers were saying on PBS, I could only imagine what they were screaming on Fox.

A writer for the right-wing *American Thinker* brought a literary flair to her attacks: "Men like Schiff have plagued mankind throughout the ages, in literature and in real life. He is as unoriginal as they come. He is Ahab of Melville's *Moby Dick*. He is Villefort of *The Count of Monte Cristo*. He's Mrs. Danvers of *Rebecca*. He is a version of Dickens's Uriah Heep, the smarmiest of all Dickens's characters, manipulative and insincere, Iago of *Othello*. . . . In short, Schiff is a bad guy, a man without a shred of an ethical or moral core. He is a reprobate." Reading this tribute, I couldn't help but take issue with her premise: Never mind the false attack on my character, how could she suggest that an amalgam of these villains—unique in all history—would be unoriginal?

On Facebook, another falsehood was going viral, claiming that my sister was married to George Soros's son, part of a long-standing anti-Semitic trope against the Hungarian-born philanthropist. "You can't make this up," read the text over a photo of Soros, myself, a woman identified as Melissa Schiff, and her husband, Robert Soros. Except that you could make it up, and they did. I called up my brother and said, "Dan, I've got some good news and some bad news. The good news is—we have a sister and she married really well. Why didn't Mom tell us? The bad news is, Sister is clearly holding out on us!"

As lopsided as the barrage was, with all the forces the president could muster arrayed against me, I did have one advantage that Mueller hadn't had—I could fight back. I was not consigned to stony silence as Mueller had been when he was demonized by the president and his mouthpieces. I tried to stay above the daily taunts (how strange it was to feel that punching back against the president of the United States was punching below my weight) and laughed them off when I could. But when I needed to hit back, I did, and with relish.

With all of the negative attention, though, the threats on my life, a regular feature of the past three years, now escalated to an unprecedented level, and my staff renewed our previous request for a security detail, made some months earlier. It was granted and was put into effect almost immediately. I had always done my best to brush off concerns over my safety and not dwell on them, but I now found myself thinking about whether someone might bring a gun to my district events, or whether it made sense for me to sit next to a window at home with the drapes open. I hated having to think that way, and still do, but there was no denying the rage that Trump, Don Jr., Carlson, Hannity, and other purveyors of hate were now inspiring on television and in social media. Eve and I discussed our home security, what we should tell the kids (we opted not to tell them very much), and what additional precautions we should take. Eli would peer out the window at the black Suburbans of my new detail, which he said were very cool, but what he was thinking, I couldn't be sure.

Eve is a very strong person, and she adjusted to the stresses of my job, our moves across country, and the demands of raising our kids without much complaint. But she was hearing the same thing I was, from our friends and family, about all the threats online, and everyone wanted to know what we were doing about them. Concern over security came over Eve in waves, especially when I was on the other side of the country and she was home alone. One night, while I was away, a man tried to open our front door at 1 A.M. and then came back the next night and sat outside in the street for hours, staring up at our bedroom window. He had a flashlight and a small sign, which Eve couldn't read. Local police were doing periodic drive-bys of our house, but they were still too few and far between. My job was already a lot to ask of Eve, but this was something quite different, and we had our share of arguments about what we should do—and whether she and Eli should stay somewhere else for a while.

The day after Maguire's testimony, Elliot Engel, chairman of the Foreign Affairs Committee, Elijah Cummings, and I subpoenaed Secretary of State Pompeo for documents related to the Ukraine scandal. Congress was about to go on recess for two weeks, but we were going to work right through it, pushing forward as aggressively as we could. We had no timetable, but this was urgent, and I think we all understood there was a psychological barrier to going beyond the end of the year. That meant we had about eight weeks to investigate what resembled a complex white collar crime case. This would require breakneck speed. Recognizing that the end of the process could be the impeachment of the president of the United States, I thought of the lines from Macbeth: "If it were done when 'tis done, then 'twere well it were done quickly."

The subpoenaed documents would be part of the impeachment inquiry and would be shared among the committees, we told Pompeo in a letter accompanying our subpoena. "Your failure or refusal to comply with the subpoena shall constitute evidence of obstruction of the House's impeachment inquiry." By separate letter, we informed Pompeo that we were scheduling five State Department witnesses for depositions: Kurt Volker, U.S. special representative to Ukraine; George Kent, deputy assistant secretary of state overseeing Ukraine and the region; T. Ulrich Brechbuhl, a close aide to Pompeo who listened in on the call; Gordon Sondland, U.S. ambassador to the European Union; and Ambassador Marie Yovanovitch.

Pompeo's response was, not surprisingly, hostile and defiant. He refused our request for the documents and said the five State Department witnesses would not appear because they had "woefully inadequate" time to prepare. Projecting, as his boss so often did, he also said that our request "can be understood only as an attempt to intimidate, bully, and treat improperly" these foreign service professionals.

I wasn't about to allow Trump or Pompeo to do what they had done in the Russia investigation and fight us in the courts until the clock ran out. With very few exceptions, I wouldn't go to court at all. Instead, I would treat every bogus assertion, or nonassertion, of privilege, every subpoena they stonewalled, every witness they sought to intimidate, every document they withheld, as evidence of obstruction. More than that, I would use the refusal to provide witnesses or documents to draw an adverse inference that the reason they were being withheld is that their testimony would be incriminating. This is true in many proceedings in civil court, and there was no reason why we could not apply the same principle here, since the president's liberty was not at stake. During Watergate, the impeachment charges against Richard Nixon included an article based on his obstruction of congressional subpoenas, and I was already thinking ahead as to how we would build such a case. Even as the administration fought to prevent us from learning the facts of the president's Ukraine-related misconduct, they would be building the case for his impeachment for obstruction.

Meanwhile, we were encountering a different problem in our

efforts to interview the whistleblower. As a result of the president's calling his accuser a traitor and a spy, there were now threats on the that person's life. Online, someone was offering a $50,000 bounty for the identity of the whistleblower. We had never encountered a situation like this before, where merely bringing someone before our committee could threaten their life. I quietly began exploring with my staff the possibility of finding a secure location off the Hill, where we could escape the attention of the press to take the whistleblower's deposition. But I immediately thought of our committee's experience during the Russia investigation, when Republican members or staff were in cahoots with the president's legal defense team. It wasn't so much that there was a back door between the White House and our committee—it was a front door. How could we protect the whistleblower's identity when half of our committee was bent on exposing that identity?

By the fall of 2019, I had begun to wonder, not whether Trump would succeed in getting Barr to investigate me for treason as he had been demanding, but whether he would prod Barr to investigate me for something else, anything else. It didn't even need to stick, it just needed to be enough to smear me, in the same way that Trump had sought to get Ukraine to smear Biden with the announcement of an investigation. I cannot describe what it is like to consider that your own government might gin up a phony investigation against you. Anyone who has lived under a dictatorship knows exactly how terrifying a prospect that is, but it was certainly not a fear that I ever imagined I would experience in the United States of America. Yet now I could simply not rule it out.

On October 2, Speaker Pelosi invited me to join her weekly press conference. After inquiries about her policy priorities and the pending United States Mexico Canada Agreement, we got into a series of questions on impeachment, and I fielded several along with her. I spoke about the administration's efforts to interfere with the witnesses we needed to depose, and how we would not tolerate it. Also, the Republican line on the Zelensky call had begun to coalesce—it "wasn't great," but "wasn't an impeachable offense"—and reporters wanted to know: Were we "making too much of one phone call"?

"Absolutely not," the Speaker said, and then yielded to me.

If you think about what the Framers were concerned about at the time of the drafting of the Constitution, I said, their predominate fears were about foreign interference in American affairs. They wanted to ensure that the president of the United States was defending the interests and security of the United States, and not secretly advancing a private agenda. It was hard to imagine a set of circumstances that would have alarmed the Founders more than what was on that call. To my Republican colleagues who said "There's nothing to see here," or that it is bad but nothing you would remove a president over, they would have to answer: "If this conduct doesn't rise to the level of the concern the Founders had, what conduct does?"

After we filed out of the press gallery, the Speaker and I paused with our staff in a small room behind the stage. Apparently, Trump had been watching our press conference, and was in a rage. "The Do Nothing Democrats should be focused on building up our Country," Trump tweeted, "not wasting everyone's time and energy on BULLSHIT, which is what they have been doing ever since I got overwhelmingly elected in 2016, 223-306. Get a better candidate this time, you'll need it!"

Ashley Etienne, the Speaker's communications director and senior adviser, read us one of Trump's Twitter attacks on me personally: "Adam Schiff should only be so lucky to have the brains, honor and strength of Secretary of State Mike Pompeo. For a lowlife like Schiff, who completely fabricated my words and read them to Congress as though they were said by me, to demean a First in Class at West Point is SAD!"

Ashley waited for our reaction. The Speaker turned to me and said "You're really in his head," smiled, and walked out.

Pelosi was right. At a White House joint press availability with the president of Finland, Trump was still fuming. He again called me a "lowlife" and also accused me of having a mental breakdown, committing a criminal act, and committing treason, and said that I should resign. Still fixated on my comments at the Pelosi presser and their implied criticism of Pompeo, he said that I "couldn't carry his blank strap." I could only imagine what the president of Finland was thinking at that moment.

A Fox News reporter asked Trump about a *New York Times* story breaking that day that the whistleblower had made contact with my staff prior to the filing of their complaint. This is what Trump had been waiting for, and, holding up a copy of the paper, he asserted, falsely, that I helped write the complaint myself. "He knew long before, and he helped write it, too. It's a scam. It's a scam."

Back on the Hill, members of the press asked the Senate Intelligence Committee leadership whether there was anything unusual about a whistleblower contacting Intelligence Committee staff for guidance before filing a complaint with the inspector general. Spokespersons for both Senators Burr and Warner confirmed that this was standard operating procedure. I thought little of it as I headed to the airport to fly to Chicago for two nights of events, including a long-planned speaking engagement at Northwestern University, where Lexi was now in college. Since my commitments were in the evenings, I could shuttle back and forth from Chicago late at night or early in the morning in order to return to Washington to work on the investigation during the day.

My new security detail met me at O'Hare airport, and as I was riding to one of my first events in a large black SUV, I got an anxious call from Boland. It was about the whistleblower's prior contact with our staff; a reporter was claiming I had been misleading during an interview with him. I told Boland that I thought I had been very careful in my remarks not to confirm or deny anything, but that he should go back and double-check. I was doing multiple interviews every day and wanted to be sure. "You weren't careful enough, apparently," Boland said, with a nervous laugh, and referred to an appearance on *Morning Joe* back in September. "Send it to me," I said. "How bad is it?"

"It's bad."

"How bad?"

"The reporter is calling you a liar."

"Jesus," I said. "Send me the clip."

I had already arrived at one of my events, and I asked the security detail to pull over a block away so I could deal with this crisis. Boland immediately sent me the clip, which I watched in the vehicle, my heart beating furiously. At the top of my segment, *Daily Beast* politics editor Sam Stein asked me: "Have you heard from the whistleblower? Do you want to hear from the whistleblower? What protections could you provide to the whistleblower?"

At that time, we had been trying to arrange the whistleblower's testimony before the committee, and I thought that was what he was referring to, but his questions were broader than that, and my answer was sloppy. "We have not spoken directly with the whistleblower. We would like to." I explained that the whistleblower needed to get advice from the ICIG or the DNI about how they could directly communicate with us, or they would not be protected under the whistleblower laws, but that we wanted them to testify. It didn't even occur to me that he was also asking about any contact my staff may have had before the complaint was filed—before the person even became a whistleblower—but Stein's inquiry was broad enough to include that. It was completely my mistake, and I needed to own up to it. "Send me his number," I said to Boland. "I want to call him and apologize."

I got Sam on the phone and told him that I made a mistake, inadvertently, but a serious mistake nonetheless. I had been thinking about securing the whistleblower's testimony before the committee, not any prior contact with my staff. But I screwed up and wanted him to know it. Sam said that he appreciated the call, and that he knew I wasn't trying avoid responsibility. As I hung up the phone, I felt sick to my stomach.

14

YOU NEED TO COME HOME
ON THE NEXT PLANE

I FLEW BACK TO WASHINGTON LATE THAT NIGHT, ARRIVING AT REAGAN National Airport at almost one in the morning, still beating myself up over the *Morning Joe* appearance. It was already clear how the president was going to exploit my mistake, and soon enough, the Republican House leadership was amplifying the false claim that I had written the whistleblower complaint myself. Kevin McCarthy said that I was "orchestrating with the whistleblower," while Steve Scalise, the second most senior Republican in the House, declared that I was part of a "deep state scheme." Jim Jordan, never a stickler for the truth, piled on, claiming that I met personally with the whistleblower. Don Jr. added a nice anti-Semitic twist to the attack. "And for those who don't know who Adam Schiff is," the president's first son tweeted, "he is not just a radical liberal, he is someone who has been hand-picked and supported by George Soros. . . . The fact that this anonymous whistleblower went first to seek partisan advice from a George Soros *puppet* tells you everything you need to know."

The next morning, October 3, I met briefly with committee legal staff to discuss the whistleblower. I had not met the whistleblower and did not know who they were, and I told my staff that unless they were coming in to testify, I did not want to know. My staff informed me that they had had contact with the whistleblower before the complaint was filed, and although they knew more than they shared with me during our brief August call, they had only a general understanding of the allegations before the complaint was filed. And they had played no role whatsoever in writing the complaint, as the whistleblower's attorney would soon publicly attest. I did not want to know more about my staff's prior contact with the whistleblower, for fear that I might say something publicly that could give their identity away. I wanted to make sure that nothing I did, or said, added to the considerable risk they already faced.

Indeed, to this day, although I have read speculation about the whistleblower's identity, I cannot be sure who they are, nor have I ever talked with them. In working on this book, I have maintained the same precautions in discussing the matter with legal staff, and I have learned only one new detail, which shapes my understanding in hindsight: Apparently, on the same day that the inspector general informed our committee that a whistleblower complaint had been withheld from us, attorneys for the whistleblower informed my legal staff of the same. Whether that was because they had also been informed by Atkinson, I do not know. But apparently the whistleblower's counsel was meeting with my staff when the letter from the ICIG arrived in the SCIF, and my staff immediately broke up the meeting to respond to it.

The fever pitch of the White House push back against the impeachment was not surprising, but the increasingly acerbic, bigoted, and divisive nature of the attacks was starting to draw broad concern, and not just among those being targeted. "If the Democrats are successful in removing the President from office (which they never will be), it will cause a Civil War like fracture in this Nation from which our country will never heal," Trump tweeted, quoting an appearance by Pastor Robert Jeffress on Fox News. Those who spoke out against the president or reported or investigated his wrongdoing were traitors, and now the president was suggesting that if his opponents were successful, it would mean war. And not just war, Trump and his supporters seemed to be increasingly implying—war along ethnic lines. As MSNBC host Joe Scarborough stated, "He's talking about civil war, he's talking about treason, talking about the possible execution of Adam Schiff and a whistleblower . . . you line all of that up, and here is a president that is trafficking in violent imagery, which of course will not lead to civil war, but will lead to the type of unmoored human beings out there who have directed pipe bombs at Donald Trump's opponents." In less than two years, Scarborough would find out just how right he was.

Undeterred by the president's increasingly incendiary rhetoric, we had moved quickly to schedule depositions in the Ukraine investigation, which we planned to conduct every week, sometimes every day or even several times a day. *If* the witness would even show up. It would be a blistering pace, yet there was great uncertainty about whether any of this would be possible, given the strong opposition of the administration. The depositions would take place in the same committee conference room where both Nunes and I had conducted closed interviews during the Russia investigation. The bunker lacked the grandeur of a stately hearing room in the Rayburn or Longworth buildings, where we conducted open hearings, but it was private, secure, and by this point all too familiar. Three years into the Trump administration, I had spent more time in our underground spaces than in my personal congressional office—and sometimes more than at home.

But depositions required a secrecy that only the SCIF could afford. The public hearings would come next. The depositions were for collecting evidence, and the hearings would be for telling the story. As we would soon discover, without the ability to coordinate their stories, witnesses would have to tell us everything they knew during the depositions or risk legal exposure. Several witnesses would have a much improved recollection during the hearings after learning that they had concealed too much in their private testimony. The threat of a perjury charge can really sharpen the memory.

Because it was a three-committee joint investigation, that meant more than a hundred members could theoretically be present for each deposition. Unfortunately for us, this included a number of the president's most devoted acolytes from the two other committees—Foreign Affairs and Oversight—including Jim Jordan, Mark Meadows, and Representative Lee Zeldin, a back-bencher from New York. The depositions would be staff-led and would alternate between the parties, with members asking questions last. For the majority, I again would have the expert assistance of Dan Goldman and two other extremely talented former federal prosecutors that I brought on to help with the Russia investigation—Dan Noble and Nicolas Mitchell.

As with many complex investigations, we wanted to bring in the most cooperative witnesses first and work our way up the chain of responsibility. That put Kurt Volker near the top of our list. Volker was a retired diplomat who returned to public service in a voluntary capacity as the Trump administration's special representative for Ukraine negotiations. After the whistleblower complaint became public, Volker had resigned his position as special representative, claiming that he could no longer be effective in the role. Volker volunteered to come in, and it was very important to him that he not be subpoenaed—he did not want to give the impression that he was being coerced to testify. After the stonewalling from Pompeo, that was certainly fine with me.

Volker appeared twice in the whistleblower complaint, which described a trip that he made to Kyiv one day after the president's call with Zelensky. Traveling with Gordon Sondland, he attended meetings with senior Ukrainian officials, including Zelensky himself. The whistleblower described the trip as a hybrid mission: part damage control, part enforcement. "Based on multiple readouts of these meetings recounted to me by various U.S. officials," the complaint said, "Ambassadors Volker and Sondland reportedly provided advice to the Ukrainian leadership about how to 'navigate' the demands that the President had made of Mr. Zelensky."

The complaint also described the alarm expressed by "multiple U.S. officials" about Giuliani's growing influence on Ukraine policy. Although the former New York mayor had no formal authority to represent the U.S. government, we knew that he was a regular presence in Kyiv—meeting with senior officials, claiming to speak for the president, spreading rumors about the Bidens, and demanding dirt to back up the rumors. "Ambassadors Volker and Sondland had spoken with Mr. Giuliani in an attempt to 'contain the damage,'" the whistleblower wrote, and they "sought to help Ukrainian leaders understand and respond to the differing messages they were receiving from official U.S. channels on the one hand, and from Mr. Giuliani on the other."

Volker's deposition would also be informed by materials we had received from the inspector general for the State Department, Steve Linick, who provided our committees with documents that Giuliani had delivered to the White House earlier that year. These documents included a cornucopia of disinformation and baseless conspiracy theories in an envelope marked "White House" and folders labeled "Trump Hotel." Giuliani claimed that after giving these materials to the White House, he received a promise from Pompeo to investigate the allegations.

Based on what was alleged in the complaint and his willingness to come forward, I considered Volker a very important witness, but it wasn't until the eve of his appearance that we understood just how truly important he was, when he forwarded to us dozens of text messages. I wasn't in the SCIF at the time—I was returning from my first evening in Chicago—but in a replay of the reading of the call record in my office days earlier, the reaction of my staff was loud and profane.

My staff emailed to me at home that night the scores of text messages between Volker, Sondland, and other U.S. officials, along with a proposed outline of our questions for the interview. As I pored over the messages into the early hours of the morning, I was stunned by how brazen they were. It seemed to me that Volker and his colleagues clearly understood that the president was abusing his power to exploit Zelensky in a political shakedown, were uncomfortable about it, but failed to put a stop to it.

The text messages revealed that less than a week before the July call between Trump and Zelensky, Volker had texted Gordon Sondland and Chargé d'affaires William "Bill" Taylor, who had replaced Yovanovitch in our embassy in Kyiv: "Most impt is for Zelensky to say that he will help investigation. . . ." Two days later, and still in advance of the call, Taylor expresses the concern that "President Zelensky is sensitive about Ukraine being taken seriously, not merely as an instrument in Washington domestic, reelection politics."

On the morning of the presidential call, there is an even more troubling text. Volker writes to one of Zelensky's top aides, Andriy Yermak, to let him know: "Heard from White House—assuming President Z convinces trump he will investigate / 'get to the bottom of what happened' in 2016, we will nail down date for visit to Washington. Good luck! See you tomorrow—kurt." This text implied that it would be necessary for Zelensky to convince Trump he would conduct the investigation that Trump wanted in order to get a White House meeting—in other words, quid pro quo.

But the most serious and damning text messages took place after the July 25 call, when Taylor sought confirmation that it wasn't just the White House meeting but also the military assistance that would be withheld unless Zelensky agreed to undertake the two political investigations sought by the president. Taylor wrote to Sondland on September 1, "Are we now saying that security assistance and WH meeting are conditioned on investigations?" To which Sondland replied in the manner of racketeering suspects everywhere: "Call me."

Apparently, Taylor and Sondland did talk, because the following week, Taylor wrote: "As I said on the phone, I think it's crazy to withhold security assistance for help with a political campaign." Then there was an almost five-hour delay before Sondland replies with what reads like a statement prepared for litigation: "Bill, I believe you are incorrect about President Trump's intentions. The President has been crystal clear no quid pro quo's of any kind. The President is trying to evaluate whether Ukraine is truly going to adopt the transparency and reforms that President Zelensky promised during his campaign I suggest we stop the back and forth by text If you still have concerns I recommend you give Lisa Kenna [executive secretary to Pompeo] or S [Secretary Pompeo] a call to discuss them directly. Thanks."

In reading these text messages for the first time, my general counsel told me that it reminded him of a scene in HBO's *The Wire* in which a drug kingpin, Stringer Bell, is trying to make peace with a group of rival drug dealers. When the discussion comes to an end, Bell sees one of his men scribbling down notes on a legal pad.

"Motherfucker, what is that?" Bell asks.

"The *Robert Rules* say we gotta have minutes for a meeting, right? These the minutes," his confederate replies.

"Is you takin' notes on a criminal fuckin' conspiracy?" Bell grabs the pad out of the man's hand and crumples up the pages he was writing on. "What the fuck is you thinkin', man?"

While there were certainly very different levels of culpability among those engaged in writing these text messages, it was remarkable that so much of the scheme was put in writing and that we would receive it prior to our first witness's testimony. If the written documents were this powerful, we could only imagine how compelling Volker's testimony would be. On this score, we would be mistaken.

ON OCTOBER 3, WE DEPOSED the first witness in the Ukraine investigation. In spite of the extensive text record of the president's scheme, and Volker's clear and central role in it, Volker began his opening statement by attempting to deny any knowledge of Trump's intentions. "[A]t no time was I aware of, or took part in, an effort to urge

Ukraine to investigate former vice president Biden," Volker said. Later he added: "In addition, I was not aware that Vice President Biden's name was mentioned or a request was made to investigate him until the transcript of the call was released. . . ."

I was incredulous. Surely Volker was not going to try to maintain the fiction that the investigation of Burisma that Trump was demanding was unrelated to the Bidens—that would be too absurd to be credible. Yet that is exactly what Volker attempted to do.

I wasn't about to let Volker maintain this bogus distinction between Burisma and the Bidens, as if Trump and Giuliani were interested in that company only by coincidence. Volker's dissembling was even more obvious when he argued that he had tried to warn the Ukrainians against getting "sucked in" to U.S. domestic politics. If the Burisma investigation had nothing to do with the Bidens, what was Volker warning them about?

I took Volker back to the record of the president's call with Zelensky and asked:

"There's no indication from the call record of any interest by the president in Burisma, but there is an interest of the president in the Bidens. Isn't it fair to say that when Rudy Giuliani uses the term 'Burisma,' it's really code for 'Biden'?"

"I think that is something I was aware of at the time, that there's a linkage between Joe Biden's son and Burisma, but Burisma stands on its own as a company that is an issue of longstanding, and so—"

"Well, maybe in your mind, but the president never mentions—"

"No, he doesn't."

"—Burisma."

"And so I think," Volker acknowledged finally, "what I hear you suggesting, if I understood correctly, is Rudy Giuliani seeing these as synonymous?"

"Yes."

"And I'm saying that I can see how that would be the case."

For their part, Republican members used the same line of summary questioning with Volker that they used during the Russia investigation. If Gowdy had then asked witnesses about "conspiracy, coordination, or collusion," now Republicans would ask generic questions about "quid pro quos."

Zeldin asked: "And in no way, shape, or form in either the read-outs from the United States or Ukraine did you receive any indication whatsoever for anything that resembles a quid pro quo?"

"Correct."

Meadows followed up with: "And that message that I heard from you very loud and clear today is that there was no quid pro quo at any time ever communicated to you. Is that correct?"

"Not to me, that is correct."

While Volker was busy prevaricating, some of the text messages were being leaked to the press—by whom, I didn't know. Since the leaked messages tended to exculpate the president, I had to assume these were coming from Republican members or staff, or Volker himself, although I assumed it was not the latter. I had a lengthy discussion with my staff, who had been consulting with the Oversight Committee, and they were urging that we do an official release of all of the key text messages, scrubbed of personally identifiable information. Since Volker's appearance before the committee was voluntary, the deposition rules did not apply, and we could release all of the text messages if we chose, to correct the misimpression the public might be getting from a selective leak. I was initially uncomfortable with the idea, but I was ultimately persuaded that it not only was proper but would help set the record straight. It would also have the salutary effect of getting good investigative journalists to track down leads. With the limited time constraints we were operating under, this was an important strategic consideration.

Even as we were questioning Volker, the president had been out on the White House lawn doing his part to strengthen our case against him. "China should start an investigation into the Bidens," he declared to the sound of the Marine One rotors in the background, "because what happened in China is just about as bad as what happened with Ukraine." The president was in the midst of trade talks with China, and he seemed to suggest that, as with Ukraine, he was willing to use the leverage of his office to compel China's help with his election. "If they don't do what we want, we have tremendous power." Hillary Clinton, no doubt as stunned by the president's continued and flagrant abuse of his office, summed up my feelings on Twitter: "Someone should inform the president," she wrote, "that impeachable offenses committed on national television still count."

The following day, we issued a subpoena to the White House demanding documents from Trump's chief of staff, Mick Mulvaney, and giving him two weeks to provide them. The president had been claiming that he was not bound to comply with our subpoenas until there was a full vote of the House on an impeachment resolution. We sought to preempt that stratagem in our letter to Mulvaney, pointing out that this argument was inconsistent with the Constitution and precedent. Article I gives the House the "sole power of impeachment," meaning we set the rules, and "Speaker Pelosi has confirmed that an impeachment inquiry is under way, and it is not for the White House to say otherwise." Moreover, as a matter of historical precedent, in the Nixon impeachment, "the Judiciary Committee had been investigating charges of impeachment for months before the House voted to open an inquiry."

While the president was making clear his defiance of our subpoenas, Republicans were continuing their strategy of deflection, and making the self-defeating argument that because a whistleblower contacted our staff seeking guidance, that meant the committee was not permitted to conduct the investigation. If that were true, no whistleblower could contact Congress, and no committee could conduct an investigation. Republicans also began claiming that the depositions were "secret interviews" in a "dungeon," or a "Soviet-style inquiry" conducted in a "Stalinist chamber." They clearly had a short memory: Nunes had conducted two years of closed interviews in the Russia investigation in the very same conference room, and Gowdy had held two years of private Benghazi depositions just one floor above, in another belowground conference room. But Republicans were desperate for a message, or a strategy, and they were trying everything, looking for anything that would resonate. So far, nothing had.

On the morning of October 8, we were set to interview Gordon

Sondland, who was not only deeply implicated in the text messages we had obtained from Volker, but also reported in *The Wall Street Journal* as having described a quid pro quo involving the military funding to Senator Ron Johnson. Shortly before Sondland was due to arrive in the SCIF, however, his counsel informed us that he would not be appearing. Apparently, Sondland, who had flown in from Brussels for his testimony, received a voicemail at 12:30 A.M. the night before from the State Department ordering him not to appear. His counsel told us that he not only had been willing to testify but had provided the State Department with relevant documents on a personal device that he was now unable to share. I held a press conference in the "Pit of Despair" to warn the White House that they were building an ever more potent case for impeachment based on obstruction of Congress. The president, however, was only getting started.

"I would love to send Ambassador Sondland, a really good man and great American, to testify," the president tweeted, "but unfortunately he would be testifying before a totally compromised kangaroo court, where Republican's rights have been taken away."

Not to be outdone, a Florida congressman named Matt Gaetz, at the time distinguished only by his exuberant support for Trump and frat boy mien, told reporters: "What we see in this impeachment is a kangaroo court and Chairman Schiff is acting like a malicious Captain Kangaroo." Hmm. Not sure the erudite Mr. Gaetz knew much about kangaroo courts or children's television, where Captain Kangaroo was a beloved figure for kids everywhere, but he was soon the subject of relentless mockery. Senators Chris Murphy and Brian Schatz, who keep up a comedic exchange on Twitter, responded this way, with Murphy writing: "Hey @brianschatz, I will buy you lunch if you somehow work 'Malicious Captain Kangaroo' into your next floor speech." To which Schatz replied: "I don't do quid pro quo Murph." Prompting Murphy to say, "Call me." My favorite, though, was from Stephen Colbert, who played Gaetz's clip and added to it: "Chairman Schiff is acting like a malicious Captain Kangaroo. Trump's being railroaded by the terrifying Thomas the

Tank Engine. This whole thing is a load of Howdy Doody, and it's brought to you by the letters F and U."

ON THE AFTERNOON OF SONDLAND's aborted testimony, we received one of the most extraordinary letters from a White House counsel in American history, and something that we understood immediately would be Exhibit A in any potential impeachment based on the president's obstruction of the lawful functions of Congress. There is advocacy on behalf of a client, and then there is an embrace of your client's alternate reality. This was the latter.

In eight pages of breathless hyperbole, White House Counsel Pat Cipollone blasted the investigation as illegitimate. The inquiry, he wrote, "violates the Constitution, the rule of law, and every past precedent." It was a breach of "the most elementary due process protections" and was a "transparent rush to judgment." Likewise, our "failure to provide co-equal subpoena power" to Republican members of the committee showed "utter disregard" for "procedural safeguards," even though that had never been the practice in any prior impeachment.

"Never before in our history has the House of Representatives— under the control of either political party—taken the American people down the dangerous path you seem determined to pursue," Cipollone wrote. "It is transparent that you have resorted to such unprecedented and unconstitutional procedures because you know that a fair process would expose the lack of any basis for your inquiry." The call with Zelensky, he added, "was completely appropriate." Anyone who thought otherwise had clearly been deceived by Schiff's "decision to create a false version of the call and read it to the American people at a congressional hearing, without disclosing that he was simply making it all up." Our true intention was not to uncover facts, he argued. It was "to overturn the results of the 2016 election and deprive the American people of the President they have freely chosen."

Cipollone's letter had been written for one purpose, which he made clear at the end. "Given that your inquiry lacks any legitimate constitutional foundation," he wrote, "the Executive Branch cannot be expected to participate in it."

For the next two days, I wondered whether the president would once again succeed in thwarting an investigation into his wrongdoing and without repercussion. Our next scheduled witness was the smeared and deposed former ambassador to Ukraine, Marie Yovanovitch, someone whom President Trump had already said was "going to go through some things" and who remained a current State Department employee. The White House was issuing talking points to Republican members to try to threaten and dissuade her from testifying by claiming that "there is serious danger that she could breach her obligations as a current employee not to reveal such information without authorization." Would she be willing to defy the president and obey a lawful subpoena? Or would she fall in line?

My staff was in constant touch with her attorney, Lawrence Robbins. Robbins had represented a witness in the Russia investigation and been incensed when Republican staff engaged in unethical conduct surrounding that witness's testimony. Robbins told us that Yovanovitch would obey a subpoena, but I was concerned that if we subpoenaed her too far in advance of her testimony, the White House would go to court to quash the subpoena and we would be stuck in endless appeals before we would ever hear a word of her testimony. My staff devised a clever work-around—we would not subpoena Yovanovitch until the morning of her testimony. That way, the department would understand that she had been compelled, but there wouldn't be time for the White House to engage in any chicanery. Everything was set to go until the night before her appearance, when someone told the press that she would be appearing under a "friendly" subpoena. We had given the Republicans notice of the deposition as required by House rules, and they must have decided to make it public.

Robbins was irate. On the phone with my staff that night, he told them what a tenuous position this put his client in, making it appear that she was eager to defy the State Department. We expressed our deep regret that someone had purposely jeopardized his client, but we impressed upon him that we had no control over what the Republicans might have said or done. Given his bad experience with the GOP staff before, this was not a hard case to make. *She will show up in the morning,* he told us, finally. And she did.

Marie Yovanovitch was a thirty-year veteran at the State Department who had served our country in some of the world's most hazardous diplomatic posts, everywhere from Moscow to Mogadishu. Small in stature, with auburn hair and glasses, she was the daughter of refugees who fled the Soviets and the Nazis, and had learned to speak Russian as a child. Yovanovitch had been appointed U.S. ambassador to Ukraine in August 2016 and held the post through most of the Trump presidency. But six months earlier, she had been summarily removed from her position after the campaign against her became so intense that her life was put in jeopardy. Why Giuliani and Trump believed it was so important to remove her, and not just remove her but humiliate and endanger her in the process, would shed light on how determined they were to get foreign help for Trump's campaign and how willing they were to destroy anyone who got in the way.

As ambassador, Yovanovitch was a fierce opponent of the corruption in Ukraine. She was especially critical of the country's top prosecutor, Yuriy Lutsenko, who had been appointed three months before her arrival in the country despite the fact that he did not have a law degree, had been convicted of embezzlement and abuse of office, and had spent years in prison. As prosecutor general, he presided over a notoriously corrupt office and used the power of his position to persecute his critics. Yovanovitch made no secret of her contempt for his tactics. She spoke forcefully and often about his abuse of his office, sometimes in meetings with Lutsenko himself.

By 2018, Lutsenko had set his sights on removing Yovanovitch from office. He endeared himself to Trump with ostentatious flattery and false allegations of corruption by the Bidens. In private meetings with Rudy Giuliani, he began spreading lies about Yovanovitch. The ambassador hated the president, he said. She told her staff to ignore Trump, because he would be impeached, he claimed. In May 2018, one of Giuliani's allies in Congress, Representative Pete Sessions, had written a letter to Pompeo claiming to have "concrete evidence" that Yovanovitch spoke "privately and repeatedly about her disdain" for the president and demanding that she be removed.

Lutsenko also made contact with an unsavory opinion writer, John Solomon, who published a story in *The Hill* that falsely suggested Yovanovitch herself was engaged in corruption. Lutsenko was quoted as saying that she had given him a list of people who should not be prosecuted for any crime, a lie he would later recant. Giuliani himself launched public broadsides against Yovanovitch in speeches and on television. Then Donald Trump, Jr., joined in, and Sean Hannity. By April 2019, she was recalled to Washington, with orders to remain silent.

Yovanovitch proved to be an immensely powerful witness. She described in vivid terms her alarm at being targeted by a powerful figure like Lutsenko, and her shock when the president's son and personal attorney joined in the smear campaign, calling her a "clown." Giuliani wanted to get dirt on the Bidens and Lutsenko was willing to provide it, in the hope that Trump might help Lutsenko retain his position in the Ukrainian government. This was exactly the kind of corrupt dealing—you scratch my back and I'll scratch yours—that Yovanovitch was fighting, and part of the reason she needed to go. And not just go, but be destroyed in the process.

Yovanovitch testified to her profound disappointment that leaders in the State Department buckled to the pressure and recalled her. "Although I understand, everyone understands, that I served at the pleasure of the president," she said, "I was nevertheless incredulous that the U.S. government chose to remove an ambassador, based, as far as I can tell, on unfounded and false claims by people with clearly questionable motives."

I asked Yovanovitch if Secretary Pompeo had tried to defend her.

"What I was told," she said, "was that the secretary, or perhaps somebody around him, was going to place a call to Mr. Hannity on Fox News to say, you know, 'What is going on? I mean, do you have proof of these kinds of allegations or not? If you have proof, tell me, but if not, stop.' And I understand that call was made."

"Did you ever get any readout on what the result of that conversation was?"

"No," she said. "But . . . it simmered down for a while."

When the attacks resumed, Yovanovitch made an explicit request for support from her superiors. "The State Department did not feel they could actually even issue, in the face of all this, a full-throated statement of support for me," she said.

"Can you explain why?" Dan Goldman asked.

"There was a concern that the rug would be pulled out from underneath the State Department," she said.

"By whom?" Goldman continued.

"The president."

"And in what way would the rug be pulled out?"

"There would be a tweet of disagreement or something," she said.

"Did you have an understanding that the State Department brass or the State Department executives understood that the president did not support you?" Goldman asked.

"That seemed to be the conclusion," she said.

"Did you understand why?"

"I understood that it was as a result of the partnership, if that's the right word, between Mr. Lutsenko and Mr. Giuliani."

Finally, in late April 2019, Yovanovitch received a late-night phone call from Carol Perez, the department's director general. "She said that she was giving me a heads-up that things were going wrong, kind of off the track," Yovanovitch recalled. "She didn't know what was happening, but there was a lot of nervousness on the seventh floor and up the street."

"What did she mean by 'up the street?'" Goldman asked.

"The White House," Yovanovitch said.

Several hours later, Perez called Yovanovitch again. This time, her message was even more ominous. "She said that there was a lot of concern for me, that I needed to be on the next plane home to Washington," Yovanovitch recalled. "I was like, 'What? What happened?' and she said, 'I don't know, but this is about your security. You need to come home immediately. You need to come home on the next plane.'"

Yovanovitch had no idea what danger she might be in, but she followed instructions, and flew to Washington early the next morning—where the deputy secretary of state, John Sullivan, withdrew her ambassadorship. "The deputy secretary said that, you know, he was sorry this was all happening," she recalled. "The president had lost confidence, and I would need to depart my post. . . . I said, 'What have I done wrong?' and he said, 'You've done nothing wrong.'"

Nicolas Mitchell of my staff directed her attention to the call record and asked about her reaction when she first read it. "I was shocked. I mean, I was very surprised that President Trump would— first of all, that I would feature repeatedly in a presidential phone call, but secondly, that the president would speak about me or any ambassador in that way to a foreign counterpart."

"At the bottom of that same page," Mitchell continued, "President Trump says, 'Well, she's going to go through some things.' What did you understand that to mean?"

"I didn't know what it meant. I was very concerned. I still am. . . . You know, I was wondering, is there an active investigation against me in the FBI? I don't know. I mean, I just simply don't know what this could mean."

Listening to Yovanovitch, my stomach turned. I could understand all too well her fear of what a corrupt Justice Department leadership might do to go after her. Here she was, in hardship post after hardship post, fighting corruption in the name of U.S. ideals, and now she was the victim of a smear campaign by her own government, and perhaps worse. For an American diplomat to be treated so poorly, after decades of public service, for such malignant and spurious reasons, was sickening. "We repeatedly uproot our lives," she said, "and we frequently put ourselves in harm's way to serve our nation, and we do that willingly, because we believe in America and its special role in the world. We also believe that in return, our government will have our backs and protect us if we come under attack from foreign interests. That basic understanding no longer holds true."

Like all employees of the State Department, she had been expressly forbidden to testify, and her decision to refuse that order cleared the way for others. She set an example for Foreign Service Officers and civil servants everywhere—not only could they testify, but it was the patriotic thing to do. Looking back, I don't know how many, if any, witnesses would have appeared if Yovanovitch had been unwilling to put herself at risk, once again, for the good of her country.

THE WEEK AFTER YOVANOVITCH'S TESTIMONY, four other witnesses followed her courageous example. The first was Fiona Hill, an intelligence analyst who served in the administrations of George W. Bush and Barack Obama before her appointment as the senior director for Europe and Russia on the National Security Council. As with Yovanovitch, we served her with a subpoena on the morning of her testimony, something the Republican members tried to take issue with, but were powerless to contest. The deposition nonetheless got off to a rocky start, when my staff alerted me to Representative Gaetz's presence. Since he was not a member of any of the three committees authorized to be present, I made it clear that he needed to leave.

"Mr. Chairman," Jordan objected. "Really?"

"Yes, really," I responded.

"You're [not] going to include members of Congress on committees that have roles in impeachment?" Gaetz protested with indignation.

"Mr. Gaines," I replied, unintentionally mispronouncing his

name—I genuinely had no idea who he was—"take your statement to the press. They do you no good here. So, please, absent yourself."

"You're going to have someone remove me from the hearing?"

"You're going to remove yourself, Mr. Gaines."

I told Jordan that we would wait until "Gaines" left, and I threatened to dock the time from the minority's opportunity to question the witness if they delayed any further. After confirming with the parliamentarian that he had no right to be present, Gaetz walked out.

Hill was smart, commanding, and direct, and her testimony was invaluable. She did not bother with an opening statement, and she responded to our questions with candor and a clipped British accent that gave her words a crisp authority. She said that she found the recall of Yovanovitch appalling. "There was no basis for her removal," she told us. "The accusations against her had no merit whatsoever." Hill then proceeded to describe her own experience, which bore an uncanny similarity to that of the ambassador: "I had had accusations similar to this being made against me as well. My entire first year of my tenure at the National Security Council was filled with hateful calls, conspiracy theories, which has started again, frankly, as it's been announced that I've been giving this deposition, accusing me of being a Soros mole in the White House, of colluding with all kinds of enemies of the president, and, you know, of various improprieties. . . . I received, I just have to tell you, death threats, calls at my home."

Hill described how dispiriting it was for her and the whole workforce at the State Department to see Yovanovitch hounded out of her post. "Because this had a really devastating effect on the morale of all of the teams that I work with across the interagency, because everybody knows Ambassador Yovanovitch to be the best of the best in terms of a nonpartisan career official. And as a woman, and you know, I don't see always a lot of prominent women in these positions, she was the highest-ranking woman diplomat."

The decision to force Yovanovitch out was engineered by Giuliani, she said, not just to appease Lutsenko, but to hijack American policy toward Ukraine more broadly. He and Gordon Sondland made no secret of that ambition. Sondland, in fact, told her explicitly "that *he* was in charge of Ukraine."

"I said to him, 'You're not,' with that kind of, you know, surprise and probably irritation in my voice. . . . And then he got testy with me," she recalled. "And I said, 'who has said you're in charge of Ukraine, Gordon?' And he said, 'The president.' Well, that shut me up, because you can't really argue with that."

Hill also recalled, "Mr. Giuliani was asserting quite frequently, on television and public appearances, that he had been given some authority over matters related to Ukraine." She got in the habit of turning on the television and searching YouTube when she got home each day, just to stay informed of Giuliani's latest claims. "The last thing I wanted to do when I went home was watch television," she said. But she felt compelled because "people were constantly saying to me, 'My God, have you seen what Giuliani is saying now?' And it was clearly starting to create this, you know, meta-alternative narrative about Ukraine."

Hill said that she was deeply skeptical of Giuliani's motives. He was pursuing "a package of issues" that extended from "the business interests of his own associates" to the effort to force an investigation of the Bidens. "I was extremely concerned that whatever Mr. Giuliani was doing might not be legal," she said.

Dan Goldman asked if she had expressed her concerns to the National Security Advisor, John Bolton.

"I did," she replied.

"And what was his reaction?"

"His reaction was pained. And he basically said, in fact, he directly said, 'Rudy Giuliani is a hand grenade that is going to blow everybody up.'"

Hill described a July 10, 2019, meeting she attended with Bolton, Sondland, Volker, Secretary of Energy Rick Perry, and a Ukrainian delegation at the White House. At this point, the Ukrainians were very eager for Zelensky to secure a White House meeting with the president, and Bolton was trying to remain noncommittal. In the middle of a discussion about Ukraine's energy sector, "Ambassador

Sondland blurted out, 'Well, we have an agreement with the Chief of Staff [Mulvaney] for a meeting if these . . . investigations into the energy sector start.'" The reference to an investigation of Burisma did not sit well. "Ambassador Bolton immediately stiffened and ended the meeting," she said.

Bolton left to go back to his office, while Sondland told the Ukrainians that he wanted to continue the meeting with them in another room downstairs, called the Ward Room. Pulling Hill aside, Bolton told her: "Go down to the Ward Room right now and find out what they're talking about and come back and talk to me." Hill left quickly to find out what Sondland was doing and "in front of the Ukrainians, as I came in, [Sondland] was talking about how he had an agreement with Chief of Staff Mulvaney for a meeting with the Ukrainians if they were going to go forward with investigations." Hill moved immediately to bring the meeting to an end, but Sondland protested, later telling her about his discussions with Mulvaney and Giuliani, "but then I cut him off because I didn't want to get further into this discussion at all."

Hill then went straight back to Bolton's office to report what she heard, and Bolton told her to go report this to the NSC counsel, John Eisenberg. "And he told me, and this is a direct quote from Ambassador Bolton: 'You go and tell Eisenberg that I am not part of whatever drug deal Sondland and Mulvaney are cooking up on this.'" And she did.

That night I flew to New York for an appearance at the 92nd Street Y. When the Y had invited me to speak, they asked who I would like to moderate the discussion, and it was a simple answer: Nicholas Kristof. Kristof is a *New York Times* columnist, and I greatly appreciated the elegance of his writing and his dogged determination to fight the genocide in Darfur. We had a wonderful discussion before a full house, and he asked me why I was conducting the depositions in closed session. I told him that the initial hearings needed to be in private so that witnesses could not tailor their stories to what others had said. I wanted the witnesses to be fully forthcoming and to know that if they held anything back that other witnesses admitted to, they would be risking perjury. But I also assured Kristof that at the appropriate time, "all these transcripts are going to be made public."

For all of the discussion we were having about Trump and impeachment, at the end of the conversation, I wanted to be sure to underscore a broader point. The larger issue was that democracy was under assault all over the world. "This is bigger than Trump. It started before Trump; it won't end with Trump," I said. "The bigger picture is democracy is hanging in the balance, and we remain its best hope."

15

THIS FOR THAT

THE IMPEACHMENT INQUIRY INTO DONALD J. TRUMP WAS DIFFERENT from prior impeachments in one key respect—in both the Clinton and Nixon impeachments, an independent counsel or special prosecutor had been appointed to conduct the investigative work and provide a report of their findings to Congress. Here, Barr's Justice Department had not only declined to appoint an independent counsel but also refused to look into the matter or allow the inspector general to do so. Forget the interests of justice—the attorney general represented Trump's interests alone. That left the matter for Congress to investigate—more particularly, our three committees. We would do those fact-finding investigations just as in the Nixon and Clinton impeachments, in closed session—followed by open hearings later.

On the evening of October 15, we had our next six-chairs meeting with the Speaker. Although the investigation of the Ukraine matter in our committee had primacy, the Judiciary Committee was still pursuing the president's obstruction of the Mueller investigation and his use of office to enrich himself in violation of the Emoluments Clause, Oversight was looking at potential fraud in his financial disclosures among a myriad of other issues, Foreign Affairs was examining misconduct at the State Department, and Financial Services was exploring potential money laundering. The Speaker had in mind that when we concluded our investigations, we would each draw up a report of our findings for the Judiciary Committee, and then we would have a discussion as a caucus as to whether impeachment was warranted and on what charges. The Ways and Means Committee was seeking the president's tax returns, but it was focused on broader oversight issues that were distinct from our efforts in the other committees. Already it was clear that there would be a significant dividing line between those who believed the president should be impeached for a broad array of misconduct on the one hand, and those, like myself, who felt that we should home in on the clearest abuse of presidential power—Ukraine. This vital difference of opinion would put me and Chairman Nadler on a collision course.

Elijah Cummings, chair of the Oversight Committee, was absent from our meeting, having been at home recovering from illness for several weeks now. Two days later, to my utter disbelief, he passed away. I had spoken to him a short time earlier by phone to see how he was doing. He was improving, and he told me that he expected to be back on the Hill within the next two weeks—only adding to my shock that he was now gone. For all of its strife, there are times when Congress is like a family, even if a dysfunctional one, and Cummings occupied a unique place among our members. In the Democratic caucus he was a moral leader, our North Star on how we ought to conduct ourselves, but he was also beloved by the Republicans, notwithstanding how polarized we had all become. His staff, who knew him best, was the most devastated. That morning, we were to begin the rescheduled deposition of Gordon Sondland, now under subpoena and willing to testify. I wrestled with what to do about this vital interview, and considered canceling it. Conferring with

Cummings's staff, however, I was convinced that Cummings would want the work to go on, and after discussing it with the Speaker, that is what we did.

I began the deposition talking about Cummings, and read a poem by Dr. Benjamin E. Mays that Cummings had recited in his first one-minute speech as a new member of Congress more than twenty years before. "I have only just a minute. Only sixty seconds in it. Forced upon me, can't refuse it, didn't seek it, didn't choose it, but it's up to me to use it. I must suffer if I lose it. Give account if I abuse it. Just a tiny little minute, but eternity is in it."

True friendships can be hard to come by on the Hill, and like all relationships, they take time. It took years, and the time we spent together on two investigations, before I really came to know, love, and admire Elijah Cummings. As a friend, I found his sudden absence shattering. And as an American, at this moment, I found his loss deeply unnerving. We would have to do our best to do right by his memory, and that meant working through our grief and defending the country he loved.

Tall, bald, and garrulous, Sondland owned and managed hotels across the country from his headquarters in the Northwest. I had run into Sondland once before, in the lobby of one of his hotels in Portland, and he struck me as every bit the hotelier and type of large Republican donor who is often chosen for an ambassadorial position.

Sondland described a meeting that he had attended with President Trump on May 23, just days after Zelensky was inaugurated. He, Volker, Perry, and others urged the president to have a phone call with the new Ukrainian leader, but the president's reaction was skeptical, even paranoid. In connection with the 2016 election, Sondland quoted the president as saying: "They tried to take me down. He kept saying that over and over." Trump told them to talk to Giuliani.

Sondland said that he had been disappointed by the president's decision to involve Giuliani, and that he "did not understand until much later that Mr. Giuliani's agenda might have also included an effort to prompt Ukrainians to investigate Vice President Biden or his son, or to involve Ukrainians directly or indirectly in the president's 2020 reelection campaign."

Like Volker, Sondland sought to downplay his culpability in the scheme by claiming that while "a public embrace of anticorruption reforms by Ukraine was one of the preconditions for securing a White House meeting with President Zelensky," this was somehow distinct from an investigation into the Bidens. Indeed, he claimed that until recent press reports, he had been unaware that Hunter Biden was even on the board of Burisma.

"So it's your testimony," I asked him, "that up until the moment you read the call record in September, you were completely oblivious to Rudy Giuliani's interest in Burisma because it involved the Bidens?"

"I never made the connection between Burisma and the Bidens," he said. "I heard the word 'Burisma,' but I didn't understand that Biden and Burisma were connected."

Nevertheless, Sondland admitted that over time there were increasing demands on Ukraine that involved both the White House meeting and the military aid. "The continuum was, first of all, an unconditional phone call and an unconditional invitation to the White House, and then I believe the next part of the continuum was some kind of a commitment to investigate corruption generally. And then the next part of the continuum was talking about Burisma and the 2016 election . . . And then at the end of that continuum I became aware that there might be a link between the White House visit and aid to Ukraine that was being held up when I couldn't get a straight answer as to why the aid was being held up . . ."

In trying to explain why he urged William Taylor to stop texting about the military aid being held up over the investigations— his "call me" message—he said, "I simply prefer to talk rather than text." Sondland also testified that after Taylor raised a concern over the linkage between the aid and the desire for the investigations, he called President Trump directly. "I asked the president, what do you want from Ukraine? The president responded, *nothing*. There is no quid pro quo. The president repeated, no quid pro quo, no quid pro quo, multiple times." Sondland said the president told him, "I want Zelensky to do the right thing." He said the call was very short and "the president was really in a bad mood."

Midway through the interview with Sondland, we took a lunch break and I left the SCIF briefly to check my phone for messages. On the television outside the SCIF, Chief of Staff Mulvaney was holding a press conference. In trying to explain why the Ukraine aid was held up, Mulvaney said it involved the president's concerns about corruption, but then he added: "Did he also mention to me in passing the corruption related to the DNC server? Absolutely. No question about that. But that's it, that's why we held up the money."

"So, so, so, the demand for an investigation into the Democrats was part of the reason that he ordered to withhold funding to Ukraine?" the ABC reporter Jonathan Karl asked.

"The look back to what happened in 2016 certainly was part of the thing he was worried about in corruption with that nation. And that is absolutely appropriate."

"In withholding the funding?" Karl persisted.

"Yeah."

Later, Karl followed up again, no doubt as astounded as the rest of us at just what Mulvaney was admitting on live television: "Let's be clear—what you just described is a quid pro quo. It is 'funding will not flow unless the investigation into the Democratic server happened as well.'"

"We do, we do that all the time with foreign policy," Mulvaney declared. Still later, he admonished the press: "Get over it. There's going to be political influence in foreign policy."

I went back into the deposition in a bit of a daze. I had thought the day would be significant on account of Sondland's much-anticipated testimony. But now, the president's chief of staff had just admitted to a quid pro quo involving $400 million in military aid tied to one of the two political investigations that Trump discussed in his "perfect" call with Zelensky on July 25. Addressing Sondland again, I made reference to the press conference and Mulvaney's admission, and after shutting down efforts by Jordan and Zeldin to interrupt the question, I asked Sondland if that was the first he was hearing of such a quid pro quo. He said that it was, reaffirming what he had said in his opening statement, that "inviting a foreign government to undertake investigations for the purpose of influencing an upcoming election would be wrong. Withholding foreign aid in order to pressure a foreign government to take such steps would be wrong. I did not and would not ever participate in such undertakings."

That statement, along with much else that Sondland had told us, was not true. And he would need to repeatedly revise and extend his testimony to keep pace with the facts we learned from other witnesses—and most particularly, Ambassador William Taylor. But before Taylor would testify, I had an important trip to take that had been too long postponed.

THE DAY AFTER SONDLAND'S TESTIMONY, I joined Speaker Pelosi on a three-day visit to Jordan and Afghanistan. The trip replaced one Pelosi had invited me to join earlier in the year. At that time, the president had shut down the government over his demand that Congress fund the border wall and said he might keep it shut for "months or even years." Pelosi sent him a letter threatening to postpone the State of the Union address, and Trump responded by canceling the military aircraft she was to use.

Now, barring any further petulant acts by the president, we were once again set to embark by military aircraft and would finally be able to visit the commanders and troops we had planned to see nine months earlier. With the Ukraine investigation well under way, the timing of the trip was difficult. But I have always felt that visiting service members on combat deployments is one of the most important responsibilities of my job. Congress alone has the power to declare war, and that authority comes with a duty—to stand with, and listen to, the men and women we send to fight those wars.

Conditions in Afghanistan were still too dangerous for a public announcement of our itinerary, so the official destination was Jordan. Trump had just announced the withdrawal of more than a thousand of our Special Forces from Kurdish territory in northeast-ern Syria, where they had spent five years fighting alongside Kurdish troops to crush the Islamic State. Our abrupt departure would leave a vacuum for Turkish forces to fill, and risk the release of ISIS fight-ers. It also meant a shameful betrayal of our Kurdish allies, and that America's reputation for standing by its friends and partners would be irrevocably tarnished. We planned to meet with King Abdullah to discuss these developments and possible responses before we con-tinued on to Kabul.

On the flight, Pelosi sat in a private section at the front, and I wandered up to speak with her. It would be a good opportunity to give her an update on the week's depositions, and I was eager to hear her thoughts on the process going forward. We had grown particu-larly close over the previous couple years, thrown into the crucible of the Trump presidency together, and I enjoyed her insights on legisla-tive strategy, the caucus, the administration, and the president. But as I settled into my seat, she brought up an issue I hadn't expected. She was planning to move forward on a bill of mine that I had been trying to pass for nearly twenty years.

My district in California is home to a large Armenian commu-nity, and one of my abiding priorities in Congress has been to pass a resolution that would recognize their unique history. A century ago, the Ottoman Empire systematically slaughtered Armenian families, destroying their villages, seizing their property, and forcing conver-sions of those left alive. By 1923, at least 1.5 million Armenians had been killed. It was at once an incomprehensible tragedy and a famil-iar current of history—a genocide rooted in religious bigotry and resentment. When Holocaust survivor Raphael Lempkin would first give a name to the crime of race slaughter and call it "genocide," he held up the Armenian experience as a preeminent case in point.

There was no credible dispute about the facts, but for a hundred years, the Turkish government had refused to accept responsibility, and threatened those that recognized the genocide. In Turkey, doing so was considered "an insult to Turkishness," and more than that, a crime for which Turkish citizens would be prosecuted. And as far as other nations were concerned, Turkey used its wealth to lobby against recognition of the genocide, and also used threats of retaliation. With an American airbase in Incirlik and Turkey's role as a NATO ally as leverage, successive American governments and congresses had shamefully succumbed to Ankara's campaign of genocide denial.

Each year, I introduced a resolution to recognize the Armenian genocide, and each year political pressures materialized to block its passage. The first time my bill was taken up in committee over a decade earlier, then-President George W. Bush began calling members personally to urge their vote against it. Many years later, when we had enough cosponsors to pass it on the House floor and began scheduling the resolution for a vote, some of my colleagues started peeling off the bill, and asking for their names to be removed. To avoid a potential loss and resulting Turkish claims that Congress had decided that there had been no genocide, our leadership held off on bringing the bill up for a vote. But now that we held the majority again, I was trying to get the resolution taken up in committee.

Pelosi had other ideas. Encouraged by my Armenian American colleague Representative Anna Eshoo, she decided, "I think we should just take it to the floor, and not even go to committee." It was an extraordinary step, bypassing any procedural logjam and leaving little time for opponents to mobilize against it. I could only hope that my sponsorship of the bill would not cause Republicans to vote against the measure.

We arrived in Jordan and spent the evening with King Abdullah, then continued to Kabul for meetings with President Ashraf Ghani and U.S. ambassador John Bass before spending time with service members. As with all of my prior trips to Afghanistan, our military leadership was optimistic that we were making progress, but from my perspective, that progress was very hard to see. There was still no resolution of the recently conducted Afghan presidential elections, and the continuing divisions in the Afghan government did not inspire confidence. The Taliban was gaining ground, with more of the country in Taliban hands every time I came to visit. Day and night we met with service members from our home states and the generals who oversaw their efforts, and one very late night, the Speaker and I met with some of our Intelligence Community professionals. I was exhausted, and I marveled at Pelosi's stamina, and her toughness. None of which surprised me. I had spent enough time with the Speaker to know just how tenacious she was, and how intrepid.

In one characteristic moment, months earlier, I had been on a sailboat with Pelosi, after a DCCC event in Hyannis Port, Massachusetts. When we left harbor, along with some of the Democratic Party's strongest supporters, the sky had been blue and the breeze fair. But not long afterward, the skies darkened, and a squall sent rough seas and cold pouring rain our way. Soon the boat was burying the rail in the water on one side, then tacking and burying the rail on the other. Teddy Kennedy, Jr., who was piloting, shouted that we could lower the sails and motor back to port. "We could," Pelosi called out, "but that would be the cowardly thing to do. I can tell you we would never do that in the San Francisco Bay." "Okay," Kennedy replied, a bit startled and with a laugh, "the sail stays up."

In the midst of our whirlwind Afghanistan itinerary, the Speaker received some heartbreaking news: Her older brother, Tommy, had passed away in Baltimore. When we had shuffled back to the plane and departed on the long flight home, I walked up the aisle to sit with her and offer my condolences. Pelosi was devastated by the loss of her brother, and as we sped through the night sky, she told me about his leadership in civil rights. Elected mayor of Baltimore in 1967, her brother had appointed a record number of Black leaders to senior positions, including the head of the fire department and the school system. His leadership during the 1968 riots earned praise from civil-rights icon Marion Bascom, who declared him "the greatest mayor in Baltimore's modern history." Pelosi was so very proud of him, and I could see just how deep the D'Alesandro family commitment to service ran.

The day I returned from Afghanistan, Republicans brought a resolution to the floor censuring me for an "egregiously false and fabricated retelling" of the president's call that "misled the American people," and brought "disrepute upon the House of Representatives," among a long list of offenses. The resolution was called up for a vote and tabled, but it had the support of the entire Republican caucus, excluding a few who declined to vote. They wouldn't stand up to this amoral president, but they would condemn anyone who did. Some of the Republicans who voted for the censure, like Liz Cheney, would soon discover that when they could no longer countenance the actions of the president, they too would be sanctioned, and by their own Republican colleagues.

The following morning, we had one of the most consequential depositions of our investigation, and members on both sides of the aisle knew it. Our first couple of interviews were sparsely attended, but by October 22 the evidence had continued to mount, and seventy-five members would crowd into our conference room for at least some portion of the testimony.

The man who took over Ambassador Yovanovitch's responsibilities in Ukraine was Chargé d'affaires William Taylor, a career diplomat. He provided our committee with a lengthy written statement that I barely had time to read before the deposition was to begin. But what I read was powerful, and if Taylor was as good a witness in person as he was on paper, the deposition was going to be a blockbuster. The moment he began speaking, I could tell that not only was he a good witness, but with his old-school gentility and a voice that struck many of us as sounding like Walter Cronkite, he was absolutely compelling.

Taylor began by describing the strategic importance of Ukraine. "First, if Ukraine succeeds in breaking free of Russian influence, it is possible for Europe to be whole, free, democratic, and at peace. In contrast, if Russia dominates Ukraine, Russia will again become an empire, oppressing its people, and threatening its neighbors and the rest of the world." When he was asked by Pompeo to return to Ukraine, where he had earlier served as an ambassador, he said he was reluctant, because he had read of Giuliani's machinations there. "I will tell you, my wife, in no uncertain terms, strongly opposed the idea." But he was guided by a senior Republican official who had been like a mentor to him and who advised: "If your country asks you to do something, you do it—if you can be effective." He would go, he told Pompeo, as long as the United States maintained its commitment to Ukraine; if that changed, he would resign.

Taylor said that once he had arrived in Kyiv, he had found "a confusing and unusual arrangement for making U.S. policy towards Ukraine. There appeared to be two channels of U.S. policy making and implementation," he said, "one regular, and one highly irregular." The regular channel consisted of U.S. diplomatic personnel. The irregular channel of U.S. policy making with respect to Ukraine included then special envoy Kurt Volker, Ambassador Sondland, Secretary of Energy Rick Perry, and Rudy Giuliani.

At first, Taylor said, both channels appeared to be working toward the goal of a stronger relationship between our country and Ukraine. By the end of June, he was no longer certain. During a call with Volker, Sondland, and Perry, he said, Volker casually referred to "what President Zelensky should do to get the meeting in the White House . . ." which included "cooperation on investigations."

"By mid-July," Taylor continued, "it was becoming clear to me that the meeting President Zelensky wanted was conditioned on the investigations of Burisma and alleged Ukrainian interference in the 2016 U.S. elections. It was also clear that this condition was driven by the irregular policy channel I had come to understand was guided by Mr. Giuliani." A few days later, on a call with a representative from the Office of Management and Budget (OMB), Taylor learned that military aid to Ukraine had been suspended "until further notice."

"I and the others on the call sat in astonishment," he said. "The Ukrainians were fighting the Russians and counted on not only the training and weapons, but also the assurance of U.S. support. All that the OMB staff person said was that the directive had come from the president to the chief of staff to the OMB. In an instant, I realized that one of the key pillars of our strong support for Ukraine was threatened. The irregular policy channel was running contrary to the goals of longstanding U.S. policy." In a July 20 conversation with the Ukrainians, Zelensky's national security adviser told Taylor that "President Zelensky did not want to be used as a pawn in a U.S. reelection campaign." The following month, when another adviser to Zelensky asked why the aid was being withheld, Taylor could provide no answer, and thought about resigning.

At the beginning of September, Vice President Pence had a brief meeting scheduled with Zelensky in Warsaw during a World War II commemoration, and Taylor hoped the meeting would result in the aid freeze being lifted. Instead, he was informed by Tim Morrison—Fiona Hill's successor on the NSC—that at the same meeting, Sondland had informed Zelensky's top adviser, Andriy Yermak, that "the security assistance would not come until President Zelensky committed to pursue the Burisma investigation."

It was now clear that when Sondland told our committee just a week earlier that "I did not and would not ever participate in such undertakings," this wasn't true. In fact, Sondland had confided in Morrison that during his conversation with Trump, when the president repeatedly declared "no quid pro quo," Trump also insisted "that President Zelensky go to a microphone and say he is opening investigations of Biden and 2016 election interference." Sondland had conveniently forgotten to tell us that part of the conversation.

According to Taylor, Sondland also said that he had told Zelensky and Yermak that "although this was not a quid pro quo, if President Zelensky did not clear things up in public, we would be at a stalemate." Taylor said that he understood a stalemate "to mean that Ukraine would not receive the much-needed assistance." Sondland told Taylor that the conversation with Zelensky ultimately ended when the Ukrainian president agreed to make the announcement of the investigations on CNN.

> Ambassador Sondland also told me that he now recognized that he had made a mistake by earlier telling the Ukrainian officials to whom he spoke that a White House meeting with President Zelensky was dependent on a public announcement of investigations—in fact, Ambassador Sondland said, "everything" was

dependent on such an announcement, including security assistance. He said that President Trump wanted President Zelensky in a box by making a public statement about ordering such investigations.

Ambassador Sondland tried to explain to me that President Trump is a businessman. When a businessman is about to sign a check to someone who owes him something, he said, the businessman asks that person to pay up before signing the check. Ambassador Volker used the same terms several days later when we were together at the Yalta European Strategy Conference in Kyiv. I argued to both that the explanation made no sense. The Ukrainians did not owe President Trump anything, and holding up security assistance for domestic political gain was crazy, as I had said in my text message [to both of them].

Taylor pushed to get the Ukraine aid released, but he learned that Bolton and others were having a difficult time getting on the president's schedule. "I think this was also about the time of the Greenland question, about purchasing Greenland, which took up a lot of energy in the NSC," Taylor explained.

"Okay," I replied, interrupting Taylor, "that's disturbing for a whole different reason."

Taylor's testimony was devastating to the president's apologists. Not only was it clear that Trump had conditioned the military aid on a political favor from Zelensky, but Taylor had taken careful and copious notes of his conversations, putting quotation marks around exact language. Nevertheless, Republicans tried to quarrel with Taylor's account, attacking it as hearsay. Ratcliffe even suggested that since Taylor wasn't a lawyer, he might not know what quid pro quo really meant. This gave me an opening to have a little fun.

"When you talk about 'conditioned,'" I asked Taylor, "did you mean that if they didn't do this—the investigations—they weren't going to get that—the meeting and the military assistance?"

"That was my clear understanding," Taylor replied, "security assistance money would not come until the president committed to pursue the investigation."

"So if they don't do *this,* they are not going to get *that,* was your understanding?"

"Yes, sir."

"Are you aware that 'quid pro quo' literally means 'this for that'?"

Ambassador Taylor betrayed a small smile, the first of his long deposition, before replying: "I am."

There was one more important revelation to come out of Taylor's deposition, but it did not come from Taylor. During the course of the Ukraine interviews, Nunes had remained relatively quiet and unengaged, leaving the role of primary Trump defender to Jordan, Meadows, and Zeldin. But he came alive for one brief moment during the Taylor deposition, informing Taylor and all of us present of another disturbing counterinvestigation that Nunes was evidently engaged in: "You may not be aware," Nunes told Taylor, "but at least the Republicans on this committee were very concerned by Ukraine's actions during the 2016 election, and they have long been a target of our investigation and have continued today to try to get to the bottom of what they were up to in the 2016 election." I looked to my staff and Democratic colleagues to see whether they knew what he was talking about or were just as surprised as I was. Their faces showed the same puzzlement. "So that is our real concern in Ukraine over the 2016 election. So I understand that you, as an ambassador, you don't like to get involved in politics, but the fact of the matter is the Ukrainians decided to get involved in politics and be, in almost all cases, supportive of the Democrats and helped to deliver dirt that was then used—"

It was at that point that I came to suspect Nunes had been using the committee to conduct the same sham investigation that Trump sought to get the Ukrainians to do, an investigation into a Kremlin talking point that it was Ukraine, not Russia, that had been interfering in the 2016 election, and to help Hillary. It was a stunning revelation, but I would soon come to find out that the problem went much deeper, and certain Republicans in the Senate were engaged in much the same conduct, including the senator whom Sondland had originally told of the quid pro quo—Ron Johnson.

Following Taylor's devastating testimony, and Mulvaney's admission, the general outlines of the president's abuse of power and many of its details were now plain. Trump had conditioned official actions—a White House phone call, Oval Office meeting, and military assistance—on Ukraine's willingness to help him cheat in the next election by smearing his opponent. The remaining depositions would be devoted to filling in the few missing pieces and corroborating the evidence we already had. We could see the evidence of Trump's guilt mounting, and so could the Republicans, who became desperate. But no one was more desperate than the president himself.

Trump invited several of the Freedom Caucus members to the White House to talk strategy with him. There, he must have repeated his claims of the previous day, when he demanded that Republicans "get tougher and fight," and said that Democrats were "vicious" in the pursuit of his Ukraine actions and "stick together." "We have some that are great fighters," he had said, "but they have to get tougher and fight, because the Democrats are trying to hurt the Republican Party before the election." It wouldn't be long before I would get a vivid taste of how the president and his most devoted supporters in the House were planning to "get tougher," in a stunt that would come to have its own name and lore: "the storming of the SCIF."

THE NEXT MORNING, I WALKED down the stairs to the SCIF and noticed a podium set up in the Pit of Despair. I wasn't aware of anyone else using such an out-of-the-way location for speaking engagements or press functions, and it struck me as odd. Boland informed me that a large group of Republican members, including some of their leadership—like second-ranking GOP whip Steve Scalise—were planning to hold a press conference in the well to attack the impeachment inquiry. "Whatever," I said, shrugging it off.

Eve and I celebrate my election to Congress in 2000 after defeating Jim Rogan, one of the Clinton impeachment House managers.

My grandfather, Harry Glovsky (right), was from the GOP side of my family, and an elector for Dwight D. Eisenhower in 1952.

Outside the criminal courts building in Los Angeles in 1991, after leaving the U.S. Attorney's Office to run—unsuccessfully—for the State Assembly. I came in eleventh.

At a hearing of
the Select Committee
on Benghazi, confer-
ring with my dear
friend Representative
Elijah Cummings,
the moral North Star
for our caucus.

After ambushing me
with a call for my
resignation, Repub-
licans couldn't look
me in the eye when
I spelled out the
corrupt conduct they
were condoning:
"You might think
that's okay."

After he blocked
early witnesses in
the Ukraine investi-
gation, I wondered
if Trump would
again escape
accountability.

Conferring on strategy for the open hearings. If I was a general, Speaker Nancy Pelosi was the Supreme Allied Commander.

William Taylor texted Ambassador Gordon Sondland, "As I said on the phone, I think it's crazy to withhold security assistance for help with a political campaign."

Sondland acted like he was at a party, even as he told us, "Everyone was in the loop."

David Holmes demonstrates how Sondland had to hold the phone away from his ear because Trump talked so loudly.

Representative Devin Nunes and I, here arguing a point during one of the Ukraine hearings, had once been close working partners. Now we were occupying two different worlds.

In the anteroom behind the Ways and Means hearing room, after Ukraine testimony, members and staff of the Intelligence Committee giving each other a hard time and watching the coverage.

Just as we began Ukraine public hearings, Representative Jim Jordan was put on the Intelligence Committee to try to make a circus out of them. He did not succeed.

Ambassador Marie Yovanovitch's courage, at home and abroad, demonstrated that you can stand up to the most powerful people in the world.

Fiona Hill warned Republicans about advancing the false Russian narrative that Ukraine, not Russia, interfered in the 2016 election.

Despite his combat tours and Purple Heart, there was an innocence to Alexander Vindman. As he told his dad, "Do not worry, I will be fine for telling the truth."

Speaker Pelosi introduces the House managers for the first impeachment trial, a team as diverse as the country.

"All right. Time to line up," the Speaker's staff would call out when the trial was resuming and it was time to head back onto the Senate floor.

Preparing for the first day of question and answer during the trial, I confer with my brilliant general counsel, Maher Bitar, and equally brilliant chief of investigations, Rheanne Wirkkala. Staff prepared hundreds of potential questions and answers.

Super Bowl Sunday, 2020, working on my closing statement, "Midnight in Washington." Eve and Eli would go next door to watch the game with our neighbors.

At trial in the Senate: "Whenever we have departed from the values of our nation, we have come to regret it, and that regret is written all over the pages of our history."

Senator Mitt Romney delivers his verdict in the first trial and answers the question of whether the president committed an act "so extreme and egregious" that it warrants impeachment: "Yes, he did."

But I could tell that Boland was concerned, which concerned me; he seemed to have a sixth sense when it came to spotting trouble. Boland had great relationships with the press, and he was often getting wind of things before anyone else in our office. Still, he couldn't make out what they were planning.

I went inside the conference room and introduced myself to Deputy Assistant Secretary of Defense Laura Cooper, who had arrived early for her deposition. She was an important witness and had knowledge of some of the circumstances behind the withholding of the aid, but I wasn't expecting any fireworks. Before we could get started, though, my staff alerted me to the presence of several Republican members who were not authorized to participate in the deposition. Soon the double doors were flung open and a cascade of GOP rabble-rousers clamored into the room demanding to be included. "So this is the secret bunker!" one of them yelled. "Oooh, this is where it's all going down!" They had stormed past the security guard and into the bunker, bringing their cellphones with them, an extremely serious breach of the SCIF security protocols. These were GPS tracking devices with high-resolution cameras and microphones that could be commandeered by an adversary, and they were now in a secure facility where highly classified information was housed. The usual suspects were among the deposition crashers, including, once again, the congressbro from Florida, Matt Gaetz, and they began to loudly attack the process we were using—even though it was the same process Nunes and Gowdy had used when they were in the majority. I apologized to Ms. Cooper for the interruption and asked my staff to escort her across the hall.

I told the Republican crashers they needed to leave, and it was urgent that they take their phones with them. I reminded Meadows and Jordan that we had already been through this once before with Gaetz, and the parliamentarian had ruled against the continued presence of members not on any of the three committees. Interestingly, some of the crashers *were* members of the three committees, but they didn't seem to be aware that they didn't need to crash the proceedings—they could have simply walked through the door. But

I could tell they were interested in a brawl, in making a circus of the proceedings, and I wouldn't let them. I simply got up and walked out. Representative Bradley Byrne of Alabama, among the most belligerent of the crashers, yelled at me as I left—*"Don't leave! Don't walk out!"*—and seemed genuinely upset that I wouldn't stay to quarrel with them. I went back to my office.

Because of the security breach, it wasn't long before Paul Irving, the House sergeant at arms, came down to my office. The crashers were still in the conference room, arguing it out with several of my Democratic colleagues, their voices loud enough to be heard all the way down the hall. I could hear Representative Val Demings, my Democratic colleague from Florida and the former police chief of Orlando, asking the Republicans if this was what they wanted to teach their children and hurling biblical injunctions against them in her beautiful deep voice.

As Irving, my staff, and a few Democratic members huddled in my small office, he laid out the options. We could have the Capitol Police come down and eject them, but that would cause a scene. We could reschedule the deposition, but that would allow them to declare victory and encourage them to crash every deposition in the future. Or we could simply allow them to stay and ignore the deposition rules. None of those options made sense to me, least of all calling the Capitol Police. They would like nothing better than to cause an altercation. We would have to let the Ethics Committee sort it out later. But for now, "We need them to get rid of their electronics." Apart from that, I said, "We will just wait them out. They will get bored and leave on their own."

"Adam Schiff just SHUT DOWN his secret underground impeachment hearing after I led a group of Republicans into the room. Now he's threatening me with an Ethics complaint!" bragged Byrne on Twitter. "Reporting from Adam Schiff's secret chamber," Representative Andy Biggs declared. "Adam Schiff, clearly peeved that he will no longer be able to hide his impeachment sham, is threatening Ethics punishment for all of us," Representative Mark Walker bragged. It was like spring break in there, and the rebels soon ordered pizza, but the violation of the security of the space where we keep some of the nation's most closely guarded secrets was no joke.

It wasn't long before Meadows wandered into my office and sought to play the role of peacemaker. He wasn't very good at it. And besides, why he thought this juvenile stunt entitled him to negotiate with anybody for anything was beyond me. He complained again about the exclusion of non-committee members, and I reminded him of the rules and Gowdy's expulsion of a non-committee member, Republican Darrell Issa, from attending his own depositions: "Non-committee members are not allowed in the room during the deposition," Gowdy had said. "Those are the rules and we have to follow them, no exceptions made." Unmoved by the hypocrisy, Meadows also complained about the fact that information was leaking to the press. It was true that several witnesses or their counsel released their opening statements to the press so they could control the public narrative of their testimony rather than let members mischaracterize it for them. But that was their prerogative; the confidentiality rules only apply to the members, and the witnesses can discuss whatever they want with the press as long as it is not classified. Finally, Meadows sought to use the crashers as leverage with which to bargain for unmonitored access to the transcripts.

Bitar, my committee's general counsel, then interjected: "Mr. Chairman, the only transcript that has leaked so far was Volker's, and that happened immediately after it was provided to the minority."

"Shut up, smart-ass," Meadows erupted, his face turning red.

"Whoa, whoa, whoa!" we all responded in unison. "That is totally out of line," I said. Embarrassed, Meadows apologized to Bitar, and the fight went out of him. We reached no resolution, however, and Meadows soon returned to the conference room, where the Republicans were still having a heck of a time.

"Let's ask the Speaker if we can move up votes," my staff suggested, as that might finally shoo the revelers from the bunker. And sure enough, not long thereafter, bored and stuffed with pizza, Gaetz and his confederates left the bunker to vote and never bothered to come back. Five hours after she had arrived, I invited Laura Cooper to return to the conference room, apologized for wasting her time, and we got back to work.

Storming the bunker wasn't the only means of "fighting harder," or the most serious. On October 24, the day after the storming of the SCIF, we learned that Barr had authorized a criminal investigation into his own department's Russia investigation. For two years, Trump had been attacking the Russia probe and calling for retribution, and now Barr was prepared to deliver it, using the awesome power of the Justice Department to go after the president's opponents and potentially deprive them of their liberty. John Durham, the prosecutor Barr chose to conduct an "administrative review" of the investigation's predication, was now empowered to convene a grand jury and pursue a criminal prosecution of the president's enemies. It wasn't at all clear what crime or crimes Durham was supposed to investigate, but the mere opening of the investigation would give Trump another opportunity to claim vindication. It was also another hammer stroke against the rule of law. In the middle of an impeachment inquiry, Trump had ordered up a criminal investigation as retribution against his investigators, further demonstrating his unfitness for office.

This dangerous new escalation was driven by the president's desperation. Not only had Taylor's testimony been devastating, but public polling was now showing an increase in support for the impeachment inquiry, *and* the conviction and removal of the president from office. An October 9 Fox poll in particular had the president worried and irate, when it showed that a slight majority of Americans now favored his removal from office. "From the day I announced I was running for President," Trump tweeted in exasperation, "I have NEVER had a good @FoxNewsPoll. Whoever their pollster is, they suck." Ever the dutiful servant, Barr took the unprecedented step of obtaining a private meeting with Rupert Murdoch, the owner of Fox's parent company, at his home, but he refused to tell reporters what they discussed.

At the same time, Florida Republican Francis Rooney, a moderate in the mold of my Republican grandparents, was the first to declare himself open to considering articles of impeachment. I was impressed with Rooney, who had participated in a couple of our depositions and defended their fairness. But his comments were a heresy to Trump and his party, and within twenty-four hours of saying he was open to impeachment, he was forced to announce he would not seek reelection.

On October 24, Elijah Cummings lay in state in the Capitol Rotunda, a tremendous honor rarely given to a member of Congress. I circled his coffin, then approached it and leaned down to whisper: "Thank you, Elijah. For giving us all an example to follow. Love you, my friend. And miss you."

I left the Rotunda to go to the Speaker's office for another meeting of the chairs. The Speaker said she thought it was time to bring a resolution to the floor to formalize our impeachment proceedings, something I favored as well, since it would allow us to structure the open hearings. We had been conducting the depositions with three committees participating, and there was no way we could hold open hearings with more than a hundred members involved. Representative Engel, chair of the Foreign Affairs Committee, said he was deeply interested in participating, but the Speaker decided that the Intelligence Committee should conduct the proceedings with only its members. I could see that Engel was devastated, and he told me privately that he thought he had been sidelined. He was in a very competitive primary back home, and he was worried this would reflect poorly on him. I tried to assure him that this was not the case, and it would have been impossible to make exceptions for individual members, even as respected as him, without opening it up to the Republicans to do the same and for people far less deserving.

Once the Intelligence Committee concluded its open hearings, we would compile the transcripts and other evidence and draft a report, which our committee counsel would then present to the Judiciary Committee during an open session. The discussion with Pelosi then moved to the rules governing additional hearings in the Judiciary Committee, the minority's right to call witnesses, and the president's ability to present a defense. Here, matters became even more uncomfortable. Congressman Jerry Nadler of New York is one of our most respected members, with a brilliant mind and expansive knowledge of the Constitution and devotion to its core principles. And, like any true New York City Democrat, he is bold and unapologetic in sharing his progressive views. It was very important to Nadler that once the matter reached his Judiciary Committee, the president be afforded all the due process provided to his predecessors when they faced impeachment. This meant, among other things, a full opportunity for the White House to participate in his committee's hearing. What's more, Nadler needed to look out for the members of his committee, who would want to be fully involved in any impeachment proceedings as well.

I agreed with Nadler that the rules governing the participation of the president should be the same as those in the Nixon and Clinton impeachments, but unlike prior impeachments, the factual investigation had been conducted in the Intelligence Committee because of the nature of the complaint. Our committee should be the one to hear from fact witnesses, I argued, and Judiciary Committee should hear from the constitutional experts. There was no need for the Judiciary Committee to duplicate our work by calling the same people, and doing so would add a lot of risk.

I could tell that Nadler wasn't thrilled with this, and knew that members of his staff would be even less pleased, particularly those who had been hired to conduct an impeachment investigation. But there was a certain undeniable logic that Nadler recognized even if he didn't like: The minority would have the right to request fact witnesses in our committee, and it made little sense to duplicate that process elsewhere. The Speaker was likewise disinclined to have fact witnesses appearing in multiple committees, and, reluctantly, Nadler agreed. There was one more issue I flagged, although we did not resolve it: What was to stop the White House from selectively submitting documents to the Judiciary Committee that they thought helped them, while withholding other documents that would incriminate them?

The pace of depositions had picked up dramatically since Marie

Yovanovitch broke the president's blockade, and we were now interviewing witnesses almost every day, using the same last-minute service of subpoenas that had worked so well with her. The next significant witness was Charles Kupperman, who had been deputy to former National Security Advisor Bolton. We knew that we would ultimately want to interview Bolton, but we thought it made sense to climb the ladder of witnesses before we got to him, and Kupperman was the next logical step.

I also didn't trust Bolton, who had no business being National Security Advisor. He was bellicose, hotheaded, and obstinate, the last three qualities you want in someone who is supposed to mediate differences among national security cabinet members. When Bolton had been appointed the previous year, I criticized him for trafficking in the most bizarre conspiracy theories on Fox in order to catch Trump's attention. He had made the astounding suggestion that the Russian hack of the DNC in 2016 might not have been conducted by the Russians at all and could have been a "false flag" operation by the Obama administration. It took me a while to get my head around it, but the idea was that Obama hacked his own party's headquarters so that he could blame the Russians, and this would somehow help Hillary Clinton. After I called him out on the reckless propagation of this conspiracy theory, Bolton's staff called my office day after day demanding a retraction. For what, it wasn't clear—we had the tape of his appearance on Fox and offered to send it to them.

"What do you think of Michael Bolton being named National Security Advisor?" a Democratic colleague had asked me on the House floor at the time. "Well," I replied, "I think you mean John Bolton. Michael Bolton is a singer. But honestly, I would feel better with Michael Bolton."

Kupperman was represented by Charles Cooper, a conservative lawyer who had hoped to be named solicitor general by Trump but was passed over. Cooper also represented Bolton, and we figured that he would take the same approach for both witnesses. Cooper implied that Kupperman was cooperative, but he demanded the subpoena be served on Friday, several days before Kupperman's

Monday testimony. This raised our suspicions, but Cooper was insistent, and we had little choice but to risk the extra time this would allow for mischief.

No sooner was Kupperman served with his subpoena than his attorney filed a seventeen-page complaint in federal district court seeking a declaratory judgment about whether he should testify. The complaint cited White House counsel's reliance on an opinion of the OLC prepared by the Justice Department that was clearly orchestrated between Kupperman and the White House days ahead of time, and which claimed that Kupperman was "absolutely immune" from testifying. This was nonsense. As we wrote back to Cooper, "The White House and Department of Justice cite no authority allowing the President to direct private citizens, like your client, to disobey a congressional subpoena." But the problem this presented was less a legal one, and more one of time, and the endless amount of it necessary to litigate the matter. For Kupperman and Bolton, we feared, delay was the whole point.

The case was assigned to Federal District Judge Richard Leon, a George W. Bush appointee who grew up not far from my hometown of Framingham, Massachusetts, and attended the same law school I did, but that's about all we had in common. Leon seemed to delight in the high-profile case, even if it plainly lacked merit. The same claim of absolute immunity had been made in the case of former White House counsel Don McGahn, and more than half a year later, it was still being litigated in court. The district judge in that case was about to rule, and we proposed to Cooper that both sides simply agree to be bound by that court's decision. Cooper claimed that Kupperman was willing to testify, but he wanted court guidance as to whether his client should. If this was true, and Kupperman wasn't merely using the court for purposes of delay, there was no reason for him not to agree to be bound by the court's decision in the McGahn case. But Kupperman refused, and that told us all we needed to know. For all of Bolton's newfound public posturing about standing up to Trump, it was clear that both he and Kupperman were unwilling to show the same courage as those who worked for them—people like Fiona Hill and our next witness, Army Lt. Col. Alexander Vindman.

OCTOBER 29 WAS ONE OF those days when everything was happening at once, and I was needed in three places at the same time. The previous evening, I had seen a draft of the impeachment inquiry resolution for the first time, and it made provision for the minority to be able to request fact witnesses in the Judiciary Committee. This ran contrary to what I thought had already been agreed to in the meeting with the Speaker and I needed to resolve any differences with the Judiciary Committee by early afternoon. But that morning, we had the Vindman deposition, and in the late afternoon, I had the Armenian Genocide resolution coming up for a vote, and I needed to be present on the House floor to whip it. I didn't know how I was going to do all that.

In my office in the SCIF at 8:30 A.M., I quickly reviewed the impeachment resolution text again and handwrote some proposed changes on the issue of fact witnesses and a variation on the idea I had raised earlier which would make some of the White House participation in the Judiciary Committee contingent on complying with the subpoenas. Then I rushed down the hall.

Vindman had already arrived and he was nervous. He had a right to be. The right-wing commentariat and other Trump defenders had been questioning Vindman's loyalty to America. Vindman, who had served two tours in Iraq and earned a Purple Heart when his vehicle was hit with an improvised explosive device, had immigrated to the United States with his parents when he was a child. That's all it took for Fox hosts to cast aspersions on the patriotism of an American soldier who had risked his life for his country. The night before his deposition, Laura Ingraham and her guests suggested that Vindman was betraying the United States by advising Ukraine on how to deal with Giuliani's meddling in their affairs. "Some people might call that espionage," former Justice Department lawyer and torture memo author John Yoo remarked. "He tends to feel simpatico with the Ukraine," *Fox and Friends* cohost Brian Kilmeade said of Vindman. And early that morning, former Republican representative Sean Duffy added: "It seems very clear that he is incredibly concerned about Ukrainian defense; I don't know that he's concerned about American policy."

Greeting Vindman before his testimony, I tried to make him feel at ease. He was still on active duty, still on the job, and he had come to tell the truth about the most powerful man in the world. Dressed in his impeccable military uniform, he struck me as shy, a straight shooter, someone who did not invite attention to himself but was guided by a strong sense of right and wrong and patriotic duty. When we began his deposition, I thanked him for his dedicated service to the country and told him that "Congress will not tolerate any reprisal, threat of reprisal, or attempt to retaliate" against him or any of his colleagues. Even as I said it, though, I fretted over whether we really had the power to protect him, given the norms the president had been shattering.

Lt. Col. Vindman was a regional expert and director for European affairs for the National Security Council, and it was that expertise that made him a target for the White House. After an opening statement, he gave us new detail on the July 10 meeting in the Ward Room, contradicting Sondland's testimony, and making it clear that Sondland told the Ukrainians "the importance that Ukraine deliver the investigation into the 2016 elections, the Bidens, and Burisma." Vindman said he told Sondland that his statements were inappropriate and that "the request to investigate the Bidens and his son had nothing to do with national security, and that such investigations were not something that the NSC was going to get involved in or push." Following the meeting in the Ward Room, Vindman was concerned enough over Sondland's efforts to tie the investigations to a White House meeting that he reported the matter to NSC legal counsel John Eisenberg.

Vindman also testified that he listened in on the July 25 call between Trump and Zelensky from the Situation Room and took notes, and that he did not think it was proper for the president "to demand that a foreign government investigate a U.S. citizen." He realized that if Ukraine was drawn into our partisan politics in this manner, "it would cause that nation to lose bipartisan support," and that this would "undermine U.S. national security." He said he had also reported his concerns about the president's call with Zelensky to Eisenberg.

Vindman said two other very notable things. The first was "I want the committee to know that I am not the whistleblower. . . ." Up until he said that, I'm not sure that I was aware of speculation that Vindman might be the whistleblower. And second, he said that he did not know the identity of the whistleblower and would not feel comfortable speculating as to their identity.

In concluding his prepared remarks, Vindman said that it was a great honor to serve the American people "and a privilege to work in the White House and on the National Security Council." He was so genuine in saying it, so proud of what he had been able to accomplish as a first-generation American, that I was moved by his words. I thought about how proud my parents were to see me elected to Congress, as the grandson of immigrants from a similar part of the world as Vindman's family had come from, and I could easily relate to his experience. "I hope to continue to serve and advance America's national security interests," he said finally, and the statement had a wistful quality about it. He knew that he was risking everything.

If the attacks on his patriotism that took place before Vindman's deposition were shameful, what took place three floors underneath the Capitol that day was every bit as much a disgrace. Ratcliffe carried on a line of questioning that sought to further the Fox narrative of disloyalty, suggesting that Vindman was working against the interests of the United States. "So you," Ratcliffe began, "a week following you listening in on a phone call with the president of the United States making a request of the Ukrainian government to assist in ongoing investigations, a member of his National Security Council subsequently told Ukrainian officials to do just the opposite and ignore his request and stay out of U.S. politics. Is that what we are to understand from your testimony today?"

"That's an interesting characterization, Congressman. I was certainly not going against the orders of my commander in chief. What I was suggesting is that . . . staying out of U.S. domestic politics is a good idea."

Ratcliffe continued to press the matter until Vindman's counsel stepped in: "If you guys want to go down this road, God be with you. But I'm telling you, it's so cynical for you to go down such a road with an individual like this."

Efforts to suggest Vindman had been disloyal to the country were not the only low road Republicans would take that day. Over the course of several hours, the Republican counsel, Steve Castor, with the full support of Meadows, Jordan, and Zeldin, sought to use Vindman to disclose the identity of the whistleblower. "Who did you speak to?" "Who is that?" "Who?" they asked. To protect the whistleblower I made a ruling that "the witness may refrain from identifying any employee, detailee, or contractor of the Intelligence Community." Nevertheless, the Republicans continued their efforts.

At 10:15 A.M., I got an urgent message from my staff. I was needed for an emergency meeting in the Speaker's office to finalize outstanding issues on the impeachment inquiry resolution. Rushing upstairs, I joined the Speaker, Nadler, Rules Committee chairman Jim McGovern, and the House general counsel, Doug Letter. Nadler was insisting on affording the right to the minority to request fact witnesses, and if they were unjustified, he would vote them down. I told him that he would be under immense pressure to allow extraneous witnesses like Hunter Biden and the whistleblower, just as we had been, and he assured us that he could take the heat. I believed him, and so did the Speaker. I wasn't thrilled with it, but the language Nadler wanted would stay in.

We then turned to my proposal to give Nadler the power to exclude certain White House documents or participation if they didn't respond to our subpoenas. I didn't want the president's lawyers, having withheld all of the documents requested by our committees, to be able to suddenly waltz into the Judiciary Committee and cherry-pick certain documents they believed would help exculpate the president and introduce them into the record. In civil cases, a rule of completeness prohibits one party from introducing a document that tells one story, and precluding the other party from revealing documents that should be considered along with it. This was a variation on that concept.

Nadler said he was uncomfortable with the idea, and so was McGovern. "That has never been done before," Nadler said. "That's true," I replied, "but no president has ever stonewalled Congress like this before. What's to stop them from selectively pulling out a few emails that help them and hiding all the rest?" I understood why Nadler was upset—he would take all the heat for any departure from precedent in his committee, and he was utterly devoted to due process. But then, so was I, including our own compulsory process. "These people are ruthless," the Speaker interjected, breaking it up. "I wouldn't trust them any further than . . . I wouldn't trust them at all. Not a single one of them. They're not on the level." The Speaker didn't think we should give them an inch, and requested that we work out language, but to do it fast.

I went back into the Vindman deposition. In my absence, the Republicans had continued their efforts to use Vindman to out the whistleblower, and I needed to make sure matters didn't get further out of control. It had already been pretty heated earlier that morning, between Swalwell and Meadows, with Meadows telling Swalwell to "shut up," just as he had with my general counsel. But within an hour of my returning to the deposition, I was interrupted again; Nadler was on his way down to the SCIF and wanted to talk to me. There were competing understandings of what had been agreed to in the Speaker's office again, and we needed to figure it out.

I thought a private talk with Nadler would help us clear the air. I had served on the Judiciary Committee with Nadler for a decade and he had a tremendous grasp of the issues, and I liked his fierce dedication to the underdog. I also felt that he was being given a bum rap by the press, which had been pushing out a story line that he was being sidelined in the impeachment inquiry. It didn't help that Republicans on Nadler's committee kept trying to needle him about the role our committee was playing. The center of gravity in the investigation had moved to the Intelligence Committee through no failing of Nadler's, only because the whistleblower was connected to the Intelligence Community and filed the complaint with our inspector general. If there was to be an impeachment, the Judiciary Committee would still be the body to draft and take up any articles, and that would be a singular responsibility. Already, Nadler was zeroing in on a potential rubric for Trump's Ukraine misconduct, focused on a single article alleging "abuse of power." And while no decision had been made about other potential articles, the Speaker's operating instructions were clear—the case against Trump must be powerful, direct, and easy to communicate to the public.

When Nadler arrived in the SCIF, though, he was not alone; he brought a phalanx of his committee staff, including his deputy chief counsel, Aaron Hiller, and three attorneys he had brought on to help him with the impeachment investigation—Barry Berke, a very talented defense lawyer who had done a remarkable job questioning the obstreperous Lewandowski during the hearing in their committee, Norman Eisen, an eccentric and accomplished ethicist and gifted writer, and Joshua Matz, an expert on impeachment and coauthor of two books with Laurence Tribe.

It was suddenly very crowded in my small office in the SCIF. I sat behind my desk and Nadler took the plush leather seat to my left. All along the back wall, standing, or sitting in chairs, or leaning against the large safe or small refrigerator, the staff were packed shoulder to shoulder. My staff, Judiciary staff, the Speaker's staff, the House counsel, it was all hands on deck when Nadler lit into me.

"I resent you dictating what the procedures should be in my committee," he said, ticking off one finger. "I resent you forcing this issue with the Speaker at the last minute," ticking off another finger. "I resent being forced to accept a provision that may be unconstitutional."

I was more than taken aback by this ambush. "Well, I resent reaching an agreement with you and the Speaker and then having to renegotiate it every time," I countered. "And I resent how you are going to throw away any leverage we might have to get them to comply, not just with my subpoenas, but with all of our subpoenas. I've been fighting these people for three years and you're unilaterally surrendering to Trump."

Boland leaned over to Wells Bennett, my deputy general counsel, and handed him a yellow Post-it that read: "This is one of the times that I regret coming to a meeting that I didn't know anything about. Oops."

Nevertheless, it was cathartic for Nadler and me to finally vent our differences and get it all out on the table. Eisen and I argued over the constitutional issues, and I told him that as we had "the sole power of impeachment," we could establish any reasonable limitation on the president's right to participate that was appropriate under the circumstances. Eisen then dropped the big guns: "Larry Tribe will tweet at us!" I had to laugh at that, and so did he, and a bit of the tension left the room. "With all due respect, Norm," I said to Eisen, "let Larry tell me his views himself."

Then I went back into the deposition and left the staff to figure it out. The staff had much cooler heads than either Nadler or myself. Maher Bitar and Wells Bennett on my staff got together with Eisen, Berke, and Matz and succeeded in crafting compromise language that everyone agreed was fully constitutional and they could live with, and presumably, so could Larry Tribe. My staff brought it to me on the House floor during votes, and Nadler's staff brought it to him, and we both gave it the thumbs-up.

The final language invited the president or his counsel to participate in the Judiciary Committee proceedings, call and examine witnesses, and provide other evidence for their defense, but it also provided that "Should the President unlawfully refuse to make witnesses available for testimony to, or to produce documents requested by, the investigative committees . . . the chair shall have the discretion to impose appropriate remedies, including by denying specific requests by the President or his counsel under these procedures to call or question witnesses."

Nadler had been right to insist on mirroring the language in the

Clinton and Nixon impeachments on due process for the minority and White House. And I was relieved that we were not giving the Trump administration carte blanche to stonewall and mislead Congress. It wasn't easy getting there, but the final result was a good one. Tribe's tweet, when it came, was supportive, and as many of us debating the matter were his former students, we were grateful for that.

Later that day, I took out a piece of personal stationery and wrote Nadler a note. I was upset about our confrontation, he was a friend and more than that, someone I liked and admired. As I recall, I told him how much I valued him, and wanted to work together. That we had a tremendous responsibility to carry out, and more than enough work for both of us. And that I had great confidence that when the matter reached his committee, we couldn't be in better hands.

I hoped that it would ease some of the friction between us; we really were all in this together.

That afternoon, I had a long-sought and poignant victory on the House floor. After nineteen years of struggle, my resolution recognizing the Armenian genocide had finally come up for a vote. I had some trepidation that Republicans would vote against the bill, so great had their animus toward my work become, and we considered asking for a voice vote. But we decided to put every member on the record and test the relative strength of their support for historical truth measured against their animosity toward the author of the bill. It passed by a vote of 405–11. I was elated. Over the years, I had sat in the homes of the few genocide survivors remaining, and as I looked up at the green "yeses" on the voting board, I thought of one in particular, Ghazaros Kademian. I had met Mr. Kademian on the occasion of his hundredth birthday, and he told me of surviving the forced marches in the deserts of Syria to escape Ottoman forces. He arrived in Kirkuk and built a family and a life there as a truck driver. During the pogroms against the Jews in Iraq in the early 1940s, this genocide survivor had risked his life to help Jews smuggle their belongings to Tehran so they could start a new life in safety. "What you are doing for the Armenian people," Ghazaros told me, "is reward for what my family did for the Jews of Baghdad." I only wished that Ghazaros had been alive to see the bill pass.

Back in my district a couple of weeks later, I attended an Armenian community function celebrating passage of the genocide resolution. About two hundred people crowded into the auditorium at the Glendale Central Library, filling the room to capacity. Many in the audience were elderly, in suit and tie, and the children of genocide survivors. But others were wearing jackets with right-wing insignia, and as soon as the event began, they took the jackets off to reveal Trump T-shirts. When I was invited up to the podium, a few protesters took out signs that said, "Don't impeach." When the children of survivors asked them to lower the signs so they could see, the protesters refused. "Liar!" one of them yelled as I began speaking. "You will be going to jail for treason!" another screamed. "No disrespect to you all," one of the Trump supporters told the audience, "I'm glad you guys are getting recognized for your genocide, but this man is a fucking liar!"

And then the scuffles broke out. I saw an eighty-year-old friend, a descendant of survivors, bring his arm back to punch one of the agitators, who looked like an extra from a ZZ Top cover band. My security team looked at me apprehensively, wanting to know, I'm sure, whether I thought it was time to get out of Dodge. I did not. I wasn't about to let these professional agitators who had come from other parts of Los Angeles County drive me away from my constituents. Supporters began yelling, "Adam! Adam!" and additional squad cars were on their way. After finishing my remarks, I walked across the stage toward the stairs, and one of the agitators reached up to grab my arm. Whether he meant to pull me off the stage or what he had in mind, I do not know, but he never got the chance. The head of my security detail, Derren Fuentes, a very muscular six foot four, grabbed his arm, wrested it from me, and shoved the man away like he was a toy. The man was taken aback, but took one look at Fuentes and that was enough to persuade him that he would be wise to go his own way.

. . .

By Halloween we had abandoned the idea of bringing in the whistleblower for a deposition, both because there was no way to ensure their security and because we now had firsthand witnesses that could attest to the allegations they raised in the complaint. Most significant, we also had a transcript of the call, which was at the core of the whistleblower complaint. That day we deposed Tim Morrison, Fiona Hill's successor at the NSC, and his testimony put Sondland at further risk of perjury. Morrison, a Republican former Hill staffer, testified that when he took over for Hill, she confided that Sondland and Giuliani were trying to get President Zelensky to "reopen Ukrainian investigations into Burisma." At the time, Morrison did not know anything about Burisma or what investigation she was referring to. "After the meeting with Dr. Hill, I googled 'Burisma' and learned that it was a Ukrainian energy company and that Hunter Biden was on its board." For all of Sondland's and Volker's false protestations that they never connected Burisma with the Bidens, it took Morrison all of about thirty seconds to find out the link with the simple expedient of a Google search.

On the same day as Morrison's testimony, and by a margin of 232–196, the House passed Resolution 660, affirming an impeachment inquiry for only the fourth time in history and setting out the rules for the proceedings to come. Only two Democrats opposed it, and it had the support of Representative Justin Amash, now an Independent.

We had interviewed almost two dozen witnesses in under a month, a remarkable feat considering the vehement opposition of the president. And we had built a powerful case that the president of the United States had betrayed his oath of office in a way that damaged our national security, and we had done so largely devoid of documentation. We didn't have "tapes" of the president's criminality, as they did during Watergate, but we had the transcript of a conversation that was every bit as incriminating.

What differentiated Trump's circumstances from Nixon's wasn't the absence of a recording, but the presence of Fox News and a whole information ecosystem that sustained Trump no matter how corrupt his conduct. If Nixon had had the benefit of Fox News, he would never have been forced to resign. Propaganda works, and it is devastating to both the truth and justice. We would need to try to break through our stratified media and make the case to the American people who had only heard the stories of these witnesses second-hand, through opening statements released to the press or through the slanders of the president and his allies. The Republicans would be planning to turn those hearings into a shameful spectacle, and we would need to be prepared.

16

HERE, RIGHT MATTERS

It was time to tell the story to the public. If we did so well, if we allowed the witnesses to speak unfiltered to the country, to show themselves not as some nefarious underground, but as the patriots they were, then we might stand a chance of holding this president accountable. But if we did not, if we allowed the Republicans to make a mockery of Congress and our committee, a Trumpian reality TV circus of a proceeding, then he would escape accountability once again, and history would judge us harshly. The potential impeachment of the president was riding on how we performed and a lot of that weight was now on my shoulders.

To help us get ready, I turned to Phil Schiliro and Phil Barnett, or, as we came to affectionately call them, the Phils. Both Phils had once served on the staff of former representative Henry Waxman, and had gone on to occupy other important positions in the

Obama administration or the private sector. They were both widely respected as gurus of congressional procedure and also had a keen sense of how Congress communicates with the public. The first issue we had to confront was how to structure our hearings given the very short timetable we were operating under. Although nothing had been firmly decided, the Speaker wanted us to conclude the hearings in November, which meant before Thanksgiving, so that we might have the first couple of weeks in December for the Judiciary Committee to take up impeachment—or not—as the case may be, and leave time for a vote on the House floor by Christmas. That left us with precious little time.

We were not going to bring in all of the witnesses we had deposed, only the most important, and we wanted to allow the Republicans to request relevant witnesses as well. On November 4, the Phils and I met in the Speaker's conference room to strategize; they advocated that we pair our witnesses at most hearings, so that we could move more expeditiously. The idea made me uneasy. It was one thing to put a bunch of legal experts on a panel, and another to have multiple fact witnesses testifying at the same time. If the Republicans were skillful, they could highlight inconsistencies in the facts and try to turn one witness against another during the same hearing. I wanted to bring in William Taylor first and not have his testimony diluted by the presence of another witness. "Okay," Phil Schiliro argued, "but you are going to be betting everything on a single witness. Are you sure you want to do that? That's putting a lot of pressure on the first hearing." Besides, the Phils argued, pairing witnesses would allow us to put a weaker witness with a stronger one, thus minimizing the downsides. Ultimately, I was persuaded by these arguments and by the tyranny of the clock. My staff started drawing up pairs of witnesses on a large whiteboard in the SCIF, erasing them, moving them around, and debating the merits of each combination.

On the same day I met with the Phils, Gordon Sondland filed a sworn declaration with our committee to amend his deposition testimony. After reading the opening statements of both Taylor and Morrison, which contradicted his earlier denials of any knowledge of the conditioning of military aid on political investigations, Sondland now claimed that these statements "have refreshed my recollection." Nothing like the fear of a perjury prosecution to improve one's memory. Sondland now declared that he recalled having a conversation with one of Zelensky's top aides, Andriy Yermak, in Warsaw, in which he told the Ukrainian that "resumption of U.S. aid would likely not occur until Ukraine provided the public anti-corruption statement that we had been discussing for many weeks." Quid pro quo.

Sondland's about-face was exactly the reason that I had wanted the depositions conducted in closed session, so that witnesses like him would have to risk perjury if they weren't honest about what they knew. The president's allies now needed to discredit Sondland, but they couldn't attack him as a "never Trumper," because after all, he had given a million dollars to Trump's inauguration committee, a donation that no doubt landed him the ambassadorship to begin with. Instead, they came up with an alternate theory. "Why did Sunderland change his testimony?" asked Lindsey Graham, mispronouncing Sondland's name. He was probably even less familiar with Sondland's testimony than he had been with the Benghazi report he had attacked without reading a couple of years earlier. "Was there a connection between Sunderland and Democratic operatives on the committee? Did he talk to Schiff? Did he talk to Schiff staffers?"

On November 6, we gave notice for our first hearings with William Taylor and Deputy Assistant Secretary of State George Kent for Wednesday of the following week, and Marie Yovanovitch by herself that Friday. Under House Resolution 660, this triggered a seventy-two-hour window in which the Republicans could request their witnesses. Pursuant to the rules that accompanied 660, those witnesses had to have testimony pertinent to three questions: (1) Did the president request that a foreign leader conduct investigations to benefit his personal political interests? (2) Did he or his agents use the power of his office, either by withholding military aid or a White House meeting to apply pressure? and (3) Did the president seek to "obstruct, suppress or cover up" evidence of the president's conduct?

We purposely did not disclose to the minority which witnesses we would be calling, beyond the three that we noticed for the following week. This would force the minority to request some of the same witnesses we were contemplating or risk that they would not be called at all.

Within seventy-two hours, I had Nunes's reply. It began with the usual litany of hyperbole, personal attacks, and complaints over process before identifying nine witnesses or categories of witnesses, including Hunter Biden; Devon Archer (a former board member of Burisma and business partner of Hunter Biden); Alexandra Chalupa (a former DNC staffer who figured prominently in conspiracy theories about Ukraine's alleged involvement in the 2016 election); David Hale, undersecretary of state for political affairs and a witness we had already deposed; Tim Morrison; Nellie Ohr (a former contractor for Fusion GPS and favorite of Fox News conspiracy theorists); Kurt Volker; the whistleblower; and "All individuals relied upon by the anonymous whistleblower in drafting his or her second-hand complaint."

Nunes's witness list said a lot about where the House Republican leadership stood under President Trump. Just as with Benghazi and the Russia investigation, they took a serious search for the truth to be an affront, and were resolved to turn the screws on anyone who exposed the guilt of their standard-bearer. They wanted to expose the whistleblower and all those who provided information to the whistleblower—in other words, all the people that Trump had declared "spies." The whistleblower had notified the committee of their willingness to answer questions in writing, but Republicans were not interested. After all, this would not satisfy the need to expose them, and to tear them down. Only two years earlier, Nunes had this to say about whistleblowers: "We don't talk about sources at this committee. We want more people to come forward. The good thing is that we have continued to have people come forward, voluntarily, to this committee and we want to continue that and I will tell you that that will not happen if we tell you who our sources are and people that come to the committee." But that was then.

Just as I observed during the deposition, Nunes seemed to be using our impeachment hearings to propagate the same smears that Trump sought unsuccessfully to have Ukraine undertake, and I was not about to let that happen. And finally, the minority hoped to use the hearings to push out the same propaganda that the Intelligence Community would later disclose the Kremlin was advancing about the 2016 election—the whole bucket of conspiratorial thinking summarized by the term "Crowdstrike." We were not going down that road either. Thankfully, we had written 660 well, and all but three of the witnesses sought by the minority were outside the scope of the parameters of the impeachment inquiry and were thus ineligible to testify. Accordingly, I informed Nunes in writing that at their request we would be calling Hale, Morrison, and Volker.

A couple of days later, I did my first dry run in preparation for the hearings. My staff put together a binder of every possible dilatory action and motion that the Republicans could bring, and the proper parliamentary response. With the Phils spread out in the member seats and my staff doing the same, the Phils mimicked the actions we anticipated, trying to interrupt me, trying to bait me, trying to derail the proceedings, and I practiced gaveling them down and ruling them out of order. "You are not recognized." "The gentleman will suspend." "That motion is not in order." "That motion is non-debatable." The Phils taught me about "the power of the gavel" and how to use it in different gradations and tones, with light taps on the handle, harder taps on the business end, and bringing it down with ear-shattering force when necessary—like a musician employing the full range of their instrument.

In anticipation of the hearings, we also began strategically releasing the deposition transcripts, giving the press time to absorb each along with a helpful guide to the most salient points. In this way, the public would hear the testimony three times, once through the transcripts, once through the House hearings, and, if it went to trial, once more in the Senate. Tell them what you're going to tell them, tell them again, and then tell them what you told them. I also gave a number of television interviews and published an op-ed in *USA*

Today entitled "Trump Betrayed America. Soon You Will Hear from Patriots Who Defended It," in order to set the stage.

After raging against the closed-door depositions, Trump now objected to my releasing the transcripts, claiming that Republicans should release their own because I would "change the words" and produce "manipulated propaganda." And then, for good measure, he called me a "freak." "They shouldn't be having public hearings," Trump protested. "This is a hoax." It wasn't hard to reply: "First, Republicans objected to private depositions," I tweeted, "even though almost fifty of their members could attend. Now, they don't want public hearings. The only consistency—They don't want the American people to learn the truth about the President's serious misconduct."

THE WEEKEND BEFORE THE HEARINGS were to begin was parents' weekend at Northwestern. There are about a million things I like about my job and only three that I don't: wearing a suit and tie, making calls to raise money, and being away from my family. For all of my children's lives, I have had to commute three thousand miles to work every week or two. That meant that I was away a lot, and even when I was home, at times like this I was working around the clock. Consequently, much of the joy and burden of raising our children fell to Eve, and I have always been conscious of how quickly the kids were growing, how soon they would be out from under our roof, and how despondent I would be over their absence. But I would like to think that within the confines of my job and its many demands, I have done my best to be a good father. I suppose that only time, and my kids, will tell. The timing of parents' weekend was unfortunate, but I wasn't going to miss a weekend at college with my family, so I went and I am so glad that I did.

Northwestern has a beautiful campus in Evanston, Illinois, on the shores of Lake Michigan. With an impressive faculty, great facilities, and a community devoted to its football team, it is a wonderful place to go to school. Lexi was now a senior, and an English major, and I loved having her come home and suddenly want to discuss Russian literature with me and my brother, Dan. Of course, college for her wasn't all Tolstoy and Dostoyevsky, and she introduced me to a whole new vocabulary of things that had changed since I was in school—including words like "darty," or daytime party, because there aren't enough nights in the week for that sort of thing. I didn't worry too much about Lexi while she was at school—she has always been centered and pragmatic—it was her younger brother, Eli, who was giving me fits. He had become a bit of a thrill seeker, leaping out of airplanes at 18,000 feet and Bungee jumping off towers and cliffs. Eve and I would look at each other and wonder—Where on earth did that come from?

Before the home game against Purdue, our family joined Lexi's boyfriend, Eric, at his fraternity, where all the parents crowded into the backyard, drank beer, and pretended to enjoy the loud music. There was a serious game of beer pong going on, but there are certain things you need to refrain from doing when you are a member of Congress, and playing beer pong at a college fraternity—parents' weekend or no parents' weekend—is certainly one of them. I did my best to stay away.

Watching Lexi and Eric enjoy themselves, surrounded by their friends and classmates, was a bittersweet joy. I looked over at Eli—it would be several more years before he would be off to college himself—and felt a pang at how quickly the kids had both grown and would be gone from our daily lives. A few of the other parents sought to engage me in a political discussion, but mostly they just wanted to enjoy their kids' experience, as I was. Eric and his father, Michael, held the beer pong table with great aplomb, taking on all comers and demonstrating considerable skill, while Lexi and Eli mingled in the crowd. Eve and I looked on and wondered where the time had gone.

It was a gorgeous day for football. The president of the university, Morty Schapiro, invited us to come watch from the sidelines, where we hustled to keep up with him as the ball moved up and down the field. I could not imagine a more wonderful relief from the stresses of the Ukraine investigation, and for one blissful weekend, I did my best to forget the rest of the world.

ON THE AFTERNOON OF NOVEMBER 12, I asked the Democratic members of my committee to join me in the SCIF so we could practice our response to Republican antics. No matter how well I had mastered parliamentary procedure, this was a group endeavor, and I might very well need their intercession if things were starting to get out of hand. More important, I wanted to underscore how important it was for them to keep their cool, even as I did my best to keep mine. The Phils walked us all through our paces, exhibiting all the same dilatory tactics I had practiced with them before, and we now practiced as a team.

I spent the afternoon reviewing a memo published by the minority, setting out their defense of Trump. The memo began in classic Nunes fashion, with a list of phony due process complaints and personal attacks, but in a triumph for the Kremlin, an entire section of their brief was entitled "Senior Ukrainian Government Officials Interfered in the 2016 U.S. Presidential Election in Opposition to President Trump." This was so much in line with Russian talking points that it took my breath away. What an extraordinary coup for the Russian psychological operations team, that Republicans in Congress were making the case that Ukraine was the meddler in 2016, not Russia. What phenomenal cover Russia was being provided courtesy of the party of Ronald Reagan. The minority also identified four key pillars of their defense of the president: The July 25 call record "shows no conditionality or evidence of pressure"; both Trump and Zelensky said there was no pressure applied to get the investigations; Ukraine was not aware of the hold on military assistance at the time of the call; and Trump eventually met with Zelensky and provided the aid.

It wasn't hard to knock down these arguments. The call record showed abundant indications of conditionality. Zelensky would *have* to say that he didn't feel pressured—did the Republicans really expect Zelensky to say he was being extorted at a joint presser with Trump? As for whether Ukraine was aware of the hold on aid on the day of the call, that was beside the point. They soon found out, and when they did, it was made abundantly clear to them what they needed to do to get the money. Finally, the argument that Ukraine ultimately got the money and the meeting amounted to little more than this—Trump got caught and had to release the funds. That was hardly the stuff of exoneration. What's more, Zelensky never did get the White House meeting.

That evening, CNN aired a profile about me as a curtain raiser to the hearings. Gloria Borger had conducted an interview with me days earlier, and she clearly had done her homework. Wrapping up the segment that covered my strengths and ample flaws, she finished with a deeply insightful question about one of my favorite films, *The Big Lebowski:* "Any words from 'the Dude' that might come up most in political life?" I didn't even need to think about it. "No, you're not wrong," I responded, quoting the Dude, "you're just an asshole." I didn't mean Gloria, of course.

On November 13, the Democrats on my committee gathered in the SCIF at 8 A.M. to do our final preparations for the 10 A.M. open hearing with Taylor and Kent. Members practiced their questions out loud, and often asked me for feedback. "Do you think I can ask Taylor this, or do you think that will be pushing him too far?" And I would respond, "I think you can certainly ask Taylor whether he thinks it is appropriate to withhold aid for a political favor, but I wouldn't ask him whether he thinks it's impeachable. He's not going to want to go there, and that's not his decision anyway. But you may be able to get him pretty close. You might ask him about his own oath to defend the Constitution; and if he were to tell the Ukrainians they needed to do this to get military aid, would that be consistent with his oath, with his commitment to the Constitution and national security?"

At about 9:40 A.M., we left the SCIF together to walk to the Longworth House Office Building and the Ways and Means hearing room, taking the tunnels below the Capitol to avoid the press. We were largely silent on the walk over, and you could hear our footfalls on the hard marble floors. I tried to use this time to settle myself, to remind myself that I knew the material as well as anyone, that I was fully prepared for whatever might come. Mike Quigley and I led our somber procession through the visitors' center and the Cannon tunnel and up the circular stairway to the hearing room. When we emerged from the stairwell, the sound was explosive from the crowd, press, and police. We passed through a gauntlet of cameras and reporters shouting questions at us—one of which penetrated the chaos. "Are you ready?" I didn't respond, but hoped and prayed that I was.

I took my place at the head of the dais and looked out on the large, elegant room. It was loud with commotion as reporters talked with each other or with members of Congress, and audience members stood chatting with one another. Those in the audience were the lucky ones who had waited in a long line outside the committee room to see if they might get a seat. On the walls, the former chairs of the Ways and Means Committee stared down at us from dark oil paintings. And above us hung an immense chandelier, something more appropriate to a luxury ship than a congressional hearing room.

Peering behind me, I could see that the Republicans had brought props, large posterboard signs they placed on easels behind their seats, including one with a bright "93," which falsely asserted the number of days "since Adam Schiff learned the identity of the whistleblower." Eight cameramen made a beeline for the row in front of me and jockeyed for position as I opened my binder and took a last look at my opening statement. Turning my attention back to the room, I could see other members of Congress seated in the audience, a rare occurrence on the Hill but one reflective of the unique nature of the proceedings. These included mostly Democratic members, but also Republicans like Meadows and Zeldin, no doubt there to act as a fast response team for the president. Only Jim Jordan had finagled a role in the hearings, persuading one of the Republican committee members to take a leave of absence so that he could temporarily take his place. I never found Jordan to be a particularly effective questioner—most of the time he would rather hear himself talk—and he does nothing but play to the base. My goal was to reach Americans who were still undecided about the president's conduct, and I knew that Jordan would not be speaking to them, only insulting them. Still, his primary mission would be to disrupt.

We had large television screens set up for the audience, having worked with the networks to enable them to televise the exhibits that we would be displaying to the witnesses. We wanted to be able to show Taylor some of the key text messages and ask him just what he was thinking when he wrote and received them; to play Mulvaney's admission of a quid pro quo; and to present other exhibits that we hoped would engage the viewers at home.

Suddenly the room became very quiet, but for the sound of camera shutters fluttering like so many insects, and flashes erupting; Taylor and Kent had arrived and were walking toward their seats. "All right, everybody back. Let's go, guys," someone from the press gallery called out to the photographers, who took a last shot before moving away from the witness table.

I gaveled the committee to order, began laying out the procedures for the hearing, and was literally in the middle of saying "it is the intention of the committee to proceed without disruptions," when the Republicans disrupted, and Ratcliffe made a parliamentary inquiry. It was easily disposed of, but already the interruption had my heart beating stronger. I moved quickly to my opening statement, giving a broad overview of the facts, and following with the issues that they presented to Congress and the country—whether the president sought to condition military aid and a White House meeting on two political investigations to help his reelection, and if he did, whether such an abuse of power was compatible with the office of the presidency.

"Our answer to these questions will affect not only the future of this Presidency but the future of the Presidency itself and what kind of conduct or misconduct the American people may come to expect from their Commander in Chief."

Turning to the president's obstruction of Congress, I made it clear that we needed to consider, as Congress had with Nixon, whether stonewalling of Congressional subpoenas constituted additional grounds for impeachment. If the president could simply refuse all oversight, particularly in the context of an impeachment proceeding, then the balance of power between our two branches of government would be irrevocably altered. The consequence of such an imbalance would mean "the prospects for further corruption and abuse of power in this administration or any other will be exponentially increased."

In his opening statement, Nunes was, well, Nunes: "Ambassador Taylor and Mr. Kent, I would like to welcome you here. I would like to congratulate you for passing the Democrats' star chamber auditions held for the last weeks in the basement of the Capitol. It seems you agreed witting[ly] or unwitting[ly] to participate in a drama, but the main performance, the Russia hoax, has ended and you've been cast in the low-rent Ukrainian sequel."

I looked out at these two public servants, with collectively almost eighty years of service to the country, for their reaction. Both of them knew well that the matter they were here to testify about was not some kind of joke. Kent, bow-tie-clad and sitting at attention, had a wry expression on his face that looked as if he were struggling to maintain his composure. For his part, Taylor merely narrowed his eyes with an expression of intense concentration.

When Nunes was finished, I swore in the witnesses, and no sooner had I done so than the Republicans resumed their efforts at disruption. Representative Elise Stefanik was the first to interrupt, wanting to know when they could have a vote on their proposed witnesses. "The gentlewoman should be aware that three of the witnesses the minority has requested are scheduled for next week," I replied. "Those were your witnesses," Stefanik responded falsely. She was either unaware of the fact that Nunes had requested the three, or didn't care. Nevertheless, I told her that she could always seek a vote on any additional witnesses—after Taylor and Kent testified. She then inquired if I would be "prohibiting witnesses from answering members' questions as you have done in the closed-door depositions?"

"As the gentlewoman should know if she was present for the depositions," I responded, since she hadn't bothered to be present for many of them, "the only times I prevented witnesses from answering questions . . . was when it was apparent that members were seeking to out the whistleblower." Representative Conaway then interrupted with his own motion to call the whistleblower for testimony in a closed session; then it was Jordan's turn, and he took advantage of the opportunity to direct a recurring falsehood at me, saying "You are the only member who knows who that individual is."

Ratcliffe later would try to engage me in a colloquy along these lines: "When are we going to find out the details of the contact between Chairman Schiff and the whistleblower, what they met about, when they met, the number of times they met, the discussions that were had—?" This was consistent with the lie being promoted by their legislative leader, Kevin McCarthy, who claimed on a Sunday show that I was "the only person who knows who this whistleblower is." "How many times did he meet with the whistleblower?" McCarthy had demanded. "What did he talk to the whistleblower about?"

It shouldn't have been striking to me, after being the subject of so many lies, that people could be so brazen about it, but there they were, on national television, repeating something they all knew was false. For Jordan—in his shirtsleeves as usual—it was the same game he'd played during the Benghazi hearing, and he was willing to do anything, say anything, if it drew attention to himself and pleased the old man watching from down the street. Ratcliffe still hoped to be appointed to something by Trump and this was merely part of an endless audition. People like Jordan, Ratcliffe, Meadows, and McCarthy were made for a presidency like Trump's, where truth was for suckers, principle meant nothing, and it was all about power and position. Their false attacks were galling, but not very effective, and I did my best to ignore them and move on.

As Kent began his testimony, I maintained the same immovable expression I would hold throughout, but I found myself reassured. The GOP efforts had amounted to nothing. If they were going to turn these hearings into a circus, they were going to have to do a lot better than that.

Taylor's opening statement was almost exactly the same as it had been during his deposition—until he got to the end. "Last Friday," he told the committee, a member of my staff told me of events that occurred on July 26." This was the day after Trump's call with Zelensky, and Taylor's staff member had accompanied Sondland to a restaurant in Kyiv, where Sondland called the president on his cellphone. The president was speaking so loudly that the staff member could hear him asking Sondland "about the investigations" and Sondland telling him that "the Ukrainians were ready to move forward." Following the call, the staff member asked Sondland what Trump thought of Ukraine, and "Ambassador Sondland responded that President Trump cares more about the investigations of Biden which Giuliani was pressing for."

I had been hoping that something new and fresh would emerge from each hearing, something that would add to our insights and the public interest, and this was it. The staff member's name was David Holmes, and I was already arranging for him to fly in from Ukraine to be deposed in just a few days. When we began the question-and-answer portion of the hearing, I immediately gravitated to this new information and drew Taylor's answers out even more fully.

Nunes began the Republican questioning period by saying that what the call record "actually shows is a pleasant exchange between two leaders who discuss mutual cooperation over a range of issues." Later, in talking points that might as well have been written by the Kremlin, Nunes also claimed that "Democrats downplay, ignore, outright deny the many indications that Ukrainians actually did meddle in the election." Nunes made little constructive use of his time before turning to Steve Castor for questions, and Castor did a serviceable job of going through the Trump defense talking points. One question in particular caused a rare break in Ambassador Taylor's demeanor.

"I want to turn to the discussion of the irregular channel you described," Castor began. "And in fairness, this irregular channel of diplomacy, it's not as outlandish as it could be. Is that correct?"

Taylor wasn't quite sure how to answer this, and he broke into a rare smile that brightened his face and caused the whole room to laugh along with him. "It's not as outlandish as it could be, yeah, I agree, Mr. Castor."

During member questioning, Ratcliffe alluded to President Zelensky's awkward statement at the United Nations meeting with Trump that he didn't feel pushed by Trump to agree to the investigations. When Representative Andre Carson was up, I caught his attention so that I might rebut these arguments, and he was generous enough to yield me his time.

"You would agree," I asked Kent, "that if President Zelensky contradicted President Trump and said, 'Of course I felt pressured, they were holding up four hundred million dollars in military assistance, we have people dying every day,' if he were to contradict President Trump directly, they would be sophisticated enough to know they might pay a heavy price with this president, were they not?"

"That's a fair assessment," Kent replied.

"And President Zelensky not only had to worry about retribution from Donald Trump should he contradict Donald Trump publicly, he also has to worry about how he's perceived domestically, doesn't he, Ambassador Taylor?"

"President Zelensky is very sensitive to the views of the Ukrainian people, who, indeed, are very attentive to Ukrainian-U.S. politics, yes," Taylor replied.

"And so, if President Zelensky were to say, 'I had to capitulate and agree to these investigations, I was ready to go on CNN until the aid got restored,' that would obviously be hurtful to him back home, would it not?"

"He cannot afford to be seen deferring to any foreign leader. He is very confident in his own abilities, and he knows that the Ukrainian people expect him to be clear and defend Ukrainian interests."

Other Democratic members would likewise yield time to me as

the hearing went on, and in this manner, we were able to rebut the president's arguments in real time, while they were fresh and before they could fix the public attitudes of those watching. But the best line of questioning went to Representative Sean Patrick Maloney, who demonstrated that—contrary to everything they teach you in law school—sometimes the best questions are the ones to which you do not already know the answer.

"Ambassador Taylor, what year did you graduate from West Point?"

"1969, sir," Taylor answered crisply.

"It was the height of the Vietnam War, wasn't it, sir?"

"The height was about that time."

"What was your class rank at West Point?" Maloney asked. Maloney did not know the answer, but he represented the district that includes West Point and knew a lot about the institution.

"I was number five."

"How many people were in your class?"

"Eight hundred."

"Eight hundred cadets. You were number five."

"Yes, sir."

"So when you're top one percent of your class at West Point, you probably get your pick of assignments, but you picked the infantry—"

"I did, sir."

"—didn't you?"

"Yes, sir."

"You were a rifle company commander?"

"Yes, sir."

"Did you see combat in Vietnam, sir?"

"I did."

"Did you earn any commendations for that service?"

"I was awarded the Combat Infantryman Badge, which is my highest—I'm proudest of. There was a Bronze Star. There was an Air Medal with 'V'—"

"That's for 'valor,' isn't it, sir?"

Maloney then walked Taylor through his experience many years later, visiting the front lines in Eastern Ukraine, where soldiers were fighting and dying at the hands of Russian troops, and asked him how it made him feel—as an infantryman—to know that the United States was withholding material support to those men. "Badly," was his reply.

Oh, it was a thing of beauty to watch an examination conducted so well. Maloney succeeded in showing the world what a patriot this soft-spoken man was, and how very small the Republicans had been who attacked him. And he brought the relevance of our military aid to Ukraine, and to our own security, home in the most personal of ways—through the eyes of a soldier who knew what it meant to fight an enemy without the resources you need. Beautiful.

When the testimony was over, I recognized Nunes for his closing statement, which he wasted, and then I looked over my notes from the day to identify what was most important. Putting numbers by my handwritten notes to organize them in a coherent order, I improvised a closing argument about what we learned from the hearing. I would use this practice in all of the hearings that would follow, and I would be told that these impromptu closes were much more effective than anything I might have scripted out in advance.

After a break to allow the witnesses to leave and to allow the press to begin analyzing their testimony, we returned to the committee room and took up Conaway's motion to subpoena the whistleblower. Representative Swalwell immediately moved to table the motion—something that is nondebatable—and Conaway bitterly objected. "A classic move," he muttered, before trying to argue the point. I moved forward with the roll call, the motion was defeated, and I adjourned the proceedings.

We were done with the first hearing, and as I gathered our members in the anteroom behind the chamber, they were exultant at how well it had gone. They huddled around me in the small space, like a team around their coach. "You all did a tremendous job," I told them. "Andre, thank you for giving me your time. And Sean Patrick Maloney, that line of questioning with Taylor was brilliant, just brilliant. Did you know that he graduated number five in his class?"

"No, I knew he graduated well, but not that well."

"Damn, better to be lucky than good," I said, and we laughed. But this day hadn't gone well because of luck—the members of our committee had prepared well, and they understood the gravity of our responsibility. They felt the same pressure I did—it was high stakes for all of us—and there would be good days and bad. But this day was a good day. Still, as we passed the Republicans who were doing a presser outside the hearing room and trashing the proceedings, it was hard to feel too confident about where we were—it was now abundantly clear that there would be no Watergate heroes in this impeachment inquiry.

TWO DAYS LATER, MY ALARM went off at 6 A.M. and as I swung my legs over the side of the bed, I thought: "I just have to get through the day. That's all I have to do. Just get through the day." This was now my daily mantra. I do not generally feel a lot of stress, or if I do, I just push it down. These days I was only getting a few hours of sleep a night—not because of restlessness, but because of the immense amount of work. Today would be our second hearing, with Marie Yovanovitch, and the security detail would be picking me up in an hour. I still had more of the outline to go over, and had been too tired to do any more when I turned out the lights only five hours earlier. I would eat a quick breakfast and mark up my binder in the back of the Suburban.

I could stand the pace, I knew, but only if I didn't think too much about how long it would go on. I had taken up doing triathlons before the Trump administration, and while the increased workload had put a temporary end to my training, one trick I learned from endurance sports was to lie to myself about how far I had to go. "Just one more mile," I would tell myself during the run or bike portions, even though I had several more after that. And then, "just one more," and so on, until there really was only one mile left. Now, I thought, I just had to get through the day. Just one more day.

But if I was girding myself for some kind of battle, our

witness—who had been the victim of smears and intimidation from the most powerful officeholder in the world, and who was defying him by simply showing up—helped me to keep all of this in perspective. The room was very still when the sergeants at arms opened the doors to allow Ambassador Marie Yovanovitch into the room. Something about her presence demanded hushed respect, and she sat down, lips drawn together in a thin line of resolve. She had served in some of the most dangerous places in the world, had stood up to dictators and their corrupt allies. But it took another form of courage for her to come into that room and sit alone at the witness table. "Get back. Butts down," the press gallery folks called out to photographers, who then sat down on the floor or cleared the way.

As I introduced her and enumerated her long service to the country, her toughness, and her credentials as an anticorruption fighter, I found myself already getting emotional about the slandering of this remarkable woman. George Kent had said that you can't fight corruption without pissing off corrupt people, and she had, in Ukraine and in the United States.

"Ambassador Yovanovitch was serving our nation's interest in fighting corruption in Ukraine, but she was considered an obstacle to the furtherance of the president's personal and political agenda," I said. "For that, she was smeared and cast aside. The powers of the presidency are immense, but they are not absolute, and they cannot be used for corrupt purpose. The American people expect their president to use the authority they grant him in the service of the nation, not to destroy others to advance his personal or political interests."

After Nunes's opening statement, Jordan and Stefanik made a few efforts to interrupt the flow of the proceedings again but were easily gaveled down, and we turned to the ambassador's testimony and the question period. About midway through Dan Goldman's opening forty-five-minute examination, Eric Swalwell called my staff's attention to the fact that the president had been tweeting about Yovanovitch in real time. I asked the staff to write down what his tweet said, and when I read it, I knew it was significant enough to interrupt the flow of Goldman's questioning. Coincidentally,

Dan had just asked the ambassador about the State Department's unwillingness to defend her from the smear campaign because they feared an errant tweet from the president, and this provided just the opening:

"Just a moment," I said, getting Dan's attention. "If I could follow up on that question, it seems like an appropriate time. Ambassador Yovanovitch, as we sit here testifying, the president is attacking you on Twitter, and I'd like to give you a chance to respond. I'll read part of one of his tweets: 'Everywhere Marie Yovanovitch went turned bad. She started off in Somalia, how did that go?' He goes on to say, later in the tweet, 'It is a U.S. President's absolute right to appoint ambassadors.' First of all, Ambassador Yovanovitch, the Senate has a chance to confirm or deny an ambassador, do they not?"

"Yes," she replied. "Advise and consent."

"Would you like to respond to the president's attack that everywhere you went turned bad?"

"Well," she said, "I don't think I have such powers, not in Mogadishu, Somalia, and not in other places. I actually think that where I've served over the years, I and others have demonstrably made things better, you know, for the U.S., as well as for the countries that I've served in."

"Ambassador," I continued a minute later, "you've shown the courage to come forward today and testify. Notwithstanding the fact you were urged by the White House or State Department not to, notwithstanding the fact that as you testified earlier, the president implicitly threatened you in that call record; and now, the president, in real time, is attacking you, what effect do you think that has on other witnesses' willingness to come forward and expose wrongdoing?"

"Well," she said, looking visibly upset, "it's very intimidating."

"It's designed to intimidate, is it not?"

"I mean," she said, carefully, "I can't speak to what the president is trying to do, but I think the effect is to be intimidating."

"Well, I want to let you know, Ambassador, that some of us here take witness intimidation very, very seriously."

When the hearing was over and Marie Yovanovitch stood up from the table, the large audience that had gathered to hear her testimony stood up with her and gave her a boisterous round of applause, shouting their approval. Yovanovitch looked briefly over her shoulder toward the dais as she approached the doors, then she was gone.

TUESDAY, NOVEMBER 19, WOULD BE another grueling endurance test. In the morning, we would be conducting an open hearing with Jennifer Williams, a foreign service officer detailed to the vice president's office, and Lt. Col. Vindman. Later that afternoon, we would bring in two of the minority witnesses, Ambassador Kurt Volker and Tim Morrison. "Tell Jennifer Williams, whoever that is," Trump tweeted the day before her testimony, "to read BOTH transcripts of the presidential calls, & see the just released statement from Ukraine. Then she should meet with the other Never Trumpers, who I don't know & mostly never even heard of, & work out a better presidential attack."

I guess I shouldn't have been surprised that, after seeing how badly his attack on Yovanovitch had gone over, Trump would still be going after the career professionals appearing before our committee, but there he was, unable to control himself. Williams's offense, apparently, was that she testified in her deposition that Trump's side of the July 25 call was not perfect but "unusual and inappropriate."

When I introduced Williams, there were no interruptions by the minority, no spurious points of order or dilatory parliamentary inquiries. It seemed that the fight had gone out of them, or maybe they just concluded that their strategy, whatever it was, wasn't working. Williams's statement was short and matter-of-fact, and it included one salient detail that I was interested in: "On May 13, an assistant to the Vice President's Chief of Staff called and informed me that President Trump had decided the Vice President would not attend Zelensky's inauguration in Ukraine." Williams did not know the reason for the cancellation, but it wasn't difficult to surmise—Giuliani had just been forced to abort his May trip to Ukraine to "meddle" in the investigation, and he complained to Trump that the Ukrainians were poisoned against him. And that meant the end of Pence's participation in the inauguration.

But it was Vindman's testimony that would leave an indelible mark on me, and on the country. "Next month will mark forty years since my family arrived in the United States as refugees. When my father was forty-seven years old, he left behind his entire life and the only home he had ever known to start over in the United States so his three sons could have better and safer lives. His courageous decision inspired a deep sense of gratitude in my brothers and myself, and instilled in us a sense of duty and service. All three of us have served, or are currently serving, in the military. My little brother sits behind me here today. Our collective military service is a special part of our family's story in America."

Vindman praised the courage of his colleagues who had come forward to testify and said that he understood that speaking out like this—about the misconduct of a head of state—would not be tolerated in many places around the world. In Russia, he said, raising such concerns would have "severe personal and professional repercussions." Offering testimony against the Kremlin leadership "would surely cost me my life," he averred. "I am grateful to my father—for my father's brave act of hope forty years ago and for the privilege of being an American citizen and public servant, where I can live free, free of fear for mine and my family's safety."

"Dad," Vindman said to his father watching from home, "I am sitting here today in the U.S. Capitol talking to our elected professionals. Talking to our elected professionals is proof that you made the right decision forty years ago to leave the Soviet Union and come here to the United States of America in search of a better life for our family. Do not worry. I will be fine for telling the truth."

The simple power of his words affected me deeply. I looked out at him, so proud of the uniform that he wore, and to be in the service of his country. He displayed a youthful awe at where he found himself, speaking to "our elected professionals" and before the entire country.

Still, I couldn't help but wonder whether he *would* be "fine" for telling the truth. It had cost Marie Yovanovitch her job and threatened her reputation. The IC inspector general, Michael Atkinson, was clearly at risk of losing his job. And the whistleblower who had put it all in motion was dealing with threats to their life. I wanted to believe Vindman's hopeful words, for what they said about our country, for how much they reflected my own idealism as a young prosecutor thirty years earlier staring down drug lords, and because my ninety-one-year-old father had the same worries for his son.

The real moment of the day came late in the hearing, and once again, it was Sean Patrick Maloney who elicited the most powerful testimony. He asked Vindman to reread the end of his opening remarks, where he told his father not to worry, and then Maloney asked him this: "You realized when you came forward, out of a sense of duty, that you were putting yourself in direct opposition to the most powerful person in the world? Do you realize that, sir?"

"I knew I was assuming a lot of risk," Vindman replied.

"And I'm struck by that word—that phrase, 'Do not worry,' you addressed to your dad . . . And he would have worried, if you were putting yourself up against the president of the United States. Is that right?" Maloney asked.

"He deeply worried about it because in his context it was, it was the ultimate risk."

"And why do you have confidence that you can do that and tell your dad not to worry?"

"Congressman," Vindman replied, "because this is America. This is the country that I've served and defended. That all of my brothers have served. And here, right matters."

Here, right matters. When he said it, Vindman paused with each word—here—right—matters. The audience applauded that simple expression of faith in our country and form of governance. It was beautiful, and it was heartbreaking. He said it so earnestly, like a prayer. Which, I suppose, it was.

17

EVERYONE WAS IN THE LOOP

AN ACT OF PATRIOTISM SUCH AS ALEXANDER VINDMAN'S FEELS LIKE IT
has the power to stop time and inspire us to be the people that we
hope to be. A simple, singular act of standing on principle and
telling the truth, with the conviction that no matter how great the
forces you are up against, nothing can hurt you because you have the
truth—I would like to believe that can change the world. It certainly
changed mine.

After Vindman's powerful testimony, we broke for a few hours
and then returned for the second hearing of the day. One of the
witnesses I was most eager to have testify under oath again was
Ambassador Volker, who had been crafty and disingenuous in his
deposition. And wouldn't you know it, Volker did claim a bit of an
epiphany after learning of the testimony of other witnesses. "In
hindsight," Volker said in his opening statement, "I now understand

that others saw the idea of investigating possible corruption involving the Ukrainian company Burisma as equivalent to investigating former vice president Biden. I saw them as very different, the former being appropriate and unremarkable, the latter being unacceptable. In retrospect, I should have seen that connection differently, and had I done so, I would have raised my own objections."

When he was deposed, Volker had conveniently neglected to tell us important information about the July 10 meeting in which Sondland had brought up the deal he had with Mulvaney to get Zelensky a White House meeting if the Ukrainians would announce an investigation into the Bidens and Burisma. Now he was acknowledging that Sondland brought up investigations and claiming "I think all of us thought it was inappropriate."

"Ambassador Volker," I asked him, "we asked you about that meeting during your deposition. . . . Why didn't you tell us about this?"

"Because that's what I remembered from the meeting . . . As I said, I've learned other things, including seeing the statements from Alex Vindman and Fiona Hill, and that reminded me that, yes, at the very end of that meeting, . . . yes, that's right, Gordon did bring that up."

Volker had served the country for decades and undoubtedly did not want to end his career caught up in the president's scandal, but he had gone along with Giuliani's scheming, trying to mitigate the damage, perhaps, but he had only ended up lending a patina of legitimacy to an illegitimate objective. I would have had more sympathy for his situation if he had simply owned it, but he took only a very grudging kind of responsibility. Volker's testimony wasn't helpful so much to the president as to himself. After seeing the courage demonstrated by Yovanovitch and Vindman—and the price they were paying for it—I found myself annoyed at Volker's continued deflection. In fact, a recording of one of Volker's calls later released by the press specifically mentioned Biden and directly contradicted his claims of ignorance.

Early the following morning, I met the Democratic members

back in the SCIF for more preparations. In an hour, we would begin one of our most important hearings, and with one of our most difficult witnesses, Gordon Sondland. He had clearly not been honest with us during his deposition, and his subsequent declaration marked a clear interest in, if not coming clean, at least avoiding perjury charges. We could go after him for being untruthful with us earlier, but we might also need him during trial as one of the few cooperating witnesses who had spoken to the president directly. I asked the members to tread lightly until we had a chance to see what kind of witness he would be. We did not want to vouch for him or his character—but unless he gave us a reason to harshly cross-examine him, we also didn't need to make him an adversary.

Sondland entered the committee room at 9:05 A.M. looking as if he were walking into a cocktail party. Sitting down at the witness table and smiling with his attorney, laughing with people seated behind him, he might as well have been chatting over hors d'oeuvres with a flute of champagne. Instead, he was about to deliver the most devastating evidence against the president, and not just the president, but the vice president, the secretary of state, and others as well.

Sondland began his opening statement as others had, telling the story of his family, of his parents' flight from Europe during the Holocaust, his upbringing in Seattle, his involvement in politics supporting members of both parties, and "the highest honor in my public life" when President Trump asked him to serve as United States ambassador to the European Union. He then told the committee that he had been hampered in his testimony, past and present, by the State Department's unwillingness to share his own records with him, and in the absence of those records "my memory, admittedly, has not been perfect." Nevertheless, he said, he wanted to begin with a few key points.

Sondland testified that he, Volker, and Perry—the "Three Amigos," as Sondland had taken to calling them—worked with Giuliani at the direction of the president, and "we made every effort to ensure that the relevant decision makers at the National Security Council and the State Department knew the important details of our efforts.

The suggestion that we were engaged in some irregular or rogue diplomacy is absolutely false." He told us that he had now been able to identify certain State Department emails and other documents in his possession that proved this statement, and that he would be quoting from. "Mr. Giuliani's requests were a quid pro quo for arranging a White House visit for President Zelensky. Mr. Giuliani demanded Ukraine make a public statement announcing the investigations of the 2016 election, DNC server, and Burisma. Mr. Giuliani was expressing the desires of the president of the United States, and we knew these investigations were important to the president."

Then Sondland went beyond affirming the quid pro quo over the White House meeting and addressed the hold on military assistance. "I tried diligently to ask why the aid was suspended, but I never received a clear answer. I still haven't to this day. In the absence of any credible explanation for the suspension of the aid, I later came to believe that the resumption of security aid would not occur until there was a public statement from Ukraine committing to the investigations of the 2016 election and Burisma, as Mr. Giuliani had demanded."

Sondland wanted to make sure that the committee understood that he was not operating on his own, or without the knowledge of other high-ranking U.S. officials while he was pursuing the investigations sought by the president. "We kept the leadership of the State Department and the NSC informed of our activities, and that included communications with Secretary of State Pompeo, his counselor, Ulrich Brechbuhl, his executive secretary, Lisa Kenna, and also communications with Ambassador Bolton, Dr. Hill, Mr. Morrison, and their staff at the NSC. They knew what we were doing and why.

"Everyone's in the loop," he added.

"Was there a quid pro quo? As I testified previously with regard to the requested White House call and the White House meeting, the answer is yes." On July 19, Sondland had sent an email to Pompeo, Mulvaney, Perry, and "a lot of senior officials" about how he had just spoken to Zelensky, and the Ukrainian president was prepared to assure Trump during their call that he would turn over every stone in the requested investigation. "Everyone was in the loop. It was no secret."

Sondland described another email he had addressed to Secretary Pompeo: "Mike, . . . Kurt and I negotiated a statement from Zelensky to be delivered for our review in a day or two. The contents will hopefully make the boss happy enough . . . to authorize an invitation. Zelensky plans to have a big presser . . . next week. . . . Again, everyone was in the loop."

And yet another appeal to Pompeo: "Specifically, on August 22, I emailed Secretary Pompeo directly . . . 'should we block time in Warsaw for a short pull-aside for POTUS to meet Zelensky? I would ask Zelensky to look him in the eye and tell him that . . . [he] should be able to move forward publicly and with confidence on those issues of importance to POTUS and the U.S. Hopefully that will break the logjam.' The secretary replied, 'yes.'"

I asked Sondland whether "the logjam" referred to both the delay in scheduling a White House meeting and the withholding of the military aid. "Correct," he said.

"And based on the context of that email, this was not the first time you had discussed these investigations with Secretary Pompeo, is it?" I asked.

"No."

"He was aware of the connections that you were making between the investigations and the White House meeting and the security assistance?"

"Yes."

Sondland had just pulled Pompeo completely under the bus with him. If others were suggesting that Sondland had been pursuing this quid pro quo on his own, he wasn't going down alone. And it didn't stop there—he'd take down the vice president of the United States too.

When Trump was unable to make the Warsaw meeting with Zelensky, Mike Pence ended up taking his place. "I mentioned to Vice President Pence before the meetings with the Ukrainians that I had concerns that the delay in aid had become tied to the issue of investigations." During questioning he elaborated further. "I just spoke up and I said, it appears that everything is stalled until this statement gets made. . . . And the vice president nodded like, you know, he heard what I said, and that was pretty much it, as I recall."

"And it was immediately after this meeting between the vice president and Zelensky that you went to speak with Yermak [Zelensky's top adviser] and you told him similarly that in order to release the military assistance they were going to have to publicly announce these investigations?" I asked.

"Yeah."

Sondland had come a long way since his deposition—from insisting there was no evidence of a quid pro quo to "Everyone was in the loop." I suspect he did so not only because he feared exposure to perjury charges, but because he wasn't going to be the fall guy for a scheme in which so many others were now implicated. The Republicans continued—as if they had been in another room while Sondland was testifying or he had been speaking another language—to insist that there was no evidence of a quid pro quo, that the Ukrainians never knew the aid was withheld, or that the president's denials of a quid pro quo were somehow dispositive.

"My colleagues seem to think," I said in my closing for the day, "that unless the president says the magic words 'I hereby bribed the Ukrainians,' there's no evidence of bribery or other high crimes or misdemeanors." But the evidence was now very powerful that the president had engaged in provably impeachable conduct. The only question that remained was whether, as Mulvaney had posited—the country should just "get over it."

In an effort to prove that up was down and black was white, Republicans during the hearings had attempted to portray the president as a great anticorruption crusader, motivated only by helping Ukraine along the path toward a firmly established rule of law. This was, of course, an absurdity. Not once in his life, I pointed out—much less in his presidency—had Trump taken a stand against corruption. Quite the opposite. When he fired Yovanovitch, that wasn't anticorruption, but corruption. When he praised the dishonest former

Ukrainian prosecutors, that wasn't anticorruption, but corruption. When he conditioned a White House meeting and aid on political investigations, that wasn't anticorruption, but corruption. In fact, before Trump and his band of enablers came along, we had a robust anticorruption policy, one devoted to the rule of law, and the great men and women in the State Department and Defense Department carried that message around the globe. But when the world witnesses a president of the United States who was not devoted to the rule of law, who was not fighting corruption, but in word and deed was the embodiment of corruption, they are forced to ask themselves, *What does America stand for anymore?*

"RIGHT NOW, YOU HAVE A kangaroo court headed by little shifty Schiff," Trump said in response to the day's testimony. "We don't have lawyers, we don't have witnesses, we don't have anything." I had no time to watch television, let alone late night, but my staff would occasionally text me highlights to give me a good laugh amid the seriousness. Late-night host James Corden read the president's tweet and mocked: "We don't have truth on our side. We don't have a credible defense. We don't have an explanation. We don't have many allies left. And the cafeteria is out of those cool toothpicks that look like little swords. He called Adam Schiff 'li'l shifty Schiff.' Now is it just me, or are Trump's insult skills getting sloppy? Is he little or is he shifty? Or is he a little shifty? Like you gotta pick a lane, dude."

November 21 would be our final impeachment hearing, and it was another crucial one, with Fiona Hill and David Holmes, political counselor in the U.S. embassy in Kyiv and staff member to William Taylor.

Holmes described the lunch that he had with Sondland on July 26, the day after Trump spoke with Zelensky. They were sitting on the outdoor terrace of a restaurant in Kyiv, enjoying food and a bottle of wine, when Sondland picked up his cellphone and said that he was going to call the president of the United States and give him an update. After placing the call, Holmes heard Sondland announce himself several times as holding for the president. Although Sond-land's phone was not on speakerphone, Holmes could hear the president's voice through the earpiece, clear and recognizable. In fact, Sondland held the phone away from his ear during part of the call because Trump's voice was so loud. To demonstrate, Holmes mimicked Sondland, putting his hand to his ear and then moving it several inches away, as if to show that the phone was loud enough to hurt his ears.

After Sondland greeted the president and told him that he was in Ukraine, he went on to tell Trump that Zelensky "loves your ass." Holmes then heard President Trump ask, "So he's going to do the investigation?" and Sondland replied that he was going to do it. Presi-dent Zelensky would do anything Trump asked him to do, Sondland said.

It was such a vivid scene that Holmes was depicting—sitting in a public place and having a bottle of wine while someone he was din-ing with called the president of the United States and almost imme-diately got through, and hearing that familiar voice on the other end. And most significant, the only question the president asked about Ukraine was whether Zelensky was going to do the investigation.

But what happened after the call was equally compelling. As Holmes testified,

> I then took the opportunity to ask Ambassador Sondland for his candid impression of the president's views on Ukraine. In particular, I asked Ambassador Sondland if it was true that the president did not give a [expletive] about Ukraine. Ambassador Sondland agreed that the president did not give a [expletive] about Ukraine. I asked, why not? And Ambassador Sondland stated that the president only cares about "big stuff." I noted there was big stuff going on in Ukraine, like a war with Rus-sia. And Ambassador Sondland replied that he meant big stuff that benefits the president, like the Biden investigation that Mr. Giuliani was pushing. And the conversation then moved to other topics.

Holmes's account of the call and the conversation that followed was particularly devastating because it was so credible, so consistent with everything we knew about the president and his obsessive focus on himself, even while there was a war going on. It was also a perfect description of Sondland, gregarious and profane, ostentatiously flaunting his connections, his penchant for cutting to the chase. In this small scene at a restaurant, I believed we could see in microcosm all we needed to know about the danger this president posed to our country and our allies.

Even then, our hearing was just getting started. Fiona Hill told the committee that she came from a working-class family of coal miners in Britain that always struggled with poverty. Her father had hoped to emigrate to work in the coal mines of West Virginia or Pennsylvania, but he had to stay home and take care of his mother, crippled from hard labor. "While his dream of emigrating to America was thwarted, my father loved America, its culture, its history, and its role as a beacon of hope for the world. He always wanted someone in the family to make it to the United States." Fiona Hill did, after winning an academic competition. "I grew up poor with a very distinctive working-class accent," Hill explained. "In England in the 1980s and 1990s, this would have impeded my professional advancement. This background has never set me back in America."

Listening to her, I was struck by how many of our witnesses were immigrants, and why their parents had been drawn to this country. I was so proud of that, and so grateful that if nothing else, these hearings were showing the country what fine people were attracted to a career in public service. Hill started with no advantage but a brilliant mind, and, like Vindman, had earned her place on the National Security Council of the United States. But as I was thinking about this, she was issuing a warning, and one that would immediately cause a furor among the Republicans. "Based on questions and statements I have heard, some of you on this committee appear to believe that Russia and its security services did not conduct a campaign against our country and that perhaps, somehow for some reason, Ukraine did. This is a fictional narrative that is being

perpetrated and propagated by the Russian security services themselves." Hill went on to confirm "the unfortunate truth" that Russia
systematically attacked our democratic institutions in 2016, just as
our agencies confirmed, and that the impacts were dire: "Truth is
questioned. Our highly professional, expert career Foreign Service is
being undermined."

"Right now," she warned, "Russia's security services and their
proxies have geared up to repeat their interference in the 2020 election. We are running out of time to stop them. In the course of this
investigation, I would ask that you please not promote politically
driven falsehoods that so clearly advance Russian interests." Hill
stated that Putin and the Russian services operate like a Super PAC
and spend millions on opposition research and false narratives. "I
refuse to be part of an effort to legitimize an alternate narrative that
the Ukrainian Government is a U.S. adversary and that Ukraine,
not Russia, attacked us in 2016. These fictions are harmful even if
they're deployed for purely domestic political purposes."

I could feel the anger rising like waves of heat to my left as Nunes and
other members of the minority fumed. In her crisp British cadences,
Fiona Hill had just told the Republicans on our committee—and not
only them but the president as well—that they were full of it, and even
worse, they were pushing out Kremlin talking points and doing Putin's
bidding. Hill's statement was a stunning rebuke. Her point was one
that I had been making for months, but delivered in much more erudite fashion and coming from a Trump appointee, it was all the more
powerful. I was glad that we could let that sink in for the next forty-five
minutes before the Republicans unloaded on her. If they did, however,
they would need to be careful; she was smart enough, and articulate
enough, to march circles around them.

As powerful an indictment as her opening statement had been, I
was even more struck with her testimony later in the hearing, during
minority questioning. Republican Counsel Steve Castor asked her
about the argument she had with Sondland, when she had asked
him, "Who put you in charge of Ukraine?" and he had answered
"the president," which she said, "shut me up."

"I've actually realized," Hill continued, "having listened to his deposition, that he was absolutely right, that he wasn't coordinating with us because we weren't doing the same thing that he was doing. So I was upset with him that he wasn't fully telling us about all of the meetings that he was having. And he said to me, but I am briefing the president, I'm briefing Chief of Staff Mulvaney, I'm briefing Secretary Pompeo, and I've talked to Ambassador Bolton. Who else do I have to deal with?"

"But it struck me yesterday, when you put up on the screen Ambassador Sondland's emails and who was on these emails, and he said 'These are the people who need to know,' that he was absolutely right. Because he was being involved in a domestic political errand, and we were being involved in national security foreign policy, and those two things had just diverged."

This was remarkable. Hill was admitting that she had been wrong about Sondland, wrong to think that he was acting without remit, wrong to be angry with him. He was, in fact, communicating directly with the president and others, including the secretary of state and chief of staff. Everyone who needed to be in the loop was in the loop, because they were engaged in skulduggery and not U.S. policy. But even as she was saying that she was being unfair to Sondland, she was also, in a brilliant kind of rhetorical jiu jitsu, pointing out how much more incriminating it was, this pursuit of a "domestic political errand," since so many top officials were involved.

I thought my closing statement that day would be my last, unless and until the matter went to trial. So I took the opportunity to go, one by one, through each of the president's defenses and knock them all down—the bogus hearsay objections, the false claims of "no pressure" on Ukraine, and the argument that because the president denied a quid pro quo, he couldn't have done anything wrong, or what I called the "I'm not a crook" defense.

I also turned to the conversation that Holmes had with Sondland, and Sondland's observation that the president only cared about the big stuff. In Trump's case, that meant stuff important to him personally. And I asked, "What do we care about? Do we care about the big stuff like the Constitution, like an oath of office, or do we only care now about party?" Harking back to Watergate, when Republican Howard Baker showed enough independence from the president of his party to conduct a genuine investigation, I asked, *Where is Howard Baker?*

As I drew to a close, I thought of my late colleague Elijah Cummings, and hoped that I had conducted the hearings in a manner that would have made him proud. And as tribute to him, I wanted the last words of the hearings to be his words, even if I could not say his name without risk of tears: "This president believes he is above the law, beyond accountability," I said. "And I would just say to people watching here at home and around the world, in the words of my great colleague, *We are better than that.*" I slammed down the gavel, and its wooden complaint echoed around the room.

"CORRUPT POLITICIAN ADAM SCHIFF'S LIES are growing by the day," Trump tweeted, in a grousing commentary on the hearings. "Keep fighting tough, Republicans, you are dealing with human scum." But for all of Trump's posturing, and all of the commentator speculation that Trump secretly wanted to be impeached because he thought it would help his reelection, a previous tweet from the president about his impeachment told the real story. "I never in my wildest dreams," he said, "thought my name would in any way be associated with the ugly word, Impeachment!"

Back in the SCIF at the end of the day, I felt that a large weight had been lifted. The hearings were over, and we had made a powerful case to the American people that the president had engaged in serious abuses of power. During the course of the three months of investigation and hearings, public attitudes had swung dramatically, from opposition to an impeachment inquiry to eventual support for the investigation—and now narrowly in favor of Trump's removal from office.

Not content to allow me to enjoy even a moment's reprieve, my staff engaged me in the process of writing our report, which would be due to the Judiciary Committee in less than ten days and needed to be scrupulously well written. I don't know how long Mueller's team took to draft their findings, but my guess is that it was closer to ten months than ten days. My staff gave me copies of the Iran-Contra Report, the Senate Watergate Report, and Ken Starr's lengthy report in the Clinton impeachment to study. I needed to go through them and decide which of these analyses we wanted our report to resemble.

I chose to model our report after the one produced by Senator Sam Ervin summarizing the results of the Senate Select Committee's Watergate investigation. It had a plainspoken preface by Ervin and read like a novel, not a thesis. I did not want to write another Mueller report.

In a matter of ten days—and working around the clock over the Thanksgiving recess—the incredibly talented staff of our committee, as well as that of Oversight and Foreign Affairs, produced a three-hundred-page report that summarized the critical evidence adduced at our depositions and hearings, cross-referencing all the key documents we had received and, in plain English, told the story of the president's egregious misconduct. Thanks in particular to the incredible work of the Oversight Committee, we were also able to incorporate new evidence gained by subpoenas served on telephone providers that suggested a level of coordination between Giuliani, the president, and others close to the president at key times in our chronology, but also implicated John Solomon, the conservative opinion writer for *The Hill*, who published a lot of the smears and allegations against Yovanovitch and the Bidens. The committee did not subpoena call detail records of any members of Congress, staff, or journalists. But, alarmingly, the phone records did lead us back to someone very close to our investigation—Devin Nunes—raising the question of whether the ranking member was engaged in the same "domestic political errand" on behalf of the president. Specifically, the records showed contacts between Nunes and Giuliani, and between Nunes and Lev Parnas, one of Giuliani's confederates.

The Democratic members of our committee read the draft and provided important edits and additions. My predominant contribution to the report, apart from proofing and editing, was writing the preface. In it, I set out a brief explanation of the impeachment power and how the Framers intended it to be used, and then gave a very straightforward summary of the facts of the president's misconduct. The Ukraine story is really quite simple, even if it involves some unusual-sounding names, and I wanted to make it as accessible as possible. But I also wanted to acknowledge the plain truth of where we found ourselves at the end of the investigation—with a set of facts that were not really in dispute, but two parties in bitter disagreement.

In his preface, Sam Ervin had proudly written that his investigation began in bipartisan fashion and ended that way. How much I wish I could have said the same. Instead, I wrote of the extreme partisanship of our era, something that the Founders called "factionalism." "If there was one ill the Founders feared as much as that of an unfit president," I wrote,

> it may have been that of excessive factionalism. . . . Today, we may be witnessing a collision between the power of a remedy meant to curb presidential misconduct and the power of faction determined to defend against the use of that remedy on a president of the same party. But perhaps even more corrosive to our democratic system of governance, the President and his allies are making a comprehensive attack on the very idea of fact and truth. How can a democracy survive without acceptance of a common set of experiences?

FOR THANKSGIVING WEEKEND, I WAS lucky enough to spend some down time with my family, and we had our Thanksgiving meal with Eric's family in New York. His folks, Michael and Shelley, were nice enough to take us all in—including the large security detail—for a fabulous meal. On the way back, we spent a day in New Jersey and stayed at a place near some stables, where we could all go horse-back riding. A couple of the guys in my detail had never been on a horse, and we all got a laugh, including members of the detail, as they struggled to stay in their saddles. Eve is a very talented rider, who grew up riding English saddle and learned to jump. I made up for far less experience with more enthusiasm—I love to ride—and I enjoyed it all the more because I had been enduring such sensory deprivation over the previous few months. Each jolt of the horse's walk, trot, and canter beat a bit of the stress out of me. The ride wasn't particularly scenic, but that didn't matter. I could have been on a mule in downtown Newark and I would have enjoyed it.

Meanwhile, Trump was participating in the annual Turkey pardon at the White House. The North Carolina turkeys that Trump was about to pardon had been bred to "remain calm under any condition," Trump said, something that would be "very important because they've already received subpoenas to appear in Adam Schiff's basement on Thursday." And he told the Turkeys that their subpoenas were very unusual, because "unlike previous witnesses, you and I have actually met." I guess this was Trump's effort at distancing himself from those I subpoenaed to testify against him. I really was in his head.

On December 2, our report was concluded and available for review, and the following night, our committee voted it out, 13–9, along party lines, and sent it to the Judiciary Committee. Comparing our report to Mueller's, one writer in *The Washington Post* observed that our report brought "light and clarity" to the president's misdeeds, observing that if "Mueller's report was 'Ulysses,' our report was 'The Sun Also Rises.'" Thanks to the brilliance of our staff, we had accomplished our objective.

Now that the impeachment proceedings had moved to the Judiciary Committee, Nadler invited the White House to call witnesses or present evidence, but they declined to participate. The lengthy argument Nadler and I had over the provision to prevent the White House from cherry-picking the evidence turned out to be moot after all. "As you know," White House Counsel Pat Cipollone had written in a bombastic five-page letter days earlier, "this baseless and highly partisan inquiry violates all past historical precedent, basic due process, and fundamental fairness." He complained the timing of the hearing was "no doubt purposely" designed to embarrass the president while he was appearing at a NATO summit in London. Despite all of the flaws of the intelligence committee hearings, Cipollone concluded, "the facts that emerged even from Chairman Schiff's carefully controlled and blatantly unfair process served only to further confirm that the President has done nothing wrong and that there is no basis for continuing your inquiry."

The president's decision not to participate in the Judiciary Committee hearings was another mistake. Trump's best chance, perhaps only chance, to derail the impeachment proceedings at this point was to call witnesses of his own and try to contest the facts. If he had made reasonable requests for relevant testimony, Nadler would have been hard-pressed to deny them, and Trump might have been able to draw out the proceedings and give his allies more to work with. But the White House was either unprepared or, more likely, had no pertinent witnesses to call. Most of those with relevant information, like Bolton, Kupperman, Mulvaney, Pompeo, Pence, and others, were already on our witness list and were far more likely to incriminate the president than to help him. Still, a better set of lawyers might have put on a good enough defense to pick off a few of our members during a vote on the House floor—and they didn't need to win over many in a majority as narrow as ours.

Across the Capitol, Senator Schumer was outlining the mechanics of an impeachment trial to his caucus during their Wednesday meeting, while Republicans were lunching with Cipollone, along with two other lawyers brought on to help with the president's defense, Pam Bondi and Tony Sayegh. McConnell was making no secret of the fact that he intended to coordinate his every action with the White House. Trump was claiming that he wanted Pelosi and me to testify, along with Hunter Biden, Joe Biden, and a host of others. But it was already apparent that Senate Republicans wanted to get a trial over with as soon as possible, even if it meant conducting the first impeachment trial in history without witnesses. As for the oath that they would be required to take to do "impartial justice," Lindsey Graham expressed the views of many GOP colleagues when he said: "I'm not trying to pretend to be a fair juror here."

On December 7, the Judiciary Committee Democrats had a long brainstorming session with Larry Tribe on potential articles of impeachment, and many of the members were leaning toward including a whole range of offenses, from Ukraine to obstruction of justice and violations of the Emoluments Clause. I was now having daily meetings with the Speaker and the other committee chairs, and when it was time to reach a final resolution, the Speaker broadened the group beyond the chairs to other members of the leadership including Majority Leader Steny Hoyer and Majority Whip Jim Clyburn. An article based on the Emoluments Clause quickly dropped out of consideration, as that matter was still pending in the courts and not as weighty as the others, but the issue of the president's obstruction of the Russia investigation remained contested. Nadler was strongly in favor of including an obstruction article based on volume two of the Mueller report, and he had considerable support among the leadership. I instinctively fell back on my strategy as a prosecutor, which was to charge only those offenses with the strongest, most compelling—and readily available—evidence.

There was no question that Trump had committed impeachable conduct by obstructing the Mueller investigation in many different ways. The problem was that the whole constellation of issues in the Mueller report was complicated and difficult to explain. Most of the witnesses to the president's obstruction of justice had never testified outside the grand jury, like Don McGahn, and it wasn't clear we could make the case without them. They were also people of low character, many of them now felons, or putative felons, like Roger Stone, Paul Manafort, Mike Flynn, and Michael Cohen. Someone was going to have to try this case in the Senate, and it would be better to rely on the Marie Yovanovitches and William Taylors than to have to drag in the whole cast of characters in the Mueller report. Just saying their names elicited a shudder from the Speaker.

I also knew that many of the Badasses and other members from marginal districts did not want us revisiting the Mueller investigation and all its baggage. That meant that if we went forward with an article or articles based on Mueller-related misconduct, we could potentially lose several votes on those articles in the House, which would only further complicate our message. Pelosi had been hearing the same thoughts from many of our members, and that was her inclination to begin with: to focus on the case that would most resonate with the American people, and that was one that emphasized the threat to our national security. We would settle on two articles, one on Ukraine and one on obstruction. We didn't need to ignore the president's misconduct in the Russia investigation completely, and we could incorporate references to those prior bad acts as evidence of the president's corrupt pattern and practice.

The last question was whether the Ukraine article should charge "bribery" or, as Nadler was recommending, "abuse of power." Bribery was a concept clearly understood by the public, and it had the merit of being an easily recognizable and stigmatized act. Abuse of power, on the other hand, was nebulous. What exactly was an abuse of power, and when did it become impeachable? Still, Trump had been withholding the money from Ukraine to coerce them into investigating the Bidens rather than offering it for that purpose; the facts seemed more like extortion than bribery, and extortion was not explicitly mentioned in the Constitution. Moreover, proving a case of statutory bribery was not a simple matter. A recent Supreme Court case involving the former governor of Virginia had raised the bar significantly on the proof required in a bribery case under existing law. It was certainly true that the Founders had a broader understanding of bribery than is embodied in current federal statutes—there was no federal crime of bribery when the Constitution was adopted, after all, because no federal crimes had yet been defined. But it wouldn't be difficult for the Trump defense to argue that we needed to prove the modern statutory crime, which would only add to our burden of proof at trial. That consideration ended up being decisive. We would go with abuse of power.

While we were hashing out the language of the articles, Rudy Giuliani was in Ukraine doing everything he could to strengthen our case. He was meeting with a former Ukrainian diplomat named Andrii Telizhenko, who the U.S. government would later acknowledge had links to Russian intelligence. Telizhenko was tweeting photos of himself with Giuliani and bragging about plans they had to meet with corrupt former Ukrainian government officials. Giuliani would also meet with Andrii Derkach, a Ukrainian lawmaker and someone that our government would also later publicly identify as an active agent of Russian intelligence and someone who had earlier sent a package of information to Devin Nunes. The package had arrived in the SCIF addressed to Nunes and we had a copy of the mailing label. It was the most demonstrable proof that the president, his lawyer, and a prominent member of our committee were doing just what Fiona Hill had warned us against—advancing a false Kremlin narrative in the service of a domestic political end.

On Monday, December 9, Dan Goldman appeared before a hostile audience in the Judiciary Committee to present our findings. I had told Dan before his appearance that he knew the facts better than anyone else in that room, and all he needed to do was keep calm. "They are going to try to bait you. Don't let them."

The rules established under H. Res. 660 specified that committee counsel would present the report, but this greatly disappointed the Republicans. They brought the usual props—this time large placards behind the dais, one of which read "Where's Adam?" and another depicted a milk carton with my face on it. (My favorite sign—"It's been zero days since Adam Schiff followed the rules"—had been retired after a prior hearing when someone must have pointed out that that meant I was always following the rules.)

I was watching from my personal office as the GOP members of the committee went after Dan Goldman, or tried to, but he was unflappable. He knew the investigation and its findings so much better than any of his tormentors, and did an excellent job answering the questions and deflecting their attacks. Dan's only frustration, he would tell me later, was that some of the questions from Democrats did not give him a chance to more fully describe key events in the report. They were asking very narrow, yes-or-no questions, as they had of Mueller, and Dan wanted an opportunity to elaborate on the report's findings. Through all the Republican barbs—and there were many—Dan kept his cool, and so did Nadler, who did a great job of keeping the train on the tracks.

The following morning, December 10, I met with Pelosi and the other chairs for a press conference in the Rayburn Room, where we unveiled the two articles of impeachment. Article I was entitled "Abuse of Power" and charged the president with a scheme that included soliciting Ukraine "to publicly announce investigations that would benefit his reelection," harm his opponent, and influence the election "to his advantage." It further alleged that he sought to pressure the Ukrainian government to do so by "conditioning official United States Government acts of significant value." And in a reference to his Russia-related misconduct, the article further alleged that "these actions were consistent with President Trump's previous invitations of foreign interference" in U.S. elections.

Article II charged Trump with "Obstruction of Congress" in directing "the unprecedented, categorial, and indiscriminate defiance of subpoenas" issued by the House of Representatives. In this article, we itemized all the subpoenas for documents that were ignored, and we listed the names of nine administration officials who defied our subpoenas. "In all of this," the article charged, "President Trump has acted in a manner contrary to his trust as President and subversive of constitutional government, to the great prejudice of the cause of law and justice, and to the manifest injury of the people of the United States." Wherefore he should be impeached, tried, removed from office, and disqualified from holding or enjoying a future office or trust.

During the press conference, I talked about the danger Trump posed to the country, and the need to move with urgency. But

I thought I should also address the one question we were getting repeatedly: Why not slow down and call other witnesses? There was a strong public desire to hear the testimony of people like Bolton, and to determine the culpability of Pompeo and Pence. But I knew that there was no way to get these witnesses before any committee in less than a year, and with an election coming up, there was every risk that Trump would continue his efforts to cheat. So I decided to address the question foursquare: "Some would argue, why don't you just wait? Why don't you just wait until you get these witnesses the White House refuses to produce? Why don't you just wait until you get the documents the White House refuses to turn over? And people should understand what that argument really means." And it means this: "Why don't you just let him cheat in one more election? Why not let him cheat just one more time?"

On December 17, the day before a House vote to impeach a president for only the third time in history, Trump sent a long personal letter to the Speaker, accusing her of an "illegal, partisan attempted coup." It was an extraordinary screed, even by the president's own low standards. "You dare to invoke the Founding Fathers in pursuit of this election-nullification scheme—yet your spiteful actions display unfettered contempt for America's founding and your egregious conduct threatens to destroy that which our Founders pledged their very lives to build." Trump then took issue with Pelosi's Catholicism, saying that she was lying by saying she prayed for him. "It is a terrible thing you are doing, but you will have to live with it, not I!" It went on like this for six pages—six pages of claims that there was more due process in the Salem witch trials, claims that Pelosi hated democracy, and claims that voters could see through the "empty, hollow, and dangerous game you are playing."

Reading this letter, I was struck once again at how unwell a man the president was, and what a danger he posed to the country—not only because of his Ukraine misconduct but because he seemed so unbalanced mentally. What kind of person in a responsible position writes a letter like that? Could he really have his finger on the nuclear button?

On the following day, December 18, after eight hours of debate, the House of Representatives passed the first article of impeachment by a vote of 230–197, the second by 229–198. Over the next several days, we quietly began preparations for trial. Pelosi had not named House managers yet, and it became Washington's biggest parlor game to guess who the managers would be. After a caucus meeting, Pelosi and I stood in the large meeting room amid two hundred empty seats, the members having departed. "Do you see those seats?" Pelosi asked me. "Everyone sitting in them has asked me to be a manager. Every single one of them. Half of them aren't even on the relevant committees and had nothing to do with it." I wasn't surprised. Other than our vulnerable freshmen, just about everyone else had been cornering me to ask for my support or to put in a good word with the Speaker. Pelosi had told me nothing about my own role in the trial, but I was operating under the assumption that I would be a manager if not the lead prosecutor. We needed to get started organizing the case, a mammoth undertaking for a trial that was only a few weeks away, and she gave me the green light to utilize my own staff, and, eventually, select members of the Judiciary and Oversight staffs to start getting ready.

I was back in my office one evening when she called me. "Do you want to be the lead manager?" she asked.

"I want to do whatever you need me to do, to help make the case. I just want to make sure it's done right."

"Okay," she said. "But do you want to lead?"

"Yes."

"Good. Done."

As I hung up the phone, I thought about what lay ahead. As a prosecutor, I had never gone into a courtroom where I thought I couldn't win. Now I would be leading the House in one of the most consequential trials in history, and I was almost certain to lose. I needed to think about this trial differently—not as a prosecutor, but as a defender of the Constitution. I needed to figure out how we could win by losing.

PART FOUR

IMPARTIAL JUSTICE

18

THE FOUR AND THE FORTY MILLION

EVE AND I HAD PLANS TO TAKE THE KIDS TO SOUTH CAROLINA FOR A few days before the holidays, where we would meet up with Eve's side of the family and rent a large house together on the beach. Before we left, I gathered our committee investigative team together in the SCIF to discuss trial preparation. There had been only two other impeachment trials involving a president, Andrew Johnson's impeachment in 1868, and the 1999 impeachment trial of Bill Clinton. Although I hadn't followed the Clinton impeachment closely, this much I knew—it consisted of thirteen angry white men talking at the Senate for weeks. The Speaker would want our team of managers to be reflective of the country, so I knew that that much would be different. But I also wanted our presentation to be different. We would be trying the case to two juries—the Senate and the American people—and while I had little hope of winning over the two-thirds of the Senate needed for conviction, I thought we had a fighting chance of winning over the public. We needed to show the country not just that the president had committed impeachable acts, but why he was an ongoing danger to our nation and democracy. To do that, we needed to hold the public's attention.

"I want this to be like an HBO miniseries or a Ken Burns documentary," I told the staff, "with as much video and audio as we can make use of." We had hours of videotaped testimony that could be interwoven with graphic exhibits that displayed emails and text messages. We should look for news footage of the war in Ukraine so that senators and the public could see the fighting and know the stakes when the president withheld military aid. "And the video of Mulvaney admitting the quid pro quo, I want them to see that so often they can recite his words in their sleep."

Schumer's staff had given us feedback from the senators who had been present for the Clinton trial, that the House managers had been too repetitive and boring. We would have to use some repetition—I couldn't assume that ordinary Americans would be watching every minute of the trial the way the senators would—and I wanted the public to be able to follow what was happening even if they only listened to the trial on the way to the barbershop, to the hay and grain, or on the evening news. But the key was to make it visually interesting, and keep it that way. We still didn't know how long the Senate would give us to try the case, but the last thing I wanted to expose the country to was a bunch of members of Congress doing nothing but talking at them for weeks.

When I left for Charleston, the shape of the trial was still very much in doubt. McConnell was refusing to negotiate the resolution which would establish the duration of the trial, what procedures would govern, and how the issue of calling witnesses would be resolved. But he made this much clear—he was not going to be an impartial juror, as his oath would require. Taking to the Senate floor on December 19, McConnell engaged in a thirty-minute rant against the impeachment, calling it the "most rushed, least thorough, and most unfair impeachment inquiry in modern history."

McConnell said the House vote was not a neutral judgment that Democrats came to reluctantly, but "the predetermined end of a partisan crusade that began before President Trump was even nominated, let alone sworn in." Only one outcome would preserve the core tenets of our system, in his view, and it was up to the Senate to put things right.

Speaker Pelosi made the decision *not* to send the articles to the Senate—which would commence the clock to trial—until we had a better understanding of what kind of a trial it would be. For one thing, the resolution transmitting the articles would also name House managers, and she did not want to have to decide on those in the absence of knowing what skills would be required by the trial. More important, she felt that the additional time would allow us to increase the pressure on McConnell to allow witnesses. McConnell had already been threatening to make this the first impeachment trial in history to prohibit live testimony, and there was even the possibility—which concerned me the most—that he would simply bring a motion to dismiss and there would be no trial at all.

The four days we spent outside Charleston passed much too quickly, and I used the time to recharge my batteries after a grueling few months. We stayed indoors a lot, making good food, playing board games, and enjoying our extended family, while I did my best to stay off the phone and email. I was only partly successful. One of the great pleasures I had during that respite, though, was running along the beach late each day. It was generally overcast and rainy, but I loved running along the hard sand, leaning in against the wind and the small bits of water it threw in my face, and staring out to sea.

I returned to Washington, D.C., just before Christmas, and I spent the next ten days sitting by the fireplace, reading and editing the trial presentations my staff were putting together and studying up on impeachment procedure. Since I had tried an impeachment case once already, I had a leg up on just about everyone, but that had involved a federal judge and was a different animal altogether. So I downloaded the complete transcripts of the Clinton impeachment trial and started reading, occasionally pulling up video of the proceedings so I could also get a sense of the optics. As I did, I sent periodic emails to my staff on what I found noteworthy, what worked and what didn't, how the managers made their arguments and how the defense responded, what kind of questions senators asked, and the role of the chief justice in presiding. My staff joked that it was as if I was live-blogging a trial that had taken place more than twenty years earlier. The most riveting moment of the Clinton trial was when former senator Dale Bumpers took to the floor to defend his friend Bill Clinton. Wearing a roving microphone that allowed him to step away from the lectern, he spoke in a folksy and unencumbered manner. Senators were there, he said, because President Clinton had committed a "terrible moral lapse," "not a breach of the public trust" or "crime against society." A sex scandal. "H. L. Mencken said one time that when you hear somebody say 'This is not about money,' it's about money." Bumpers paused to let that sink in, and as he did, laughter spread throughout the chamber. "And when you hear someone say this is not about sex, it's about sex."

Bumpers was more effective than any of the other managers or defense counsel, because he spoke plainly about what was at stake, in terms that both the senators and the public could appreciate, and because he was not held captive to a script. I would try to learn from that. The Clinton House managers were complaining about the procedure in the trial, that the format was "not particularly helpful to the trial managers," as one of them said—even though the Senate, like the House, was controlled by Republicans—and they came across as constantly whining, as if the process were unfair to them, not to the country. Even as McConnell stacked the deck against us, I would have to learn from that too. In the debate we were destined to have over witnesses, I needed to make the case why they were important to the Constitution and the country and not some matter of personal privilege.

"Do you think this is leverage," McConnell asked reporters, referring to Pelosi's decision to withhold transmission of the articles, "to not send us something we'd rather not do?" He smiled at the thought, even as public sentiment moved swiftly against his entrenched position. We had been making the argument that the choice was between a fair trial—fair to the president and fair to the American people—and a cover-up. Seventy percent of the American people agreed that the trial needed to include witness testimony in order to be credible, and the pressure continued to mount. The delay exposed the degree to which McConnell was working in lockstep with the president, and McConnell's thin margin for error. McConnell could not afford to lose more than four Republican senators on any vote on witnesses, and there were at least four who refused to commit one way or another, including: Senators Susan Collins of Maine, Lisa Murkowski of Alaska, Mitt Romney of Utah, and Lamar Alexander of Tennessee.

The delay in transmitting the articles had another salutary effect—new evidence was continually coming to light. In late December, partially redacted Pentagon emails were released as part of a Freedom of Information Act request by the Center for Public Integrity, and they showed one of the president's political appointees asking for the military aid to be suspended just hours after the July 25 call; other emails detailed serious concerns at the Defense Department over whether delaying the aid might prevent some of it from going out at all. That a private litigant could get discovery more quickly than Congress with its subpoena power was a powerful indictment of how much Trump had neutered our oversight capability.

And the disclosures kept coming. In early January, the publication *Just Security* released unredacted copies of the same documents that shed additional light on the president's role in withholding the military aid from Ukraine. "Clear direction from POTUS to continue to hold," one document read. The records also showed concerns within the Defense Department that the hold was violating the law. As part of our impeachment inquiry, we had subpoenaed all of these records and now we had them, or at least some of them. Their production also reinforced our argument that the Senate should use its subpoena power to compel witnesses *and* documents, and "if they were not produced, the Senate and the American people would be justified in asking, what else is the president hiding?"

Soon we learned about something even more consequential that the president had been doing in secret—authorizing the killing of Iranian Quds Force leader Qasem Soleimani, one of Iran's top generals. There was no question that Soleimani had played a major role in all kinds of deadly and malign activities in the region, and I was glad that he would no longer pose a danger to our troops and the region, but the timing of his assassination on the eve of trial alarmed me. I had been receiving intelligence briefings on Iran, and while there was a growing threat to our personnel in the region, I wasn't made aware of any imminent threat. Moreover, it stood to reason that killing Soleimani was likely to increase the near term risk to our troops and diplomatic personnel. Given the president's earlier reluctance to use force against Iran that I had witnessed during our meeting in the Cabinet Room, what had changed?

After a top level briefing on the matter, I was still not convinced of the urgency or the specificity of the threat, and I urged the administration to take all possible steps to protect our troops in the region from the likely Iranian retaliation. Days later, Iran did attack, launching missiles against two of our bases in Iraq. It was a miracle that none of our troops was killed, but dozens suffered serious head trauma from the blasts, something the president tried to dismiss as "headaches." The killing of Soleimani while he was on Iraqi soil was also turning Iraqis against us, and calls for our forces to be expelled from the country were increasing.

Meanwhile, the administration's rationale for the strike was continuing to evolve, with the president now claiming that Soleimani was plotting to strike four U.S. embassies, and Pompeo was backing him up. I was aware of no such specific intelligence, and Defense Secretary Esper would soon acknowledge that he wasn't either. Trump and Pompeo were fudging the intelligence again, this time to justify a strike that had the potential of leading us into war. Was it really possible that Trump would take such consequential action at least in part to gin up Republican support prior to his impeachment? Of course it was—and no one who had watched his destructive narcissism over the last three years could rule it out.

As I worried that Trump might be wagging the dog into war, Kevin McCarthy was arguing that I was somehow responsible for the strike on Soleimani and the prospect of war, since I had not been "trying to protect us." As if acting in defense of the Constitution was somehow inconsistent with our national security. At the same time, Trump was making his own links between impeachment and the targeted killing, while trying to deflect criticism that he failed to notify the Gang of Eight about the strike in advance. Apparently, he told Lindsey Graham about the planned strike while they were together in West Palm Beach for a golf outing, but not the Speaker or any other Democratic leader. At a rally in Toledo, Ohio, Trump complained, "Now they want us to call—can you imagine calling crooked Adam Schiff? He's so crooked. He's so crooked. Shifty Schiff. Say, 'Gee Adam, how you doing? Listen, we have the world's number one terrorist. Killed thousands and thousands of people. We'd like to set up a meeting so we can discuss his execution . . . We've got him lined up, Adam. You little pencil neck. Nine inches. He buys the smallest shirt collar you can get, and it's loose." And, pretending to be me, he replied, "But I can't make it now, because I'm trying to impeach Trump. I'm trying to impeach him. Even though he did nothing wrong."

Sometime later, Trump would get bored of the "pencil neck" routine and start calling me "watermelon head." I'm sure there was some explanation deep in his psyche for the change, but I took to telling my supporters that having a pencil neck and a watermelon head made for a very difficult balancing act.

On January 6, John Bolton announced—out of the blue—that he was willing to testify in the Senate trial. He gave no explanation for his change of heart, or for why he needed a court order before he could testify before the House, but now a mere Senate subpoena would do. I suspect that his upcoming book had a lot to do with it, and it wasn't just the increasing public criticism that he was withholding important information from the country so that he could sell more books. The Trump White House was refusing to complete its classification review of his book, and unless he could make its contents public—as through a trial—he might never be able to publish. If patriotism was not sufficient motive to testify, greed would have to do. But whatever his motivation, I would take it.

Lev Parnas, now an indicted associate of Rudy Giuliani, also expressed a willingness to testify, and he provided a trove of documents to us, including significant correspondence with Giuliani. Most concerning were text messages to and from a Republican operative named Robert Hyde, suggesting that Hyde had been surveilling the ambassador, or worse. In a cryptic message, he had written, "They are willing to help if we/you would like a price. Guess you can do anything in the Ukraine with money . . . what I was told."

The documents we received from Parnas contained other deeply disturbing material as well, about a member of Nunes's staff who, from February to May 2019, had had numerous contacts with Parnas in which the staff member raised questions about aid to Ukraine and discussed arranging interviews with discredited Ukrainian officials like former prosecutors Shokin and Lutsenko. These messages tracked all too closely with Nunes's disclosure that committee Republicans were engaged in some undisclosed Ukraine investigation of their own, and one that I believed was aligned with Russian propaganda and the president's goal of discrediting Joe Biden.

Parnas was eager to testify about the work he had been doing for Trump and Giuliani, perhaps too eager, but Bolton and Mulvaney remained higher priorities, since they had had the most direct contact with the president. Despite my lack of trust in Bolton, I was willing to risk the uncertainties of his testimony for the near certainty that I would lose the trial without him. In a normal trial, I would be reluctant to call witnesses without knowing exactly what they had to say in advance, but this was not a normal trial. All of the risk of their testimony lay on the other side, and if we could just get them on the stand, it was possible that their testimony might lead to other witnesses and discoveries and break the trial right open.

The president's allies had reached the same conclusion. For all of Trump's talk of calling me, the Bidens, or Pelosi to the stand, possibly as a trade for Mulvaney and Bolton, there was a growing consensus among Republican strategists and media advocates against calling any witnesses at all. "Let me address all of you . . . in the U.S. Senate tonight," Hannity threatened on January 9, "all of you Republican senators. You do not and should not ever lend any credibility to this despicable corrupt Schiff show. . . . You Republican senators are weak and timid if you give credibility to this repulsive, corrupt political stunt."

On January 13, the cybersecurity firm Area 1 disclosed that the Main Intelligence Directorate of the General Staff of the Russian Army (GRU) had hacked Burisma only weeks earlier, launching a spear phishing campaign and stealing user names. While we had been conducting open hearings in the House and looking into Trump's efforts to coerce Ukraine to investigate the Bidens, the Russians were once again leaping into the void in an obvious effort to dig up dirt they could use to help Trump again. Mueller had indicted Russians in this same unit of the GRU for hacking Democratic organizations in 2016, and now they were back at it. It was like the previous election all over again, and in the middle of an impeachment proceeding, no less.

Throughout the first two weeks of January, the Speaker and I had numerous conversations about the managers, and we were constantly comparing lists of who we thought would bring trial skills, communications skills, and geographic, ethnic, and gender diversity to the team. Little by little we were coming together on a final list, and as we agreed on a particular manager, we would send them down to the SCIF to start getting up to speed. Representative Jason Crow of Colorado, a former Army Ranger and talented new member, was among the first to be picked, and I wanted him to begin studying the file right away since he didn't serve on either the Intelligence or Judiciary Committees and would need the most time to prepare. He was sworn to secrecy about his own selection, and we didn't even share with him who he would be working with—when the managers were announced, we wanted to make a statement. Jerry Nadler would also be a manager, but for all of the Speaker's confidence in Nadler, she also wanted to make sure there would be clear lines of authority and only one lead. "One good general," she told me, "is better than two great generals." Then, she added with a laugh, "Not that you're not a great general."

On the morning of January 14, Pelosi and I addressed the caucus. I told the members what to expect, assuming the trial resembled the Clinton impeachment. We would have twenty-four hours to make our case, spread out over a number of days, and the defense would have the same. The issue of witnesses might be decided later, only after we and the defense put on our cases and answered questions. This process made little sense to me, but it seemed to be where McConnell was headed. Pelosi told the members that we would soon be sending the articles to the Senate, perhaps as early as the following day. Whatever happened in the Senate, and whatever McConnell might do about the procedure, we had done our constitutional duty. The president had been impeached, and he would be impeached *for life*. He would be impeached *forever*. As the members filed out, Pelosi and I remained behind, once again alone in the room with all of the empty chairs. And by the end of that day, if not that meeting, all of the managers would be selected.

Later that afternoon, I made a fateful decision. I had a loose filling in one of my teeth that was not painful, but I was worried that it might break off during the trial. I sneaked away from the Capitol and had the filling redone. When I left the dentist's office, I had the usual pain and numbness, and I assumed that whatever sensitivity I was now feeling would dissipate in a day or two. But I was wrong—in the process of refilling the cavity, a nerve had been inflamed, and the pain was only going to grow.

"And today is an important day," the Speaker said the next morning, after the other six managers and I followed her onto the stage in the press gallery for the first time, "because today we go to the floor to pass the resolution to transmit the articles of impeachment to the Senate, and later in the day, when we have our engrossment, that we march those articles of impeachment to the U.S. Senate." After naming me as the lead manager, she introduced Jerry Nadler and Representatives Zoe Lofgren of California, Hakeem Jeffries of New York, Val Demings of Florida, Sylvia Garcia of Texas, and Jason Crow of Colorado. It was a very diverse group of managers, with three women, two African Americans, and a Latina, from both coasts, the South, and the West. In short, it was a group of managers that looked like America. The selection emphasis, she said, was on litigators, on comfort level in the courtroom, and on making the strongest possible case in an impeachment "that will last forever."

After the presser, my fellow managers and I gathered in the SCIF for our first strategy session as a group, and Speaker Pelosi stopped by briefly to urge us on and wish us success. But apparently she also had another motive. Surveying the conference room and finding the long table empty of anything but water, she said: "I thought there might be food." We all laughed.

We discussed the procedure for the trial, how long we would have for certain argumentation, and the creation of a war room through the Speaker's office for messaging. Jeffries underscored the need to be disciplined and not freelance on communications, while Garcia offered to handle Spanish-language media requests and Crow suggested we develop talking points. I wanted all press hits to be run through Boland, but also wanted the managers out there to amplify our position, since they were such good communicators. If anyone raises concerns about our process on this, I told the managers, they could blame me. "Why not," Demings replied. "Everybody else is."

I recommended to my colleagues that they take their interns off the phones, since the calls they were about to receive from around the country were going to be ugly. I also said that we should be respectful of the senators, but they should feel free to spotlight McConnell and anything he was doing that would make a fair trial difficult to achieve. We needed to be particularly careful about the key senators and not give any impression that we were trying to put pressure on them back home, which I thought would backfire. I also emphasized the need to keep our private discussions private, and spoke about how the press would love to write about any differences on strategy. "As Ben Franklin said," I commented, "we must hang together or surely we shall hang separately." Demings furrowed her brow and said: "Thanks a lot." And we all laughed again.

"Get ready for a hell of a roller coaster," I said as we wrapped up the meeting. "Some days are going to be great and some days will be shitty. These are historic times and we should all feel a sense of mission about the work ahead of us. We did our duty in the House, and now we seven will do our duty in the Senate."

The resolution of transmittal passed the House later that morning on a near party line vote, with one Democrat voting no and one independent representative voting yea. We then gathered in the Rayburn Room in the Capitol, where Pelosi signed the transmittal and handed each of the managers and the chairs of the six committees one of the pens she used. "Today we will make history," she said. "This president will be held accountable."

When she was done, I lined up behind the House clerk and sergeant at arms, Nadler at my side and the other managers falling in behind us, and we proceeded away from the House, under the dome of the Capitol, and over to the Senate side. None of us spoke as we made that solemn pilgrimage through the marble hallways, cordoned off with red velvet ropes. Sun shone through the windows high above, covering us in light and shadow, and we passed by a series of risers where photographers took photos from on high, their shutters filling the silence like so many angry insects. When we reached the Senate doors, we waited outside until the senators were ready and we could be admitted, then stood in the rear of the chamber as we were announced by our clerk.

"The House has passed House Resolution 798, a resolution appointing and authorizing managers of the impeachment trial of Donald John Trump, president of the United States," she declared. Having received the articles, McConnell pledged that the Senate would "rise above the petty factionalism" and "serve the long-term best interests of our nation," but it was hard to see how he could mean it, given what he had already said. Perhaps he was hopeful that the Senate would reject the evidence against the president on a bipartisan basis.

At noon the following day, Wednesday, January 16, 2020, we reprised our march across the Capitol and were brought to the well of the Senate. "Hear ye, hear ye, hear ye," the Senate sergeant at arms called out, in language that had echoed down through the ages of our nation's history. "All persons are commanded to keep silent on pain of imprisonment." The chamber was full and quiet as I was invited to read the articles to the body. I was struck by how intimate the Senate chamber was, how I could hear every sound around me and see the expressions of everyone in the room. The microphone was sensitive, and as I turned to make eye contact with the senators, I could hear the amplification begin to trail off—I would need to remember that too. My voice was steady and I read slowly, not wanting to have a single word out of place. Still, it was hard not to let my mind wander as I read the final words of the articles and thought what an extraordinary moment it was to be in that place and for that purpose.

Later, after being sworn in himself, Chief Justice Roberts swore in the senators with an oath that required them to "do impartial justice according to the Constitution and laws." The trial itself would begin in earnest in five days. In the interim, McConnell gave us until Saturday to file our trial brief, with defense briefs and replies due on Monday. Trump had been filling in his legal defense team, adding retired Harvard Law professor Alan Dershowitz and Clinton-era independent counsel Ken Starr to a team that included White House Counsel Pat Cipollone, the president's longtime personal lawyer, Jay Sekulow, Pam Bondi, and a growing list of others. The commentators on Fox liked their matchup. "So you compare that all-star lineup," Laura Ingraham gushed, "serious legal people, astute legal minds, to the partisan hacks that Nancy Pelosi tapped for the prosecution. . . . Do we really think Schiff is going to be somehow more convincing in the Senate chamber than Alan Dershowitz, a constitutional scholar . . . ? Well, it's going to be a blowout for the Republicans, and we're going to be covering it every step of the way."

WORKING AROUND THE CLOCK, THE combined staff of our three committees quickly produced a 111-page brief, which included the meaning and history of the impeachment clause, its applicability to Trump's misconduct, a rebuttal of their defenses, and more than sixty pages of findings of fact. The Trump defense brief, filed two days later, called the articles "an affront to the Constitution and to our democratic institutions." Apart from the familiar, and factually unsound, claims of a "perfect call" to President Zelensky and "no pressure," the brief took issue with Article I for not alleging a statutory crime, claiming that the president could not be impeached for abusing his power—an assertion that would have come as a rude awakening to the delegates to the Constitutional Convention of 1787, who believed it to be the highest of constitutional crimes.

They also took issue with Article II, claiming that the House should have exhausted court remedies before resorting to impeachment when the president obstructed Congress. This argument was not without its irony, since the Trump administration was in court arguing that Congress could not go to court to enforce its subpoenas. None of these arguments was unexpected, but one of the appendices was a surprise—the defense brief attached an opinion from the Office of Legal Counsel (OLC) of the Justice Department dated January 19, 2020, only one day earlier, which argued that witnesses subpoenaed by the House could not be compelled to testify if they had been called prior to the House vote formalizing the impeachment inquiry. The brief also appended another OLC opinion, written weeks earlier, which asserted that senior advisers to the president were absolutely immune from testimony.

Both OLC opinions had been requested by White House Counsel Cipollone, the same lawyer who had played an integral role in obstructing Congress, and had written the eight-page diatribe announcing the president's intention to stonewall the impeachment inquiry. If that conflict of interest wasn't brazen enough, OLC was the same office that told the DNI that the whistleblower complaint did not need to be provided to Congress—that the "shall" in the law didn't really mean "shall." It was the most obvious demonstration yet that Barr had dragooned this otherwise independent office into complete servitude to the president's corrupt cause. People outside the department, unaware of OLC's purported role as a neutral legal adviser to executive branch agencies, might not recognize how shocking a betrayal of its history and responsibilities this was, but there it was, in all its inglorious pages. The argument it made was nonsense—Trump hadn't even asserted a privilege, and had merely instructed the administration to stonewall all subpoenas—but the fact that OLC was trying to give the president a "get out of jail free" card, and as part of the president's impeachment trial brief, no less, meant that another check on the executive had come crashing down.

On Tuesday, January 21, I met with the other House managers in one of the Speaker's conference rooms, H-236. This had become our hideaway, where we could work outside the scrutiny of the press and away from the distractions of our offices. In the short time since their appointment, I had sought to pair the material we would cover in our initial presentations—our case-in-chief—with the respective strengths of each of the managers and their particular interests. Nadler had an extensive knowledge of the legal and constitutional issues and understood the procedures used in prior impeachments as well as the historical framework. Zoe Lofgren had been a House staffer during the Nixon impeachment and a member of the Judiciary Committee during Clinton's impeachment, so this was now her third experience with the process. She was a particularly great resource on many of the same historical and procedural issues, with a soft-spoken and nonpartisan manner of communicating that would be very effective with senators of both parties. Hakeem Jeffries had been a litigator in his prior career, very quick on his feet, with a rare talent for both improvisation *and* staying on message. Demings, as a former police chief, had a commanding presence and the ability to talk convincingly about right and wrong. Sylvia Garcia had been a judge in South Texas, and with a demeanor much like Zoe's, carried herself with the gravitas of an officer of the court. She was also fluent in Spanish, and could help convey our message in Spanish language media. And finally, Jason Crow, a former Army Ranger and litigator, would be superb in discussing the military aid to Ukraine and how important that was in the fight against the Russians.

"We have to remember," I told the managers, "we are talking to the four and the forty million." "The four" referred to the handful of swing Republican senators who might be persuaded to allow witnesses or to convict, and forty million was the number of Americans watching at home that I assumed were still undecided about the president and his conduct. This was our target audience.

Each day we were in trial, the managers would get an outline of their presentations from staff at least one evening in advance, and I wanted them to own the material, make it theirs with personal touches and edits; if they thought it needed restructuring, to do so with staff; and if they had any questions about the facts or their presentations, to discuss them with me. "We have a fine line to walk," I explained. "We want to hold the Senators accountable for their votes, but we also want to be respectful and avoid alienating any of them, and particularly the four."

The first day of trial was supposed to be all about process, and a debate over the rules that would govern the trial. McConnell waited until the night before to finally release his organizing resolution setting out the trial process. As expected, McConnell's resolution deferred until the end of the trial the question of whether witnesses could be called. He had claimed to be following the Clinton precedent, but when we received the resolution, it was clear that he was sharply deviating from past practice. In the Clinton case, the former president had provided all of the relevant documents, more than ninety thousand of them, before the trial. McConnell was not requiring Trump to provide anything. Even more consequential, the Clinton managers were permitted to call witnesses, and McConnell was already making it very clear he would fight that tooth and nail.

Schumer would be offering a series of amendments to the McConnell resolution, authorizing subpoenas for Mulvaney and Bolton, but also several amendments to subpoena documents from the relevant agencies. We would have two hours to debate each of these matters, and the Trump defense team expected that debate to be no more than a sterile discussion over process. But I had something else in mind. I wanted to present our case on the merits—through these motions—and get a head start. So we had multimedia presentations ready to go, using each witness and agency document request to explain the case against the president, with slides, footage from the hearings, public statements of the president, and other visuals to hammer home the president's misconduct. If we were lucky, we could catch the president's team unprepared to address the substance of the articles.

Trial was to begin at 1 P.M., and we left the Speaker's conference room about half an hour in advance, making our way to S-239, the ceremonial office of the Senate Rules Chair, just down the hall from the Senate chamber. This elegant space, with fine couches and chairs, a chandelier and gilded mirror, a marble fireplace, high-speed printers, computers and television screens, and a beautiful view of the West Capitol grounds and Washington Monument, was to be our home away from home while we were in the Senate trying the case. It would be the room to which we would retreat during breaks to discuss strategy, make final changes to our arguments, and get a bite to eat. When we arrived in our new workspace, McConnell was on the Senate floor making the case for his resolution, and Schumer was making the case against it. Shortly thereafter, Ashley Etienne on the Speaker's staff announced "It's time, everyone," and we processed into the Senate chamber.

I sat down at the table reserved for the House managers, in the seat closest to the podium, and my fellow managers took up their seats next to me in order of seniority. I was carrying my grandfather Frank Schiff's old Waltham pocket watch with me for luck, and I set it down on the table in front of me so I could keep time without checking my wristwatch. As I looked at its beautiful face, with small lines marking its age on the delicate porcelain, I imagined what the immigrant who carried it in his pocket for so many years would have thought about where it ended up—keeping time during the impeachment of a president.

After the formal reading of McConnell's resolution, the chief justice recognized Pat Cipollone to make the first argument in support of the measure. Cipollone was pale and thin, wore glasses, and looked more like a corporate transactions attorney than a litigator. He gave some very brief and perfunctory words of support for the measure, before reserving the remainder of his time for rebuttal. I was amazed that he had so little to say, and that he seemed disorganized, so much so that I began to wonder whether the Trump defense wasn't sufficiently aware of the time that they would have for debate. Perhaps they expected the senators to debate the process, not the managers and defense? It was also possible that they were merely reserving all of their time so that we could not rebut their arguments.

This gave us a chance to make the first strong impression on the senators and the more important jury at home. As I approached the microphone, I was more than aware of the hopes that I carried, of my fellow managers and the Democratic members of the House and Senate, but also of millions of Americans who had been watching the destructive actions of the president and wanted someone to speak for them, and to hold this lawless man to account. It was hard not to think of the historic figures who had stood where I now stood, and I felt a grave sense of responsibility, along with a nervous excitement.

I began with a brief recitation of the facts and could hear, in the slightly tremulous quality of my voice, that I was not completely settled. That was okay, I just needed time. I described the president's abuse of his office, and how his defense team would have us believe that there was nothing that the House or Senate could do about it. There were two questions the Senate would ultimately need to answer: whether the House had proved its case, and whether, having done so, the remedy provided by the Founders was warranted. "And so you will vote to find the president guilty or not guilty, to find his conduct impeachable or not impeachable."

But those would not be the most important decisions the Senate would make. How could that be?

"I believe . . . the most important question is the question you must answer today: Will the president and the American people get a fair trial? Will there be a fair trial? I submit that this is an even more important question than how you vote on guilt or innocence, because whether we have a fair trial will determine whether you have a basis to render a fair and impartial verdict. It is foundational—the structure upon which every other decision you will make must rest."

This was the point I wanted to drive home during the entire day's proceedings—a fair trial required witnesses, documents, and testimony, like any other trial, and the McConnell resolution sought to have us try the case first and reject witnesses later. No courtroom in America tried a case that way, and in the long history of impeachments—of judges and presidents—neither had the Senate.

Already I was starting to feel more at home in the chamber. My voice was growing stronger, and I began to look away from the page, at the senators and to the gallery above where the cameras—and the American people—were watching. I acknowledged that people were already saying that McConnell had the votes to prevent witnesses, and that McConnell was a very good vote counter. But I said that I hoped McConnell was wrong, because "whatever Senators may have said or pledged or committed has been superseded by an event of constitutional dimension. You have all now sworn an oath—not to each other, not to your legislative leadership, not to the managers or even to the chief justice. You have sworn an oath to do impartial justice. That oath binds you. That oath supersedes all else."

Most Americans thought the result was precooked and the president would be acquitted, not because he was innocent, but because his party had the votes, and that meant the votes to make sure the evidence never came out, that the public would never get to see it. "Let's prove them wrong," I said. "Let's prove them wrong."

For much of the next hour, I walked the senators through the many reasons we wanted Bolton and Mulvaney to testify, and why senators should insist on seeing the documents the administration was withholding. I was convinced that the Senate paid little attention to the House proceedings, and what they did know had been filtered through the distorting lens of Fox prime time. So I played video clips of the president, just a month earlier, saying that he would "love" to have Pompeo, Mulvaney, and Perry testify in the Senate trial, where it was "fair." Later we would show them slides of the documents we had obtained through other means, displaying their redactions and asking senators whether they would like to see what was blacked out. I directed Senators to a visual with a quote from McConnell himself, in the impeachment trial of Judge Claiborne, describing how the Senate "labored intensively for more than two months, amassing the necessary evidence and testimony." In that trial, the Senate heard from nineteen witnesses and allowed for the admission of two thousand pages of documents.

Finally, I warned the senators that the facts would come out in the end. I wanted the senators to know that when the full truth of the president's misconduct emerged, they would be held accountable.

JAY SEKULOW BEGAN THE PRESENTATION for the defense. With a handkerchief folded neatly in his pocket, stylish glasses, and an elegant suit, he was very much at home in a courtroom, even this one, and he would be formidable. No sooner had he introduced himself than the attacks began. "Manager Schiff just tried to summarize my colleague's defense of the president. He said it not in his words, of course, which is not the first time Mr. Schiff has put words into transcripts that did not exist." Well, that certainly didn't take long. After attacking me, he moved on to Nadler, complaining about the process in his committee, and misrepresenting it, badly. "During the proceedings that took place before the Judiciary Committee, the president was denied the right to cross-examine witnesses; the president was denied the right to access evidence; and the president was denied the right to have counsel present at hearings."

Nadler, sitting next to me at the managers' table, leaned over, indignant. "Adam, that's a lie. They had the right to participate and they refused. You need to stand up and tell them, it's a lie." Nadler was right, but I told him that I couldn't do that, that Sekulow was also lying about me, but I wasn't going to interrupt their opening statement. He said that if I didn't, he would. I told him that we needed to let it go and we would address it later. They were trying to bait us, to turn the trial into an ugly brawl, and we couldn't allow them to succeed. We were just going to have to suck it up for now and stick to the plan. But I understood Nadler's anger. He had worked hard to make sure that the president was granted full due process rights, consistent with prior impeachments, and had been willing to go even further to accommodate the president's participation than I thought wise. Nadler and I had had a bitter fight over whether to do so, and Nadler had won. It was the president who had refused his committee's offer to participate.

Sekulow had no prepared remarks and seemed to be winging it, which gave his argument a certain incoherence. There was no defense of the president's Ukraine misconduct, and little defense of his obstructive conduct, apart from the argument that he had a right to vindicate his interests in executive privilege. He went through a list of the president's grievances—the desire of Democrats to get rid of Trump, the Mueller investigation, and more, before turning it over to Cipollone again. Clearly, he was playing to an audience of one, which was fine with me, since I had a completely different audience in mind.

Cipollone resumed the attacks on me. Not content with Sekulow's misrepresentation that I had doctored transcripts, Cipollone repeated the president's fictitious narrative that I had made up false allegations about the July 25 call, forcing the president to release the call record. He then attacked the conduct of the investigation in the House, making the obviously false claim that "Not even Mr. Schiff's

Republican colleagues were allowed into the SCIF." Cipollone also attacked Nadler again, and I could feel Nadler's anger rising. After four years of unrelenting false and negative attacks, I had grown accustomed to them. They still bothered me—no one likes to be the subject of endless smears—but I had come to accept that they were part of the job, just as Speaker Pelosi had had to endure years of villainization. But the egregiousness of the falsehoods, here, in front of the world, was something that Nadler had not experienced, and certainly not to this degree. He was furious.

BACK IN OUR SENATE WORKPLACE for a fifteen-minute break, I spoke with Nadler and separately with his staff, to make sure that he was okay and holding up as well as could be expected under the attacks. As disturbing as they were, Nadler had far more on his mind than the Trump team's many falsehoods. His wife, Joyce, had been recently diagnosed with cancer. How Nadler was holding it together, I couldn't imagine. I also gave the managers my critique of the Trump defense team and their strategy. Clearly, they were unprepared to debate the merits of these amendments with us, and they were even less prepared to address the president's underlying misconduct.

When debate on the McConnell resolution concluded, I took the opportunity to respond "before certain representations became congealed." First, I pointed out how the Trump defense made no effort to defend McConnell's resolution, or conducting a trial with no witnesses. They did not because they could not, since every Senate precedent, including the most recent presidential impeachment, that of Bill Clinton, ran contrary to their position. I batted away their argument about executive privilege, since the president never invoked one. And I took aim at the only really substantive argument that they did make: that the House should have taken whatever time was necessary to exhaust its remedies in the courts before impeaching the president, even if it had taken years to do so. If the Founders had wanted to require the exhaustion of legal remedies, they would have said so, I argued. Instead, they gave Congress the sole power of impeachment.

Turning to our most powerful case for witnesses—Bolton—I tried to tantalize the Senate into hearing from him—and not just the Senate, but the American people. "He is willing to come and talk to you. He is willing to come and testify and tell you what he knows. The question is, Do you want to hear it? . . . Do you want to hear from someone who was in the meetings, someone who described what the president did—this deal between Mulvaney and Sondland—as a drug deal? Do you want to know why it was a drug deal? . . . You should want to know." Pointing at Trump's defense team, I said: "They don't want you to know. The president doesn't want you to know. Can you really live up to the oath you have taken to be impartial and not know?"

Then, alluding to Cipollone's assertion that Republicans were not allowed in the depositions, I said, "I am not going to suggest to you that Mr. Cipollone would deliberately make a false statement . . . but I will tell you this. He is mistaken." I then pointed out that every Republican member on three committees had been allowed to attend and had had equal time to question the witnesses. I wasn't going to call Cipollone a liar, or even use the word "lie," as I thought it too inflammatory, but I wanted the senators to know that they could not trust what he was saying, not now, and not later in the trial.

Trump's lawyers had also claimed that the president was not allowed to present evidence—or even be in the room—in Nadler's committee, and I wanted to set the record straight there as well. "I am not going to suggest to you that they are being deliberately misleading here," I said, "but it is just plain wrong." Although I did not say this to the senators, I recognized that these were tactical lies by Trump's lawyers, meant to rattle us, and in the absence of a legitimate defense. But I did tell senators that we would not waste their time by responding to all of the attacks against us. It was important for them to know that when they heard attacks on the House managers, what they were really hearing was *We don't want to talk about the president's guilt.* When they heard Trump's defense team going after us, I wanted the senators (and the forty million) to ask themselves, "What are they trying to deflect my attention from? Why don't they have a better argument to make on the merits?"

I yielded the floor to Lofgren to discuss the first Schumer amendment and sat down. I realized, with some surprise, that I had completely forgotten where I was and the unique nature of the setting. The Senate was now a courtroom like any other, and I was focused on the arguments of opposing counsel, jotting down notes and extemporizing my responses. I hadn't tried a case in years and hoped it was like riding a bike, and to some degree it was. I didn't know my evidentiary objections the way I used to, but then I didn't need to. The senators could admit whatever evidence they wanted. Even the standard of proof was open to their discretion. Of course the president's team was arguing that it should be proof beyond a reasonable doubt, but the Constitution said nothing about that except this—"The Senate shall have the sole Power to try all Impeachments"—which meant that the burden of proof was whatever they said it was.

Lofgren's presentation was perfect—methodical, persuasive, and, for a discussion about trial procedure, pretty darned interesting. Using slides to demonstrate past impeachments, she displayed how many witnesses and documents were introduced in each, paying particular attention to the Clinton trial, given her direct experience with that impeachment. She marched through our efforts to get documents in the House investigation, and Cipollone's eight-page response. While the president's team offered various excuses for obstructing the witnesses, it had provided no basis for obstructing the production of documents. She played videos of witnesses in the House hearings, talking about the notes they took, the emails they wrote, and the text messages they sent—all of which were in the possession of the administration. In so doing, she was proving the president's guilt, even as she was making the case for Senate action.

Pat Philbin, deputy White House counsel, took over for the defense team to rebut Lofgren's presentation. Tall, lanky, and academic-looking, Philbin presented a credible defense argument for the first time that day. He argued that the subpoenas were invalid because the House had not yet authorized the impeachment inquiry. This argument was flawed as a constitutional matter, since no such resolution was needed, and it didn't apply to the many subpoenas issued after the House passed such a resolution, but at least it was an argument and not an attack. He next asserted that the House was not ready to go to trial and was seeking to have the Senate do the work it should have done before impeaching the president. "If the House has not done the investigation and cannot support its case, it is not the time, once it arrives here, to start doing all that work. That is something that is the House's role."

This would be a recurrent defense theme for the rest of the day—that the Senate could only consider the cold record sent it by the House and could not actually hear testimony or gather new evidence. When he was finished, Lofgren deferred to me for rebuttal, and I immediately responded. "Mr. Philbin says that the House is not ready to present its case," I said, looking at Philbin. "Of course, that is not something you heard from any of the managers. We are ready. The House calls John Bolton." I paused, as if he were about to enter the Senate unexpectedly and be sworn in. "The House calls John Bolton. The House calls Mick Mulvaney. Let's get this trial started, shall we? We are ready to present our case. We are ready to call our witnesses. The question is," I said, turning to the senators, "will you let us?"

Trump's defense would have the Senate believe they were appellate court justices, confined only to the record of the court below, rather than empowered to try the case as the Constitution provides. *None of you are appellate court judges,* I had told them earlier, before turning to look behind me at the chief justice. *Okay, one of you is.* When debate on Schumer's amendment concluded, McConnell called a vote, and the result broke down along party lines, 53 to 47, against the amendment. McConnell had counted his votes well, and each subsequent amendment met the same fate, if not precisely the same margin.

Although we were losing the amendments in the Senate, I felt

confident we were winning the arguments with the American people, and I was very pleased with the quality of our presentations.
Jason Crow drew on his own military experience in a highly affecting and effective manner. One of the points that we wanted to hammer home was why Americans should care about Ukraine and its
war with Russia. Crow began with that question and explained that
before he was a member of Congress, he had been an American
soldier serving in Iraq and Afghanistan. "Although some years have
passed since that time, there are still some memories that are seared
in my brain. One of those memories is scavenging scrap metal on
the streets of Baghdad in the summer of 2003, which we had to
bolt onto the side of our trucks because we had no armor to protect
against roadside bombs. When we talk about troops not getting the
equipment they need, when they need it, it is personal to me."

It was a powerful beginning to his presentation, and just what I
hoped the managers would do to make the material their own. We
carried on this way all day and well into the night, the managers
using each amendment to graphically make the case for witnesses
and documents even as we proved the president's guilt. Because the
Trump defense team was so ill-prepared for the kind of presentation
we were making, they could not address the substantive points about
the evidence against the president, and their presentations became
shorter and shorter as the night progressed. We kept winning the
message, and they kept winning the votes. Until just after midnight.

The most important amendment of the day was that requiring
the testimony of John Bolton as a witness. I had assigned that argument to Nadler, at his request, and we saved that for the end of the
day so that we could finish just as strong as we started. But it was late,
we were all tired, and the long day and night had left Nadler stewing over the attacks against him. I had done my best to rebut them,
and his script contained no mention of these issues and was solely
focused on Bolton—or should have been. But Nadler had something
else in mind.

"Mr. Chief Justice, senators, counsel for the president," Nadler
began, "the House managers strongly support this amendment to

subpoena John Bolton. I am struck by what we have heard from the president's counsel so far tonight. They complain about process, but they do not seriously contest any of the allegations against the president. They insist that the president has done nothing wrong, but they refuse to allow the evidence and hear from the witnesses." *So far, so good,* I thought, *he is sticking to the script.* And then, all of a sudden, he wasn't: "They will not permit the American people to hear from the witnesses, and they lie and lie and lie and lie."

Nadler went on to discuss Bolton, and his willingness to testify. But then Nadler went further: "The question is whether the Senate will be complicit in the president's crimes by covering them up. Any senator who votes against Ambassador Bolton's testimony or any relevant testimony shows that he or she wants to be part of the cover-up. What other reason is there to prohibit a relevant witness from testifying here? Unfortunately, so far, I have seen every Republican senator has shown that they want to be part of the cover-up by voting against every document and witness proposed."

Nadler returned to the script and went through the multimedia presentation that the staff had prepared for him before returning to this theme once again at the end of his remarks, that a vote to deny witnesses was a "treacherous vote" and senators either wanted the truth to come out or were part of a "shameful cover-up." His words were strong, too strong, and not aimed at the four or the forty million. Cipollone quickly moved to exploit them.

Cipollone claimed, with practiced indignation, that the defense had been respectful to the Senate and they did not deserve Nadler's attacks—even though Cipollone's presentations had been laden with falsehood. He said that Nadler was accusing senators of being part of a cover-up and that he should be embarrassed and owed an apology to the president, the president's family, and the American people.

In rebuttal, Nadler said the president was attempting to become a monarch, and he went after Cipollone again, calling the president and Cipollone both liars. It was the kind of ugly back-and-forth with Trump's team that I was hoping to avoid. Nadler is a street fighter, and I admire his passion for the Constitution, a passion I share, and the president's lawyers *were* lying—but this wasn't the place for a street fight.

"I think it is appropriate at this point," the chief justice said, after debate had concluded, "for me to admonish both the House managers and the president's counsel in equal terms to remember that they are addressing the world's greatest deliberative body. One reason it has earned that title is because its members avoid speaking in a manner and using language that is not conducive to civil discourse." The chief justice referred to the 1905 Swayne trial when a senator objected to one of the managers using the term "pettifogging" and the presiding officer said that that word should not have been used. And Roberts said, "I don't think we need to aspire to that high a standard, but I think those addressing the Senate should remember where they are."

At just prior to two in the morning, we concluded all debate, and the Senate voted to approve the McConnell resolution by the usual partisan margin of 53 to 47. It had been a very long day, and, I thought, a productive one for the managers. The result on the amendments was baked in—McConnell likely had the commitment of his members to vote down all of the amendments before the first words were spoken—but we had already made a powerful case on the facts of the president's guilt, and the defense had been unprepared for it.

19

DOES HE REALLY NEED TO BE REMOVED?

We now had three days to present our case-in-chief. I would start the presentations with a summary of what senators could expect: First, a detailed discussion of the facts of the president's Ukraine misconduct and cover-up, weaving in House testimony from depositions and hearings, text messages and emails, television footage of key figures like the president and his cabinet and more. Second, we would present the law and constitutional provisions governing impeachable offenses and apply them to Article I. And finally, on day three of our case, we would apply the law to the facts of Article II, and conclude by showing why the president must be convicted and removed from office.

At 1 p.m., we began with a prayer led by the Senate chaplain, Dr. Barry C. Black, in his bow tie and beautiful baritone voice. Channeling the chief justice's comments from the night before, he prayed that we would "remember that patriots reside on both sides of the aisle, that words have consequences, and that how something is said can be as important as what is said." Apropos of those sentiments, I started by thanking the chief justice for the manner in which he was presiding and thanked the senators for the close attention they paid to both sides until two in the morning. And then I turned to the Framers for my initial presentation.

Reciting the prophecy of Alexander Hamilton about the "man unprincipled in private life" who seeks to "throw things into confusion that he may 'ride the storm and direct the whirlwind,'" I described how our Founders had achieved a kind of mythical status. We were aware of their flaws, and yet "we cannot help but be in awe of their genius." Still, they were human beings and acutely aware of human failings. They knew what it was like to live under a despot and risked their lives to be free of it.

"These are politically charged times. Tempers can run high, particularly where this President is concerned, but these are not unique times," I said. Deep divisions and disagreements were not alien to the Founders, and so they entrusted the decision over impeachment to our greatest deliberative body. "Where else than in the Senate," Hamilton had written, "could have been found a tribunal sufficiently dignified, or sufficiently independent?" It was up to the Senate to be that tribunal that Hamilton envisioned and to show the American people that their confidence was well placed.

Over the next couple of hours I gave the senators and public a summary outline of our case, using but a fraction of the media they would see and hear from my colleagues. But I wanted to make sure that if the public saw nothing else of the trial except the very beginning, they would understand what the president had done and why he should be removed from office. I put a particular focus on three days in July, which in microcosm told a lot of the story. The twenty-fourth, when Mueller testified and Trump thought he had escaped justice for seeking Russia's help in 2016. The twenty-fifth, when he spoke to Zelensky and tried to get Ukraine's help cheating in his next campaign. And the twenty-sixth, when he got confirmation that

Ukraine would indeed help him by announcing the sham investigations he sought. I explained why Trump's misconduct could not simply be addressed during the election, now only nine months away, since he was seeking to use the powers of the presidency to pervert the results of that very election.

In wrapping up this introduction to the case, I told the senators that we were nearly two and a half centuries into this beautiful experiment of American democracy, but that our future was not assured. Then, returning to our Founders and a story the Speaker loves to tell, I brought senators back to Benjamin Franklin leaving the Constitutional Convention. "What have we got?" someone had asked him. "A republic or a monarchy?" Franklin had responded: "A republic, if you can keep it."

"A fair trial," I told the senators, with "impartial consideration of all of the evidence against the president is how we keep our republic."

As we recessed subject to the call of the chair and returned to our Senate hideaway, we watched commentary of the proceedings on television screens tuned to the different stations. The president was at a conference of global leaders in Davos, watching the trial and firing off a Trumpian record of over 140 tweets in a single day, at one point averaging a tweet every eighty-eight seconds. At a news conference before leaving Davos, he called me a "con job" and a "corrupt politician" and Nadler a "sleaze bag." He told reporters that he would like to "sit right in the front row and stare into their corrupt faces." On the subject of John Bolton, Trump said he did not want Bolton to testify, claiming it was a "national security problem." "He knows some of my thoughts," Trump said. "What happens if he reveals what I think about a certain leader and it's not very positive?"

But what really caught my attention was something else the president said while professing confidence about the proceedings. "We're doing very well. I got to watch enough. I thought our team did a very good job. But honestly, we have all the material. They don't have the material." There he was, being impeached for obstructing

Congress and saying the quiet thing out loud—they had the incriminating evidence and were keeping it to themselves.

Over the next several hours, my colleagues walked the senators through the early months of the scheme, the effort to smear and remove Ambassador Yovanovitch, Zelensky's inauguration, and the arrival of the "Three Amigos" on the scene. During Jeffries's presentation, a man entered the third floor of the gallery and started bellowing that Schumer was the devil. He had a powerful set of lungs and I was startled at just how well his voice projected through the chamber. He was a large man, and it took the Capitol Police what seemed like a long time to pull him away, his voice still reverberating in the chamber as they struggled with him down the hall. When we broke for dinner, I told Demings that I was about to call on her, as a former police chief, to remove the man. "I can tell you this," she said, laughing, "it wouldn't have taken me so long if you had." I believed her.

When we returned to the floor, Senator Menendez of New Jersey approached me and said that senators were extraordinarily impressed with just how comprehensive and integrated our case had been, and even conservative Republicans like John Kennedy of Louisiana were expressing surprise at the volume of evidence. It was confirmation of what I had suspected—the senators had not been watching the House proceedings and were accepting everything they heard on Fox News as the gospel.

"Keep it up," Menendez said, "but don't keep it up too long." He smiled and I laughed. "I'm going to use that," I replied, and a few minutes later I did, quoting him—anonymously—and telling the senators that I appreciated their patience. Two hours later, when the last of my fellow managers had spoken for the day, I returned to the well for the day's closing presentation. As I brought the factual chronology up to the present day, I continued to deviate more and more from the script, still using its basic outline and multimedia exhibits but feeling free to extemporize as I had done during the House hearings. Nicolas Mitchell of my staff, sitting anxiously at our counsel table, had the nerve-racking responsibility of keeping track of where I was in the outline and displaying the corresponding exhibit or footage when I returned to the page.

Putting aside my notes, I reminded the senators of what had brought us here, and the fact that courageous people had come forward and, in doing so, risked everything. I was struck by the fact that while these public servants were willing to meet their lawful obligations and testify, others, with less to lose, refused to do so. These other potential witnesses, like Bolton and Kupperman, had every advantage, sat in positions of power, and yet lacked the basic commitment to put their country first and expose wrongdoing.

Referring to Yovanovitch, I said: "I think this is some form of cosmic justice that this ambassador, who was so ruthlessly smeared, is now [regarded as] a hero for her courage. There is justice in that. But what would really vindicate the leap of faith that she took is if we show the same courage. They risked everything—their careers—and yes, I know what you are asked to decide may risk yours too, but if they could show the courage, so can we."

Before we adjourned, McConnell and Schumer acknowledged that the next day would be the last day for the term's Senate pages, the young men and women who had been dutifully delivering water, notes, and messages throughout our long proceedings. We all stood and applauded them for their good work, and Judiciary Committee counsel Norman Eisen leaned over to me and whispered: "Let history record that shortly after you finished speaking, the entire Senate rose in a standing ovation."

That night, returning home for a few hours of rest before the next long day, it took a while for the adrenaline to stop coursing through my system. Eve asked me how I thought everything went, and I told her, and she shared her impressions from listening throughout the day. For as long as I had been involved in politics, she has retained a really important detachment, able to share the perspective of people who did not live, eat, and breathe politics. Her observations were always insightful, even when they were critical—perhaps most of all when they were critical. "Do you have to be so harsh on the Republicans?" she would ask me after one of my television appearances before the trial. "You're awfully harsh." And I would try to tone it down. But now, in the midst of the trial, she had few criticisms, understanding that I needed encouragement more than anything else. When we were done talking and I put aside my trial book for the next day, I let out a long breath. "I'm still standing," I said to myself, and then popped a couple more Advil. My toothache, already bad, was getting worse, and I could fend off the pain during the trial, but when the Advil wore off at night, the pain would wake me up and I would have to take more. These two expressions—"I just need to get through the day," in the morning, and "I'm still standing" in the evening, had now become the bookends of my days and nights.

The next morning, the managers gathered in the Speaker's conference room for our daily pretrial preparations. We took our usual seats around the table, and the room was quiet but for the flipping of pages, murmured conversations of staff, or the sound of highlighters working their way across the page. Silent for all of us, except Jason Crow, who worked with earbuds in place. "What are you listening to?" I asked him. "Oh," he said, in that midwestern drawl, "it's a playlist, mostly rock and pop, stuff from the seventies and beyond." We all deal with pressure in different ways, and this was Jason's way. I told him that when this was all over I'd love to get ahold of Jason's rocking playlist. "You got it," he replied.

On a break from our preparations, we would discuss what we were seeing and hearing in the Senate chamber. We were paying close attention to the "four," of course. Collins and Murkowski sat close to each other, their faces studious and unreadable, but always focused on the presentations. Lamar Alexander would get up and pace, which some took as a sign of inattentiveness, but I did not; if I were sitting for long hours on end listening to colleagues in the House or Senate, I would be up and roaming no matter what they were discussing, just to get some blood flowing. Romney was near the back and to my far left, and he would often rise from his chair and lean against the back wall.

When I would make a particular point, I would sometimes look to these senators to gauge their reaction, but I didn't want to be too obvious about it. And it was not just the Republican potential swing votes that concerned me. Democrats Joe Manchin, Kyrsten Sinema, and Doug Jones were also key "jurors," and in the case of Manchin and Jones came from states that were arguably more "pro-Trump" than those of any of the four Republicans. There was no guarantee that they would side with us on the second round of votes on witnesses that would take place at the end of the trial, let alone on conviction.

During each day's proceedings, some of the senators would wander down to the well during breaks and mingle with the managers or Trump defense lawyers. Senator Tom Carper made it a point after several of our presentations to give us much appreciated words of encouragement, and Senator Elizabeth Warren visited S-239 to congratulate our staff on the remarkable work they were doing. There was no rule against this, but it took some getting used to. In the courtroom, it would be unthinkable for a lawyer to be talking privately with a juror. But these were no ordinary jurors—hell, half of them had just had lunch with the Trump defense team before the trial even started, and the jury foreman, Mitch McConnell, had said he was coordinating with the defendant!

Before we lined up to make our procession into the Senate chamber that afternoon, I told my colleagues that I would be making some short introductory remarks before handing it off to others. "I will be very brief," I reiterated, "though you may not believe me."

"We believe you," Demings replied, "we just don't know how you define 'very brief.'"

As WE KICKED OFF THE third full day of proceedings, I told the chief justice that he might not be fully aware of how extraordinary it was for senators to give House members their undivided attention for even a few minutes, let alone hours on end. "Of course," I said, "it doesn't hurt that the morning starts out every day with the sergeant at arms warning that if you don't, you will be imprisoned." Today, the House would go through the underpinnings of Article I, applying the facts of the president's scheme to the law and the Constitution.

Nadler began the presentation and did a masterful job. This was his great strength, walking senators through the meaning of "high crimes and misdemeanors" and the history, rationale, and intent behind the constitutional provisions. "Explaining why the Constitution required an impeachment option," Nadler said, "Madison argued that a president 'might betray his trust to foreign powers.'" And Nadler cleverly used the words of House Republicans' own impeachment expert, Jonathan Turley, against them: "The use of military aid for a quid pro quo to investigate one's political opponent, if proven, can be an impeachable offense," he said, quoting Turley's testimony. Nadler also quoted Dershowitz from more than twenty years earlier: "It certainly doesn't have to be a crime. If you have somebody who completely corrupts the office of president and who abuses trust and poses great danger to our liberty, you don't need a technical crime." Even Bill Barr had written in his 2018 memo that although the president could not be indicted, he could be impeached for "any abuses of discretion" and for "his misdeeds in office."

After Nadler, Sylvia Garcia had one of the most challenging presentations to make. I needed her to describe the two sham investigations sought by the president and his allies, without giving the Trump defense team too much of an opening. The decision to spend time debunking the conspiracy theories about 2016 and Joe Biden was a strategic one that we made as a team. It was the type of issue that was larger than just the trial, and that I would consult the Speaker on, since there were other equities to consider. On this, as on other issues, she usually deferred to my judgment—*You're the general*, she would say—but not without sharing her own thoughts and questions and helping me work through the issue. As managers, we didn't want to amplify the false narratives that the president and Giuliani were continuing to peddle in real time, or give them any credibility, but we expected the Trump team to go after the Bidens, and we wanted to defang their efforts as well as we could in advance. Garcia handled this task with great deftness.

Garcia pointed out that it wasn't until 2019 that Trump began pushing for an investigation into Joe Biden's Ukraine efforts as vice president. Trump was apparently indifferent to the matter in 2017 and 2018, and he never sought to withhold military assistance in those years. "So what changed?" Garcia asked rhetorically. "Senators, you know what changed in 2019 when President Trump suddenly cared. It is that Biden got in the race." If I had said that, or Nadler, or any number of others, the senators might have written it off to partisanship, but Garcia was no fire-breathing liberal, no Fox News villain, and her words carried the convincing and objective aura of truth. To drive the point home further, Garcia displayed polling data, taken at the time of Trump's sudden concern over corruption in Ukrainian energy companies, showing the considerable strength of Biden in a head-to-head with Trump.

When I returned to the podium after a short break, I felt the need to address an unspoken issue in the chamber. Several of the senators present, including Amy Klobuchar, Elizabeth Warren, Michael Bennet, and Bernie Sanders, were running for president, and the Iowa caucuses were only days away—and I didn't want them to think we were gratuitously promoting Biden's competitiveness in a general election matchup. "This is an appropriate point," I said, "for me to make the disclaimer that the House managers take no position in the Democratic primary for President." Then, jokingly, I added: "I do not want to lose a single more vote than necessary."

I also harked back to a part of Garcia's presentation in which she quoted something Putin had said only months ago: "Thank God nobody is accusing us anymore of interfering in U.S. elections. Now they're accusing Ukraine." I don't think we want Vladimir Putin to be thanking God for the president of the United States. "Well," I said, "you have to give Donald Trump credit for this—he has made a religious man out of Vladimir Putin." There was a lot of laughter, mostly from Democrats; I peered over at Romney, but his face was in shadow and I could not read it.

During one of Romney's 2012 presidential debates, Obama had attacked him over his position on Russia. In a mocking tone, Obama said: "When you were asked 'What's the biggest geopolitical threat facing America?' you said Russia. Not al-Qaeda, you said Russia. And the 1980s are now calling to ask for their foreign policy back, because the Cold War's been over for twenty years." In the time that had since passed, Romney's view of the continuing threat from Russia had proved far more prescient than Obama's, and it stood to reason that Romney would have been alienated by Trump's betrayal of our interests to the Kremlin leader. (We would later play clips of John McCain on the subject of Russia and demonstrate how much the Trump administration had subverted the Republican Party's position on standing up to Russia. I tried to take special notice of Romney's reaction then as well, but again his face betrayed nothing.)

One reaction that day was not the least bit ambiguous, and that was from Democratic senator Tim Kaine of Virginia. He was seated to my right and several rows up, but like so many of the senators, he was close enough that I could watch how our argument was resonating—or not resonating as the case may be. We were displaying video of the testimony of Col. Vindman, and his emotional appeal to his father not to be worried, that he was going to be all right for speaking out, because here in America, right mattered. Kaine's eyes glistened with tears as he watched, and I could tell that he was as moved as I had been when I first heard it. If Vindman's words could carry such power for others, even on video, I needed to take note.

A few hours after we began, Jeffries took the floor. He had become more comfortable with his presentations and began taking greater liberties in deviating from the script. Jeffries has a nice cadence to his speech, pausing frequently to emphasize a point, not rushing to get to the next sentence, and gesturing broadly. He also made a real effort to inject levity into his remarks, a very important balm amid the unrelenting seriousness of what we were engaged in. "Earlier this morning," he said, beginning his presentation, "I was on my way to the office, and I ran into a fellow New Yorker who just happens to work here in Washington, D.C. He said to me: 'Congressman, have you heard the latest outrage?' I wasn't really sure what he was talking about. So, to be honest, I thought, *Well, the president is back in town.*

What has Donald Trump done now? So I said to him: 'What outrage are you talking about?' He paused for a moment, and then he said to me: 'Someone voted against Derek Jeter on his Hall of Fame ballot.'" The Senate burst into laughter, and Jeffries continued: "Life is all about perspective." That kind of humor, deftly delivered as it was, buys you a lot of credibility.

Late in the evening, just as we were about to get under way for our last presentations, I received some of the most important feedback of the trial. Dan Goldman approached me and related that he was hearing from senators that we had proven the president's guilt, but they needed to know why Trump must be removed from office. I didn't have time to ask Dan what his source of information was—often it came through Schumer's staff—or which senators he was referring to, Democrats or Republicans, and that made a big difference. It was possible that senators could find Trump had committed the offenses he was charged with but still conclude that they should let the voters sort it out at the polls. I had seen Republican senators speaking to the press, like Senators Josh Hawley of Missouri and John Barrasso of Wyoming, echoing White House talking points that Democrats were trying to nullify the votes of tens of millions of Americans in the last election and disqualify Trump from running in the next one. I could tell that this argument had resonance politically, and it could provide an easy way out for Republican senators who did not want to deny or minimize the president's misconduct, but were reluctant to convict him because of what it would mean to their own future in the party.

I suddenly understood how important it was for me to address this question more directly, in simple and personal terms, and I needed to do so in my closing remarks; I didn't want senators to go home for another night still unresolved on why they ought to risk their careers by removing this man from office. That was the heart of the matter, but I just didn't know how to do it, and time was running out. Jason Crow was speaking and I was up next. I don't think I heard a word of his presentation as I agonized over what to say. When I rose and made my way to the lectern, I brought with me some notes on the

July 25 call record that I had planned to go through, culling out new details and explaining their significance. Even as I did so, a part of me kept asking myself, why should they risk it all?

Finally, I told the senators, "This brings me to the last point I want to make tonight." When we were done, I said, I believed that we would have demonstrated the president's guilt overwhelmingly—that is, we would have proved that he did what he was charged with doing: withholding the money and the meeting in order to coerce Ukraine, then covering it up and obstructing Congress. "But I want to address one other thing tonight . . . Okay. He is guilty. Does he really need to be removed? We have an election coming up. Does he really need to be removed? You know, is there really any doubt about this? I mean, do we really have any doubt about the facts here? Does anybody really question whether the president is capable of what he is charged with?" And then it occurred to me that the president's supporters had been completely silent on one very basic point, and I might as well say it out loud: "Nobody is really making the argument 'Donald Trump would never do such a thing' because, of course, we know that he would, and, of course, we know that he did."

I gazed around the chamber to check for the reaction from GOP senators to a statement as provocative as this, but there was no head shaking, no denial, nothing but their rapt attention. If I was to have a "Dale Bumpers" moment, this would be it. I was speaking a truth they all knew and understood, even if they could not say it them-selves. "It is a somewhat different question, though, to ask: Okay. It is pretty obvious. Whether we can say it publicly or we can't say it publicly, we all know what we are dealing with here with this presi-dent, but does he really need to be *removed*?" Even as I posed the question, I was still not sure how I was going to answer it. I knew of the danger that he posed to the country if left in office, but I wasn't sure how to articulate it. "This is why he needs to be removed," I said as a preface, not so much to underscore the point I was about to make as to give me another moment to formulate the thought. If there was anything in what my parents taught me about right and wrong, or my professors taught me about history or the law, or what

I learned as a prosecutor or in Congress, I needed to draw on that life experience at that moment to answer that question. I went on:

> Donald Trump chose Rudy Giuliani over his own intelligence agencies. He chose Rudy Giuliani over his own FBI director. He chose Rudy Giuliani over his own national security advisers. When all of them were telling him this Ukraine 2016 stuff is kooky, crazy Russian propaganda, he chose not to believe them. He chose to believe Rudy Giuliani. That makes him *dangerous* to *us*, to our country. That was Donald Trump's choice.
>
> Now, why would Donald Trump believe a man like Rudy Giuliani over a man like [FBI director] Christopher Wray? Okay, why would anyone in his right mind believe Rudy Giuliani over Christopher Wray? Because he *wanted* to, and because what Rudy was offering him was something that would help him personally. And what Christopher Wray was offering him was merely the truth. What Christopher Wray was offering him was merely the information he needed to protect this country and its elections, but *that was not good enough*. What's in it for *him*? What's in it for Donald Trump? *This* is why he needs to be *removed*.
>
> Now, you may be asking how much damage can he really do in the next several months until the election? *A lot. A lot of damage.* We just saw last week, a report that Russia tried to hack or maybe did hack Burisma. I don't know if they got in. I am trying to find out. My colleagues on the Intel Committees of the House and Senate are trying to find out. Did the Russians get in? What are the Russians' plans and intentions?
>
> Well, let's say they get in, and let's say they start dumping documents to interfere in the next election. Let's say they start dumping some real things they have from Burisma. Let's say they start dumping some fake things they didn't hack from Burisma, but they want you to believe they did. Let's say they start blatantly interfering in our election again to help Donald Trump.

Can you have the least bit of confidence that Donald Trump will stand up to them and protect our national interests over his own personal interests? You know you *can't*, which makes him dangerous to this country. *You know you can't. You know you can't count on him.* None of us can.

What happens if China got the message? Now, you can say: Well, he is just joking, of course. He didn't really mean China should investigate the Bidens. You know that that is no *joke*. Now, maybe you could have argued it three years ago when he said: Hey, Russia. If you are listening, hack Hillary's emails. Maybe you could have given him a freebee and said he was joking, but now we know better. Hours after he did that, Russia did, in fact, try to hack Hillary's emails. There is no mulligan here when it comes to our national security.

"So what if China does overtly or covertly start to help the Trump campaign?" I asked the senators. Did they think he was going to "call them out on it," or did they think he was going to "give them a better trade deal" because of it? I continued,

Can any of us really have the confidence that Donald Trump will put national interests ahead of his personal interests? Is there really any evidence in this Presidency that should give us the ironclad confidence that he would do so? You know you can't count on him to do that. That is the sad truth. You know you can't count on him to do that. The American people deserve a president they can count on to put their interests first—to put their interests first.

Colonel Vindman said: Here, right matters. Here, right matters. Well, let me tell you something. If right doesn't matter—if right doesn't matter—it doesn't matter how good the Constitution is; it doesn't matter how brilliant the Framers were; it doesn't matter how good or bad our advocacy in this trial is; it doesn't matter how well written the oath of impartiality is. If right doesn't matter, we are *lost*. If the truth doesn't matter, we are lost. The Framers couldn't protect us from ourselves if right and truth don't matter. And you know that what he did was not *right*.

You know, that is what they do in the old country that Colonel Vindman's father came from or the old country that my great-grandfather came from or the old countries that your ancestors came from or maybe you came from, but here, right is supposed to matter. It is what has made us the greatest nation on earth. No Constitution can protect us if right doesn't matter anymore.

And you know you can't trust this President to do what is right for this country. You can trust he will do what is right for Donald Trump. He will do it now. He has done it before. He will do it for the next several months. He will do it in the election if he is allowed to. This is why, if you find him guilty, you must find that he should be *removed*—because right matters. Because right matters. And the truth matters. Otherwise, we are lost.

When I was finished, my voice was trembling and I could barely say a word more. I didn't even have the presence of mind to yield back to the chief justice, or wasn't sure I could do so and retain my composure. So I just walked away from the podium.

McConnell asked that we adjourn for the night and I walked back to our table. Before I could get there, Schumer greeted me in the well and there were tears in his eyes as he clapped me on the shoulders. Senators broke whatever norms there were and came down to shake my hand. "Save something," a couple of them said, smiling. "Save it for the end." Others, maintaining a respectful distance, nodded at me or gave a thumbs-up. I sat back down at the table, even as others departed the chamber, and gathered my thoughts. When I returned to S-239, my colleagues and staff were waiting for me and broke into applause as I entered the room.

"All you needed to do was drop the mic," Demings said.

"Yeah," Crow added, "except that the mic is attached, so you would have had to push the podium over."

Leaving the Capitol that night, I walked out at the same time as Senators Lindsey Graham and Sheldon Whitehouse of Rhode Island, two other former prosecutors. Whitehouse had already complimented me on my work that day, and Graham stepped forward to shake my hand. "Good job," Graham said. "Very well spoken." A *Huffington Post* reporter captured the moment on camera, although I wished they hadn't. Such moments of private connection for members across the aisle were increasingly rare over the last few years, and I hated to discourage them any further by exposure.

REACTION TO MY SPEECH THAT night seemed to break out of the usual partisan mold. Democrats were effusive, but even some Republicans showed a grudging respect. "If you accept that every politician, except for me," Louisiana Republican senator Bill Cassidy said, "occasionally does something for their own political gain, the question is at which point does it cross the threshold by which they have to be removed from office, right? And he's asking that. That's a good thing to ask."

But of course it was entirely a different story on Fox. AMATEUR THESPIAN SCHIFF TRIES OUT SOME NEW LINES, Fox declared in an alarming font across the screen, while Tucker Carlson called me a "wild-eyed conspiracy nut." Despite their pledges to bring their viewers all the coverage of the trial, Fox frequently cut away from broadcasting my remarks and those of other managers, or placed them in a postage-stamp-sized box on the side of the frame with the sound off. "He is a lunatic," Hannity declared one night. "If you watched him talk, he was totally unhinged. He looked like a lunatic who has lost his mind." But the most disturbing reaction came from Republican senator Marsha Blackburn of Tennessee, who picked up where House Republicans had left off and used my speech to attack Vindman's patriotism, tweeting, "Adam Schiff is hailing Alexander

Vindman as an American Patriot. How patriotic is it to badmouth and ridicule our great nation in front of Russia, America's greatest enemy?"

When the trial began the next day, I talked about my father, and how he would say that you couldn't understand someone until you walked in their shoes. I always thought that he invented that wisdom until I watched *To Kill a Mockingbird* and found out that Atticus Finch said it first. So I invited the senators to stand in Marie Yovanovitch's shoes and imagine that the president of the United States was asking a foreign nation to conduct a sham investigation of them—what would we think then? "Would we think that is good U.S. policy? Would we think that he has every right to do it? Would we think that is a perfect call?"

I asked senators to imagine themselves the victims of a vicious smear campaign, to imagine that the president was bragging that "some things" were going to happen to them. Why should it matter that it was Marie Yovanovitch? And then I warned them: "The next time, it just may be you. It just may be you. Do you think for a moment that any of you, no matter what your relationship with this President, no matter how close you are to this President—do you think for a moment that if he felt it was in his best interest he wouldn't ask you to be investigated?" I turned from senator to senator to senator, and much as when I had made a similar accusation against the president less than twenty-four hours earlier, not a person sought to contradict me—indeed, several of them had already been smeared by the president. "If somewhere deep down below you realize that he would, you cannot leave a man like that in office when he has violated the Constitution.

"It goes to character," I continued. "You don't realize how important character is in the highest office in the land until you don't have it." It wasn't necessary for the House to prove that the president lacked character, was dishonest, and couldn't tell right from wrong. None of that was really vital to showing that the president coerced Ukraine or obstructed our investigation. But by this point in the trial, I felt it was essential to show the country what a danger he posed to our security and our democracy. If the senators would not rise to the occasion, the country needed to be warned in the most powerful terms I could muster, so that they could hold the president accountable, yes, but also so that they could hold senators accountable if they did not do their constitutional duty.

Val Demings laid out much of the case against the president on the charge of obstruction of Congress, and she did a magnificent job. She has the ability to read from a prepared script and make it sound improvised, spontaneous, and compelling. "I love Val Demings's voice," Eve would tell me later that night. "I was listening to her in the car, and she's terrific. Her voice just commands respect, and she has such a good grasp of the facts." "I agree," I said. "And she's even better in person." The Article II presentation was among the most challenging because the conduct was not as vivid as the Ukraine scheme, but, as Demings would demonstrate, it was every bit as important an abuse of power and threatened to do even longer-term harm to our system of checks and balances. "If you can't have the ability to enforce an impeachment power," I would tell the senators a couple of hours later, "you might as well not put it in the Constitution."

When my colleagues had completed our case on obstruction, I returned to the podium to close out the day. We would soon be handing it over to Trump's defense for up to three days, and I wanted to give the senators a preview of what they could expect. I had been keeping a running list of the defenses I anticipated the Trump team to make, and I wanted to do my best to disarm them, using humor when I could. After ticking through a series of them, and their flaws, I got to the "The managers are just awful" defense. "They are terrible people," I cried, mimicking the defense's theatrics, "especially that Schiff guy. He is the worst. He is the worst . . . He mocked the president. He mocked the president as if he was shaking down the leader of another country like an organized crime figure. . . . Well, I discovered something very significant by mocking the president, and that is, for a man who loves to mock others, he does not like to be mocked." The chamber erupted in laughter, including many

Republicans. "As it turns out, he has got pretty thin skin. Who would have thought?"

Then I turned to the president's false exculpatories. "Now, you will also hear the defense that the president said there was 'no quid pro quo.' . . . I guess that is the end of the story. This is a well-known principle of criminal law—that if the defendant says he didn't do it, he couldn't have done it." With this, there was more laughter in the chamber.

"So what do all these defenses mean?" I asked, after I had addressed dozens of other arguments, ridiculing them in like fashion. "What do they mean collectively when you add them all up? What they mean is, under Article II [of the Constitution], the president can do whatever he wants. That is really it. That is really it, stripped of all the detail and all the histrionics."

To conclude our case, I turned to one of my idols, Robert Kennedy. "Moral courage," he once said, "is a rarer commodity than bravery in battle or great intelligence. Yet it is the one essential, vital quality for those who seek to change a world that yields most painfully to change." When I first read that quote, I wasn't sure that I agreed—could moral courage really be so rare? I asked the senators. I described visiting our troops all over the world and discovering how common was their "uncommon bravery." I talked about my father's own service in the Army, and going to college on the GI Bill. My dad had left college after only a couple of years and had always regretted it. I had planned to tell the senators more about my father, but I found myself growing too emotional and veered away. I told the senators that I thought in many ways that my dad had received a better education than I did, that those who serve in the military learn things that there is no other way to learn. Even so, I wasn't sure that I believed Robert Kennedy—that moral courage was more rare than courage on the battlefiled—until I read what else he wrote. "Few men are willing to brave the disapproval of their peers, the censure of their colleagues, [and] the wrath of their society." Then I understood just how rare moral courage was.

If what I had said the previous night had resonated with anyone in the chamber, it was not because it required moral courage. My views, I told the senators, as heartfelt as they were, reflected the views of the people who had sent me to Congress. "But what happens when our heartfelt views of right and wrong are in conflict with the popular opinion of our constituents? What happens when the devotion to our oaths, to our values, to our love of country departs from the momentary passion of the large number of people backing us? Those are the times that try our souls.

"CBS News reported last night that a Trump confidant said that GOP senators were warned: 'Vote against the president, and your head will be on a pike.' I don't know if that is true." Several senators indicated that it was not, including Collins, and I responded by saying that I hoped it was not true. But I pointed out the irony of a reported threat to use the remedy of a monarch in a trial of a president who would be king. And, although I left it unsaid, I hoped that the senators would display the kind of moral courage Robert Kennedy described, even if it meant the censure of their friends and colleagues.

Coming full circle to the question of witnesses raised during the first day of the trial, I addressed an argument that Trump's defense team had been making to the cameras outside the chamber: that if senators allowed witnesses, the proceedings would go on indefinitely, because the president's lawyers would raise the same issues of privilege they had failed to raise earlier. I told the senators that we had a perfectly good judge in our midst, the chief justice of the Supreme Court, who could quickly resolve any issue of privilege. What's more, if a majority of senators did not like Roberts's rulings, under impeachment rules, they could overturn him by a majority vote. "How often," I asked, "do you get the chance to overrule a chief justice of the Supreme Court? You have to admit, it is every legislator's dream." The senators laughed again, because it was so very true.

In his pamphlet of 1777, Thomas Paine had written: "Those who expect to reap the blessings of freedom must . . . undergo the fatigues of supporting it." And then I asked them, "Is it too much fatigue to call witnesses and have a fair trial? Are the blessings of freedom so meager that we will not endure the fatigue of a real trial with witnesses and documents?" My last words that night were these: "So I am asking you. I implore you. Give America a fair trial. Give America a fair trial. She's worth it."

Later that night, Republicans attacked me for citing the CBS story, with faux outrage that I would suggest Trump might be vindictive to those who crossed him. That was about as incontrovertible a proposition as I could imagine. Nonetheless, Collins felt it necessary to issue a statement: "Not only have I never heard the 'head on the pike' line, but also I know of no Republican Senator who has been threatened in any way by anyone in the administration." Murkowski was less indignant, but still critical: "I thought he was doing fine with moral courage until he got to the head on the pike. That's where he lost me. He's a good orator . . . you got to give him that." "I have not been told that my head is on a pike," she said, laughing. The manufactured outrage from others I could understand; that was calculated strategy. But Collins and Murkowski were different, and I wondered if I had unintentionally provoked them rather than appealed to their sense of duty. Were senators afraid that if they voted to acquit, they would be perceived as having done so out of fear?

Saturday, January 25, began the defense case. In a bizarre way, I had been looking forward to this; as difficult as it would be to hear their arguments and attacks, our role would be less demanding and give our team a chance to catch our breath. Cipollone began with a very brief presentation, and, I thought, made the most succinct and powerful point of the defense: "They are asking you not only to overturn the results of the last election, but as I have said before, they are asking you to remove President Trump from the ballot in an election occurring in approximately nine months." If I had been representing the president, this is the point I would have been arguing over and over again. But as soon as he said it, he and the defense team moved on to a potpourri of factual, legal, and constitutional arguments that were distributed among a team of high profile lawyers, and the core theory of their defense, if they had one, was lost.

Mike Purpura was the first of the large Trump defense team to appear after Cipollone, and no sooner had he reintroduced himself to the senators than he hit Play and showed video of me mocking the president over his "classic organized crime shakedown." I'm not sure what purpose this served, since it was not integrated into the rest of his presentation, but I suspect it was just a nod to the man down the street. He then went through six defenses to the Ukraine allegations, but he placed particular reliance on one argument: "Not a single witness testified that the president himself said that there was any connection between any investigations and security assistance, a presidential meeting, or anything else." All of which he said pointed to what he claimed everyone knew from the start: "The president did absolutely nothing wrong." He was definitely playing to an audience of one.

But no one on the defense team made more of an effort to gratify the president than his longtime lawyer Jay Sekulow. Taking me up on my father's (and Atticus Finch's) admonition about walking in someone else's shoes, he asked the senators to put themselves in the shoes of Donald Trump. What followed in that presentation, and another he would make later, was a lengthy set of presidential complaints that went back to Crossfire Hurricane, Robert Mueller, James Comey, the Carter Page FISA, Peter Strzok, Lisa Page, Christopher Steele, and more. It was a veritable who's who of presidential grievances.

In my view, only Pat Philbin would give a methodical and effective argument that day, focused on the obstruction of justice article. As I would tell the managers after we returned to S-239 for our daily wrap-up, Philbin repeated many of the falsehoods from earlier in the week about process, so it was difficult for me to credit him too much, but he had done a very competent job of articulating what sounded like plausible legal bases for Trump to oppose each particular subpoena. It was a fairly common defense tactic to ignore the big picture—that Trump had ordered the stonewalling of all subpoenas—and focus on a hundred discrete acts, offering an innocent explanation for each. None of the individual explanations held up well to scrutiny, but how many senators were going to read the specific cases he was citing to see that they did not support the proposition he was arguing? It was enough to make any nonlawyer, and a great many lawyers, want to throw up their hands and say "This is too confusing and therefore not clearly impeachable." We would not seek to rebut the myriad errors of law he was making, but would return senators to the big picture: Trump fought all subpoenas, and the rest was noise.

For whatever reason, the Trump defense team cut their Saturday presentations very short—perhaps because Trump did not want them making their case on a day with lower ratings. Much as the Trump defense had done during our case-in-chief, we took advantage of the opportunity to do a joint press availability and push back against the defense claims. But I didn't linger at the Capitol too long; I had something else very important to do that didn't involve trial strategy. I raced to my dentist's office to get some relief from the pain. But not even that visit would end up resolving the problem, and I would eventually need a root canal.

On Sunday morning, I awoke to a Twitter attack from the president calling me "a CORRUPT POLITICIAN, and probably a very sick man." What followed was more disturbing: "He has not paid the price, yet, for what he has done to our Country!" Coming so quickly after the faux outrage over my citing the CBS report about the president's vindictiveness, the president seemed to be fact-checking my critics. Appearing on *Meet the Press,* the Novocain fully worn off and the pain returning, I was asked if I took that as a threat. "I think it's intended to be," I replied. James Lankford, one of the senators who said he was most "offended" by the suggestion that the president "has threatened all of us," nevertheless defended the president's comments. Again, the president would help me make the case. On Fox's *Sunday Morning Futures,* Trump said that it would be a mistake for Republican senators to support calling witnesses. "Some of them are running, and I think it would be very bad for them."

On Sunday afternoon, I gathered with the managers in the Speaker's small conference room to go over our preparations for the question-and-answer period that would follow the conclusion of the defense case. Trump's team still had two days left of presentations, but our staff was amassing a huge database of potential questions and scripted answers, and it would be helpful to go over them as a team. Around six o'clock that night, Etienne, Boland, and Simons abruptly interrupted the meeting. *The New York Times* had just broken a story about Bolton's still unpublished book, and it had all of us scrambling to our phones.

TRUMP TIED UKRAINE AID TO INQUIRIES HE SOUGHT, BOLTON BOOK SAYS read the headline, which outlined what his potential testimony in the Senate would reveal. The *Times* reported that Bolton's book alleged that "President Trump told his national security advisor in August that he wanted to continue freezing $391 million in security assistance to Ukraine until officials there helped with investigations into Democrats including the Bidens." The article also suggested that Bolton's account would implicate Pompeo, Mulvaney, and Barr. "Oh my God," I said, "he's throwing everyone under the bus."

"We should issue a statement with the headline, YIKES!" said Lofgren. Looking around the room, I was amazed at the transformation; a subdued and studied preparation for trial had become a kind of nervous celebration. Members and staff were marveling with each other over the news, and what it might mean, before turning to a very practical discussion of how we could use this new information as a bludgeon.

Bolton had given his book to the White House days after Trump was impeached—no wonder the president's defenders were fighting so hard to keep Bolton off the stand. Trump's comments in Davos, in which he said Bolton's testimony might threaten national security, also took on new meaning: Clearly, Trump was once again confusing his own personal interests with those of the nation. Over the past few days, it had felt like some of the four swing senators were moving against us on the question of witnesses. Now we had a fighting chance after all. And the timing could not have been better, coming right in the middle of the defense case. Trump's lawyers had argued there was no direct evidence that Trump personally connected the aid and the investigations, which wasn't true, but nonetheless, how could senators refuse to hear from Bolton now?

20

ONE MAN HAD SAID "ENOUGH"

On Monday morning, January 27, the managers gathered with the Speaker in a new and very special venue in the Capitol to discuss the impact of the Bolton revelations. Pelosi told us that the hideaway where we were meeting was known as the "Board of Education" and had been used for more than a hundred years as a spot where legislative leadership gathered with members to strategize, drink, and play poker. When Sam Rayburn was Speaker, he called it "the little room" and served bourbon while he gained insights from his members, including then-representative Lyndon Johnson, and others, like Vice President Harry S. Truman. Each time the members drank—including during Prohibition—they said that it was "to strike a blow for liberty." This was also the place where Truman got the news that Franklin Roosevelt had died.

"I want to thank you," the Speaker told us, "for the solemnity and dignity you are displaying to the country, and for the enormous preparation that you and the staff have put into your presentations. You set the pace and the tone—"

"Sorry," Dan Goldman said, rushing into the room and interrupting the Speaker. "I got lost."

Alluding to the fact we were in a hideaway, Pelosi quipped, "That was the whole point!"

Goldman sat down at the table. "Wouldn't you know it," I added, "now Goldman is taking Truman's seat!"

After the Speaker concluded her message of thanks to the managers and staff, we turned to a discussion of Bolton. "We warned that the truth would come out," I said, "and now it has, again. Anyone who doesn't support calling Bolton now, when this witness goes right to the heart of it—how do they not allow us to call him? And if we get him, it could break the dam. I still believe it is somewhat uphill, but we need to keep the pressure on, and respectfully but forcefully make the case for a fair trial."

Pelosi castigated Bolton's decision to withhold what he witnessed in order to save it for his book. But she said, "And this is important—we don't even need [Bolton] to make the case to remove the president from office. And unless the Republican senators think they have a price to pay with voters, they won't do it. Trump is undermining our Constitution, and the public must know how he has committed numerous impeachable offenses and what it means *to them*. Trump is giving carte blanche to Putin, and we must communicate to the public that allowing Russian interference in our elections is undermining *their* vote."

Demings said that when she was home for Martin Luther King Day parades, people were yelling to her, "So proud you are a manager" and "Impeach this president," because they knew what it meant to their lives. Garcia echoed Demings, relating her own experience at an event over the weekend when Spanish-speaking staff at the site told her how happy they were that she was a manager and, in Spanish,

"You need to get him." In the nations where they came from, Garcia explained, "they are familiar with dealing with dictators," and they understood that if we don't act, "we won't have free elections" either.

As we made our way back to the Senate chamber, and with the Bolton book revelations careening through the Capitol and scrambling expectations about witnesses, I wondered how the Trump defense team planned to handle it, going into day two of their case. Just as their defense (and much of the Trump presidency) seemed to exist in a world where facts could not intrude, for a long time it appeared that they were just going to try to ignore it. Sekulow began his presentation by arguing that Vindman's alarm over the president's Ukraine misconduct really amounted to nothing more than a quibble over policy. "Every time there is a policy difference . . . are we going to start an impeachment proceeding?"

He was followed by Ken Starr, the independent counsel in the Clinton impeachment investigation, who decried an "age of impeachment" and, with no sense of irony or self-awareness, asked, "How did we get here, with presidential impeachment invoked frequently in its inherently destabilizing as well as acrimonious way?" Listening to him, I was incredulous. Was the man who pursued Bill Clinton with such a messianic zeal over an extramarital affair really going to lecture the Senate on the perils of impeachment? Yes, he was. "And I respectfully submit that the Senate, in its wisdom, would do well in its deliberations to . . . return to our country's traditions when presidential impeachment was truly a measure of last resort."

The Trump defense team was evidently not satisfied with only one Clinton-era independent counsel, but invited another, Robert Ray, to pick up where Starr left off, just as he had done decades earlier. "Today, twenty years later, what have we learned from that experience? I fear that the answer to that question is nothing at all." His argument might have had more force if he was expressing a mea culpa for his involvement in the Clinton impeachment, but he was not. Clinton had been impeached for obstruction of justice, which Ray evidently thought was fine, but impeaching Trump for obstructing a different branch of government, Congress, was beyond the pale. Although Ray did not say it, the implicit logic of his position was that Clinton's big mistake was acquiescing to the threat of subpoena—had he simply refused to testify and fought the matter endlessly in the courts, he would have been just fine. "When I hear Mr. Schiff's complaint that the House's request for former White House counsel Don McGahn's testimony . . . has been drawn out since April of last year," Ray declared, "I can only say in response: Boo-hoo." Ray emphasized that the election was only nine months away and, quoting Dale Bumpers, said that is the day when members of both parties could hold hands and say "win or lose, we will abide by the decision." Of all claims he would make that day, nothing would prove more tragically wrong.

As if Starr and Ray were not gaslighting enough, there was this pearl from another Trump lawyer, Eric Herschmann, who was brought in to dirty up Joe and Hunter Biden for the president's political benefit. "One thing he [Joe Biden] apparently did not do, however, was to tell his son not to trade on his family connections." Where were they getting these people? Another Trump lawyer, Pam Bondi, had been considering, as Florida attorney general, whether to join multistate litigation against Trump for fraudulent marketing in connection with Trump University. Four days later, the Trump Foundation, a charitable nonprofit, contributed $25,000 to a Bondi PAC, and Bondi declined to join the litigation. Someone, it appeared, had correctly priced Bondi's devotion to her defrauded constituents, and it was shockingly low. Not only that, but the IRS would later determine that the contribution had been unlawful. With that stellar record behind her, Bondi joined in the attacks on the ethics of the Bidens.

And then came Dershowitz.

In law school, I had audited a class from Alan Dershowitz, but I gave up after a few weeks when I found that I was not learning enough about the law and learning a little too much about Alan Dershowitz. But he was brilliant, and I admired his effortless advocacy. I remember attending a debate between Dersh, as we called him then, and Rudy Giuliani, about the Prince of the City corruption cases they had tried against each other, and it was like watching two talented legal gladiators going at it. It was marvelous.

Now he was standing in the well of the Senate, holding a dusty law book as a prop and telling the senators that he was going to "transport you back to a hot summer in Philadelphia and a cold winter in Washington. I will introduce you to patriots and ideas that helped shape our great Nation." For the next hour, that is what he did, or tried to do, and I have to confess that it was very engaging. For sixty minutes, I was transported, if not to the 1700s, at least to the 1980s, and I was back in law school again. Except now my youthful blinders were off, and instead of the brilliant if egocentric professor, I watched an aging scholar struggling for relevance. Dershowitz had shed the position he took during the Clinton impeachment and was now trying to convince senators that unless we had explicitly charged Trump with a crime, he could not be impeached.

To his credit, and unlike Starr and Ray, he did not pretend his position now was somehow consistent with his position then. "During the Clinton impeachment, I stated in an interview that I did not think that a technical crime was required but that I did think abusing trust could be considered. I said that." At that time, Dershowitz claimed that he had not done extensive research on the issue because it was not implicated in the Clinton impeachment, and he had "simply accepted the academic consensus." Now he had gone back and read the relevant historical material and had come to a different conclusion.

You could say a lot of things about Alan Dershowitz, but to claim he didn't do his homework during the last impeachment wasn't particularly plausible, nor was the idea that he would simply go along with the academic consensus. Later in his presentation, Dershowitz seemed to contradict himself when acknowledging that his current position was out of step with the academic consensus. "I do my own research, and I do my own thinking, and I have never bowed to the majority on intellectual or scholarly matters." Except that he had just told us that he had, and in the prime of his academic career.

Even if the Senate were to conclude that a crime was not

required for impeachment, Dershowitz argued that abuse of power and obstruction of congress did *not* constitute impeachable offenses. This was why Dershowitz had been brought in: to make the argument that even if the Senate found the president guilty of everything he had been charged with, the Senate still could not convict. It was the ultimate fallback argument.

Then Dershowitz addressed the elephant in the room: "Now, it follows from this that, if a president—any president—were to have done what the *Times* reported about the content of the Bolton manuscript, that would not constitute an impeachable offense. Let me repeat it. Nothing in the Bolton revelations, even if true, would rise to the level of an abuse of power or an impeachable offense." Except that it didn't follow at all. Dershowitz's examples of unimpeachable quid pro quos (then and later) all involved the suspension of aid for legitimate public purposes, not illicit efforts to gain foreign help in an election. He was using the same moral equivalence argument that I had earlier described as an insult to our intelligence. I still felt that it was, even if coming from a law professor I had once admired. Back in S-239 for the day's recap, the managers were poking holes in Dershowitz's arguments. "I rather enjoyed it," I said to their surprise, and they began heckling me. "What?" I replied, mocking offense. "It was like being in law school again."

But all kidding aside, a serious lawyer had just tried to argue that there was no such thing as presidential abuse of power, at least none that was impeachable. That his presentation was entertaining and cloaked in a facade of scholarship did not remedy its destructive implications. Why was he using his intellect in this way? Did he not see what this man had done, and was capable of doing, if left constitutionally unshackled in the manner that he was advocating?

That night we received an additional assist from Trump's former chief of staff, General John Kelly, who was now saying that he believed Bolton's account over that of the president he once served, and that there should be witness testimony during the trial. Meanwhile, the usual group of GOP senators defending Trump held another press briefing. They refused to comment on the witness issue, but the Iowa caucuses were only a week away, and Senator Barrasso delighted in saying that no one had been listening more attentively to the attacks on Biden than Senators Warren, Sanders, Klobuchar, and Bennet, who were all running for president. Republican senator Joni Ernst was all smiles as she questioned whether Iowa voters would be supporting Biden at this point. They didn't even try to hide the Trump defense goal of using the trial to smear Joe Biden, and weaken his candidacy.

Just after midnight, Trump was on Twitter attacking Bolton. "I NEVER told John Bolton that the aid to Ukraine was tied to investigations into Democrats, including the Bidens . . . If John Bolton said this, it was only to sell a book." This was helpful—if Trump was denying Bolton's allegations, there was a simple way to get to the truth: Call Bolton to testify. Already, the whirling impact of the *Times* story seemed to be dislodging Republican senators. The next day, Lankford and Graham proposed getting hold of Bolton's manuscript and reading it in a SCIF before making a decision on witnesses. Apparently, the Republicans had a use for the bunker after all. "We've got to be able to see it in advance to be able to make that decision on witnesses in a couple days," Lankford said. Schumer quickly rejected the idea, viewing it as an effort to defang the drive to call Bolton as a witness, which it almost certainly was. But if staunch Trump defenders like Lankford and Graham were getting cold feet about holding a trial without witnesses, the ground was clearly moving.

When the defense argument resumed that afternoon, Sekulow felt he could no longer ignore the growing clamor over Bolton. Still maintaining that the president's Ukraine conduct was nothing more than a "foreign policy decision," he cited Dershowitz and claimed that the articles of impeachment needed to be rejected "even if it was a quid pro quo." Clearly in disarray, the defense concluded its case using less than half of the time allotted to their arguments. If they had been planning to continue the fallacious claim that there was no evidence Trump had directly sought to condition the aid on investigations, that argument was now even more untenable.

Trump's defense could not have ended on a weaker note, and that night, after we returned to our study room to work on further preparations for the Q&A, we were greeted with even more good news. According to *The Washington Post,* McConnell had just informed his Senate colleagues that he did not have the votes to block witnesses. I wanted to believe it, and so did all of my fellow managers, and staff intensified preparations for a Bolton examination. But I knew never to count McConnell out, and it occurred to me that the leak of McConnell's vote count might have been strategic, even if accurate. He was sounding the alarm, and in the home states of any wavering senators, McConnell may have just unleashed the dogs of hell.

On Wednesday, we began two days of questions and answers from senators. The questions would be submitted in writing to the chief justice on large index cards and senators would indicate to whom they wanted to direct the questions—managers, defense, or both. In the Clinton trial, Roberts said, Chief Justice Rehnquist had advised counsel that there would be a rebuttable presumption that each question could be answered fairly in five minutes—and that Rehnquist's comment had been met with laughter. So too was Roberts's citation of it.

We divided up the topics among the House managers so that they would be fully prepared for me to quickly turn to individual managers to answer particular questions. Hakeem Jeffries summed up the various roles beautifully in an interview with *Vanity Fair:* "Adam Schiff is the prosecutor. Jason Crow is the soldier. Val Demings is the chief. Sylvia Garcia is the judge. Jerry Nadler is the scholar. Zoe Lofgren is the oracle, and I'm just a boy from Brooklyn trying to play my position." Of course Jeffries was doing much more than that, and I could count on him to answer some of the most difficult and delicate questions.

We had two primary goals in responding to questions—underscore the need for Bolton's testimony and pay particular attention to any issues raised by the four senators, whether the question was proposed to us or the defense. The very first two questions gave us the opportunity to do both. Right out of the gate, Senators Collins, Murkowski, and Romney asked the defense how the Senate should consider the president's conduct if he had more than one motive for withholding the aid, including both personal and policy interests. It was a good question and gave us a window into their thinking—at a minimum, these senators had an open mind and were taking the issues seriously. Philbin, addressing the chamber first, argued that any mixed motive made the president's conduct unimpeachable because it would be impossible to divine the proportions of his various motivations. I made a note to come back to that question at my earliest opportunity, which would come sooner than I thought.

The very next question came from Schumer, and he asked managers whether there was any way for the Senate to render a fully informed verdict without hearing from Bolton, Mulvaney, and other key witnesses. Most, though not all, of the questions would take this form—directed by Democratic senators to the managers and by Republicans to Trump's defense team. "The short answer," I said, "is no." When you had a witness as plainly relevant as Bolton, whose testimony went to one of the central allegations in the case and who was volunteering to come in, to turn him away was at odds with the obligation to be an impartial juror. I then used the time I had left to pivot back to Collins's question. If the president's corrupt motive was any part of his decision to withhold the aid, I said, that was enough to convict. Under well-established principles of criminal law, if a corrupt motive was part of the defendant's decision, then they should find him guilty. Later in the trial, I would cite an example given at the Constitutional Convention, where the Framers were concerned that a president might bribe an elector to win his election. Certainly, it would not be a defense that in addition to buying the vote, the president was also rewarding the elector for their legislative service. Here, I reiterated, there was really no question about what was driving the president, but if there was, if they had any doubt, there was a simple way to find out: Call Bolton.

With time still left on the clock, I played a video to underscore my point. It was from earlier in the trial, when Cipollone said that the goal of House managers should be to give you all the facts. "Impeachment shouldn't be a shell game. They should give you the facts." As the video was playing and Cipollone was occupying the screens around the chamber, I looked over at the defense table—he was white as a ghost.

I would soon have another opportunity to hammer home the duplicity of the defense case when Senator Markey of Massachusetts asked about a Trump tweet claiming we never asked Bolton to testify in the House. I told the senators that this was false; we had asked him and he had refused and threatened to sue us if we subpoenaed him. I then referred to the McGahn litigation in which Trump's lawyers—a different set of them—had just filed their appellate brief. It could not have been worse timing for Trump's impeachment defense, because this is what they were arguing: "The committee," I quoted, "lacks Article III standing to sue to enforce a congressional subpoena demanding testimony from an individual on matters related to his duties as an Executive Branch official." Here, Trump's lawyers were arguing that we couldn't impeach the president for obstruction and we should have gone to court, and in court, other Trump lawyers were arguing the opposite. Was the Senate really prepared to accept such hypocrisy?

As a practical matter, the Trump defense position would mean the House could never investigate presidential misconduct. Combine that with Alan Dershowitz's argument that presidential abuses of power are unimpeachable, and you have a president who is truly above the law. "Even sixty-year-old Alan Dershowitz doesn't agree with eighty-one-year-old Alan Dershowitz, and for a reason—because where that conclusion leads us is that a president can abuse his power in any kind of way, and there is nothing you can do about it." At the next break, I was approached by Republican senator Pat Roberts of Kansas. In his eighties himself, he asked me, good-naturedly, if I was making a commentary on Dershowitz's age. "No, no," I assured him, "just using a different way of making the point." The last thing I needed to do was gratuitously offend!

In fact, it would be another question to Dershowitz that would prove the most consequential of the day. Senator Cruz asked whether, as a matter of law, it mattered if there was a quid pro quo. Although I didn't know it at the time, Cruz had told Trump's defense team privately that they should stop pretending there was no such thing. "Out of a hundred senators," Cruz was reported to have said, "zero believe you on the argument there is no quid pro quo." Dershowitz responded, much as Mulvaney had, by saying it was done all the time and then Dershowitz gave inapt analogies about a president holding up aid to Israel unless they stopped settlement growth, or aid to the Palestinians unless they stopped supporting terror. But then he made a terrible blunder, and one that would haunt Trump's defense for the rest of the trial. "Every public official whom I know believes that his election is in the public interest," Dershowitz continued. "Mostly, you are right. Your election is in the public interest. If a president does something which he believes will help him get elected—in the public interest—that cannot be the kind of quid pro quo that results in impeachment."

This idea, the Dershowitz doctrine as it became called, was breathtaking in its destructive permissiveness. A president could abuse his power in any way he liked, as long as he believed that his reelection was in the public interest. The worst despot in the world will tell you that his people need him—Dershowitz, a once esteemed scholar, had now endorsed this philosophy. The next question came from Schumer, and he asked if I would like to respond to the prior answer. I said that I would be delighted to, prompting laughter in the chamber. Applying Dershowitz's own "shoe on the other foot" test, I hypothesized a situation in which Obama had told the Russian leader, Medvedev, that he would withhold military aid from Ukraine and help Russian soldiers on the front line if Russia would conduct an investigation of Obama's presidential opponent, Mitt Romney. By this point in the trial, I could look up at Romney without being too self-conscious about it, and he seemed amused by the analogy. "Do any of us have any question that Barack Obama would be impeached for that kind of misconduct?" Even closer to home, I raised the hypothetical situation of the president's telling a state governor that he wouldn't send disaster relief unless the state attorney general announced an investigation of his rival. If all quid pro quos are fine, I told the senators, then all bets were off and the next investigation that the president called for just might be into any one of you.

Senator Sullivan of Alaska asked "how long the Senate might be tied up" if it allowed witness testimony. "A very long time," Sekulow responded, "many weeks," "months." "Here's what I want. I want Adam Schiff. I want Hunter Biden. I want Joe Biden. I want the whistleblower." And he added several people on the House Intelligence Committee to the mix.

Senator Schumer asked me to respond to Sekulow. "I think we can all see what is going on here," I said. "If you want to hear what John Bolton has to say, we are going to make this endless . . . if you have the unmitigated temerity to want witnesses in a trial, we will make you pay for it with endless delay. The Senate will never be able to go back to its business . . . So Mr. Sekulow wants me to testify. I would like Mr. Sekulow to testify about his contact with Mr. Parnas or Mr. Cipollone about his efforts to implement the president's fight on all subpoenas. I would like to ask questions . . . of the president and put him under oath. But we are not here to indulge in fantasy or distraction; we are here to talk about people with pertinent and probative evidence.

"And you know something? I trust the man behind me [referring to the chief justice], sitting way up, whom I can't see right now, but I trust him to make decisions about whether a witness is material or not, whether it is appropriate to out a whistleblower or not . . . whether a particular passage in a document is privileged or not. It is not going to take months of litigation, although that is what the president's counsel is threatening."

They were doing the same thing that they had done in the House, which was promise to tie up the Senate for months with litigation if they wanted to hear witness testimony. I told the senators they did not have to allow this, that the chief justice could make privilege decisions, reviewing materials in camera. Privately, I knew that the chief justice would not relish the task and might not be willing to engage in it, but I wanted the senators to know that I trusted this Republican-appointed justice to do the right thing, even if the defense team, aware of the president's guilt, did not. In fact, we would later offer to take all witness depositions in a week, while the Senate conducted other business—just as in the Clinton trial.

The Trump defense was not about to let the chief justice decide. "Mr. Schiff is up here: Let's make a deal," Cipollone argued. " 'How about we have the chief justice—' and we have great respect for the chief justice. Here is the problem. . . . There are critical constitutional issues that will alter our balance of power for generations if we go down that road." It wasn't at all clear how that differed from the decisions Roberts made every day on the Supreme Court, and I had no trouble responding. "Mr. Chief Justice," I said, "it may be different in the court than it is in this chamber and in the House, but when anybody begins a sentence with the phrase 'I have the greatest respect for,' you have to look out for what follows." I couldn't observe Roberts's reaction from where I was facing, but I could certainly see the senators laughing. It wasn't that the defense didn't trust Roberts to be fair, it was precisely because they believed he *would* be fair that they did not want him to decide the question of witnesses.

Like much of the other portions of the trial, Q&A had its comedic moments. Bernie Sanders asked why we should credit Trump's denials of a quid pro quo when he had lied more than 16,200 times in the course of his presidency as of the prior week. "Well," I said, struggling not to laugh, "I am not quite sure where to begin with that question, except to say that if every defendant in a trial could be exonerated just by denying the crime, there would never be a conviction. It doesn't work that way." Given that I didn't need five minutes to answer Sanders's question, I returned to the first question Collins had asked about mixed motive. Over the break, our staff had done some amazing research and found that Dershowitz had argued a high-profile criminal case in the Seventh Circuit and made the same argument there—that mixed motive must result in acquittal. He lost.

That argument, I said, "shouldn't be any more availing here than it was there."

The debate I was having with Dershowitz continued when Marco Rubio asked how the Framers would have viewed an impeachment that had not been bipartisan in the House and for which there was no national consensus. Dershowitz responded that the Framers would have disapproved of such an impeachment, but then he felt the need to return to our discussion of the president's motivation. "The argument has been made," he said, "that the president of the United States only became interested in corruption when he learned that Joe Biden was running for President." For the sake of argument, Dershowitz assumed that this was true. But instead of seeking to limit or correct the dangerous license granted by his previous argument, Dershowitz doubled down on it, claiming that the fact that Biden was now running for president made it *more* appropriate for Trump to seek his investigation. "The fact that he has announced his candidacy is a very good reason for upping the interest in his son. If he wasn't running for president, he is a has-been. He is the former vice president of the United States. Okay, big deal. But if he is running for president, that is an enormous big deal."

I was again incredulous. Dershowitz was effectively saying that not only was it appropriate for Trump to withhold money from Ukraine to get that country to investigate Biden, but it was even *more* appropriate for him to do so because Biden might win. The higher the political stakes, the more the president was allowed to abuse his position. Wow.

Returning to the Dershowitz argument, I said that there was no way to reconcile that line of thinking unless you believed that the president *was* the state and that his interests were synonymous with those of the state. "I mean, you really have to step aside from what is going on to imagine that anyone could make that argument . . . running for President now means that you are a more justified target of investigation than when you weren't. *That cannot be* . . . But that is essentially what is being argued here."

As I headed back to S-239, I had a chance encounter with Senator Romney. We almost bumped into each other on the way through the lobby behind the chamber, and he remarked that he was interested in knowing more about how the hold on military aid was communicated to the Ukrainians. I imagine he brought it up with me then because he wasn't getting called on very often for questions—that is a prerogative McConnell would grant his own members—and Romney had a genuine interest in the answer. I was encouraged by his focus on the matter, as it signaled to me that he was taking his responsibility very seriously and would make his judgment based on the facts, something that I hoped others would do, and I resolved to come back to that issue in our coming presentations.

The debate over the Dershowitz doctrine carried on to the second day of questioning, but without Dershowitz. Not only had he been benched from the Trump defense, but the remaining lawyers tried to walk back the extreme consequences of his argument. We wouldn't let them. The first question I received came from Democratic senator Jon Tester of Montana. Quoting Dershowitz from the day before, he asked whether, under the Trump defense theory, there would be any limit to the kind of quid pro quo that a president could engage in with a foreign power if he thought it would help his reelection. No, I responded, there was no limiting principle to their position. It was a "descent into constitutional madness." Their argument would permit the president to offer military funding as well as withhold it from another nation unless they agreed to help his reelection, by hacking his opponent or through any other means. "Now, the only reason you [make] that argument is because you know your client is guilty and dead to rights. That is an argument made of desperation." I pointed to Nixon's famous claim to an interviewer after Watergate that when a president does it, it's not illegal, and asked, "Have we learned nothing in the last half century?" In fact, I argued, we had moved backward, not forward, since that Nixonian argument had failed, because it was at risk of succeeding here. "That is the normalization of lawlessness."

Senator King would play this argument out in devastating fashion, asking the defense if it would be permissible for a president running for reelection to inform the Israeli prime minister that he was withholding military aid "unless the prime minister promised to come to the United States and publicly charge his opponent with anti-Semitism." Philbin "thanked" him for the question and back-pedaled furiously from Dershowitz's argument, claiming that he had been misinterpreted. But Philbin still wouldn't declare such conduct impeachable, because misinterpretation or no misinterpretation, this was very much like the kind of conduct Trump had been engaged in.

DURING OUR LUNCH BREAK, I returned to S-239 and pumped down more ibuprofen. Sitting on the couch, leaning over with my head in my hand, Jeffries tried to spur me on. "It's like you're in the championship game. You're playing injured!" he said excitedly. "You've got to play through the pain." Jeffries had a sports metaphor for everything, but I have to say, it was working. His words didn't take the pain away, but they did give me a way of visualizing the challenge of keeping my focus on the work and not letting the pain get in my way. When lunch arrived, I had a different problem. I had become vegan, like Eve, three years earlier for health reasons. But today's meal was barbecue, and the vegan options were worse than awful. I made myself a full plate of the barbecue and Demings took a photo, saying that she would blackmail me later. I do allow myself to cheat occasionally, as long as I keep the exceptions very narrowly drawn. When I was on the overseas trip to Jordan with Pelosi, for example, we had dinner with King Abdullah and there was nothing vegan for me to eat, so I created the "King Abdullah exception." Now, I told the managers, I was declaring a presidential impeachment exception. After all, how often could that happen?

Back in the chamber, several of the Republican questions pertained to the whistleblower, but the chief justice had made it clear to the parties that he was not going to allow the Senate trial to be used to expose the whistleblower any more than I had been willing to let Republicans do so in the House. Nevertheless, Senator Rand Paul submitted a question purporting to identify the whistleblower, and after reading it, the chief justice declined to ask it. It would be the only question that he would refuse, and Senator Paul responded by going outside the chamber to read it to reporters.

One key question came from Republicans Collins and Murkowski and Democrats Manchin and Sinema, and it concerned whether private citizens could conduct foreign policy, since that would appear to violate the Logan Act. Philbin said that "there was no conduct of foreign policy being carried on here by a private person." This was a remarkable admission, but I wasn't sure that everyone caught it. They were conceding that Giuliani's pursuit of the two political investigations was *not* policy. "So what *were* they?" I asked. "They were, in the words of Dr. Hill, 'a domestic political errand,' not to be confused with policy."

When it came time for the last question of the night, Senator Klobuchar asked the managers if there was anything the Senate would benefit from hearing before we adjourned. What happened next would be the subject of endless memes, and would cause the president some merriment of his own. As I got up to give a five-minute closing statement, Nadler rushed past me to the lectern. He moved so fast it took me by surprise. I whispered "Jerry, Jerry, Jerry" to get his attention, but it was too late, and we would miss the opportunity to give a summation of the import of the last two days of interrogatories. Nadler said he wasn't aware it was the last question, and with all he had on his mind back home and the critical decisions to be made about his wife's care, I could understand why. It was a feat of incredible mental strength and discipline that he had been able to perform as well as he did. Still, it was a lost opportunity and made for some endless ribbing. One very popular meme showed LeBron incensed at teammate J. R. Smith for holding onto the ball as seconds were counting down on the clock. J.R. believed their team was ahead—they were not—and it may have cost them the game, since they went on to lose in overtime. I needed Hakeem Jeffries to explain it to me. "Don't worry," he told me, smiling, "in this scenario, you're LeBron. You're LeBron!"

We soon put our heads together to figure out where we were with the key senators. Manchin, Sinema, and Jones had all asked questions that seemed to cut in both directions, but were more sympathetic than hostile to our cause. The questions from the Republican four were even more difficult to divine. But one question in particular gave us room for optimism. Late in the evening, Senator Murkowski had asked "Why should this body not call in Ambassador Bolton," since a "dispute about material facts weighs in favor of calling additional witnesses with direct knowledge." Philbin's answer was predictable—that the Senate should not do investigative work that the House should have done on its own—but the answer was far less important than the question, and who was asking it. If Murkowski was leaning in favor of Bolton's testimony, and Collins and Romney had already indicated their receptiveness to witnesses earlier in the trial, that meant we needed just one more—Lamar Alexander, who had told reporters he would announce his decision at the end of the night.

It wasn't long before he did. Senator Alexander would *not* support calling witnesses. It was a grave disappointment. Alexander was retiring—so he was under less pressure from Trump voters back home—but he was very close to McConnell, and those personal ties make a big difference in legislative life. Sometimes too big a difference. In an effort to justify his decision, Alexander issued a statement trying to have it both ways. "I worked with other senators to make sure that we have the right to ask for more documents and witnesses, but there is no need for more evidence to prove something that has already been proven and that does not meet the United States Constitution's high bar for an impeachable offense," he said. "The question is not whether the president did it, but whether the United States Senate or the American people should decide what to do about what he did."

Senator Alexander was conceding that we had proved the president's guilt, and other senators, including Ben Sasse of Nebraska, would soon make it clear that Alexander spoke for many of them as well. But there were several flaws in Alexander's further reasoning. What did it mean to say that you had worked to make sure there was a right to call witnesses if your vote precluded senators from doing exactly that? But more to the point, how could you argue that voters should make the decision and then withhold some of the most critical information that voters would need to inform their judgment—like Bolton's testimony? And how could you rely on the election to remedy the president's abuse of power when he was still trying to undermine the integrity of that very election?

We had lost Alexander, but with Collins and Romney in support of calling witnesses, that still left Murkowski, who said that she would announce her decision in the morning. If Murkowski went our way, the vote on witnesses would be 50–50, and that would raise a constitutional question not heard in over a century: Would the chief justice break the tie?

On the afternoon of Friday, January 31, we convened at the usual time and began final debate on "the question of whether or not it shall be in order to consider . . . any motion to subpoena witnesses and documents." It was not even a direct vote on witnesses, but a vote on whether there should be a vote on witnesses, part of the McConnell strategy to deflect accountability from the pivotal decision on whether to have a fair trial. I began my presentation with yet another development in the case, another breaking story in *The New York Times* that Bolton's manuscript would reveal that he had been instructed by Trump to help Giuliani with his pressure campaign as early as a meeting in May. That meeting included not only Mulvaney but also Cipollone, meaning that the man leading Trump's defense during the trial had also been "in the loop" about the scheme. Talk about a fact witness, I told senators, referring to the article and Cipollone. I looked over at Cipollone, who had accused managers of hiding the facts, and he sat frozen in place with his arms crossed. I had warned senators that the facts would continue to come out, and they had, again.

As my fellow House managers ran through the now familiar arguments for a fair trial, we got the news: Murkowski had issued a statement—she would *not* support calling witnesses. "Given the partisan nature of this impeachment from beginning and throughout, I have come to the conclusion that there will be no fair trial in the Senate . . . the Congress has failed." It was a remarkable statement, and one, like Alexander's, that I had difficulty fathoming. Murkowski was bemoaning the failure to provide a fair trial when her vote might have been decisive in bringing about such a result. It was as if she were a spectator to the proceedings that were taking place around her, powerless to do anything about them.

When I returned to the chamber after a short recess, I knew that the cause of calling witnesses had been lost. Even if Murkowski had voted with us, we now understood from the Senate parliamentarian that the chief justice would not cast a deciding vote. Asked by Schumer later in the day if he was aware that Chief Justice Chase had cast deciding votes twice during the impeachment of President Andrew Johnson, Roberts replied in an exchange that was scripted out in advance: "I do not regard those isolated episodes a hundred fifty years ago as sufficient to support a general authority to break ties. If the members of this body, elected by the people and accountable to them, divide equally on a motion, the normal rule is that the motion fails. I think it would be inappropriate for me, an unelected official from a different branch of government, to assert the power to change the result so that the motion would succeed."

As I returned to the podium for another closing statement, I rebutted the defense arguments that had preceded me, but my heart wasn't in it. How could it be? And so I focused less on the senators in the chamber whose minds were made up than on those who would come later to serve in that body.

"Senators," I said, "there is a storm blowing through this Capitol. Its winds are strong, and they move us in uncertain and dangerous directions. Jefferson once said: 'I consider trial by jury as the only anchor . . . yet imagined by man, by which a government can be held to the principles of its constitution.' I would submit to you, remove that anchor, and we are adrift, but if we hold true, if we have faith that the ship of state can survive the truth, this storm shall pass."

The vote was 49–51, with Senators Collins and Romney the only Republicans voting in favor of witnesses, and the impeachment trial of Donald J. Trump became the first in history in which witness testimony would not be allowed.

The following morning I went to the dentist and had a root canal, and no one was ever more grateful for a root canal. My wonderful dentist, who came in on the weekend for the second time during the trial to rescue me from pain, told me that he had been watching the trial in agony himself, and that if I had brought my hand to my mouth it would have killed him. "I wanted to tell my wife," he said, "'I broke Adam Schiff'—but I couldn't even commiserate with her because your privacy would not allow me to tell her you were my patient." "You can tell her I'm your patient," I said, "and please let her know how grateful I am for everything you've done."

The trial would not resume until Monday for closing arguments, and that was fine—I needed to spend more time preparing, and recovering from my root canal. I hadn't written a single word, because I could not have predicted just what course the trial would take. But first I had a much more joyous experience ahead. My cousin Steve and his longtime partner, Ira, were getting married in Philadelphia. For quite a while, they had not planned on marrying—originally because it was not lawful for them to do so and later for other reasons. But now Ira had been diagnosed with cancer, and they didn't know how much more time they would have together.

On the way to the wedding, we stopped for lunch at a wonderful restaurant, Germano's Piattini, in the Little Italy section of Baltimore. Eve had picked this restaurant at random, based on its rating from a vegan app on her phone. On the wall over our table was a beautiful oil painting of a large, elegant family, with a young girl in a white dress sitting in the center. The girl was Nancy Pelosi, and the restaurant happened to be right across the street from her childhood home. The owner told us the portrait had been rescued from disrepair and they were proud to have it, and I called the Speaker to let her know the happy coincidence. We both considered it a good omen.

The wedding was beautiful, and being able to celebrate with family an event both joyful and tinged with sweet sadness gave me a chance to recover my strength surrounded by love and affection. As I walked into the reception with my father and Fuentes, the head of my security detail, my father, once a tall man but now a bit shrunken with age, looked up at him and said: "Thank you for taking care of my son. I know you don't believe this, but there are a lot of crazy fuckers out there."

We returned home on Sunday night in time for the Super Bowl. Eve and Eli went next door to watch the game with our neighbors, and I sat in my favorite place for thinking and writing—a big comfortable leather chair by the fireplace. My closing argument would not be impromptu, and I wanted to think through every word. We were at a very dangerous moment in the history of our country, at risk of embracing a doctrine of unchecked presidential power at a time when autocracy was gaining favor around the world and we had the most unscrupulous of leaders. If there were any open minds in the Senate, I wanted to reach them. If there were any open minds in the country—and I believed there were—I wanted to reach them too. But failing to do either, I wanted to speak to the future, in the hope that we might learn from the tragic mistakes we were making, before it was too late.

ON THE MORNING OF CLOSING arguments, Pelosi invited the managers to join her in a ceremonial room just off the House floor. She wanted to thank us again for the dignity with which we had presented our case, on behalf of the caucus and the American people. She knew that we were not going to get a conviction, but she wanted to assure us that we had done our constitutional duty and earned a place in history. Our efforts had been worthy of the Founders, she said, and we should be enormously proud of what we had already achieved. It was a very uplifting talk, and so characteristic of the Speaker. If I was a general, she was the Supreme Allied Commander, marshaling her forces and sending us in for one last fight.

For the closing statements, I gave my fellow managers wide latitude to address the issues they thought most important, in the manner they thought most effective, and when they did, I could not have been more impressed. Many of us did not know one another well before the trial began, and we had grown extremely close, with bonds forged by the rigors of our work together. I had come to have enormous respect for each of them, and we had developed a profound trust and confidence in one another. There were a few notable frictions at times, but in a body known for its division and competitiveness, we really were a team, bound for life by this remarkable shared experience.

Jeffries spoke last of my colleagues before handing off to me for the final words of the trial. He ended by citing Scripture. "Second Corinthians," he said, "encourages us to walk by faith, not by sight. Faith is the substance of things hoped for, the evidence of things not seen. We have come this far by faith." He urged that all of us, in the chamber and out, walk by faith. With a pastor's cadence he said: "Through the ups and the downs, the highs and the lows, the peaks and the valleys, the trials and the tribulations of this turbulent moment, walk by faith—faith in the Constitution; faith in our democracy; faith in the rule of law; faith in government of the people, by the people, and for the people; faith in almighty God. Walk by faith."

As I thought about his words, I had a new appreciation for the faith—and the courage—our Founders must have had to trust their lives to this unproven experiment, now centuries old. Everything they had experienced should have caused them to distrust its success, but they walked by faith, and we were the lucky beneficiaries of that step into the unknown.

When I walked to the lectern, I looked out at those hundred faces, by now so familiar. Before I stepped into that chamber weeks earlier, many of them had thought me a monster; that's what the leader of their party had told them, in any case. Now I couldn't tell what they thought. "Senators," I said, "we are not enemies but friends. We must not be enemies. If Lincoln could speak these words during the Civil War, surely we can live them now and overcome our divisions and our animosities."

The room was very still, and whether they thought me an enemy or not, I could tell at least this much: They wanted to hear what I would say.

"It is midnight in Washington," I began. "The lights are finally going out in the Capitol after a long day in the impeachment trial of Donald J. Trump." Late Friday night, as senators were leaving town, one of Trump's lawyers at Justice had waited until just before the clock struck twelve to make another duplicitous filing in court. One that again argued that the House could not use the courts to enforce its subpoenas—and directly contradicted their impeachment defense. The last-minute filing was designed to land in court so late at night that senators would not find out.

"Midnight in Washington. All too tragic a metaphor for where the country finds itself at the conclusion of only the third impeachment in history and the first impeachment trial without witnesses or documents, the first such trial—or nontrial—in impeachment history. How did we get here?"

In the beginning, senators did not know whether the House could prove its case, but now they had seen what we promised, overwhelming evidence of the president's guilt. Unable to overcome our proof of the president's corrupt quid pro quo, his team opted "in a kind of desperation" for a different kind of defense. First they would seek to prevent the Senate and the public from hearing from witnesses with the most damning accounts of the president's misconduct, and second, they would rely on a theory of presidential power so broad and unaccountable that the occupant of the Oval Office could be as corrupt as he chooses while Congress would be powerless to do anything about it. "That defense collapsed of its own dead weight," I said. If abuse of power was unimpeachable because the president considered his reelection in the public interest, there would be no limit to the damage he could do to our nation or its security. This was such an extreme view that the president's own lawyers had run away from it.

So the president had to retreat to his final defense, which I summed up in these words:

> He is guilty as sin, but can't we just let the voters decide? He is guilty as sin, but why not let the voters clean up this mess? And here, to answer that question, we must look at the history of this presidency and to the character of this president—or lack of character—and ask, can we be confident that he will not continue to try to cheat in that very election? . . . And the short, plain, sad, incontestable answer is, no, you *can't*. You can't trust this president to do the right thing, not for one minute, not for one election, not for the sake of our country. You just *can't*. He will not change, and you know it.

As I said the words, I found my pace accelerating and the intensity grow. It was not something I did consciously, but I allowed the anger over what he had done to show, and my conviction that he would do it again, or worse. I went through the history of Trump's effort to get Russia to help him in 2016, and his efforts to cover it up. I reminded senators of his decision after Mueller to invite foreign interference again, only this time he could use the powers of his office to coerce it, and this time he could use the Justice Department to help cover it up. Trump had no more Jeff Sessions. He had just the man he wanted in Bill Barr, someone who would do his bidding and would refuse to investigate the president's misconduct.

"He has not changed," I said of Trump. "He will not change. He has made that clear himself without self-awareness or hesitation. A man without character or ethical compass will never find his way." I itemized Trump's continuing efforts to get other countries, like China, to help him cheat, even as he was continuing, through Giuliani, to try to dig up dirt in Ukraine.

The plot goes on; the scheming persists; and the danger will never recede. He has done it before. He will do it again. What are the odds, if left in office, that he will continue trying to cheat? I will tell you: one hundred percent. Not five, not ten or even fifty, but one hundred percent. If you have found him guilty and you do not remove him from office, he will continue trying to cheat in the election until he succeeds. Then what shall you say?

So how, I asked, given the gravity of the president's offense, and the abundance of evidence, given that senators from both parties were now acknowledging that we had proved our case—how had we arrived at this place with such little common ground? I traced the history of the Nixon and Clinton impeachments, how our process in the House had been largely the same, and how the harm Trump had done was so much greater. Why, then, was there such a disparate result in the level of bipartisan support for Trump's removal? What had changed?

"The short answer is," I said,

we have changed. The members of Congress have changed. For reasons as varied as the stars, the members of this body and ours in the House are now far more accepting of the most serious misconduct of a president as long as it is a president of one's own party. And that is a trend most dangerous for our country. Fifty years ago, no lawyer representing the president would have ever made the outlandish argument that if the president believes his corruption will serve to get him reelected, whether it is by coercing an ally to help him cheat or in any other form, that he may not be impeached, that this is somehow a permissible use of his power. But here we are. The argument has been made, and some appear ready to accept it. And that is dangerous, for there is no limiting principle to that position.

It must have come as a shock—a pleasant shock—to this president that our norms and institutions would prove to be so *weak*. The independence of the Justice Department and its formerly proud Office of Legal Counsel now are mere legal tools at the president's disposal to investigate enemies or churn out helpful opinions not worth the paper they are written on. The FBI painted by a president as corrupt and disloyal. The Intelligence Community not to be trusted against the good counsel of Vladimir Putin. The press portrayed as enemies of the people. The daily attacks on the guardrails of our democracy, so relentlessly assailed, have made us numb and blind to the consequences. Does none of that matter anymore if he is the president of our party?

I told the senators that I hoped we would never have a president like Donald Trump in the Democratic Party, but that if we did, I hoped we would impeach him and Democrats would lead the way. But I recognized that it was difficult for me to stand in their shoes. Nonetheless, Republican senators had to confront the danger now, and if they didn't, I wanted to let them know how they would be judged by history. This may seem like an ephemeral consideration to many, but elected officials think in these terms—I know that I do. I continued:

> History will not be kind to Donald Trump—I think we all know that—not because it will be written by Never Trumpers, but because whenever we have departed from the values of our nation, we have come to regret it, and that regret is written all over the pages of our history.
>
> If you find that the House has proved its case and still vote to acquit, your name will be tied to his with a cord of steel and for all of history; but if you find the courage to stand up to him, to speak the awful truth to his rank falsehood, your place will be among the Davids who took on Goliath. If only you will say *"Enough."*

When we look at the sweep of history, there are times when our nation and the rest of the world have moved with a seemingly irresistible force in the direction of greater freedom: more freedom to speak and to assemble, to practice our faith and tolerate the faith of others, to love whom we would and choose love over hate—more free societies, walls tumbling down, nations reborn. But then, like a pendulum approaching the end of its arc, the outward movement begins to arrest. The golden globe of freedom reaches its zenith and starts to retreat. The pendulum swings back past the center and recedes into a dark unknown. How much farther will it travel in its illiberal direction, how many more freedoms will be extinguished before it turns back we cannot say. But what we do here, in this moment, will affect its course and its correction."

Every single vote, even a *single* vote, by a single member, can change the course of history. It is said that a single man or a woman of courage makes a majority. Is there one among you who will say *"Enough"*?

America believes in a thing called truth. She does not believe we are entitled to our own alternate facts. She recoils at those who spread pernicious falsehoods. To her, truth matters. There is nothing more corrosive to a democracy than the idea that there is no truth. America also believes there is a difference between right and wrong, and right matters here. But there is more. Truth matters. Right matters. But so does decency. Decency matters. When the president smears a patriotic public servant like Marie Yovanovitch in pursuit of a corrupt aim, we recoil. When the president mocks the disabled, a war hero who was a prisoner of war, or a Gold Star father, we are appalled because decency matters here. And when the president tries to coerce an ally to help him cheat in our elections and then covers it up, we must say *"Enough. Enough!"*

He has betrayed our national security, and he will do so again. He has compromised our elections, and he will do so again. You will not change him. You cannot constrain him. He is who he is. Truth matters little to him. What is right matters even less. And decency matters not at all. I do not ask you to convict him because truth or right or decency matters nothing to him but because we have proven our case and it matters to you. Truth matters to *you*. Right matters to *you*. You are decent. He is not who *you* are.

It may be midnight in Washington, but the sun will rise again. I put my faith in the optimism of the Founders. You should too. They gave us the tools to do the job, a remedy as powerful as the evil it was meant to constrain: impeachment. They meant it to be used rarely, but they put it in the Constitution for a reason—for a man who would sell out his country for a political favor, for a man who would threaten the integrity of our elections, for a man who would invite foreign interference in our affairs, for a man who would undermine our national security and that of our allies—for a man like Donald J. Trump.

They gave you a remedy, and they meant for you to use it. They gave you an oath, and they meant for you to observe it. We have proven Donald Trump guilty. Now do impartial justice and convict him.

Over the next three days, and continuing through a State of the Union presentation in which the president refused to shake Pelosi's hand and lied so frequently that she tore up her copy of his speech when he had concluded, senators filed onto the Senate floor to announce their verdicts to a mostly empty chamber. Lisa Murkowski addressed the Senate on February 3, calling the president's conduct "shameful and wrong," and saying that his personal interests do not take precedence over those of the nation. Nevertheless, she would not convict. For her part, Susan Collins said the House had done little to support its assertion that the president would "remain a threat to national security and the Constitution if allowed to remain in office." She would later tell reporters, "I believe that the president has learned from this case. The president has been impeached.

That's a pretty big lesson . . . I believe that he will be much more cautious in the future."

Manchin, Sinema, and Jones were all voting to convict. Only Mitt Romney remained a mystery. I was alone in the House cloakroom when he finally addressed the Senate. Boland stuck his head in the door to tell me that he was hearing that Romney might convict. I had heard so many false rumors over the weeks, months, and years that I was not prepared to believe it. Then Romney started speaking. The allegations made in the articles were very serious, he said. "As a Senator juror, I swore an oath before God to exercise impartial justice. I am profoundly religious. My faith is at the heart of who I am." At this point, Romney became very emotional and paused to collect himself. "I take an oath before God as enormously consequential."

He went through the president's defenses and knocked them down, one by one. Still, I was not convinced where this was going. I was waiting for the inevitable "but"—but it never came. "The grave question the Constitution tasks Senators to answer is whether the president committed an act so extreme and egregious that it rises to the level of a high crime and misdemeanor." Romney paused, and the moment stretched on. "Yes, he did."

"My God," I said out loud, sitting up from where I had been slouching on one of the leather couches. Romney was about to become the first senator in American history to vote to convict a president of his own party. "The president asked a foreign government to investigate his political rival," Romney continued.

The president withheld vital military funds from that government to press it to do so. The president delayed funds for an American ally at war with Russian invaders. The president's purpose was personal and political. Accordingly, the president is guilty of an appalling abuse of public trust. What he did was not "perfect." No, it was a flagrant assault on our electoral rights, our national security, and our fundamental values. Corrupting an election to keep oneself in office is perhaps the most abusive and destructive violation of one's oath of office that I can imagine.

Romney described the anger his decision was likely to provoke, and the cries of disloyalty he would hear, but his promise before God was to apply impartial justice, and he needed, he said, to put party loyalty and other considerations aside. Were he to ignore the evidence and what he believed his oath and the Constitution required, it would expose his character "to history's rebuke and the censure of my own conscience." Romney was looking to his children and grandchildren, and would tell them that he did his duty to the best of his ability, "believing that my country expected it of me."

I will be only one name among many—no more, no less—to future generations of Americans who look at the record of this trial. They will note merely that I was among the senators who determined that what the president did was wrong, grievously wrong. We are all footnotes at best in the annals of history, but in the most powerful nation on earth, the nation conceived in liberty and justice, that distinction is enough for any citizen.

I was breathless. In his humility and his truthfulness, in his devotion to his faith and the seriousness with which he took his oath before God, this one brave man had validated my belief and that of the Founders, that the people possessed sufficient virtue to be self-governing. One man had made a majority. One man had said, *"Enough."*

PART FIVE

SOMEONE'S GOING TO
GET KILLED

21

HEADS ON PIKES

THE STORY OF THE YEAR FOLLOWING THE FIRST IMPEACHMENT OF DON-
ald Trump reads like the chronicle of a presidential disaster fore-
told. On February 5, 2020, the very same day that Trump would be
acquitted in his impeachment trial, the House of Representatives
would have its first hearing on the novel coronavirus that would soon
paralyze the world. Covid-19, as it became known, would challenge
the United States' capacity to respond to a global pandemic unseen
in more than a hundred years. And it would test a proposition I
raised during the trial—whether the American people could trust
their president to do what was best for the country, or only what was
best for Donald J. Trump.

But Covid-19 was not the only serious danger facing the country.
Our democracy was also under attack, and on multiple fronts. The
Russians were ramping up a disinformation campaign designed to

help Trump and hurt Biden in the upcoming election. Much as they had done with Hillary Clinton four years earlier, and as the Intelligence Community would later publicly acknowledge, the Russians began pushing out information attacking Biden's health and casting doubt on his capacity to serve as president. Trump's response to the gathering storm of intelligence on Russia's renewed efforts to help his campaign met with the same response that characterized his earlier approach—to disavow the intelligence and remake the leadership of the Intelligence Community to reflect and embrace his preferred, and false, narrative of events. The politicization of intelligence, a problem since the beginning of the Trump presidency, would become far worse.

Perhaps the most destructive Russian misinformation was the Kremlin's renewed attack on the integrity of American elections. As the U.S. government would later reveal, the Russians were disseminating propaganda that absentee voting, a necessity during the pandemic, would be plagued by fraud, and that the election would be stolen from Donald Trump. But the Russians were not inventing this fictitious narrative, only amplifying it—its architect was none other than the president of the United States. As states embraced voting by mail so that their citizens could vote safely, Trump saw this effort to facilitate turnout as a threat to his reelection. Democrats, he believed, were less frequent and disciplined voters, and Trump wanted to further chill their participation by forcing them to choose between their franchise and their health, so he began a systemic and fraudulent effort to discourage mail-in voting.

Much of the president's disenfranchisement push was aimed at communities of color and deliberately aggravated racial tensions in the country, already raw after more than three years of his divisive presidency. Systemic racism would catapult to the top of the national consciousness during the summer, with the slow strangulation of George Floyd at the knee of a Minnesota policeman. As marchers took to the streets in protests all across America, Trump saw an opportunity. He would stoke racial tensions further and capitalize on the theme of "law and order" even as he encouraged violence and disorder. He would use fear, anger, and division to drive his voters to the polls, just as I had observed Vladimir Meciar do in Czechoslovakia so many years ago.

Trailing in the polls, his response to the pandemic a deadly disaster, the country convulsed with frustration over its inability to make progress against a pernicious bias present since its founding—here was a chance to change the topic and the trajectory of his campaign, and recast himself as the only thing standing between civil society and anarchy. Kellyanne Conway echoed the president's thoughts when she acknowledged that increased violence would help the Trump campaign: "The more chaos and anarchy and vandalism and violence reigns, the better it is for the very clear choice on who's best on public safety and law and order," she declared on *Fox and Friends*.

Of all the iconic images of the period, the one that stands out most vividly for me is that of Donald Trump standing in front of St. John's Church, holding a Bible and posing with the grim expression of a Grant Wood portrait. Peaceful protesters had been gassed and beaten to put up fencing nearby, while Trump made his way to the church. Trump was accompanied by, among others, the chairman of the Joint Chiefs of Staff, General Mark Milley, who wore full combat fatigues, a tangible demonstration of the president's threat to use military force to quell the protests nationwide. In that one obscene image before the church, and all that preceded it, one sees the entire Trump presidency: a skilled contrivance, a desecration of that which is holy, and a dangerous projection of power divorced from both principle and the law.

There was a common element to Trump's reaction to these crises convulsing the country during the months after his acquittal, and one far more sweeping than his mere pursuit of self-interest at the expense of the nation. And it was simply this: Trump believed that he could make his own truth. Covid-19 was no worse than the flu and the virus would go away on its own. The Russians weren't helping him, it was all a hoax. Voting by mail was plagued with fraud, and millions of counterfeit ballots would be sent from abroad. And the danger of domestic terrorism came not from white nationalists who supported him, but from antifa radicals who did not.

All of Trump's falsehoods would play a role in his biggest deception of all—that our election was rigged and stolen. A big lie does not take shape on its own, but must be carefully built upon a scaffold of lies.

Susan Collins had said that Trump would learn a lesson from his impeachment, and he did, though not the lesson she thought. She was not alone in her misapprehension. Lamar Alexander made very similar comments, observing that "We all learn lessons as we go through life . . . hopefully we learn from those things." Indiana Republican senator Mike Braun rationalized his decision to acquit, saying, "Hopefully it'll be instructive . . . I think he'll put two and two together."

Trump did put two and two together, and what it added up to was this: He had an iron grip on the base of the Republican Party and he could say whatever he wanted and they would believe him, or at least profess that they did. And as for the Republican members of Congress or people who served in his administration, none of them would dare contradict his falsehoods again, and anyone who did, would pay.

The postimpeachment bloodletting began almost immediately.

At a prayer breakfast the morning after the verdict, Trump jarred the peace of those assembled, when the former president of a conservative think tank urged those in attendance to love their enemies, and Trump later responded by saying, "I don't know if I agree with you." In a reference to the one Republican who had voted to convict him, Trump went on to question Senator Romney's faith—at this event celebrating people's belief in God. "I don't like people who use their faith as justification for doing what they know is wrong." Then, referring to Pelosi, who was present at the event, he added: "Nor do I like people who say 'I pray for you' when they know that's not so."

Later that day, Trump invited his most devoted followers from Congress and elsewhere to a packed celebration in the White House. Unlike Bill Clinton, who, after his own impeachment, expressed sorrow for what he had done and the burden it placed on Congress and the public, Trump filled the East Room with fury and vitriol. Holding up a newspaper whose front page declared him "acquitted," Trump played the victim and railed against his opponents. "It was evil, it was corrupt, it was dirty cops. . . . It was all bullshit." In a bit of prophecy, he held out the prospect that he might be impeached again in the future, but only "because these people have gone stone cold crazy." And he had a few choice words for me: "Adam Schiff is a vicious, horrible person."

The following day, Trump fired Sondland, and Lt. Col. Vindman was marched out of his office at the White House by security. The Colonel's twin brother, Yevgeny Vindman, an ethics lawyer at the National Security Council, also lost his position, in retaliation for raising his own concerns over Trump's efforts to coerce Ukraine, but also for reporting alleged misconduct involving National Security Advisor Robert O'Brien. Don Jr. was ecstatic about the retribution, and thanked me for "unearthing who all needed to be fired." Trump apologists in the House also praised Alexander Vindman's firing, like Representative Zeldin, who said it "is a good move based on the fact that there is a lack of trust." Yes, a lack of trust in anyone who would not applaud the president's misdeeds.

A few days later, the president's former chief of staff, John Kelly, once again pushed back against Trump. Drawing on his own experience as a general in the Marine Corps, Kelly issued a forceful defense of Vindman's decision to testify in the trial. Vindman, he explained, was bound to a strict code of military ethics. He was trained, and also required, to report misconduct by a superior. Listening to the president's call with Zelensky was akin to hearing a commander give an illegal order. "We teach them, 'Don't follow an illegal order,'" Kelly said. "He did exactly what we teach them to do, from cradle to grave—he went and told his boss what he just heard." As much as I appreciated Kelly's words, I couldn't help but reflect on the irony: How much misery could Kelly have saved the country if he had been as outspoken as Vindman about the presidential misconduct he had witnessed in the White House?

I shed no tears over Sondland's departure from federal service—in my view, he was fortunate not to be charged with perjury. But the treatment of the Vindman brothers disturbed me deeply. Months later, Alexander Vindman left the Army altogether, after his promotion was withheld without justification and he was forced to conclude that his military prospects were limited. I thought back to his hopeful testimony and felt sick. We had not been able to protect him from the president's vindictiveness after all. I sent him a letter thanking him for his service, but it felt too impersonal, so I called him.

"I just wanted to thank you personally," I said, after he got over the surprise of my call. "You did a very courageous thing, and the country is in your debt." I told him that his comments at the hearing about his father reminded me of my own dad, the son of immigrants and also an Army veteran. "Please say hello to your father from mine," I said. "I think they have a lot in common."

Trump's campaign of retribution was only getting started—and soon there would be many more heads on pikes. To propagate a big lie, you must get rid of the truth tellers, and Trump's ax fell hardest on the corps of inspectors general serving in key posts throughout the federal government. On April 3, Trump fired Intelligence Community Inspector General Michael Atkinson, calling him a "disgrace." Once again, Trump said the silent part out loud, admitting that his firing was punishment for providing the whistleblower complaint to Congress, though in fact Atkinson had done no such thing. It had been Maguire's office that, facing considerable pressure, ultimately had made the complaint available to members. "I thought he did a terrible job, absolutely terrible. . . . He took a fake report and he brought it to Congress with an emergency, okay? Not a big Trump fan, that I can tell you."

Atkinson wrote a lengthy statement following his dismissal, defending his actions and encouraging people in the Intelligence Community to continue exposing unethical, wasteful, or illegal conduct. "Please do not allow recent events to silence your voices," he urged.

But silence—or, worse, complicity—was just what the president had in mind, and he was not done cleaning house. On May 15, Trump fired Steve Linick, the State Department inspector general who had provided Giuliani's documents to Congress. Equally significant, Linick had been investigating the use of political appointees and diplomatic security officials by Mike Pompeo and his wife, Susan, to run personal errands for the secretary. Linick had been fired on Pompeo's own recommendation. In short order, Trump had fired or replaced five inspectors general. He was not only seeking revenge and cleaning house, he was also replacing many of these truth tellers with political operatives chosen for their loyalty to him and not to the facts.

At the Justice Department, the president's loyal lieutenant Bill Barr was playing his own role rewarding those who had lied to protect Trump, and punishing those who had stood up to him. In February 2020, when prosecutors recommended that Roger Stone receive a lengthy sentence after he was convicted of lying to our committee and witness intimidation, Trump tweeted his displeasure, calling the sentence unfair and demanding that something be done about it. The same day, Barr intervened and the Justice Department announced a more lenient sentencing recommendation, overruling the career attorneys. Four of the prosecutors on the case quit in disgust, one of them leaving his job altogether.

The following month, we gained greater insight into why Barr would take the extraordinary step of overturning a sentencing recommendation in a specific case. On March 5, Federal District Judge Reggie Walton found that Barr had misled the country with his summary of the Mueller report, citing Barr's "lack of candor" and "misleading public statements" when he claimed there was no evidence of conspiracy. After the judge reviewed redacted sections of the Mueller report, the Justice Department provided more public disclosure, including the fact that Roger Stone had given Trump advance notice that stolen Clinton documents would soon be released by WikiLeaks. "Oh good, alright," Trump had responded. Trump had lied to Mueller about his knowledge of campaign contacts with WikiLeaks, and

Barr had concealed evidence of that lie from the American people. Now the attorney general was intervening to reward Stone's role in the cover-up. Trump would later commute Stone's sentence, before granting him a full pardon.

Barr's efforts to protect and defend the liars continued in May 2020, when the Justice Department moved to dismiss the case against Michael Flynn, who twice pleaded guilty to lying to the FBI about his secret contacts with the Russian ambassador over sanctions. The federal judge in that case, Emmet Sullivan, took the extraordinary step of challenging the department's decision to drop the case. Nearly two thousand former DOJ officials would call on Barr to resign over improper intervention in the Flynn matter, charging that Barr was repeatedly using "the Department of Justice as a tool to further President Trump's personal and political interests." Efforts to fight the Flynn dismissal would become moot when Trump also granted Flynn a full pardon. Paul Manafort, the Trump campaign chairman convicted of witness tampering and numerous other crimes, would also be pardoned by Trump, as if, in granting these pardons, he could make their guilt—and his own—go away.

Having used the department to reward those who lied to cover up for the president, Barr also went after those who held the president and his men to account. On Friday night, June 19, Barr announced that the U.S. attorney for the Southern District of New York, Geoffrey Berman—who had prosecuted the president's personal lawyer, Michael Cohen, and was also investigating another of the president's lawyers, Rudy Giuliani—was stepping down. The only problem: He wasn't. "I have not resigned, and have no intention of resigning," Berman said when he read the news in a Department of Justice press release. "Our investigations will move forward without delay or interruption." After ensuring that his second-in-command would not be replaced by a Trump loyalist, as Barr had intended, Berman did resign.

But the most high-profile casualty of Trump's vengeance was not one I expected, since it was the man who had withheld the whistleblower complaint from Congress at White House urging in the first place—Acting DNI Maguire. The story of his firing would be an object lesson for everyone in the Trump White House: that no matter what you did for the president, no matter what sacrifice you made, he would always ask for more, and if you failed to fully debase yourself before him, you would be gone. In Trump's view, Maguire's sin began, as so many had, with a hearing.

On February 13, 2020, the House Intelligence Committee had held a closed briefing with officials from the DNI's office and FBI on the subject of the 2020 elections and foreign interference. As would be publicly disclosed in the National Intelligence Council (NIC) report the following year, Russia was again interfering in the U.S. presidential election, and, much as they had four years earlier, preferred Donald Trump to win reelection. The intelligence agencies would come to have high confidence in this assessment, which so closely aligned with Russia's overt and covert media messaging. When the analysts shared their assessment during their opening remarks, they did so in understated terms, and I came back to it in my questioning so that there would be no misunderstanding. The Russians wanted Trump and were denigrating Biden while advancing other Democratic primary candidates that they viewed as outside the mainstream opposition to Russian ambitions. As the NIC report later revealed, the Intelligence Community assessed that "Russian leaders viewed President Biden's potential election as disadvantageous to Russian interests" and "this drove their efforts to undermine his candidacy."

This was important information to help guard against a repeat of Russia's unfettered interference in yet another presidential race, but it was hardly surprising—at least to me. For the Republicans, it was another matter. Just as they had three years earlier, they aggressively challenged the conclusion that the Russians wanted to help Trump and reacted angrily to the idea that the Russians could have preferred someone they believed was strengthening America's defenses. Whether they really believed this, or they had other motives—more than one of the GOP members of our committee harbored ambitions to become agency heads themselves—it was impossible to know, but there was no mistaking their vehemence. "I'd challenge anyone to give me a real-world argument where Putin would rather have President Trump and not Bernie Sanders," Republican Chris Stewart, a member of our committee, later told the press.

After the briefing, Republicans complained to the White House, and the president was livid. The following day, he demanded to see Maguire and berated him for briefing our committee and not informing him of his agency's findings first. It is difficult to believe that Trump had not already been briefed on Russian interference in our election; if true, this was a separate problem and would have been the result of an Intelligence Community that had made the strategic decision not to tell the president things that he didn't want to hear. Trump was reportedly most irate that the information about Russian interference to help his campaign had been provided to me, complaining that I would weaponize the information.

A few days later, Maguire was fired—by tweet. He had risked his reputation after a lifetime of service by ignoring the clear letter of the law and withholding a whistleblower complaint from Congress, but that was not good enough. With Trump, nothing ever was. Maguire had allowed members of his staff to tell us the truth about Russian interference in the upcoming election, so he had to go.

On Sunday, February 23, the White House dispatched Robert O'Brien to appear on *Face the Nation,* where he claimed: "There's no briefing that I've received, that the president's received, that says that President Putin is doing anything to try to influence the elections in favor of President Trump. We just haven't seen that intelligence." I knew O'Brien, a constituent of mine, and he had always struck me as a decent person, even if he was in way over his head as the National Security Advisor. But here he was, plainly misleading the country about the intelligence. If he hadn't seen it, it was because he didn't want to, but it also meant that the administration was taking no steps to stop the Russian interference. The president of the United States was welcoming Putin's help, again.

Until a permanent replacement for Maguire could be found, Trump selected Richard Grenell—a Trump loyalist and the U.S. ambassador to Germany—to serve as acting director. Grenell had been a media consultant whose notable clients included a U.S. non-profit funded by the government of Hungary's autocratic ruler, Viktor Orban, and a fugitive oligarch from Moldova. As I would hear at the Munich Conference, Grenell was despised by many Germans and was losing the United States friends and influencing people in all the wrong ways.

These were ludicrous credentials for a leader of the Intelligence Community, but Grenell's second-in-command was even more disturbing. After firing Maguire's deputy, a thirty-year veteran of the CIA named Andrew Hallman, Grenell announced the appointment of none other than Kash Patel—the same former Intelligence Committee staffer who worked with Devin Nunes to promulgate the right-wing narrative about "unmasking" by Obama officials. Until the president put forward, and the Senate confirmed, a formal nominee, Grenell and Patel would command the agencies that I believed Patel had spent the previous three years working to undermine.

If there was any question about the president's determination to appoint loyalists who would weaken the Intelligence Community, it vanished with the announcement of his formal nominee for the DNI position. Just seven months had passed since Trump had attempted to install John Ratcliffe, as a reward for Ratcliffe's ardent defense of Trump in the Mueller hearings. Ratcliffe had been forced to withdraw his name from consideration when Republican senators balked at the choice of a partisan with such minimal and, as it turned out, exaggerated experience. But the impeachment had shown Trump how easily those senators would capitulate under pressure, and on February 28, he nominated Ratcliffe again.

The idea of Ratcliffe, Grenell, and Patel leading the Intelligence Community of the United States was chilling on many levels. They were purely political actors. By historic standards, none was qualified for his position. All three had taken actions I viewed as openly hostile to the agencies they would lead. And their inexperience would diminish our capacity to protect the country, and the upcoming election, from our adversaries. But what many intelligence analysts viewed as their disqualifying characteristics were exactly the reasons why they would be perfect Trump appointees.

In Congress, Mitch McConnell and Senate Republicans were determined to do their part to prevent a robust response to the latest threat of Russian interference in our election, killing three election security bills the month that Maguire was fired. Two would have required campaigns to alert the FBI and Federal Election Commission about foreign offers of election assistance, and the other provided more funding for election security and a prohibition on connecting voting machines to the Internet, where they would be easier to hack.

The Republican Senate was not only killing bills that would have hardened election security, it was also playing a leading role in the president's continuing counteroffensive. If the intelligence agencies were reporting Russian interference on the president's behalf, GOP senator Ron Johnson of Wisconsin, chairman of the Homeland Security Committee, would use his perch to push the counternarrative and investigate Hunter Biden and Burisma. In doing so, he would employ the resources of the committee to tear down the candidacy of Joe Biden while actively advancing Kremlin propaganda about Ukraine and Burisma—it was Benghazi Select Committee meets Rudy Giuliani—and Russian intelligence was successfully laundering its misinformation through committees in Congress.

One of Johnson's sources was a former Ukrainian diplomat named Andrii Telizhenko, who had long engaged in smearing the Bidens, and was pushing the same debunked conspiracy theory that it had been Ukraine, not Russia, that had interfered in the 2016 American election. Telizhenko and a Ukrainian parliamentarian, Andrii Derkach, had appeared with Giuliani in a "documentary" on OAN the previous winter as part of a Kremlin disinformation campaign to push both narratives. Johnson said he planned to issue a "report" prior to the November election on Hunter Biden's activities in Ukraine. Pushing back against Johnson's probe, his fellow committee member Mitt Romney said that "it's not the legitimate role of government or Congress, or for taxpayer expense to be used in an effort to damage political opponents."

On March 10, we had an "all hands" classified briefing for the entire House of Representatives in the Congressional Auditorium. Grenell had been expected to attend, but he didn't, and in his place, Bill Evanina, a veteran intelligence official leading the National Counterintelligence and Security Center, appeared, along with FBI director Wray; NSA director Nakasone; Cybersecurity and Infrastructure Security Agency (CISA) director Christopher Krebs; and others. When he learned that the hearing was to take place, Trump was again infuriated. "There is another Russia, Russia, Russia meeting today," he tweeted. "It is headed up by corrupt politician Adam 'Shifty' Schiff, so I wouldn't expect too much!"

Once again, he had it wrong. This wasn't my hearing at all, and the witnesses were all his own agency heads and senior officials. But if he was worried, he should not have been, because Evanina gave a dumbed-down briefing to House and Senate members, based on unclassified talking points—which no one would later accept responsibility for writing—that walked away from the conclusions of the briefers we had heard from just weeks earlier in my committee.

I wasn't going to let him get away with it, and neither was Speaker Pelosi. I challenged him, in blunt terms, with watering down the findings of the Intelligence Community; I told all of the agency heads present that they needed to speak truth to power, and they were failing. Because we were in a closed setting, I shared with House members what we had been told about Russian intentions only two weeks earlier, and pointed out that they were not getting the full truth. Evanina, I believed, was dissembling, and hiding Russia's efforts to denigrate Biden. The briefing would be repeated throughout the day, so all House members could attend, and I used each opportunity to call Evanina on the carpet.

Meanwhile, Grenell wasted no time in taking actions that I believed were undermining the DNI's essential mission and thoroughly politicizing the Intelligence Community, by firing the career professionals who ran the National Counterterrorism Center, selectively declassifying information he thought would be useful to Trump's reelection, promoting the president's false narrative about Christopher Steele and the deep state, releasing documents relating to the unmasking of Flynn's identity, and taking over election security briefings for political candidates.

In April, Trump was presumably still smarting over Christopher Wray's statements that accepting foreign assistance in a presidential campaign—or any other—was wrong and should be reported to the FBI. He wanted to fire Wray and replace him with Evanina, but was talked out of it. Had the plan gone through, Trump wanted to make Kash Patel the deputy director of the FBI. From my perspective, Evanina's willingness to shade the intelligence to suit the president's preferred narrative, and Patel's lack of any scruple, came perilously close to earning them both a substantial promotion.

As of July, Evanina was still unwilling to tell the American people the full facts concerning Russia's active interference in our election. In a statement he released on July 24, Evanina said that the Intelligence Community was "primarily concerned with China, Russia and Iran," although other nation-state and nonstate actors could also do harm to our elections. His statement began by representing that China was expanding its influence efforts to shape policy in the United States and recognized that its actions "might" affect the presidential race. Evanina then claimed that Russia's goal was to weaken the United States and that it was continuing to "spread disinformation" designed to undermine confidence in our democratic processes and "denigrate what it sees as an anti-Russia 'establishment' in America." And finally, Iran was seeking to undermine our institutions and divide the country.

This statement was misleading. Placing China first was designed to suggest that that country was the greatest threat to our elections. This undoubtedly pleased Trump, but as the NIC report would later acknowledge, China had *not* made the decision to interfere in our election, as Beijing believed that neither election outcome warranted the risk of being caught meddling. Russia *had* made the decision to interfere and was doing so in real time. Evanina's July statement tracked the misleading presentation he had made to Congress months earlier, by suggesting that Russia merely wanted to denigrate some ill-defined anti-Russia establishment. But as he must have known, Russia was actively undermining Joe Biden, and for a reason—Putin had benefited mightily from his 2016 investment in Donald Trump, and he wanted him to win again.

Although I could not disclose the intelligence we were seeing, I publicly and sharply criticized Evanina for misleading the country, and two weeks later, he was forced to issue a more accurate statement. He still placed his emphasis on China, now saying that "We assess that China prefers that President Trump—whom Beijing sees as unpredictable—does not win election." His statement went on to enumerate several of the administration's statements and actions that China did not like. But again, China had not made a decision to interfere, and the fact that it might have a preference—as most nations do—was irrelevant unless it was acting to effectuate its preference, and it was not. By falsely suggesting again that China was a bigger threat to our election, Evanina was hampering our ability to address the real threat—Russia.

Significantly, his statement did acknowledge for the first time that "We assess that Russia is using a range of measures to primarily denigrate former Vice President Biden." It also specified that the Ukrainian parliamentarian Andrii Derkach was "spreading claims about corruption, including through publicizing leaked phone calls [of Biden] to undermine Vice President Biden's candidacy," and that the Kremlin was again seeking to boost Trump's candidacy through social media. The mention of Derkach was notable, since he had been supplying information to both Ron Johnson and Devin Nunes and now he was being identified as part of a Russian disinformation campaign. After this, if Ron Johnson placed any further reliance on information provided by Derkach or his associates, including Andrii Telizhenko, Johnson could not pretend to be unwitting of what he was doing.

Both Telizhenko and Derkach would later be sanctioned by

Trump's own Treasury Department—Telizhenko as part of a "Russia-linked foreign influence network," and Derkach as an "active Russian agent for over a decade." After the election, the Intelligence Community would publicly disclose that Putin himself "had purview over the activities of Andriy Derkach," and that the Russians had been laundering their disinformation through prominent Americans.

When Trump was confronted at his Bedminster golf resort with the intelligence that Russia was again helping his campaign, his response was that of a petulant child: "I don't care what anybody says." That much was true enough. Donald Trump was demonstrating anew, if anyone needed further convincing, that he would not do what was right for the country or its elections, only what he deemed to be in his narrow self-interest. The intelligence did not support his preferred narrative—that nobody had been tougher on Russia than Donald Trump—and therefore he would ignore it. Where that left our nation's defenses was not his concern.

Appearing on CNN that fall, Bill Barr did his part to amplify the false narrative about China's actions in the upcoming election. Wolf Blitzer asked him which country, Russia, China, or Iran, was the most assertive and aggressive in interfering in the election. "I believe it's China," Barr replied. "Which one?" Blitzer asked again. "China," Barr replied. "Why do you say that?" Blitzer asked. "Because I've seen the intelligence." Barr also took the opportunity to promote the president's false narrative regarding the security of absentee voting. "Elections that have been held with [sic] mail," he declared, "have found substantial fraud and coercion."

It was a full court press to mislead the American people by hyping the China threat and downplaying Russia's actual interference. Robert O'Brien told reporters: "We know the Chinese have taken the most active role," and China has "the most massive program to influence the United States politically." Appearing on Fox News on Sunday, August 30, DNI Ratcliffe added his voice to the deception. When host Maria Bartiromo asked him, "What can you tell us about China and what they're trying to do in this election?" he responded: "Well, in an unclassified setting, I can't get into a whole lot of details, other than to say that China is using a massive and sophisticated influence campaign that dwarfs anything that any other country is doing."

At the same time, Ratcliffe informed our committee that his office would no longer provide briefings to Congress on election security. Under the National Security Act, he was required to keep us fully informed of significant intelligence matters, and this was a gross dereliction of duty, if not a violation of the law. His office had just reached out to me to schedule our next briefing before the committee, and something, or someone, had intervened to prevent Ratcliffe from doing so. Given Trump's rage every time we were briefed, I certainly had a suspect in mind.

Blaming Democrats and leaks, Ratcliffe said that he would put future information in writing instead. This, of course, made no sense—since written materials could be leaked just as easily as an oral briefing. But the problem wasn't leaks, it was his own duplicity. If Ratcliffe appeared in person, he could be pressed, by me and others, on why he was telling the public that China posed the biggest threat to our elections when his own analysts had reached a very different conclusion.

"Director Ratcliffe brought information into the committee," Trump told reporters, "and the information leaked. Whether it was Shifty Schiff or somebody else, they leaked the information. . . . And what's even worse, they leaked the wrong information. And he got tired of it. So he wants to do it in a different forum, because you have leakers on the committee." This was another fabrication, and Trump's default deflection, and it wasn't long before even Senate Republicans rejected the excuse and demanded a resumption of briefings. Facing a storm of public criticism, Ratcliffe was forced to reverse himself again, reinstating the briefings, but only for our committee and Senate Intelligence, leaving most members of Congress of both houses in the dark.

But Ratcliffe's most overtly partisan abuse of his office came on the day of Trump's first presidential debate with Joe Biden in late September. In a letter to Lindsey Graham, released only hours before the debate, Ratcliffe revealed the following: "In late July 2016, U.S. intelligence agencies obtained insight into Russian intelligence analysis alleging that U.S. Presidential candidate Hillary Clinton had approved a campaign plan to stir up a scandal against U.S. Presidential candidate Donald Trump by tying him to Putin and the Russians' hacking of the Democratic National Committee." Ratcliffe admitted that the Intelligence Community "does not know the accuracy of this allegation or the extent to which the Russian intelligence analysis may reflect exaggeration or fabrication." A week later, at the direction of the president, Ratcliffe would declassify and release notes of a briefing that former CIA director Brennan had given Obama on the matter, along with a redacted memorandum from the CIA to the FBI.

Ratcliffe's actions were inexcusable. In a hastily arranged meeting with congressional leadership in the Senate SCIF, I questioned Ratcliffe on why he would release such information on the eve of a presidential debate and politicize the Intelligence Community that way. Ratcliffe acknowledged that the information came from sensitive sources and methods—so why on earth would he risk revealing such sources by releasing information that he acknowledged may have been completely fabricated? He disagreed that he was politicizing the intelligence and tried to defend the decision, but it was indefensible. As far as I could tell, his own agency heads disapproved of the decision, which made its political motivation all the more obvious. To declassify information of this kind, Ratcliffe had to determine that the "public interest in disclosure outweighs the damage to national security," and there was no way to do so.

During the debate, Trump made use of the disclosure, saying "You saw what happened today with Hillary Clinton, where it was a whole big con job." The vice president would likewise try to exploit the declassified material in his own debate. Although the administration and its allies sought to hype it into a scandal, the reality was that there was nothing remarkable about the information. The Russians did hack the DNC in 2016 and were in fact helping the Trump campaign—of course the Clinton campaign would make an issue of it. Given the inconsequential nature of the information Ratcliffe was releasing, the risk of exposing sensitive sources of collection was all the more unconscionable.

By the late fall of 2020, our country's election was headed toward a dark and uncertain finish. Foreign intervention was picking up and the president was ignoring it. Agency heads who would speak honestly about Russian meddling were fired, impairing our ability to deter further interference and ensure a well-informed electorate that could recognize and reject it. The president was continually attacking the integrity of our elections and absentee voting, and the Russians were amplifying those lies. The threat of domestic terrorism was growing, fueled by a rise in white nationalism and stoked by a president bent on using racial divisions as a lever for his reelection. And a vicious pandemic was on track to kill more Americans than had died in any war in which our country had ever been engaged, including the Civil War.

22

RIGHT WOULD HAVE TO WAIT

TRUMP SAW THE VIRUS, LIKE ALL THINGS, THROUGH THE LENS OF HIS own self-interest. And the virus would become the most devastating example of what happens when self-interest, mendacity, and incompetence collide on a tragic scale. As the pandemic raged across the country, he raged at the pandemic—not about the loss of life, or about the fear and uncertainty gripping the nation. He raged about the unfairness of a pandemic striking so close to the election. He raged about the effect on the stock market, and the collapse of the "Trump economy." He raged against his own government's sensible public health measures, encouraging voters to abandon the safety precautions that kept them largely confined at home. Return to work, he said. Ignore public health edicts. Resume normal life. He claimed the virus would disappear "like a miracle." He suggested injecting bleach might kill it. He caught the virus himself, and he might have died without the best treatment available anywhere in the world. When a White House reporter asked him what he would say to Americans who were scared, his answer was fury: "I say that you're a terrible reporter. That's what I say. I think that's a very nasty question."

If the truth was bad—and it was—then Trump would go after these truth tellers too. The acting inspector general of the Department of Health and Human Services, Christi Grimm, a career professional, reported, all too accurately, that hospitals were experiencing "severe shortages" of Covid-19 testing kits and "widespread shortages" of protective gear like surgical masks. This contradicted Trump's preferred narrative that he was doing a marvelous job securing tests and protective gear, and Trump was incensed. Assuming Grimm was a man, Trump bellowed at reporters who had cited her report: "Where did he come from, the inspector general? What's his name? No, what's his name? What's his name?" Within a month, her replacement would be announced.

When testing began showing just how many tens of thousands of Americans were infected, Trump raged against testing, as if the disease wouldn't exist if we didn't look for it. And so Trump sought to slow down the testing, or push out the false narrative that we were leading in infections only because we were doing more tests. And it wasn't just the tests, of course—it was the deaths too. When the CDC's weekly reports on morbidity and mortality made the numbers look too bleak, the White House intervened to change them. If the truth was too damning and deadly, it needed to be rewritten.

Trump had never been interested in facts. They were stubborn; they were inconvenient. You could not bully a fact or harass it into submission. Facts were fussy. Facts were elitist. Only pencil necks believed in facts. "They're Democrats! They're against me!" he claimed of the nation's top scientists and physicians. When Trump couldn't get the answers he wanted from experts in infectious disease, like Dr. Anthony Fauci, he sought other experts, like Dr. Scott Atlas, a neuroradiologist, whom he discovered through watching Fox News. Atlas was well out of his medical depth, as this was not his specialty, but his opinions aligned with Trump's preferred version of events—there was too much emphasis on testing, deaths were exaggerated, masks might not work, and we ought to let the virus run its course through nonvulnerable populations. It was another familiar echo from the trial, paralleling Trump's decision to side with Rudy Giuliani over Christopher Wray: Atlas would offer Trump what he wanted to hear. Fauci was offering him only the truth and what he needed to do to save American lives—but what was in that for Trump?

Against the advice of his own pollster—who showed him campaign polling data that the simple expedient of wearing a mask would be embraced by a majority of Republican voters—he chose instead to make it a cultural wedge issue, and we will never know how many thousands of lives were lost as a result. He organized rallies, cramming thousands of supporters together in settings where some of them would catch the virus and later die. "All you hear is Covid, Covid, Covid, Covid, Covid, Covid, Covid, Covid, Covid, Covid, Covid," he said at a rally, repeating the word eleven times, as if the nation's fixation on a disease that was killing them was somehow nonsensical.

Trump gave his acceptance speech at the Republican National Convention on the South Lawn of the White House, where guests sat shoulder to shoulder, many not wearing masks in an event that violated not only the health guidelines of his own administration, but Hatch Act prohibitions on using federal resources for a campaign. The violation of the law was not incidental—it was the point. Trump was proud of his defiance of the law and wanted to showcase it during his own nomination acceptance speech. Some White House functions, like that celebrating the confirmation of Justice Amy Coney Barrett—who he hoped would be the deciding vote to strike down the Affordable Care Act—became documented superspreader events. As Shakespeare wrote in *Twelfth Night:* "If this were played upon a stage now, I could condemn it as an improbable fiction." But it was no fiction, and no comedy, but a terrible tragedy that was ravaging the country.

And in an awful harbinger of things to come, Trump would provoke Covid-19 uprisings. With the loudest megaphone in the world, the president denounced mayors and governors who insisted on using facts to set public policy. Each time a state imposed a mask mandate or a stay-at-home order, he would fulminate on Twitter. "LIBERATE MINNESOTA!" he wrote. "LIBERATE MICHIGAN!" "Liberate VIRGINIA, and save your great 2nd Amendment. It is under siege!"

He was telling his supporters to revolt, and they did. On April 30, a crowd of hundreds gathered in front of the Michigan state capitol to protest a lockdown order from Governor Gretchen Whitmer. They brought Confederate flags to the rally. They waved swastikas and held up nooses. They repurposed the president's chant from 2016, directing it from Hillary Clinton to Whitmer with shouts of "Lock her up!" Soon a group of men in camouflage pressed toward the front doors of the capitol building, bursting inside with semiautomatic rifles and clashing with police at the doorway to the state house of representatives. Others breached the gallery of the state senate, screaming at their elected officials with rifles slung over their shoulders. As I watched videos of this, I felt a sickening recognition. If the president was willing to incite a mob to attack the state government of Michigan, he was not just a destabilizing force in our democracy, he was a threat to its very existence.

That threat manifested itself again a short time later, when a dozen people gathered to plot against what they considered state efforts to violate the Constitution and discussed killing officials they deemed "tyrants" and capturing a governor. As a force multiplier, the plotters approached a Michigan-based militia group and began discussing plans to storm the capitol in Lansing and take hostages, including Whitmer. The conspirators conducted tactical training, tried to make bombs with black powder and BBs for shrapnel, surveilled the governor's vacation home repeatedly, and acquired a Taser to aid in her abduction. They would hold off police by using Molotov cocktails, and after capturing the governor, they would "try" her for treason.

Less than a month before the presidential election, law enforcement broke up this domestic terrorism plot and charged several individuals with planning to kidnap the governor among other crimes. The President's reaction was typical and appalling. After stating that the governor "has done a terrible job" and boasting that "my Justice Department and Federal Law Enforcement" just foiled the plot, he made himself the victim: "Rather than say thank you, she calls me a White Supremacist—while Biden and Democrats refuse to condemn Antifa, Anarchists, Looters and Mobs that burn down Democrat run cities. . . . Governor Whitmer—open up your state, open up your schools, and open up your churches!"

Throughout the course of the year, and with tensions at the boiling point, Trump had kept up a drumbeat of attacks on early voting and made preemptive claims of fraud. Time after time Trump took to Twitter to claim "It will be the greatest Rigged Election in history" and that it would be the biggest "scandal of our times"—the most inaccurate and fraudulent election in history. "Because the only way we are going to lose this election is if the election is rigged. Remember that." And his supporters believed him. Free and fair elections in the United States could no longer be trusted, because Donald Trump said so.

Knowing that it would take days to count all of the absentee ballots, and that many of those late votes would come from Democrats, Trump began predicting that he would win on election day, but that the election would then be stolen from him. Trump donor turned postmaster general Louis DeJoy heavily cut overtime for postal workers and took postal sorting machines offline, jeopardizing the timely delivery and return of absentee ballots. Trump was setting the stage for a contested result, for an effort to stay in power even if he lost, through litigation, through the efforts of his enablers in Congress, or worse—much, much worse. Asked by a reporter whether he would "commit here today for a peaceful transferral of power," Trump refused to do so. "Get rid of the ballots and you'll have a very peaceful—there won't be a transfer, frankly. There will be a continuation."

There would be no continuation, but then, there would be no peaceful transfer of power either.

On November 3, 2020, election night, I couldn't have my usual rooftop party at the Burbank Bar and Grille because of the pandemic, and what's more, like many politicians, I'm superstitious, and after the debacle four years earlier, I wasn't sure that I wanted to anyway. So we rented the parking lot behind American Legion Post 43 in Hollywood and arranged for the election results to be projected on a huge screen. Founded in 1919 by World War I veterans who worked in the motion picture industry, the post has a legendary past, and it once included members like Clark Gable, Mickey Rooney, Ronald Reagan, Gene Autry, and more. Because of pandemic-imposed space restrictions—people had to watch from their cars—attendance was limited to several dozen family members, friends, and supporters listening to the feed on their radios.

The big screen was tuned to MSNBC, and a twenty-foot-tall Rachel Maddow brought us the results state by state. The very early returns were promising, but they were expected to be, since Democrats disproportionately tend to take advantage of voting by mail and the first results are from the early absentee ballots. But soon the same-day voting totals arrived and began erasing Democratic leads in key states. The mood at our "victory" celebration began to sour, just as it had four years earlier, and I grew anxious, even as I tried to hide it from the crowd—please God, don't tell me it's going to happen all over again. As results came in from House races, I saw our challengers, every bit as talented and promising as the class from the midterm elections, get wiped out. It was the same in the Senate, where many Democratic candidates started out with substantial polling leads only to see them evaporate in the hours after the polls closed. We picked up two Senate seats but lost one, which was not enough to gain the majority, unless we swept the Georgia special election that was still weeks away, and prospects for doing that were slim. And then the down-ballot results grew worse, and several of the wonderful members I helped get elected two years ago lost—and lost badly. But this was not the worst of it.

Just after midnight, as late absentee votes were narrowing Trump's lead in pivotal swing states and Biden was gaining ground, Trump increased his agitation: "They are trying to STEAL the Election," he raged on Twitter. "We will never let them do it." A couple of hours later, and days before all the ballots would be counted, he declared victory: "This is a fraud on the American public. This is an embarrassment to our country. We are getting ready to win this election. Frankly, we did win this election."

In the days that followed, Trump would continue to urge state officials to stop the count, and stop the "fraud." Dozens of Trump supporters, some armed with rifles, would mob an elections center in pivotal Maricopa County, Arizona, to intimidate officials into stopping the count. Similar confrontations were taking place in Detroit, Milwaukee, Atlanta, and Philadelphia. "We were winning in all the key locations," Trump declared on November 5, "by a lot, actually, and then our numbers started miraculously getting whittled away in secret." There were large midnight vote dumps, he would declare. It was all rigged, he insisted. In places like Detroit—places, not coincidentally, where there was a large Black population—Trump's falsehoods were even more insidious. "It's like more votes than people," Trump claimed. "Dead people voting all over the place." The scaffolding was going up, and the big lie was taking shape.

On November 7, when most networks had declared Biden the winner, Trump refused to accept the results, just as he said that he would. When CISA director Krebs affirmed that the November 3 election "was the most secure in American history" and that there was "no evidence that any voting system deleted or lost votes, changed votes, or was in any way compromised," the president responded by firing him.

Trump dispatched his lawyers all over the country to file phony lawsuits and make claims of massive fraud based on no evidence. Judge after judge threw them out, and the language of their decisions reflected the baseless nature of the lawsuits' causes of action. The Trump campaign provided "strained legal arguments without merit and speculative accusations . . . unsupported by evidence," a federal judge in Pennsylvania wrote. "In the United States of America, this cannot justify the disenfranchisement of a single voter, let alone all the voters of its sixth most populous state." Trump could find fewer and fewer lawyers to make these bad faith claims, until he was down to a handful of unscrupulous lawyers like Sidney Powell, or Rudy Giuliani, holding press conferences with hair dye running down his face at the Republican National Committee Headquarters, or standing outside the Four Seasons landscaping company with a registered sex offender.

Trump would call local election officials to personally urge them not to certify the results; he would call state legislators in the hope that they would declare fraud and certify an alternate slate of electors, one that would ignore the votes of millions of their residents and send Congress electors who would declare Trump the winner. The lives of elections officials became threatened, and a Georgia voting system implementation manager, Gabriel Sterling, spoke for many of them when he said: "Death threats. Physical threats. Intimidation. It's too much . . . I can't explain the level of anger I have over this." He pleaded with the president, "You need to step up and say this . . . stop inspiring people to commit potential acts of violence. Someone's going to get hurt, someone's going to get shot, someone's going to get killed."

He was right. More right than he knew. And as I watched him speak to the cameras, felt his anger at a death threat to a twenty-something member of the county staff, I was glad to hear him speak out, but I also thought of my own staff and what they had gone through and wondered—where were you when my young staff was being threatened? Why did it have to happen to your people before you thought it was time to say—*enough!*

On December 14 the Electoral College certified its results, confirming that Joe Biden had officially beaten Donald Trump by the same margin, 306–232, by which Trump had beaten Clinton four years earlier when he had declared the margin a landslide. Recount after recount had confirmed the results, Trump campaign litigation was an unmitigated failure, and yet he would not concede. On the phone with Georgia secretary of state Brad Raffensperger on January 2, he urged the Republican official to "find" 11,780 votes—the precise number he would need to retake the state from Joe Biden. "Fellas, I need eleven thousand votes," he said, using shorthand later in the call. "Give me a break." Trump even threatened a criminal prosecution if Georgia officials didn't come through for him. Raffensperger refused, even though this was no idle threat, since Bill Barr had authorized the Justice Department to investigate "substantial allegations of voting and vote tabulation irregularities" when there was no evidence of any such thing.

In the weeks leading up to January 6, the Trump campaign spent tens of millions of dollars on advertising touting the president's big lie about the election, alleging massive fraud and urging supporters to "stop the steal." He tweeted out an invitation to come to Washington for a big protest on the day of the joint session, promising it would be "wild!" If a Democratic president had their election stolen as he had, Trump declared, Democratic senators would consider it "an act of war" and "fight to the death." On the night before the insurrection, Trump tweeted that he hoped Democrats and Republicans in Congress were "looking at the thousands of people pouring into D.C. They won't stand for a landslide . . . victory to be stolen."

When the day finally came and the mob assembled before him on the National Mall, Trump put the focus on his loyal vice president, urging Pence to violate his constitutional oath and refuse to certify Biden the winner. That morning he had tweeted: "All Mike Pence has to do is send them back to the States, AND WE WIN. Do it Mike, this is a time for extreme courage!" When Pence acknowledged the obvious—that he lacked constitutional authority to do any such thing—Trump turned on him, and so did the crowd. "Hang Mike Pence," they shouted. "Traitor!" Trump told the crowd that they needed to "fight like hell" if they were going to save our country—a few hours later, they did. Several would die that day, and in the weeks that followed, multiple Capitol and Metropolitan Police officers would lose their lives, including by suicide.

Looking back on these events, I am struck not only by the inevitability of the violent insurrection, but by how perilously close Trump came to overthrowing the American government and remaining in office without benefit of being elected. The Texas attorney general filed suit to overturn the election results in four other states, and more than a hundred members of the House filed an amicus brief in support. The Supreme Court declined to hear the case. What if they hadn't? In a key county in Michigan, two of the Republicans on the four-member board charged with tallying the results temporarily capitulated to Trump's demands to block certification before reversing themselves. What if they had gone through with it? What if the Republican legislature in Pennsylvania had sent an alternate slate of electors to Congress to be counted? What if Maricopa officials had given in to the demands of armed protesters in Arizona? What if Georgia's Raffensperger had said yes? The brutal assault on the Capitol was never going to succeed in permanently stopping Congress from certifying the results, but only because the House was in Democratic hands. What if Kevin McCarthy had been Speaker, and the majority of the House had voted as he did to overturn the decision of the majority of Americans?

We came so close to losing our democracy. So very, very close.

ON JANUARY 8, TWO DAYS after the insurrection, the Speaker invited me to address the caucus on our response to that violent assault on the Capitol. Representatives Jamie Raskin, David Cicilline, and Ted Lieu had already begun drafting an article of impeachment based on the president's incitement of insurrection, and Pelosi asked me to brief the members on what we could expect if we moved forward with an unprecedented second impeachment of the president. I told members that the president was again guilty of an impeachable offense, even more serious than the first, and that no lengthy investigation would be necessary, given that we were all witnesses to his crime. We could move with great alacrity and take a privileged impeachment resolution to the floor.

But I also informed the caucus that it would be up to Mitch McConnell to set the timing in the Senate, and we had to expect that he might delay scheduling the trial until *after* President Biden was sworn in—both to disrupt the new president's first weeks in office, but more to the point, so that the remedy of removing Trump from office would no longer be available. Trump could still be disqualified from ever holding office again, but the dynamic at trial would be different, since his lawyers would then be free to argue that the impeachment was no more than a Democratic Party attempt to prevent him from running for office again, and only because we were afraid that he might win.

Word of my comments to the caucus leaked, as I knew it would, and was misinterpreted as an argument against impeaching the president. Boland worked with me to quickly put out a statement affirming my belief that the president should be immediately removed from office, through impeachment or through operation of the Twenty-fifth Amendment, on account of his obvious incapacity.

In the days that followed the insurrection, we had numerous leadership conference calls to discuss the impeachment. I favored a very simple article that set out the facts of Trump's role in spurring the attack on the Capitol and his refusal to lift a finger to stop it once it began. Congressman Jamie Raskin of Maryland was leading the effort at drafting, and I sent him some proposed language that did not require us to prove "incitement" or "insurrection," two terms that might be unfamiliar to most Americans. In retrospect, there was an undeniable power to an article based on "incitement of insurrection," and if senators were going to acquit because they didn't find each element of that crime, they were going to acquit regardless. The article, as my colleagues had drafted it, helped to shape the understanding of that tragic event, and that may have been far more important than any other consideration.

The bigger issue for me was not whether to impeach—of that I was certain—but whether to go to trial once the president was out of office. I expressed the concern to the Speaker that Trump had been so discredited by the insurrection, and had become so completely toxic to the body politic, that I worried that a trial based solely on whether he should be disqualified from running again might allow him to play the victim, or somehow rehabilitate himself. But an interesting thing happened post-insurrection that alleviated my fear that Trump might use a trial to his purposes. As the images of the assault became more widely available, as members of the House and Senate realized just how close they had come to being assaulted or killed, as the public saw police officers beaten and their Capitol besieged, the reaction to the insurrection grew more serious over time, not less—more furious at the assault on our democracy with each passing day—and the chance that Trump might be convicted was suddenly very real.

On January 13, Trump was impeached in the House for the second time. Democrats were unanimous in their support and were joined by ten Republicans, including Liz Cheney, the third-ranking member of the GOP conference. Kevin McCarthy voted against the impeachment, but acknowledged that Trump "bears responsibility" for the attack. Soon, he would be making a pilgrimage to Mar-a-Lago to pay fealty to the Republican Party's insurrectionist leader once again. Privately, McConnell was said to be pleased with the impeachment, and hoped it would help his party extricate itself from Trump's destructive hold. And publicly, McConnell said that he was keeping an open mind on whether he would vote to convict or acquit. But whether either was true or merely posturing remained to be seen.

I was in my office again when Pelosi called me to tell me that she was picking a whole new team of managers to try the case, led by Jamie Raskin. It was exactly the right decision. Had I played a prominent role, Trump and his allies would have made it about me, not him. The second impeachment was not a continuation of the first, even if the verdict in the first had led inexorably to the second. The new team, like the first, represented a beautiful cross section of the country and all its diversity, with Representatives David

Cicilline, Ted Lieu, Diana DeGette, Joaquin Castro, Eric Swalwell, Stacey Plaskett, Joe Neguse, and Madeleine Dean. And Raskin was a perfect choice to lead—a brilliant constitutional scholar, with a warm and affable air, and the ability to give the impeachment a non-partisan cast. Yet asking Raskin to take on such a responsibility was no small matter; he had just gone through the most terrible trauma any parent could endure—he had lost his beloved son, Tommy, to suicide.

Walking from the House floor to the Speaker's conference room for a private lunch together where we could talk strategy about the trial, I asked Jamie how he was coping, and whether his son's memory would give him strength through the ordeal ahead. He told me that Tommy, a student at Harvard Law School, had been just as devoted to country and constitution as he was and would be a source of inspiration. Still, he was grieving, and told me how he kept thinking, over and over, whether he might have missed any sign, something that might have made a difference, and it kept playing out in his head in an endless destructive loop. I marveled at his fortitude, and still do. I knew all the pressures he would face during the trial, and was in awe of his mental discipline and the ability to remain focused on the hard work ahead while his heart was breaking. I didn't have many words of wisdom for my good friend, mostly because he didn't need them. I knew that he would do a tremendous job.

He asked me what role the Speaker played in the first impeachment trial, and I told him that she was a great resource. She would not seek to micromanage his conduct of the case, but he should not hesitate to reach out to her, as her instincts at trial were as good as any trial lawyer. And what's more, the judges and jurors were all senators, and there was no one who understood what made them tick better than Nancy D'Alesandro Pelosi.

"Don't assume the senators know all the facts," I told him, "even though they were there." Most of us had learned the background of what took place on the Mall, and the magnitude of the attack, only when the events were over, and there was a long, compelling narrative about the actions leading up to January 6 that would be unfamiliar to many of them. I told Jamie about the "four" and the "forty million," and said that I hoped there would be many more than four senators with an open mind. In fact, I believed that some of the senators who voted to acquit the first time might be looking to redeem themselves now that they saw where Trump's acquittal had led. But mostly, I wanted Jamie to know that I was there for him, and the entire team. I would help, or not help, as much as he liked. The last thing he needed was a backseat driver.

A week later, Eve and I sat on a riser on the West Capitol and waited to watch Joe Biden sworn in as the forty-sixth president of the United States. By now the Capitol was an armed fortress, with streets blocked off, tall metal fences, concrete barriers, and thousands of National Guard troops patrolling the streets with assault rifles. It looked more like the Green Zone in Baghdad than the nation's capital. I got up to stretch my legs and say hello to some of the dignitaries who processed in ahead of President-elect Biden. Barack Obama saw me and quickly walked over. "I just want to thank you for all you did over the last four years to keep it all together," he said, and shook my hand. I had rarely had the opportunity to speak with the former president since he left office and wasn't sure how carefully he had been watching events on the Hill, let alone my own work. As he returned to his seat, I was very touched by his words and realized for the first time that I was starting to see the Trump presidency through the rearview mirror, and that was a great relief.

Four years earlier, the skies had darkened as Donald Trump stepped forward to give his inaugural address and describe what he saw as American carnage. Now, as if by some equally divine intervention, bright sunlight filtered through the clouds to greet the new president and his hopeful remarks. "We have learned again," he said, "that democracy is precious. Democracy is fragile. And at this hour, my friends, democracy has prevailed." I wanted to believe him, and on that day, I think I did. But I also knew that we were not out of the woods, not by a long shot, and certainly not as long as the specter of Donald Trump hung over the Republican Party and the nation.

On February 9, the second impeachment trial of Donald Trump

began, and much like the first, it started with a debate, in this case, over whether the now former president was subject to the jurisdiction of a court of impeachment notwithstanding the fact that he was no longer in office. Constitutionally, it was not a difficult question. The history of impeachment proceedings in Britain and in the United States, in which officials had been tried after leaving office, militated strongly in favor of jurisdiction, as did the constitutional text, which provides for disqualification as a remedy separate from removal. But the most powerful argument was common sense: If a president were to abuse their power to stay in office, it would likely come at the end of their term—the most dangerous period for democracies. Surely the Founders would not have envisioned a system in which if a tyrant abused their office to stay in power and succeeded, they would be president for life, and if they failed there could be no repercussions. Or as Raskin pointed out more succinctly, it would "create a brand-new January exception to the Constitution."

The most powerful moment of the trial came during the course of this debate. Every member who was present on January 6 had a personal story about its impact on them, but few had one as poignant and powerful as Raskin himself. His youngest daughter had come to the Capitol with him that day, so that he would not be alone with his grief or she with hers, since it was the day after the family had buried Tommy. She and her brother-in-law holed up in an office off the House floor during the rioting, and when Raskin could finally get to them, hug them, and tell them how sorry he was, he also promised his daughter that the next time she came to the Capitol it would not be like this. "And do you know what she said? She said: 'Dad, I don't want to come back to the Capitol.' Of all the terrible, cruel things I saw and heard that day and since then, that one hit me the hardest." Jamie's voice caught, and he choked back a sob. I don't know how my friend could say these things and still hold it together, but he did, and when he fought off the tears, he was not alone.

While the constitutional issue was a fairly simple one, that did not mean it would be easy to persuade Republican senators to go forward with the trial. The merits were strongly with the House managers, but the politics was another matter. For senators looking for a way out, a way not to have to condemn the president's conduct but at the same time not to have to defend it, the motion gave them an easy out: They could claim that the Constitution did not permit them to try a former president so they never had to consider the underlying offense. When the vote was called, forty-four Republican senators took that path of least resistance and voted to dismiss the case. The motion failed, but it was a pyrrhic victory for the managers, since only six Republican senators concluded they could even hear the case, and that number did not include Mitch McConnell. After delaying the trial so that it would not begin until after Trump was out of office, McConnell now took the position that his own delay was fatal to moving forward. The House managers would later argue that the motion having been resolved in their favor, all senators could proceed to the merits as if they had never voted to dismiss—but still, it would be hard to persuade senators to convict when they had earlier found that the case should not be tried at all.

During the trial, Raskin and the House managers did a masterful job of weaving together video and audio from the insurrection, some which had never before been seen or heard, showing the vice president fleeing the chambers; Senators Romney, Schumer, and others being rushed in one direction or another, to avoid the mob; the brutal assault on police who were beaten with flagpoles, fire extinguishers, and fence posts, crushed by doors, gouged and bear-sprayed, pleading for help, pleading for reinforcements. It was traumatizing to see it all again and so graphically, to realize how close we came to even greater calamity, and it had a visceral impact on the senators. Equally important, it showcased the barbarity of the attack for the whole country. Though Republicans in the House would later try to reinvent history, spuriously claiming that these violent attackers were no different from tourists and that lawmakers were not in serious jeopardy, their falsehoods would gain far less traction because the House had shown the world what took place.

In both talent and presentation, it was an unequal fight. If the House managers were a completely new team, so was the Trump defense, but with a lot less time to prepare and less experience with the issues. Cobbled together seemingly at random, with personnel changes on the eve of trial and infighting during the trial, their initial presentations on the motion to dismiss were rambling, disconnected, and sophomoric. None of them was a constitutional scholar, and few of them had much experience with Congress.

When they did settle on a unified message, its tenor was aptly captured by a personal injury lawyer named Michael Thomas van der Veen, in his first statement during the defense case: "The Article of Impeachment now before the Senate is an unjust and blatantly unconstitutional act of political vengeance." He went on to claim that the impeachment was divisive, a politically motivated witch hunt, a sham, and "a deliberate attempt by the Democratic Party to smear, censor, and cancel not just President Trump but the seventy-five million Americans who voted for him." Defense counsel would also argue that the president's speech and actions concerning the election were "squarely focused on how the proper civic process could address any concerns through the established legal and constitutional system," as if efforts to shake down the secretary of state in Georgia to find 11,780 votes, or incite a mob to attack the Capitol should be taught in civics courses. David Schoen, another of the president's lawyers, and a criminal defense attorney who also represented Roger Stone and agreed to represent Jeffrey Epstein, took a similar tack, stressing "the hatred, the vitriol, the political opportunism that has brought us here today."

There was a lot of "whataboutism" to the defense presentation—what about Democrats who didn't condemn the violence in Portland, and what about Democrats who also use the word "fight" as Trump had done during his January 6 speech? One video reel of Democrats using the word "fight" in numerous inapposite contexts was played so often—"the fight club," it was pejoratively named—that senators began laughing at it, and not in sympathy with the defense case.

Trump's lawyers took issue with the due process afforded the president and claimed that he had a First Amendment right to say whatever he wanted. The First Amendment argument had some superficial appeal—why can't a president say whatever he wants?—until you realize it is not about whether he has a right to say something, but whether he is fulfilling his oath to defend the country and Constitution. As Raskin pointed out, a private citizen may have a First Amendment right to say that he thinks we should abrogate the Constitution, adopt a totalitarian form of government, or swear an oath to a foreign despot, but for a president, such speech would surely be impeachable. An ordinary citizen may have the right to say that he will not respond to a fire at the mayor's home and is content to let it burn, but if he is the fire chief, he would be terminated immediately. It is no less disqualifying for a president.

When both the managers and defense had presented their case-in-chief and responded to questions from the senators, it was time to consider the issue of witnesses. Raskin informed the senators of a statement released the previous evening by Republican representative Jaime Herrera Beutler, a moderate who had supported Trump's impeachment in the House. According to Herrera Beutler, McCarthy had called the president during the middle of the insurrection to beg for help, and Trump's response was this: "Well, Kevin, I guess these people are more upset about the election than you are." Raskin announced they would like to subpoena Herrera Beutler for her testimony, as it provided strong corroboration of the president's willful dereliction of duty. The defense naturally opposed the motion, and as they had done during the first trial when we sought to subpoena Bolton and Mulvaney, Trump's lawyers claimed that they would need time to call lots of witnesses of their own, including Nancy Pelosi and Vice President Harris—in other words, they would drag it out indefinitely and make the trial a circus. When the vote was called, the managers prevailed, 55–45, and it would be in order to call witnesses.

At this point, the proceedings recessed while senators, managers, and the defense tried to determine what this meant for the course of the trial. When the trial resumed about an hour later, the managers and defense stipulated that Herrera Beutler's statement would be admitted as evidence without the necessity of calling her as a witness. This result caused consternation among many commentators and certainly within the progressive base. If the managers had the votes to compel witnesses, why did they not do so and bring in Herrera Beutler, McCarthy, and potentially others?

I can only imagine the pressure on Raskin and his team as they deliberated whether to accept the stipulation or press on in a new and uncertain direction with witnesses. I had been in that room, walled off from the rest of the world, and making strategic decisions that might affect history and understood what they were going through. In the first trial, the calculus had been different—if we couldn't get witnesses, if we couldn't inject uncertainty in the proceedings, if we couldn't open the door to new and even more graphic testimony, we were going to lose. The dynamic was not the same in the second trial, in which the senators themselves had been firsthand witnesses to many of the events at issue. The risk of losing votes by protracting the proceedings was every bit as serious as whether the managers could win over additional votes by bringing in Herrera Beutler or others. I would not then, or now, second-guess the decision the managers made to forgo additional testimony.

In his closing argument, Raskin quoted Ben Franklin, who said that "I have observed that wrong is always growing more wrong, till there is no bearing it, and that right, however opposed, comes right at last." Listening to him, I wondered how long it would take, how many more wrongs would be countenanced by my colleagues in Congress, how many more excuses and obfuscations we must endure, how many more dangerous assaults on our democracy, before right came right at last. The vote was 57–43 that the president was guilty, the most bipartisan in history, but not enough to convict. Right would have to wait.

IN A SPEECH FOLLOWING HIS vote to acquit, Mitch McConnell called the events of January 6—when fellow Americans beat police, stormed the floor of the Senate, and tried to hunt down the Speaker and vice president—a disgrace. "They did this because they had been fed wild falsehoods by the most powerful man on earth—because he was angry he'd lost an election. President Trump's actions preceding the riot were a disgraceful dereliction of duty." McConnell said the president was both practically and morally responsible for provoking the attack, the foreseeable consequence of "the growing crescendo of false statements, conspiracy theories, and reckless hyperbole which the defeated president kept shouting into the largest megaphone on planet earth."

Two weeks later, McConnell said he would "absolutely" support Donald Trump if he became the nominee in 2024. The remarkable swiftness of that capitulation—from condemnation of a disgraceful and deadly dereliction of duty by the former president, to absolute support for him—demonstrated how feeble were his protestations of conscience compared to his desire to hold on to power. In the House, Liz Cheney showed that there was at least one Republican leader who prized something more than their position, and she would be quickly forced out of Republican leadership for refusing to adopt the big lie. She would be replaced by Elise Stefanik, who proved that she was more than willing to do what Cheney, in good conscience, could not. There was no room left in the GOP for people committed to telling the truth about our elections, or who refused to pledge the most absolute fealty to Trump. McConnell understood that, and he made his deal with the devil. So did Stefanik. Liz Cheney would not.

Our system of government depends on two functional parties, and now we had only one. The GOP had become an antitruth, antidemocratic cult organized around the former president. For a brief moment, when emotions around the insurrection were high and public sentiment against Trump was powerful and deep, McCarthy and McConnell had flirted with casting him aside, but like a candle in the breeze, their flirtation with truth quickly flickered and died. And when that small light was extinguished, prospects for a swift recovery from the damage inflicted by the most grandiose of liars died along with it.

In states around the country, Republican legislators took the big lie and ran with it, using false claims of voter fraud to usher in a new generation of Jim Crow laws targeting minority voting populations and seeking to cut off their access to the polls. Democrats had prevailed in both Senate races in Georgia's special election, electing Raphael Warnock, a senior pastor at the Ebenezer Baptist Church and the first African American senator in the state's history, along with Jon Ossoff, the first Jewish senator elected from the deep South since 1879. If Republicans couldn't succeed with their backward ideas in Georgia anymore—if a state as reliably red as Georgia could not be counted on to elect Republicans—they would not change their policies, they would change the voters.

Under a new law, Georgia voters would now need identification to vote by mail, the period to request and return your ballot would be shortened, it would now be against the law to provide voters with water while waiting in the hot sun to vote—and, most threatening to election integrity, the five-person state election board would no longer be chaired by the secretary of state. If Raffensperger would not find Trump 11,780 votes, perhaps next time the legislature would appoint someone who would.

In Arizona, the state legislature ordered a private firm to do an audit of the election results in pivotal Maricopa County months after the polls closed. It would be conducted by Cyber Ninjas, a Florida-based outfit that had no election auditing experience but was led by a Trump supporter who promoted his baseless conspiracy theories about the election. When the Arizona secretary of state criticized the move, Republican legislators introduced a bill to strip her of her ability to defend the vote count against frivolous election lawsuits. Texas Republicans introduced a voter disenfranchisement bill so severe that Democratic members of the state legislature fled the state capitol to deprive the body of a quorum and were later threatened with arrest by Texas officials.

If there was any doubt about the antidemocratic direction the GOP was now taking, or any question about whether Republicans would shake off their dangerous devotion to the former president and his rampant falsehoods, these laws were testament to the fact that Trump's GOP was here to stay, and a danger to us all. Months after Biden won with the most votes in American history, a majority of Republicans still believed the lie that he had lost.

Of all the terrible *ifs* of the previous four years, the most terrible of all was this: What if Trump had been just a little smarter, a little more competent or capable, with an agenda beyond his own self-aggrandizement, and had delivered on his promises or actually cared about the lives of the people who voted for him? Had any of these things been true and Donald Trump been motivated by something other than self-interest, he might have gained such a stranglehold on our country that he would have obtained another four years and little of our democracy would have been left.

How is that possible? Wasn't Trump just the kind of potential despot that Alexander Hamilton warned of when he described how an unprincipled man who was "desperate in his fortune" would seek to "fall in with all of the non sense of the zealots of the day" and "throw things into confusion"? Wasn't the Constitution meant to protect us from just such a man?

Indeed it was. And indeed it did. The system held, if barely, but our constitutional order sustained great damage in the process. With fantastic speed—in four short years—Trump marginalized the free press and caused millions of Americans to distrust it. He politicized our intelligence agencies and made their top leadership align their views with his false narratives. He used the Justice Department as his personal law firm to shield him from criminal liability and as a sword to go after his enemies. With the revelation that my own records had been subpoenaed by the Department of Justice, I may have been one of them. Inspectors general were fired for speaking out and replaced with political loyalists who Trump hoped would put their allegiance to the president above their duty to the nation.

And no institution suffered more under the Trump presidency than Congress, which saw its oversight powers emasculated and its impeachment power rendered obsolete. Shockingly, many of the injuries to Congress were self-inflicted, when members of the president's party abdicated those powers to the executive in the failure of one institution to jealously guard its interests against those of another. In the wake of Trump's many abuses of office, I introduced a broad set of reforms—the Protecting our Democracy Act—to strengthen the guardrails once again, by giving previous norms the force of law. Even so, they may not be enough when faced with an unscrupulous president who enjoys a zealously partisan majority. The Founders warned that their carefully calibrated system of checks and balances might give way to excessive factionalism and it has, with devastating impacts on our ability to combat metastasizing corruption within the executive branch. Even our greatest capacity to constrain the administration, by cutting off its funding, has been willingly abdicated when the president demanded it of his party, as when he diverted military funding to build a wall that Congress had rejected.

Nevertheless, the fault was not in our Constitution but in ourselves, that the checks stopped checking and the balances became unbalanced. Nothing that is written by man or woman cannot be erased by time, neglect, indifference, artifice, or design. The genius of the Constitution lay not in fending off all manner of attack by a scheming executive—no piece of parchment, no matter how brilliantly conceived, could do that—but in holding a despot at bay for as long as it did. Yet, if the failure was ours, where exactly did we go wrong?

HE IS NOT WHO YOU ARE

IT IS MIDNIGHT IN WASHINGTON, AND EVE HAS GONE TO BED. MY SON IS in his room, watching a Formula One race from the 1960s on his laptop, earbuds in, soon to doze off to the sound of their engines. I am downstairs in the den, and all is quiet. Outside my window, the cars have stopped climbing the hill, and the pavement glistens from a light rain. I love this time of night, when things seem so peaceful and I can see clearly, though everything is obscured. What is it about human nature that best shapes our understanding when our most powerful senses are in the dark? The cicadas, awake after seventeen long years, are resting, and will not resume their riotous cries until morning. In a few weeks, they will crawl back underground and go into that long sleep. What kind of America, I wonder, will await us when they emerge again? What kind of world?

At any other time, we might have answered those questions with more confidence than we can right now. But the presidency of Donald Trump has weakened America's commitment to its ideals, and emboldened dictators around the globe. The last four years have left us suddenly contemplating an America in which the values of liberal democracy have been degraded, in which elections are deemed valid only by the side that wins, in which self-governance falters, making us vulnerable to the appeal of an autocrat—an appeal that is anathema to all that we have believed in for two and a half centuries. The Trump presidency was a stress test for our system, and the results must wake us up. The survival of our institutions and the rule of law depend on what we do next.

It was almost exactly two years after Donald Trump was elected, when he was again confronted outside the White House with evidence of a big lie he had told during the campaign, the one in which he had claimed to have no business interests in Russia. It had taken a long time for journalists to discover that up until the eve of the Republican convention he had actually been pursuing a Moscow Trump Tower so tall that it would look down on the rest of Europe. Standing a few yards from Marine One, his hair unmoved by its large rotors, Trump did not deny the lie. Acknowledging that he might have lost the election, Trump explained: "Why should I lose lots of opportunities?"

For someone who lied constantly during the course of his presidency, Trump could also at times be quite revealing. Listening to the president's remarks, I was struck by an overriding and terrifying impression: What if he still wants to build the tower? What if he will never stand up to Putin during his presidency, because, after all, he might not be reelected—and why should he miss out on all those opportunities? Could it be that Trump's otherwise inexplicable fondness for the Russian dictator was no more complicated than that? That the *kompromat* was out in the open?

It was apparent from the beginning of his presidency that Trump was guided by little more than self-interest, and that he would always value personal gain above the good of the country. But what of America's meek acceptance of the scandalous revelation of this lie, every bit as tall as the tower itself? In this one small vignette, played out against the *thwack, thwack, thwack* of the rotors, we can see so much of the country's transformation and that of one of America's two great political parties.

By the time Trump stood on that grass, he had already lied thousands of times as president. Part of Trump's genius was to understand that in order to get away with his rampant falsehoods, he needed to make everyone else out to be liars. Of all the thousands of Twitter diatribes that would emanate from his executive time, one of the most frequent calumnies he leveled against his opponents was to call them a "liar." In this way, he could lead his supporters to believe that everyone lies, and at least Trump was giving them what they wanted. The same was true of his corrupt self-dealing. After running on a platform of draining the swamp, he continued his rallying cry against opponents, claiming, without evidence, that they, not he, were corrupt, even though "they" were often his own agency heads, former cabinet officials, or inspectors general who were blowing the whistle. It is a stratagem of other autocrats, like Turkey's Recep Tayyip Erdogan, caught up in a web of his own familial corruption: Don't bother trying to refute the charges, since they are true; simply accuse the other side of the same and leave a confused public to conclude that they're all corrupt, but he's corrupt and he's ours.

Of all the damage that Trump would do to our democracy, nothing has been as deleterious as his constant attack on the truth, a strategy Steve Bannon once described as "flooding the zone with shit." Democracies depend on shared experience, on a common acceptance of most facts, and, at rock bottom, an understanding that there are such things as "facts." A people cannot govern themselves if they do not have a common basis for evaluating whether this candidate or that, this party or that, has the capacity to deal with the world as it is. In the absence of that shared understanding—if indeed each party is entitled to its own alternative facts—then what basis is left for judging the merits of any particular agenda or platform? If everything could be true, then nothing is true. And there is no confusion more inviting to the autocrat.

But what was Trump offering that was so compelling to people that they could embrace his lies and obvious corruption? What need was he satisfying? That this reality television personality, this modern-day carnival barker who claimed Ted Cruz's father was consorting with John F. Kennedy's killer and that Obama was born in Kenya, could easily vanquish sixteen primary opponents was bewildering enough, but that tens of millions of Americans—almost half the country—would still support his reelection after seeing what he was, and what he represented, would still support him after losing hundreds of thousands of our fellow citizens to his incompetent handling of the pandemic, demands examination.

Before Trump took office, powerful changes in the global economy were already disturbing the democratic world. Through a combination of globalization and automation, hundreds of millions of people at home and around the world were suddenly experiencing tremendous job insecurity in an economic rending just as disruptive as the Industrial Revolution. Certainly there were beneficiaries of the new economy, but the most powerful driver of social change is not the prospect of gaining security and status but of losing them, and now, suddenly, an entire middle class was at risk of collapsing.

A democracy, like any other form of government, must deliver for its people, and America's democracy has been failing to meet the economic needs of our people. In the last quarter century, our country's promise of an accessible and burgeoning middle class has been breaking down, giving way to an increasingly constrained working class and a cadre of uber-rich that would come to own a staggering portion of the nation's wealth. Between 1979 and the great recession of 2008–2009, the income gap between the top one percent and everyone else more than tripled, and it would grow worse during the following few years, when 95 percent of economic gains went to that same tiny slice of the American population.

Supreme Court Justice Louis Brandeis is believed to have said of rising income inequality early in the last century that "we may have a democracy, or we may have great wealth concentrated in the hands of a few, but we cannot have both." During the pandemic, the nation's billionaires got more than fifty percent richer, while millions of people lost their jobs and many others their homes. Even before the pandemic, three men, Warren Buffett, Bill Gates, and Jeff Bezos, owned as much as the bottom half of all Americans. No wonder Trump's claims of a rigged system landed with such resonance; for millions of Americans, the system was rigged against them; no matter how hard they worked, they could simply not get by while others were accumulating staggering fortunes.

As a candidate and as president, Trump's most potent appeal was to the "forgotten men and women," those some described as living in "flyover country" and who had felt abandoned for decades. Trump played on a sense of grievance that was rooted in a harsh reality for many who struggled in dying manufacturing towns with unemployment and opioids, telling them that the coastal elite looked down on them, that they laughed at them, their culture, and their values. And he promised them that he would make their lives better, that he would upend the system that was rigged against them, that they would never be forgotten again. In fact, while Trump was expert in exploiting their pain, he hadn't the slightest idea of how to help them, nor the inclination. And it is perhaps Trump's cruelest lie of all that he made things measurably worse for those very Americans—championing a tax cut for the wealthy and large corporations that rewarded accumulated wealth even more and stripped the country of the resources it needed to assist families in crisis.

If he would not deliver on his promises, he could at least give millions of Americans a simple explanation for their predicament. Hewing strictly to the autocrats' playbook, Trump promoted the divisive narrative that America's economic troubles were caused by those who looked different. Hispanic immigrants took the full brunt of Trump's bigoted wrath—they were murderers and rapists bent on finding new victims in a country whose previous leadership had been too weak, too "politically correct," to stop them—but he demonized a range of other ethnic minorities as well, from Asians during the pandemic to the Muslim community (always), and most especially, Black Americans.

But if Trump used surging economic anxiety coupled with racial and religious divisions to mobilize and organize a political base, that still doesn't explain why he was able to tear down so many of our democratic norms and institutions in the process, and with such apparent ease.

Power revealed Donald Trump to be what he always was, too unprincipled and selfish to be placed in a position of responsibility over anyone but himself and his family. But it has revealed a lot about us, too, as Americans. Somewhere along the way, we stopped believing in a greater good than winning, in something larger than ourselves. Somehow we lost confidence in our system of governance, no longer believed that it was capable of delivering a fair result, and prosperity that was shared. The Republican Party in particular went from envisioning our country as a shining city on a hill and an example to the rest of the world, to seeing an "American carnage" of "rusted-out factories scattered like tombstones across the landscape of our nation," as Trump declared in his inaugural address. The GOP went from seeing a bold future with unlimited promise to one of scarce resources and a bitter struggle for survival. But even among many Democrats there was a foreboding, bordering on conviction, that as wealth grew more concentrated and the wealthy deployed their resources to perpetuate their dominance, through lobbyists and dark money, in Congress and through the courts, the system had become broken and unsalvageable.

The paramount challenge to the success of our republic lies in our present inability to address these disparities in economic opportunity through the electoral process. The moment we start to believe that elections no longer work, that they no longer reflect the popular will, that they no longer deliver results or change, that they are no longer fair, that they are somehow rigged against us, and we are unwilling to accept any result other than total victory—that is the moment we start to believe democracy is not the answer and give ourselves up to the autocrat. For millions of Americans, that moment has already arrived.

There have been harbingers along the way, signposts to our present unraveling. When Mitch McConnell gave up being an institutionalist and decided that it was more important to withhold a Supreme Court appointment from Barack Obama, it was a warning, or should have been, that America was entering a dangerous new phase in which the preservation of power was more important than the preservation of our constitutional order. When a Democrat was elected governor of North Carolina in 2016 and the Republican legislature responded by stripping the new governor of some of his powers, it was another profound indication that something was changing in America, that at least one of our parties no longer felt constrained by electoral loss, no longer responded by seeking to do better the next time but instead chose to ignore the will of the people and retain power by legislative fiat.

All of Trump's agitation before the election, his insistence that if he didn't win it would be because of fraud, was a staggering rejection of the greatest norm and common understanding of all—the peaceful transfer of power following a presidential election. The bloody insurrection on January 6 was a foreseeable consequence of an ethos that rejects any loss as illegitimate. But if we thought that the insurrection was the explosive climax of this power-at-all-costs mentality, we were wrong. More than half a year after his loss at the polls, Trump and his acolytes still talked about his "reinstatement" as president. His former National Security Advisor told QAnon conspiracy theorists that there was no reason we shouldn't have a military coup like Myanmar's. In Washington, Republicans are seeking to erase and sanitize the history of January 6, as if the entire world hadn't witnessed the violent breach of the Capitol. It was a "normal tourist visit," said one member of Congress. A "peaceful protest," added a senator. Vladimir Putin himself weighed in, concurring with these Republicans. These are dangerous lies, of course, and erasing history, however shameful that history might be, is better left with the propagandists in the Kremlin than brought to our seat of government.

When Speaker Pelosi offered to establish a bipartisan commission to investigate January 6, modeled after the September 11 commission—with an equal number of Democrats and Republicans—Trump weighed in against it, and McConnell did everything he could to stop it. He succeeded, and the commission proposal died in the Senate. Soon thereafter, the Speaker established a select committee to investigate the facts leading up to the insurrection, what happened on that bloody day, and make recommendations on how to prevent it from ever happening again—and asked me and six other Democrats to serve on it. The Speaker also asked two Republicans—Liz Cheney and Adam Kinzinger of Illinois—who accepted; notwithstanding the obstructionism of McConnell and McCarthy, the investigation would be bipartisan after all.

But as if the insurrectionists had a valid point, Republican legislators all across the country have continued Trump's big lie about massive voter fraud, initiating phony new audits of the election results and replacing independent election officials with ones beholden to partisan legislatures. They are preparing the battlefield for the struggle to overturn the next presidential election if it doesn't go their way, and should they regain majorities in Congress, they just might be successful. Even as I write these words, the idea is an astonishment—the effort to overturn the next presidential election might be successful.

To avoid the necessity of overturning the election, Republican legislators are also passing laws aimed at making it as hard as possible for people of color to vote so as to predetermine the outcome. This return to Jim Crow signals that the end of Trump's presidency was not the apogee of racial discrimination, but merely a new waypoint on the road to further exploitation of race as a tool of political organization. The pendulum continues its illiberal swing with no sign of slowing. Of all the horrible images from January 6, among the most awful were the sight of Confederate flags paraded through Statuary Hall and of insurrectionists in Camp Auschwitz T-shirts. As he struggled to protect the nation's democratic citadel, a Black Capitol Police officer, Harry Dunn, was called the n-word dozens of times. When it was over, he asked the question we must all struggle to answer: "Is this America?" For the insurrection was not a Trumpist insurrection alone, but a white nationalist one as well, and addressing that systemic problem has been, and will be, the work of generations. These new Jim Crow laws are nothing less than insurrection by other means.

If Congress fails to curtail these efforts at disenfranchisement, we the people must succeed nonetheless. If Republican state legislators mandate a purge of the voter rolls, we must reregister. If local GOP elections officials close down our polling site, we must go to another. If they shut down voting on Sunday, we must vote on Monday. If they force us to wait for long hours in the hot sun to vote, we must bring our own shade. We must love our democracy more than they wish to destroy it. We must defend it as democrats, and as Democrats, until the Republican Party breaks free from Donald Trump and the siren song of his depravity.

And our government must again meet the needs of its people. It must be responsive to a majority of its citizens, even as it is respectful of the minority. In the House, that means an end to the gerrymander, so that a popular vote of the people controls the majority of that body. And in the Senate, it means an end to the filibuster. The Senate vote on establishing the January 6 Commission was 54 yeas to 35 nays—and the nays won. How long can a democracy survive when, on issue after issue, priority after priority, a minority of nays wins? And in the highest office in the land, it means a multistate compact to mandate that the winner of the popular vote become our next president. Always. When a president can win office by more than seven million votes nationally in an election that might have been lost but for fifty thousand votes in a handful of states, then the Electoral College, too, threatens us with a tyranny of the minority. Too many Americans have given up on democracy because they believe that democracy has given up on them.

That we are in trouble is undeniable. That this trouble is of our own making—even as it is being stoked by our adversaries overseas—is also undeniable. Democracy is hard. Civilization is not inevitable.

Progress is not a straight line. Freedom is not assured. It is, as ever, something we have to fight for every day. So let us fight. Unlike Trump's violent insurrectionists, our weapon of choice must be the truth, wielded relentlessly. And even as we fight, especially in this fight, we must never lose hold of our basic decency.

It is often said that America is a great country because America is a good country. We love that idea, because it attributes our success not to our bounteous natural resources, the oceans that have protected us, or our climate, but to our generosity, our fundamental decency, our courage, and our compassion for the stranger. Viscerally, we understand that the moment we stop being a good people, we will stop being a great nation. Can we be a good people, then, can we be a great nation, if we are led by a fundamentally indecent human being who knows nothing of and cares nothing for our values? Who separates children from their parents and locks them in cages? Who consorts with dictators, defiles our Constitution, and sunders our country? Four years of Donald Trump have answered that question with a resounding "No, we cannot."

Our present circumstances are desperate, but we do not have the luxury of despair. American history gives us good reason to be hopeful, for it demonstrates an almost endless capacity for renewal, and a depth and breadth of talent, genius, and devotion that inhabit every part of our country from sea to shining sea. In the crucible of Congress, I watched the Trump presidency reveal the degree to which some of my colleagues valued nothing so much as their own position and power. But it also introduced me, and the country, to William Taylor, who chose the infantry in Vietnam and never stopped serving, and Alexander Vindman, who braved roadside bombs in Iraq and claims of disloyalty at home, and Fiona Hill, who brought her considerable intellect and talent to a country that her father loved but never got to see, and Marie Yovanovitch, whose parents fled communism and fascism, and Capitol police officers like Eugene Goodman, who risked his life to lead violent insurrectionists away from senators, and Harry Dunn, and Sergeant Aquilino Gonell, an immigrant and decorated veteran who was almost suffocated while defending the Capitol, and D.C. Metropolitan police officers like Michael Fanone and Daniel Hodges, and so many others. Seeing their courage, their selflessness, and their love of country, and knowing that such wonderful public servants populate all of our agencies and departments—and people like them inhabit all of our fifty states—was enough to reassure me that we will be okay for telling the truth. And that here, right still matters.

During the first impeachment trial of Donald J. Trump, I told the senators that Trump couldn't tell right from wrong, couldn't tell the truth from a lie, and was fundamentally indecent. He certainly had no appreciation for what a democracy is or why it should matter to us or the rest of the world. But, I said, "He is not who you are." We are a better people than that, more generous to our neighbors and to strangers, more caring and kind, and more devoted to something other than self. James Madison believed that there was sufficient virtue among us to govern ourselves, that we did not need the chains of despotism to restrain us "from destroying and devouring one another." He was right. We are the proud heirs of the greatest experiment in self-government in history. It is time we remembered that.

For all its imperfections, America remains the best hope of freedom-loving people around the world. If the United States continues its illiberal slide, much of the rest of the world will slide with us, if not into autocracy, then into something that is not quite democracy either, something more ruthless, more intolerant, less representative, less accountable, and less free. The burden of championing democracy is one we have always been proud to bear, though it has cost us dearly in blood and treasure. We should be proud to bear it still.

Seventeen years from now, when the present is a distant memory for all but the cicadas, we will look back on this time as a decisive moment for our country, when we were at sea and our destination remained unknown, our future obscure, the great enterprise in self-rule in doubt. Did we turn back toward the shores of our Founders, or was this the moment when the clouds descended, the stars disappeared, and we became irretrievably lost? We must understand that we are not passengers on this journey, unable to steer the country we all love in one direction or another. It is within our power to take hold of the rudder, choose the future we want for our children and grandchildren, and, with the grace of God, make it so.

ACKNOWLEDGMENTS

For the last twenty years, I have had the good fortune of representing the people of California's Twenty-eighth District in Congress, which stretches from West Hollywood to West Pasadena, through Burbank and Glendale, and from Echo Park to the Angeles National Forest. I want to thank my wonderful constituents for the opportunity to serve, and for all of their encouragement during my tenure in Congress—but over the last few years in particular. It would have been impossible to carry out the difficult responsibilities I had during this period without their steadfast support. I will always be grateful to you.

I cannot imagine how we would have persevered and remained a democracy without the extraordinary leadership of Speaker Nancy Pelosi. She may be the most gifted and tenacious leader the House has ever had, and thank God for that. Speaker Pelosi led us through one of the most difficult periods of congressional history with a rare combination of personal strength, strategic vision, organizational ability, and love of country. There will never be another like her, and I will be forever proud to say that I served in the House with the greatest Speaker in modern history, Nancy D'Alesandro Pelosi.

To my colleagues on the House Intelligence Committee, I could not have asked for a more committed group of public servants and friends. If you have to be in a foxhole, or in the bunker we were in, you couldn't do better than to be facing all of the incoming fire with Representatives Jim Himes, Terri Sewell, André Carson, Jackie Speier, Mike Quigley, Eric Swalwell, Joaquin Castro, Peter Welch, Sean Patrick Maloney, Val Demings, Raja Krishnamoorthi, Jim Cooper, Jason Crow, and former representative Denny Heck. I also want to acknowledge my dear friend, and fellow writer, former representative Steve Israel, who co-founded our Study Group on National Security and is one of Congress's most gifted thinkers and alumni.

There are few impeachments in history, and those who go through that harrowing experience together as House managers are bound to each other for life. To my fellow managers, Representatives Jerry Nadler, Zoe Lofgren, Hakeem Jeffries, Val Demings, Sylvia Garcia, and Jason Crow, I could not be more appreciative of the hard work, dedication, and talent you brought to the task of holding the president accountable. You represented our caucus and the American people with great dignity and devotion. And to the dedicated public servants who make up the diplomatic corps and who serve America at home and all over the world, I am deeply grateful for your service. In particular, I want to acknowledge the courage of Fiona Hill, David Holmes, William Taylor, Alexander Vindman, and Marie Yovanovitch for showing the country what patriotism means by standing up to the most powerful man in the world when duty required it, and for showing us that right still matters here.

As any member of Congress will tell you—or should, if they are being candid—we are only as good as our staff, and seldom as good as that. I have been truly blessed with the most remarkable public servants in my district office, under the leadership of Ann Peifer and including Michael Aguilera-Gaudette, Sierra deSousa, Margarita Gutierrez, Mary Hovagimian, Haig Kartounian, Qiao Li, Pamela Marcello, Colleen Oinuma, Alejandro Rosa, Teresa Lamb Simpson, and Elizabeth Vuna. In my Washington office, Patrick Boland leads the way, and we have been blessed with many wonderful staff over the last several years, including Heather Connelly, Courtney Fogwell, Jen Fox, Lauren French, Jenna Galper, Joseph Jankiewicz, Naree Ketudat, Allison Lewis, Dao Nguyen, Caroline Nicholas, Emilie Simons, Zach Sorenson, and Anthony Theissen. On the Intelligence Committee, and under the leadership of Jeff Lowenstein, I am equally grateful to my staff during this trying time, including Michael Bahar, Wells Bennett, Tim Bergreen, Maher Bitar, Carly Blake, Christine Bocchino, Patrick Boland, Kris Breaux, Linda Cohen, Thomas Eager, William Evans, Patrick Fallon, Daniel Goldman, Abigail Grace, Shannon Green, Kelsey Lax, Robert Minehart, Sean Misko, Nicolas Mitchell, Daniel Noble, Krishna Pathak, Diana Pilipenko, Ariana Rowberry, Lucian Sikorskyj, Conrad Stosz, Kathy Suber, Amanda Rogers Thorpe, Aaron Thurman, Raffaella Wakeman, Rheanne Wirkkala, and William Wu. During the impeachment investigation and trial, we also had the wonderful assistance of Perry Apelbaum, Barry Berke, Sophia Brill, Norman Eisen, Arya Hariharan, Aaron Hiller, Sarah Istel, and Joshua Matz from the Judiciary Committee; Krista Boyd, Aryele Bradford, Susanne Sachsman Grooms, Peter Kenny, Janet Kim, and Dave Rapallo from the Oversight Committee; James Bair, Laura Carey, and Tim Mulvey from the Foreign Affairs Committee; Jennifer Read from the Financial Services Committee; and, from the Speaker's office, Mia Ehrenberg, Ashley Etienne, Drew Hammill, Terri McCullough, Dick Meltzer, and Wyndee Parker; as well as House General Counsel Doug Letter. I am also deeply indebted to my campaign team over the years: Katharine Abrahamson, Audrey Abrell, Tariq Almani, Steve Barkan, Adam Blackwell, Phillip Blake, Jackie Brot-Weinberg, Katy Blake Burch-Hudson, Shannon Fitzgerald, Jennifer Frost, Laura Galanter, Justin Gevertz, Eric Hacopian, Renee Hatchwell, Patty

Horton, Malcom Johnson, Mitchell Lester, Roger Lis, Jordan Markwith, Kevin Meehan, April Mininsohn, Elizabeth Tauro Mitchell, Terri New, Jessica Prusakowski, Mike Shimpock, and Parke Skelton.

I want to acknowledge my cherished friend and staff colleague Christopher Hoven, who passed away on Christmas Day 2020. Chris was my executive assistant, budget chief, Washington scheduler, adviser, and friend for almost twenty years. Bright, passionate about public service, learned, generous, funny, and profane, he was a joy to work with and I miss him dearly. Chris was seldom seen without a volume of history or biography under his arm; how much I would have loved to see him carry this one.

I am deeply grateful for the wisdom, good counsel, and friendship of Professor Laurence Tribe, who has taught generations of aspiring lawyers and teaches us still, and for some of the other great educators in my life: my college professors David Danelski, Ron Rebholz, and William Lyttle, and my high school speech coach, Al Gentile, and Shakespeare teacher, Barbara Abbott. And to the late Wm. Matthew Byrne, Jr., former federal district judge, who was, without knowing it, my mentor. A special thanks to former California attorney general Bill Lockyer for encouraging me to run for the state senate, and to former minority leader Dick Gephardt and former representative Patrick Kennedy for spurring me on to run for Congress.

I am from Los Angeles, so of course I have written screenplays, but this is my first book and it would not have been possible without the extraordinary help of my new friends and colleagues at Random House. In particular, I want to thank executive editor Mark Warren, who approached me years ago and encouraged me to put my thoughts and experiences on paper and write a book in defense of our democracy. He said that I had a unique purchase on this moment in history; unique or otherwise, it would not have seen the light of day without his endless support, his fabulous insights, and his ruthless and essential editing. I will miss our midnight zooms after a long day at the office and his trenchant observations on the events of the times. It was such a pleasure working together, and I cannot thank him enough for the exceptional effort he put into this project. To my terrific agents at Javelin DC, Matt Latimer and Keith Urbahn, thank you for your expert help in guiding me through the business end of publishing and for your notes on the manuscript. I am also deeply appreciative of the support of Andy Ward, executive vice president and publisher at Random House, and Thomas Perry, senior vice president and deputy publisher, for believing in the importance of *Midnight in Washington* and helping to guide me all along the way; to assistant editor Chayenne Skeete for all of her help with many aspects of the book, including securing the rights for the photographs; to Carlos Beltran for the beautiful design of the jacket; to Susan Turner for the gorgeous design of these pages; to our excellent production editor, Evan Camfield, and our scrupulous copy editor, Emily DeHuff, for taking such great care of the sentences in this book; to our extraordinary researcher, Christopher Massie, for the stellar fact-checking memos; and to publicity director Susan Corcoran and deputy publicity director London King and our marketer, Michael Hoak, for getting out the good word about the book. I am also deeply grateful to Maher Bitar, Patrick Boland, and Norman Eisen for their detailed notes and observations, and to Theodore J. Boutrous, Jr., for his careful review of the manuscript.

Finally, I want to thank all the members of my family who supported me all along the way: my wonderful wife, Eve, and our children, Lexi and Eli; my father, Ed, and my mother, Sherrill, may her name be for a blessing; Jim and Marion Sanderson of blessed memory; my brother Daniel and his wife, Amy; my brother David McMillan and his mother, Angela Sellers; Eric Sanderson, Lisa Sanderson, and Dan Engel; Claire Zimmers; my nephews and nieces, Rachel, Frank, Talia, Maddie, Jordan, Jacob, and Tiffany; my Schiff cousins and my Glovsky cousins; and my dear friends who make everything in life fun as well as worthwhile, and especially the droogs—you know who you are.

PHOTO CREDITS

Jim Jordan: Redux Pictures

Marie Yovanovitch: Redux Pictures

Fiona Hill: Redux Pictures

Alexander Vindman: Getty Images

Pelosi introduces the House managers: Getty Images

Heading onto the Senate floor: Getty Images

Preparing for the first day: Getty Images

Working on the closing statement: courtesy of the author

Schiff speaking at trial: Getty Images

Mitt Romney: Getty Images

INDEX

ABOUT THE AUTHOR

ADAM SCHIFF is the United States representative for California's Twenty-eighth Congressional District. In his role as chairman of the House Permanent Select Committee on Intelligence, Schiff led the first impeachment of Donald J. Trump. Before he served in Congress, he worked as an assistant U.S. attorney in Los Angeles and as a California state senator. He and his wife, Eve, have two children, Lexi and Eli.